The Corporation as Technology

The Corporation as Technology

Re-Calibrating Corporate Governance for a Sustainable Future

CHRISTOPHER M. BRUNER
Stembler Family Distinguished Professor in Business Law
University of Georgia
School of Law

OXFORD
UNIVERSITY PRESS

OXFORD
UNIVERSITY PRESS

Oxford University Press is a department of the University of Oxford. It furthers the University's objective of excellence in research, scholarship, and education by publishing worldwide. Oxford is a registered trade mark of Oxford University Press in the UK and certain other countries.

Published in the United States of America by Oxford University Press
198 Madison Avenue, New York, NY 10016, United States of America.

Library of Congress Cataloging-in-Publication Data
Names: Bruner, Christopher M., 1972- author.
Title: The corporation as technology : re-calibrating corporate governance
for a sustainable future / Christopher M. Bruner.
Description: New York, NY : Oxford University Press, 2022. |
Includes bibliographical references and index.
Identifiers: LCCN 2021045595 (print) | LCCN 2021045596 (ebook) |
ISBN 9780197635179 (hardback) | ISBN 9780197635193 (epub) |
ISBN 9780197635186 (updf) | ISBN 9780197635209 (online)
Subjects: LCSH: Corporate governance—Law and legislation.
Classification: LCC K1327 .B785 2022 (print) | LCC K1327 (ebook) |
DDC 346/.0664—dc23/eng/20211105
LC record available at https://lccn.loc.gov/2021045595
LC ebook record available at https://lccn.loc.gov/2021045596

DOI: 10.1093/oso/9780197635179.001.0001

1 3 5 7 9 8 6 4 2

Printed by Integrated Books International, United States of America

For my students

Contents

List of Figures

Preface

This book was written during a period of rising global temperatures, growing inequalities, and deepening market instabilities, reflecting a complex web of environmental, social, and economic crises that only intensified with the onset of a global pandemic. The corporate form and corporate law have contributed to these crises, and the exigencies of the moment animate the urgent calls for reform presented in this work.

At the same time, in the face of such difficult circumstances, it pays to remain grateful for one's blessings—and in that spirit, I express my deepest thanks to all those who have supported this endeavor in various ways. For helpful comments, suggestions, and conversations regarding various aspects of the project at various stages in its development, many thanks to Alessio Bartolacelli, Stephen Bottomley, Vincent Buccola, John Burke, Eric Chaffee, Alwyn Fouchee, Martin Gelter, Andrew Johnston, Mervyn King, Jonathan Klaaren, Tshepo Mongalo, Florian Möslein, Marc Moore, Stephen Kim Park, Martin Petrin, Madimetja Phakeng, Usha Rodrigues, Emily Sherwin, Beate Sjåfjell, D. Daniel Sokol, Andrew Verstein, Edward Webster, and Harwell Wells, as well as to workshop participants at the International Monetary Fund, the University of Macerata, the University of Oslo, and the University of the Witwatersrand. I am also grateful for the constructive feedback offered by anonymous reviewers, and to Jamie Berezin and David Lipp of Oxford University Press for their support and encouragement.

For professional and financial support, I am grateful to the University of Georgia School of Law, and particularly to Bo Rutledge. For excellent research assistance, thanks to Samuel Baker, Victoria Carballo, Sydney Hamer, Sean O'Donovan, Jacob Weber, Victoria Williams, and Rayan Yassin. For their expertise and research support, I am grateful to the staff of UGA Law's Alexander Campbell King Law Library, and particularly to Anne Burnett, T.J. Striepe, and Stephen Wolfson. Thanks to Shawn Lanphere for superb administrative assistance throughout. In pursuing this work, I also benefited greatly from the opportunity to conduct comparative research at the Oliver Schreiner School of Law at the University of the Witwatersrand in Johannesburg, South Africa. Many thanks to Wesahl Domingo, Jonathan Klaaren, Tshepo Mongalo, and Adanma Yisa, as well as to Mashidila Ramaala of the Wits Law Library.

I am most grateful to, and for, my family—Lia Pierson Bruner and our kids, Cullen and Claire. I dedicate this book to my students, whose intellect and engagement remain sources of inspiration and optimism.

I note the following housekeeping items for the reader's reference. First, dollar values throughout the book refer to U.S. dollars unless indicated otherwise. Second, citations to websites are believed to be current as of this writing, but may not remain stable moving forward. Third, each chapter is independently and consecutively footnoted. Accordingly, cross references within a given chapter generally refer to the relevant footnotes, whereas cross references to material elsewhere in the book generally refer to the relevant chapters, parts, or sections. Finally, while I am indebted to those named above, they do not necessarily share all of the views expressed in the book, and any errors or omissions are naturally mine.

Athens, Georgia
July 2021

PART ONE

THE DYNAMISM OF THE CORPORATION

1
Introduction and Overview

The early decades of the twenty-first century have brought extraordinary environmental, social, and economic upheaval, spawning a multitude of interconnected crises. The Intergovernmental Panel on Climate Change (IPCC) estimated in 2018 that human activity had "caused approximately 1.0°C of global warming above pre-industrial levels," and that this would likely reach 1.5°C by 2052, threatening extreme temperature fluctuations, droughts, floods, and sea-level rise that would compound "risks to health, livelihoods, food security, water supply, human security, and economic growth."[1] A 2021 IPCC assessment that "incorporates subsequent new evidence from climate science" finds global warming of 1.09°C, estimates that this is "more likely than not" to reach 1.5°C by 2040, and concludes that it is now "unequivocal that human influence has warmed the atmosphere, ocean and land."[2] Humanity's climate impact has become so clear and pervasive that environmental scientists now speak of "a new epoch, the Anthropocene, where humans constitute the dominant driver of change to the Earth System."[3]

In response, an international and interdisciplinary team of scientists has sought to identify and define Earth's "planetary boundaries"—in essence, precautionary boundary levels keyed to the planet's estimated environmental bearing capacity that collectively establish "a safe operating space for humanity," and which "should not be transgressed if we are to avoid unacceptable global environmental change."[4] The project remains a work in progress as environmental

[1] VALÉRIE MASSON-DELMOTTE ET AL., SUMMARY FOR POLICYMAKERS, *in* GLOBAL WARMING OF 1.5°C. AN IPCC SPECIAL REPORT ON THE IMPACTS OF GLOBAL WARMING OF 1.5°C ABOVE PRE-INDUSTRIAL LEVELS AND RELATED GLOBAL GREENHOUSE GAS EMISSION PATHWAYS, IN THE CONTEXT OF STRENGTHENING THE GLOBAL RESPONSE TO THE THREAT OF CLIMATE CHANGE, SUSTAINABLE DEVELOPMENT, AND EFFORTS TO ERADICATE POVERTY 4–10 (2018). *See also* United Nations, *UN Warns Climate Change Is Driving Global Hunger* (Sept. 12, 2018), https://unfccc.int/news/un-warns-climate-change-is-driving-global-hunger.

[2] VALÉRIE MASSON-DELMOTTE ET AL., SUMMARY FOR POLICYMAKERS, *in* CLIMATE CHANGE 2021: THE PHYSICAL SCIENCE BASIS 4-5, 18 (2021) (emphasis removed). See also Christopher Flavelle, *Climate Change Is Making Big Problems Bigger*, N.Y. TIMES, May 12, 2021, https://www.nytimes.com/2021/05/12/climate/climate-change-epa.html; Paul Voosen, *Earth's Climate Destiny Finally Seen More Clearly*, 369 SCIENCE 354 (2020).

[3] Johan Rockström et al., *Planetary Boundaries: Exploring the Safe Operating Space for Humanity*, 14 ECOLOGY & SOC'Y, article 32 (2009), at 2.

[4] *Id.* In general, the precautionary principle calls for preventive action where the threat of harms is uncertain, meaning that stable probabilities cannot be assigned to potential outcomes, and incommensurate, meaning that potential harms cannot be measured by reference to the same scale

The Corporation as Technology. Christopher M. Bruner, Oxford University Press. © Christopher M. Bruner 2022.
DOI: 10.1093/oso/9780197635179.003.0001

conditions and scientific understanding evolve, but as of 2015, four of the nine planetary boundaries identified had already been exceeded, including climate change and biosphere integrity—two "core" boundaries that "provide the planetary-level overarching systems within which the other boundary processes operate."[5] Overall, it would require 1.7 Earths to sustain humanity's present use of ecological resources, but of course the intensity of resource use varies considerably around the world; indeed, five Earths would be required if all of humanity lived like the U.S. population does.[6]

These environmental realities intersect, in complex ways, with a range of significant social and economic development challenges. The present era of intense economic globalization has seen the global economy more than double in value in just three decades, and annual growth in gross domestic product (GDP) "has been higher in low- and middle-income countries"—meaning that "incomes in poorer countries are catching up with those in richer ones, and inequality between nations is falling," notably due to the rise of China and India.[7] Likewise, the worldwide rate of extreme poverty has fallen dramatically—from 36 percent in 1990 to 16 percent in 2010—although this, again, is largely attributable to these two countries.[8] In fact, desperate poverty and enormous inequalities remain pervasive around the world. In 2019, "more than 630 million workers worldwide—that is, almost one in five, or 19 per cent, of all those employed—did not earn enough to lift themselves and their families out of extreme or moderate poverty," defined as "earning less than US$3.20 per day in purchasing power parity terms."[9] One-third of the world's population is

as potential outcomes associated with another course of action. *See generally* Jonathan Aldred, *Justifying Precautionary Policies: Incommensurability and Uncertainty*, 96 ECOLOGICAL ECON. 132 (2013). Climate change exemplifies these conditions because scientific understanding of the range of potential outcomes is constantly evolving, and the potentially catastrophic losses differ in kind from any gains that declining to mitigate climate change might offer (e.g., marginally greater near-term economic growth). *See id.* at 132, 136–38.

[5] Will Steffen et al., *Planetary Boundaries: Guiding Human Development on a Changing Planet*, 347 SCIENCE 1259855-8 (2015). The four boundaries found to have been exceeded were climate change, biosphere integrity, biogeochemical flows, and land-system change. The remaining five are stratospheric ozone depletion, ocean acidification, freshwater use, atmospheric aerosol loading, and introduction of novel entities. *See generally id.*

[6] *Infographics & Videos*, EARTH OVERSHOOT DAY, https://www.overshootday.org/newsroom/infographics/. *See also* U.S. Energy Information Administration, *Frequently Asked Questions (FAQs): What is the United States' share of world energy consumption?*, https://www.eia.gov/tools/faqs/faq.php?id=87&t=1 (updated Dec. 15, 2020) (observing that the United States accounted for 17 percent of global energy consumption in 2018, but only 4 percent of the global population).

[7] Deborah Hardoon et al., *An Economy for the 1%: How Privilege and Power in the Economy Drive Extreme Inequality and How This Can Be Stopped* 8 (210 Oxfam Briefing Paper, Jan. 18, 2016).

[8] *Id. See also* INTERNATIONAL LABOUR ORGANIZATION, WORLD EMPLOYMENT AND SOCIAL OUTLOOK: TRENDS 2020, EXECUTIVE SUMMARY 5 (2020) (reporting that "labour income inequality at the global level has declined over the past 15 years," but that this is "a result of economic convergence driven by countries such as India and China, which have enjoyed a rise in average labour income").

[9] INTERNATIONAL LABOUR ORGANIZATION, *supra* note 8, at 3.

malnourished,[10] conditions intensified by the impacts of climate change on agriculture.[11] As of 2018, "some 773 million adults—two-thirds of whom are women—remained illiterate in terms of reading and writing skills."[12] While population growth is expected to slow, and the global population to stabilize, over this century, substantial growth is nevertheless expected among the least developed countries over coming decades (due largely to current age structures), exacerbating "challenges of providing adequate health care and nutrition . . . as well as access to high quality education," and compounding problems already faced by small island developing countries, which are uniquely vulnerable "to climate change, climate variability and sea-level rise."[13]

Meanwhile, global wealth inequalities have risen dramatically. As of 2015, it took "just 62 wealthy billionaires to equal the wealth of the bottom half of the world's population"—who, it bears noting, were "responsible for only around 10 percent of total global emissions," contrasting starkly with the carbon-intensive lifestyles of the rich.[14] Such staggering concentrations of wealth and resulting levels of inequality not only impede further poverty reduction, but more generally tend to undermine social stability[15]—dynamics affecting developed and developing countries alike. In the United States, from 1980 to 2014, while pretax income "doubled for the top 1% and tripled for the top 0.1%, there was little change for the bottom 50%," who increasingly struggle in low-wage jobs. Indeed, "40% of Americans are living so close to the edge that they cannot absorb an unexpected $400 expense."[16]

[10] World Food Programme, *Zero Hunger*, https://www.wfp.org/zero-hunger.

[11] United Nations, *supra* note 1.

[12] U.N. Secretary-General, *Progress Towards the Sustainable Development Goals*, ¶ 12, U.N. Doc. E/2020/xxx (May 14, 2020) (report of Secretary-General António Guterres).

[13] UNITED NATIONS DEPARTMENT OF ECONOMIC AND SOCIAL AFFAIRS, WORLD POPULATION PROSPECTS 2019: HIGHLIGHTS 5–10, 24, 37.

[14] Hardoon et al., *supra* note 7, at 11–12. By contrast, "the average carbon footprint of the richest 1 percent of people globally could be as much as 175 times higher than that of the poorest 10 percent." *Id.* at 12.

[15] *Id.* at 9, 18. *See also* THOMAS PIKETTY, CAPITAL IN THE TWENTY-FIRST CENTURY (Arthur Goldhammer trans., 2014).

[16] Zeynep Ton, *Raising Wages Is the Right Thing to Do, and Doesn't Have to Be Bad for Your Bottom Line*, HARV. BUS. REV., Apr. 18, 2019, https://hbr.org/2019/04/raising-wages-is-good-for-employees-and-doesnt-have-to-be-bad-for-your-bottom-line. *See also* Press Release, Economic Policy Institute, The incomes of the top 1 percent grew faster than the bottom 99 percent in 43 states and the District of Columbia from 2009–15 (July 19, 2018), https://www.epi.org/press/the-incomes-of-the-top-1-percent-grew-faster-than-the-bottom-99-percent-in-43-states-and-the-district-of-columbia-from-2009-15-new-york-florida-and-connecticut-top-the-list-of-most-unequal-states/; Zohar Goshen & Doron Levit, *Common Ownership and the Decline of the American Worker* 23–33 (ECGI Law Working Paper No. 584/2021), https://ssrn.com/abstract=3832069; PolicyLink, *An Overview of America's Working Poor*, https://www.policylink.org/data-in-action/overview-america-working-poor; Anna Stansbury & Lawrence H. Summers, *The Declining Worker Power Hypothesis: An Explanation for the Recent Evolution of the American Economy* 17–24 (NBER Working Paper No. 27193, 2020), https://www.nber.org/system/files/working_papers/w27193/w27193.pdf.

Global initiatives have certainly taken aim at these global problems, but progress to date remains limited. The 2015 Paris Agreement "aims to strengthen the global response to the threat of climate change, in the context of sustainable development and efforts to eradicate poverty," by establishing a goal of limiting global warming "to well below 2°C above pre-industrial levels and pursuing efforts to limit the temperature increase to 1.5°C."[17] More generally, the United Nations' 2015 Sustainable Development Goals (SDGs) aim, by 2030, to achieve "sustainable development in its three dimensions—economic, social and environmental—in a balanced and integrated manner," through pursuit of several specific goals across these domains.[18] However, these and other global efforts fundamentally remain non-binding. The Paris Agreement operates through "nationally determined contributions" toward the articulated goals,[19] requiring only that parties "put forward their best efforts" to achieve those self-determined contributions.[20] Similarly, the SDGs represent "aspirational and global" goals, "with each Government setting its own national targets" and deciding for itself how they ought to be "incorporated into national planning processes, policies and strategies."[21] The UN's *Agenda for Sustainable Development* takes pains to emphasize that the SDGs in no way impinge upon national sovereignty.[22] Progress toward achieving the SDGs was at best inconsistent as of late 2019, but according to UN Secretary-General António Guterres, by early 2020 the COVID-19 pandemic and measures taken in response had already "overwhelmed the health systems globally, caused businesses and factories to shut down and severely impacted the livelihoods of half of the global workforce, kept 1.6 billion students out of schools, disrupted global value chains and the supply of products, and [was] expected to push tens of millions of people back into extreme poverty and hunger"—impacts falling most heavily upon the "poorest and most vulnerable people . . . including women, children, older persons, persons with disabilities,

[17] Paris Agreement, Dec. 12, 2015, art. 2(1).

[18] United Nations, *Transforming Our World: The 2030 Agenda for Sustainable Development*, ¶¶ 2, 59 et seq., U.N. Doc. A/RES/70/1 (Sept. 25, 2015).

[19] Paris Agreement, *supra* note 17, art. 4(2).

[20] United Nations, *Key Aspects of the Paris Agreement*, https://unfccc.int/process-and-meetings/the-paris-agreement/the-paris-agreement/key-aspects-of-the-paris-agreement. The Paris Agreement may factor into domestic legal analysis. For example, a Dutch court referenced Paris Agreement commitments in its May 2021 order that Royal Dutch Shell must cut emissions more aggressively, a ruling based on "a 'duty of care' clause in the Dutch system which provided judges some liberty to interpret unwritten rules and consider links to human rights and the effect climate change has on the right to a healthy environment." However, the prospects for this legal strategy remain uncertain. "While the Dutch government signed up to the Paris Agreement, Shell's existing targets don't violate Dutch law," and appeals "could last many years." Diederik Baazil & Laura Millan Lombrana, *What a Dutch Court Ruling Means for Shell and Big Oil*, BLOOMBERG QUICKTAKE, June 4, 2021, https://www.bloomberg.com/news/articles/2021-06-04/what-a-dutch-court-ruling-means-for-shell-and-big-oil-quicktake.

[21] United Nations, *supra* note 18, ¶ 55.

[22] *Id.* ¶ 18.

migrants and refugees and informal sector workers," particularly in less developed countries.[23]

Given the non-binding nature of such global initiatives, from a regulatory perspective the real action remains at the national level, and recent developments in the domestic politics of numerous countries reflect growing distaste for multilateralism and real tensions among sustainability-oriented goals. The global wave of nationalism sparked by Donald Trump's 2016 election to the U.S. presidency has reinforced skepticism and even prompted hostility toward "globalist" efforts like the foregoing in many countries around the world.[24] This has emerged hand in hand with science denialism[25] and impatience regarding environmental initiatives and regulations thought to impede domestic job creation—tendencies culminating in the U.S. withdrawal from the Paris Agreement, which then-Secretary of State Mike Pompeo branded an "unfair economic burden imposed on American workers, businesses and taxpayers."[26] Although Joseph Biden's 2020 election brought a swift U.S. return to the Paris Agreement[27] and an ambitious target for emissions reductions,[28] achieving this would require legislative action by a deeply fractured and polarized Congress, reflecting a deeply fractured and polarized American public.[29]

The longer-term sustainability impacts of such developments remain to be seen, and widespread health and social crises further complicate the corporate sustainability landscape. Some expect that the COVID-19 pandemic, associated

[23] U.N. Secretary-General, *supra* note 12, ¶¶ 3–4. *See also* José Manuel Moller Dominguez & Fiona Broom, *SDG Setback "Tremendous" as COVID-19 Accelerates Slide*, GREENBIZ, June 5, 2020, https://www.greenbiz.com/article/sdg-setback-tremendous-covid-19-accelerates-slide.

[24] *See, e.g.*, Julian Borger, *Donald Trump Denounces "Globalism" in Nationalist Address to UN*, GUARDIAN, Sept. 24, 2019, https://www.theguardian.com/us-news/2019/sep/24/donald-trump-un-address-denounces-globalism; Gideon Rachman, *Donald Trump Leads a Global Revival of Nationalism*, FIN. TIMES, June 25, 2018, https://www.ft.com/content/59a37a38-7857-11e8-8e67-1e1a0846c475.

[25] Editorial, *Debunking Science Denialism*, NATURE HUM. BEHAV., Sept. 2019, at 887.

[26] Emily Holden, *Trump Begins Year-Long Process to Formally Exit Paris Climate Agreement*, GUARDIAN, Nov. 5, 2019, https://www.theguardian.com/us-news/2019/nov/04/donald-trump-climate-crisis-exit-paris-agreement (quoting Pompeo).

[27] Paris Climate Agreement: Acceptance on Behalf of the United States of America (Jan. 20, 2021), https://www.whitehouse.gov/briefing-room/statements-releases/2021/01/20/paris-climate-agreement/. *See also* Nathan Rott, *Biden Moves to Have U.S. Rejoin Climate Accord*, NPR, Jan. 20, 2021, https://www.npr.org/sections/inauguration-day-live-updates/2021/01/20/958923821/biden-moves-to-have-u-s-rejoin-climate-accord.

[28] Fact Sheet: President Biden Sets 2030 Greenhouse Gas Pollution Reduction Target Aimed at Creating Good-Paying Union Jobs and Securing U.S. Leadership on Clean Energy Technologies (Apr. 22, 2021), https://www.whitehouse.gov/briefing-room/statements-releases/2021/04/22/fact-sheet-president-biden-sets-2030-greenhouse-gas-pollution-reduction-target-aimed-at-creating-good-paying-union-jobs-and-securing-u-s-leadership-on-clean-energy-technologies/.

[29] *See, e.g.*, Lili Pike, *The US Is Back In the International Climate Game*, VOX, Jan. 20, 2021, https://www.vox.com/22241348/president-biden-climate-change-paris-agreement-executive-order-keystone-pipeline; Corinne Purtill, *How Climate Policy Will Change in 2021*, N.Y. TIMES, Dec. 14, 2020, https://www.nytimes.com/2020/12/14/business/dealbook/climate-policy-debate.html.

shutdowns, and consequent economic damage will, in the near term, only reinforce nationalist tendencies and tend to delegitimize policies that appear to prioritize the environment over economic growth.[30] Others, however, suggest that the pandemic "has become a dry run for the sustainability agenda"—vividly demonstrating the benefits of flexible workforce policies, shorter supply chains, and governing with an eye toward "adaptability and resilience"—and observe that, from an investment perspective, "companies with strong ESG [i.e. environmental, social, and governance] credentials have proven a safer haven in this period of market disruption."[31] Meanwhile, development of and access to vaccines has shone a bright light on corporate incentive structures and prompted renewed debates regarding the appropriate balance between financial and other goals. Although "rapid development of highly effective vaccines is a once-in-a-generation scientific breakthrough with huge dividends for the entire world" for which private pharmaceutical companies have rightly been praised, questions have arisen regarding the degree to which they have profited from the pandemic—notably given their reliance on government support and "taxpayer-funded research," as well as the staggering global inequities that quickly emerged as many around the world were effectively priced out of the vaccine market.[32] At the same time, widespread protests over police violence resulting in the deaths of unarmed Black victims have "shone a spotlight on the long-standing racial divide" in the United States. "This, along with the coronavirus pandemic that has disproportionately killed black Americans, has drawn renewed attention to

[30] James Temple, *The Unholy Alliance of Covid-19, Nationalism, and Climate Change*, MIT TECH. REV., Apr. 10, 2020, https://www.technologyreview.com/2020/04/10/998969/the-unholy-alliance-of-covid-19-nationalism-and-climate-change/. On the opportunistic use of COVID-19 to advance authoritarian and nationalistic policies, see Helen Davidson, *Hong Kong Using Covid-19 Crisis as "Golden Opportunity" for Crackdown, Says Arrested Leader*, GUARDIAN, Apr. 20, 2020, https://www.theguardian.com/world/2020/apr/20/hong-kong-using-covid-19-crisis-as-golden-opportunity-for-crackdown-says-arrested-leader; David Smith, *Trump Says He Will Impose Immigration Ban in Bid to Tackle Coronavirus*, GUARDIAN, Apr. 21, 2020, https://www.theguardian.com/world/2020/apr/21/trump-says-he-will-impose-immigration-ban-in-bid-to-tackle-coronavirus.

[31] Jenny Davis-Peccoud & Jean-Charles van den Branden, *Covid-19 Gives Sustainability a Dress Rehearsal*, BAIN & CO., Apr. 17, 2020, https://www.bain.com/insights/covid-19-gives-sustainability-a-dress-rehearsal/. *See also* Emily Chasan, *Covid-19 May Change Corporate Sustainability as We Know It*, BLOOMBERG, Apr. 8, 2020, https://www.bloomberg.com/news/articles/2020-04-08/covid-19-may-change-sustainability-as-we-know-it-green-insight. *See also* U.N. Secretary-General, *supra* note 12, ¶ 20 (suggesting that the COVID-19 pandemic may offer an opportunity to "change our consumption and production patterns towards a sustainable future").

[32] Rebecca Robbins & Peter S. Goodman, *Pfizer Reaps Hundreds of Millions in Profits from Covid Vaccine*, N.Y. TIMES, May 4, 2021, https://www.nytimes.com/2021/05/04/business/pfizer-covid-vaccine-profits.html (reporting that Pfizer's vaccine generated $3.5 billion in revenues in the first quarter of 2021, and that in "wealthy countries, roughly one in four people has received a vaccine" while in "poor countries, the figure is one in 500"). *See also* Rick Newman, *Let Drugmakers Keep Their Covid Vaccine Profits*, YAHOO! FINANCE, May 6, 2021, https://finance.yahoo.com/news/let-drugmakers-keep-their-covid-vaccine-profits-205407247.html (acknowledging that responses to "unfairness and wealth inequality" are required but arguing that "punishing companies that solve huge problems"—here, by suspending patent protections—"is a dumb way to do it").

the persistent inequalities in wealth, health and opportunity between blacks and whites despite economic prosperity in recent years."[33] Increasingly, "engaged consumers . . . push companies to take sides in political disputes" reflecting such dynamics.[34]

Against this background, it becomes all the more imperative to think deeply about how private actors themselves make decisions that impact sustainability—and from this perspective, large business corporations and their various constituencies take center stage. As a threshold matter, it can hardly be gainsaid that these entities represent "the most consequential economic actors on the planet."[35] The Fortune 500, comprised of the largest U.S. companies, accounts for "$13.8 trillion in revenue, or some two-thirds of the U.S. economy,"[36] and such corporations now rival many countries in their economic magnitude. If each were a country with GDP equivalent to recently reported annual revenues, then Starbucks would have the 104th largest national economy in the world. McDonald's would come in at 103rd, Nike at 96th, Coca-Cola at 95th, Facebook at 90th, Disney at 78th, Johnson & Johnson at 67th, Microsoft at 65th, Alphabet (Google's parent) at 59th, Amazon at 58th, and Apple at 47th. Walmart, with 2017 revenues of almost $486 billion—exceeding the GDP of Belgium—would have the 24th largest national economy in the world.[37] A ranking based on corporate revenues versus tax revenues collected—closer to an apples-to-apples comparison—only further underscores the economic clout of such corporations. Walmart would rank 10th by this measure—between Canada and Spain—and corporations would represent 71 of the top 100 revenue generators in the world.[38] As the University of Amsterdam researchers compiling this data concluded, "global corporations' current power position vis-à-vis other actors is unprecedented."[39] Meanwhile,

[33] Tami Luhby, *US Black-White Inequality in 6 Stark Charts*, CNN.COM, June 3, 2020, https://www.cnn.com/2020/06/03/politics/black-white-us-financial-inequality/index.html. *See also* Kristine Phillips, *Joe Biden's Centrist Dilemma: Police Groups Say He's Gone Too Far Left; Activists Say He Hasn't Gone Far Enough*, USA TODAY, Dec. 10, 2020, https://www.usatoday.com/story/news/politics/2020/12/10/biden-reform-plan-tests-black-lives-matter-police-support/6422611002/; Erin Schumaker, *Vaccination Rates Lag in Communities of Color, but It's Not Only Due to Hesitancy, Experts Say*, ABC NEWS, May 8, 2021, https://abcnews.go.com/Health/vaccination-rates-lag-communities-color-due-hesitancy-experts/story?id=77272753.

[34] *Corporate America Weighs in on Georgia's Voting-Rights Law*, ECONOMIST, Apr. 8, 2021, https://www.economist.com/news/2021/04/07/corporate-america-weighs-in-on-georgias-voting-rights-law.

[35] Christopher M. Bruner, *Managing Corporate Federalism: The Least-Bad Approach to the Shareholder Bylaw Debate*, 36 DEL. J. CORP. L. 1, 3 (2011).

[36] *Fortune 500*, FORTUNE, https://fortune.com/fortune500/.

[37] Fernando Belinchón & Qayyah Moynihan, *25 Giant Companies That Are Bigger Than Entire Countries*, BUS. INSIDER, July 25, 2018, https://www.businessinsider.com/25-giant-companies-that-earn-more-than-entire-countries-2018-7 (comparing 2017 corporate revenues with 2016 GDP reported by the International Monetary Fund).

[38] Milan Babic et al., *Who Is More Powerful—States or Corporations?*, THE CONVERSATION, July 10, 2018, https://theconversation.com/who-is-more-powerful-states-or-corporations-99616.

[39] *Id.*

the sheer number of private enterprises continues to grow at a staggering rate across developed and developing economies alike.[40]

In this light, it is hardly surprising that the many constituencies transacting on behalf of, or with, such entities—their directors, officers, and investors; their employees and contractors; suppliers of their raw materials and other inputs; consumers of their goods and services; and the communities and societies they inhabit—would have enormous impacts on all facets of sustainability, both domestically and globally.[41] The U.S. Environmental Protection Agency has identified various forms of business as major contributors to U.S. greenhouse gas emissions.[42] Strikingly, businesses "directly control roughly three-quarters of all US energy use and consequent emissions."[43] Accounting for both direct and downstream emissions from sold products, 100 fossil fuel companies "account for 71% of global industrial GHG [greenhouse gas] emissions" since 1988—and of those 100 entities, 41 are "public investor-owned companies" and 16 are "private investor-owned companies."[44] Meanwhile, redistribution of corporate gains from labor to capital over recent decades and a corresponding rise in inequality—particularly in the United States—have been linked with "the policy environment [having] become less supportive of worker power," leading to "pressures on companies to cut labor costs, resulting in wage reductions within firms and the 'fissuring' of the workplace as companies increasingly outsource and subcontract labor."[45] It is true that "corporations alone cannot address society's most pressing

[40] *See* COLIN MAYER, FIRM COMMITMENT: WHY THE CORPORATION IS FAILING US AND HOW TO RESTORE TRUST IN IT 22 (2013) (observing that "there are around 6 million firms in the US (28 million if one includes sole enterprises)," an increase of approximately one-third since 1992, and that "the number of private enterprises increased by approximately 80 per cent in China between the first and second economic censuses in 2004 and 2008, and by approximately 40 per cent in India between their economic censuses in 1998 and 2005").

[41] *See generally* THE CAMBRIDGE HANDBOOK OF CORPORATE LAW, CORPORATE GOVERNANCE AND SUSTAINABILITY (Beate Sjåfjell & Christopher M. Bruner eds., 2019). *See also* MAYER, *supra* note 40, at 23–25.

[42] *See* U.S. Environmental Protection Agency, *Sources of Greenhouse Gas Emissions*, https://www.epa.gov/ghgemissions/sources-greenhouse-gas-emissions (updated Apr. 14, 2021). The EPA reports that, as of April 2021, "Industry" accounts for 23 percent and "Agriculture" accounts for another 10 percent. At the same time, businesses account for some portion of other sources of emissions, including "Transportation" (29 percent), "Electricity" (25 percent), and "Commercial & Residential" (13 percent). *Id.*

[43] LOWELL UNGAR & ANDREW WHITLOCK, ENERGY EFFICIENCY AND CORPORATE SUSTAINABILITY: SAVING MONEY WHILE MEETING CLIMATE GOALS 3 (2019).

[44] PAUL GRIFFIN, THE CARBON MAJORS DATABASE: CDP CARBON MAJORS REPORT 2017, at 5, 8 (2017). The remainder are state-owned companies and producers. *Id.* at 5. Including both "upstream" and "downstream" emissions in this manner underscores that consumers share responsibility with these companies. *See* Madison Hunter, *100 Companies Aren't Solely to Blame for Global Emissions*, CLIMATE CONSCIOUS, Nov. 13, 2020, https://medium.com/climate-conscious/100-companies-arent-solely-to-blame-for-global-emissions-f59345761c96.

[45] Stansbury & Summers, *supra* note 16, at 2. For additional background, *see generally id.*; Goshen & Levit, *supra* note 16. *See also* GRANT M. HAYDEN & MATTHEW T. BODIE, RECONSTRUCTING THE CORPORATION: FROM SHAREHOLDER PRIMACY TO SHARED GOVERNANCE 184–85 (2020).

problems," but by the same token "it is hard to imagine any solution to these problems that does not entail a change in corporate behavior."[46]

In terms of their governance, such corporations inhabit a complex regulatory ecosystem, ranging from influential international soft-law standards to binding domestic hard-law regulations. Various international organizations have provided useful mechanisms to facilitate discussion regarding corporate sustainability, to transmit ideas, and to promote coordination—including, among others, the Global Reporting Initiative's standards;[47] the International Integrated Reporting Council's International Framework;[48] the International Organization for Standardization's ISO 26000 guidelines;[49] the Organisation for Economic Co-Operation and Development's Guidelines for Multinational Enterprises;[50] and various United Nations initiatives, such as the Global Compact, the Guiding Principles on Business and Human Rights, and the Principles for Responsible Investment.[51] Meanwhile, other international organizations have emphasized corporate sustainability issues in carrying out their particular mandates—for example, the International Monetary Fund and the World Bank have brought such issues to bear upon their efforts to promote economic and financial development and stability.[52]

Binding regulation pertaining to corporate sustainability, however, remains a domestic matter. This includes both external regulation such as environmental and labor laws, and internal regulation addressing various dimensions of corporate law and governance. While influential corporate scholars have argued

[46] Stavros Gadinis & Amelia Miazad, *Corporate Law and Social Risk*, 73 VAND. L. REV. 1401, 1474 (2020).

[47] *See* Global Reporting Initiative, *The Global Standards for Sustainability Reporting*, https://www.globalreporting.org/standards/; Global Reporting Initiative, *Resource Center*, https://www.globalreporting.org/how-to-use-the-gri-standards/resource-center/.

[48] *See* INTERNATIONAL INTEGRATED REPORTING COUNCIL, THE INTERNATIONAL FRAMEWORK (2013).

[49] *See* INTERNATIONAL ORGANIZATION FOR STANDARDIZATION, DISCOVERING ISO 26000: GUIDANCE ON SOCIAL RESPONSIBILITY (2018).

[50] *See* ORGANISATION FOR ECONOMIC CO-OPERATION AND DEVELOPMENT, OECD GUIDELINES FOR MULTINATIONAL ENTERPRISES (2011).

[51] *See* PRINCIPLES FOR RESPONSIBLE INVESTMENT, A BLUEPRINT FOR RESPONSIBLE INVESTMENT (2017) ("An investor initiative in partnership with UNEP Finance Initiative and UN Global Compact"); UNITED NATIONS, GUIDING PRINCIPLES ON BUSINESS AND HUMAN RIGHTS (2011); United Nations Global Compact, *The Ten Principles of the UN Global Compact*, https://www.unglobalcompact.org/what-is-gc/mission/principles.

[52] *See* INTERNATIONAL MONETARY FUND, GLOBAL FINANCIAL STABILITY REPORT: LOWER FOR LONGER 81–91 (2019) (discussing the significance of "sustainable finance"); International Monetary Fund, *IMF and the Sustainable Development Goals*, Feb. 16, 2021, https://www.imf.org/en/About/Factsheets/Sheets/2016/08/01/16/46/Sustainable-Development-Goals, World Bank, *Global Program on Sustainability: Overview*, https://www.worldbank.org/en/programs/global-program-on-sustainability/overview (aiming "to integrate environmental and other sustainability considerations into public and private decisions, by providing policy makers and the financial sector with the necessary metrics and tools"); World Bank, *Global Program on Sustainability: GPS Pillars*, https://www.worldbank.org/en/programs/global-program-on-sustainability/priority-themes.

that sustainability goals are most efficiently pursued through external regulation, freeing up corporate law and governance to exclusively prioritize financial returns for shareholders,[53] there is growing skepticism that reactive ex post regulation can effectively constrain such powerful private actors.[54] Indeed, even those favoring shareholder primacy as a normative goal have increasingly acknowledged that the growing capacity of such corporations to influence the content of the rules purportedly constraining them effectively undermines the argument that we can rely exclusively on external regulation as means of forcing businesses to internalize the full costs of production.[55] Accordingly, it becomes essential to understand how domestic corporate law and governance affect the ex ante incentives of corporate decision makers—and to investigate how these fields might be reformed to help us achieve corporate sustainability.[56]

Given the scope of their operations and consequent impacts, the domestic laws and regulations that structure and condition the governance of large business corporations have far-reaching significance, and corporate managers and institutional investors themselves generally agree—in the abstract, if not in the mechanics—that achieving corporate sustainability has become a fundamental imperative.[57] This book represents an effort toward that end, investigating the degree to which the corporate form itself—and accordingly, the rules and standards of corporate law and corporate governance—could better align business practices with long-term sustainability goals. Specifically, the book advances a new understanding of the corporate form and associated rules of corporate law

[53] *See, e.g.*, FRANK H. EASTERBROOK & DANIEL R. FISCHEL, THE ECONOMIC STRUCTURE OF CORPORATE LAW 35–39 (1991).

[54] *See* Christopher M. Bruner & Beate Sjåfjell, *Corporate Law, Corporate Governance and the Pursuit of Sustainability*, *in* THE CAMBRIDGE HANDBOOK OF CORPORATE LAW, CORPORATE GOVERNANCE AND SUSTAINABILITY, *supra* note 41, at 713, 714.

[55] *See, e.g.*, John Armour et al., *Beyond the Anatomy*, *in* REINIER KRAAKMAN ET AL., THE ANATOMY OF CORPORATE LAW: A COMPARATIVE AND FUNCTIONAL APPROACH 267, 271–72 (3d ed. 2017). *See also* Daniel J.H. Greenwood, *Introduction to the Metaphors of Corporate Law*, 4 SEATTLE J. SOC. JUST. 273, 295 (2005); Leo E. Strine, Jr. & Nicholas Walter, *Conservative Collision Course?: The Tension Between Conservative Corporate Law Theory and* Citizens United, 100 CORNELL L. REV. 335, 379–87 (2015).

[56] *See* Bruner & Sjåfjell, *supra* note 54, at 714. *See also* Brett McDonnell et al., *Green Boardrooms?*, 53 CONN. L. REV. 335, 408–09 (2021).

[57] For prominent examples, compare Business Roundtable, *Statement on the Purpose of a Corporation* (Aug. 19, 2019), https://www.businessroundtable.org/business-roundtable-redefines-the-purpose-of-a-corporation-to-promote-an-economy-that-serves-all-americans (statement by 181 CEOs, departing from strict "shareholder primacy" in favor of "a fundamental commitment to all of our stakeholders" and to "protect the environment by embracing sustainable practices across our businesses"), with Larry Fink, *A Fundamental Reshaping of Finance* (Jan. 14, 2020), https://www.blackrock.com/us/individual/larry-fink-ceo-letter#:~:text=A%20Fundamental%20Reshaping%20of%20Finance&text=It%20belongs%20to%20people%20in,to%20promote%20long%2Dterm%20value. (letter from BlackRock CEO to corporate CEOs, similarly emphasizing the importance of "considering the needs of a broad range of stakeholders" and addressing climate risks, but justifying this as a shareholder-centric means to "achieve long-term profits" and "attract investment," and citing shareholder voting power as a means of enforcing shareholder preferences).

and governance, and then builds upon that descriptive account to explore the corporation's potential to contribute to environmental, social, and economic sustainability.

The corporate form is widely described, and on some accounts defined, by reference to a core set of purportedly fixed, intrinsic attributes—notably, legal personality, limited liability, freely transferable shares, centralized board management, and shareholder election of directors.[58] Such depictions of the corporate form typically reflect strong assumptions about which corporate constituencies should be regarded as internal participants in the corporation—as opposed to contracting with it from the outside—and go hand in hand with strong theoretical claims about the corporation's core utility and corporate law's correlative content. I argue, however, that such rigid and static depictions of the corporate form and corporate law have fundamentally misconstrued the nature of the entity, reinforcing a host of corporate pathologies that include excessive risk-taking, cost externalization, and insufficient regard for environmental and social impacts. Hidebound conceptions of the corporation have effectively sacrificed the flexibility and dynamism of the corporate form, thereby obscuring potential governance-related regulatory options that could offer promising solutions to a host of vexing problems.

This book presents the corporation not as a fixed and rigid set of legal characteristics, but rather as a dynamic legal technology[59] that can be calibrated and re-calibrated in varying contexts, and over time, in response to a dynamic landscape. On this view, the corporation is not a set of fixed attributes, but rather a set of flexible capacities—including differing approaches to the structure and operation of the board, the allocation of governance powers among various corporate stakeholders, and exposure to potential liability for corporate decision-making. These flexible capacities are best conceptualized as governance levers that can be adjusted in various ways, and in different combinations, to achieve a range of decision-making structures and levels of risk tolerance, toward a range of potential ends.[60] The book explores both theoretical and practical ramifications of this

[58] For an influential formulation along these lines, see John Armour et al., *What Is Corporate Law?*, *in* KRAAKMAN ET AL., *supra* note 55, at 1, 1–2, 5–15.

[59] The corporation has occasionally been described as a legal or social "technology," typically to emphasize its failure to perform desired social functions. *See, e.g.*, L. Metcalf & S. Benn, *The Corporation Is Ailing Social Technology: Creating a "Fit for Purpose" Design for Sustainability*, 111 J. BUS. ETHICS 195, 197 (2012); Benjamin K. Sovacool, *Broken by Design: The Corporation as a Failed Technology*, 15 SCI., TECH. & SOC'Y 1, 2 (2010). *Cf.* Lynn Stout, *The Troubling Question of Corporate Purpose*, 3 ACCT. ECON. & L. 61, 65 (2013) (characterizing the corporation as "a multifunctional tool" that performs "something like a Swiss army knife," which "can be employed by different people to serve different purposes").

[60] For preliminary analysis along these lines, see Christopher M. Bruner, *The Corporation's Intrinsic Attributes*, *in* UNDERSTANDING THE COMPANY: CORPORATE GOVERNANCE AND THEORY 60 (Barnali Choudhury & Martin Petrin eds., 2017). *Cf.* Stout, *supra* note 59, at 63, 67 (arguing that a "multifunction theory" of corporate purpose could represent a superior alternative to shareholder primacy).

new conception of the corporation, focusing on how the corporate form—properly understood—could help secure an environmentally, socially, and economically sustainable future.

The analysis begins with a discussion of taxonomic challenges and controversies that have plagued efforts to define the corporation, and correlatively corporate law, in a singular and stable way.[61] Chapter 2 opens with a brief exploration of general challenges of legal taxonomy, focusing on the tension between internal and external views of law and the dynamic relationship between legal doctrine and social context. The analysis then turns to predominant extant modes of defining the corporation and corporate law. These include frameworks emphasizing core constituencies, describing corporate law as the body of law governing relations among constituencies thought to represent the central corporate actors; core features, describing corporate law as the body of law providing features thought to be central to the corporate form's utility; and core theories, describing corporate law as the body of law reflecting the central purposes and goals of corporate activity. In light of the inconsistencies and limitations of prior efforts, Chapter 2 closes with a brief discussion of the shift toward corporate governance as a predominant frame of reference—a development that I characterize as a trans-doctrinal lens through which to think about corporate power relations.

Chapter 3, then, explores various contextual drivers of difference in terms of how the corporation and corporate law are conceptualized—notably, factors relating to legal, cultural, market, and historical contexts. To convey the significance and impact of these contextual features, this chapter explores how divergences driven by politics, a jurisdiction's state of economic development, the degree of share ownership concentration, and prevailing social and cultural values can affect not only how a particular doctrinal subject is addressed, but even whether that subject is treated as structurally relevant to the corporate form, and correlatively whether it falls within the given jurisdiction's conception of corporate law. In so doing, I draw upon a range of comparative examples, exploring how defining the corporation and corporate law may become bound up with constitutional idiosyncrasies, impacting the formulation of regulatory goals and the division of regulatory competence within a given jurisdiction; how regional integration efforts, such as the European Union's common market project, expose the strength and persistence of culturally contingent conceptions of the corporate form and the desirable scope and content of corporate law; how varying commercial and capital market structures can impact these issues; and how conceptions of the foregoing may evolve within a given jurisdiction over

61 For preliminary analysis along these lines, see Christopher M. Bruner, *What Is the Domain of Corporate Law?* (University of Georgia School of Law Legal Studies Research Paper No. 2019-04, 2018), https://ssrn.com/abstract=3308611.

time, as ideas and background conditions change. Overall, I argue that these contextual dynamics foreclose a single, stable conception of the corporation and corporate law across all places and times, and that this contingency ought to be regarded as a feature rather than a bug—a capacity for adaptation that allows the corporation and corporate law to respond to social and economic needs that may differ markedly from one jurisdiction to another, and change over time.

The book then takes up the task of re-conceptualizing the corporation toward the aim of more fully and accurately describing its fundamental features and governance capacities, focusing on publicly traded corporations due to the significance of their scale, scope, and impacts, as well as the vigor of contemporary debates regarding their nature and purposes.[62] Chapter 4 sets the stage for this analysis by providing an overview of the emergence of the modern public corporation in the United Kingdom and the United States. Although Anglo-American scholars, in particular, have come to approach this topic with a singular archetype in mind—widely dispersed ownership of freely transferable stock by passive investors, highly centralized management through a powerful board of directors, fiduciary obligations strongly emphasizing shareholders' interests, and substantial insulation from liability exposure for boards and shareholders alike—my analysis emphasizes the flux and dynamism that in fact characterized the emergence of the modern public corporation. This further indicates that the intrinsic attributes of the corporate form are less static and rigid than contemporary accounts suggest. I acknowledge that trends toward limited liability for shareholders, free transferability of stock, and centralized management are readily discernible since the early nineteenth century and correlate with the advent of industrialization, but I argue that causal claims along these lines tend to be overstated, and that such generalizations provide little insight regarding fundamental questions of corporate governance that remain hotly contested today. These include the core issues of power, purpose, and risk, and the chapter concludes with a discussion of various ways in which we continue to grapple with issues fundamental to the corporate form and corporate law. These include who ought to have the last word in corporate decision-making, whose interests ought to guide corporate decision-making, and how much risk-taking is desirable—either generally, or in a particular business context.

[62] *See generally* CHRISTOPHER M. BRUNER, CORPORATE GOVERNANCE IN THE COMMON-LAW WORLD: THE POLITICAL FOUNDATIONS OF SHAREHOLDER POWER (2013). *See also* WILLIAM T. ALLEN & REINIER KRAAKMAN, COMMENTARIES AND CASES ON THE LAW OF BUSINESS ORGANIZATION 284 (5th ed. 2016); MARC MOORE & MARTIN PETRIN, CORPORATE GOVERNANCE: LAW, REGULATION AND THEORY 10–16 (2017) (focusing on publicly traded corporations "due to the especially vexing governance challenges" they raise, "the general . . . synonymy of 'public' and 'largeness' when it comes to correlating companies by status and relative size," and their "unique capacity . . . to attract capital from the many notionally 'passive' investors").

Chapter 5 builds on the foregoing to develop a different conception of the corporation—not as a fixed and rigid set of legal characteristics, but rather as a dynamic legal technology that can be calibrated and re-calibrated in varying contexts, and over time, in response to a dynamic contextual landscape. Here I do not refer to the presently existing legal capacity under corporate law to address the sorts of issues noted earlier on a firm-by-firm basis—for example, through corporate organizational documents, or statutory election to be treated as a "public benefit corporation" or other form of social enterprise made available on an opt-in basis.[63] Nor, for that matter, do I refer to unincorporated hybrid entities, such as the U.S. limited liability company, which are designed to permit a higher degree of contractual flexibility in terms of financial and governance arrangements.[64] Indeed, the fact that the crises described have emerged despite long-standing flexibility to adopt differing governance structures on a firm-by-firm basis only tends to demonstrate the insufficiency of reliance upon private parties to affirmatively opt into such structures. Rather, I emphasize the capacity and responsibility of lawmakers and regulators to think critically and creatively about the structure of the standard corporate form and the regulatory content of generally applicable corporate law in a given jurisdiction—which might involve structuring default rules to favor different outcomes or, in some cases, imposing mandatory constraints.[65] This process should be informed, I argue, by recognition that core issues of corporate governance have been addressed in varying ways in response to differing legal, cultural, market, and historical contexts, resulting in context-specific approaches in numerous jurisdictions around the world that deviate from the static conceptions that prevail in contemporary corporate literature.

On this view, the corporation represents not a set of fixed attributes, but rather a set of flexible capacities—governance levers that policymakers can adjust in various ways to achieve a wide range of potential outcomes, as Figure 1 reflects.

This conception of the corporation responds to the prevailing static conceptions by focusing on governance-related attributes and then re-conceptualizing each of them as a spectrum, inviting critical thought about how each

[63] Such forms of social enterprise could do more harm than good to the extent they give rise to a negative implication that the standard corporate form and generally applicable corporate law focus solely on shareholders' interests and provide no capacity to account for the sustainability-oriented concerns discussed here. *See* BRUNER, *supra* note 62, at 45 n.95; Carol Liao, *Social Enterprise Law: Friend or Foe to Corporate Sustainability?*, *in* THE CAMBRIDGE HANDBOOK OF CORPORATE LAW, CORPORATE GOVERNANCE AND SUSTAINABILITY, *supra* note 41, at 655, 667.

[64] Such entities appeal primarily to those engaged in smaller, closely held, and/or early stage businesses in which investors themselves typically engage directly in management, and to those organizing investment funds. *See* ALLEN & KRAAKMAN, *supra* note 62, at 63–73. *See also* Christopher M. Bruner, *Opting Out of Fiduciary Duties and Liabilities in U.S. and U.K. Business Entities*, *in* RESEARCH HANDBOOK ON FIDUCIARY LAW 285 (D. Gordon Smith & Andrew S. Gold eds., 2018).

[65] *See infra* Chapter 2.B.iii, Chapter 5.A.iv.

governance centralization	Decision-making power may be more centralized, through a board of directors, or dispersed, in the hands of shareholders or other stakeholders.
board liability exposure	Directors may be given more or less insulation from liability exposure—less exposure prompting more comfort with risk-taking and more exposure prompting less comfort.
shareholder representation	Composition of the board may be determined solely by shareholders, or other stakeholders may be granted some degree of representation.
shareholder orientation	Boards may be duty-bound to focus narrowly on shareholders' interests, or may be permitted—or even required—to consider the interests of other stakeholders.
shareholder enforcement	Shareholders may be given more or less capacity to advance their own interests through lawsuits, either exclusively or in common with other stakeholders.
share transferability	Shareholders may be given more or less freedom to move capital into and out of corporate equity investments unilaterally.
shareholder liability exposure	Shareholders may be given more or less insulation from liability exposure—less exposure prompting more comfort with risk-taking and more exposure prompting less comfort.

Figure 1 Levers of Governance

governance lever ought to be calibrated to achieve various goals. At the same time, it remedies shortcomings of prevailing conceptions by directly addressing the degree of board liability exposure and, related to that, the degree of shareholder enforcement capacity—both widely regarded as critical determinants of corporate decision-making.[66] This corporate technology can readily be depicted visually, as in Figure 2 below.

Figure 2 effectively represents a blank slate, summarizing a range of important choices to be made regarding the calibration of corporate governance in any particular jurisdiction. Depicted in this manner, then, one might present the archetypal U.S. public company as in Figure 3 below. Here, the various levers of governance are set to reflect what we have come to expect of the archetypal U.S. public company with widely dispersed stock ownership—strong boards elected by shareholders; greater emphasis on generating financial returns for shareholders, who possess substantial capacity to further prioritize their own interests through shareholder lawsuits; a high degree of investment liquidity for shareholders; and limited liability exposure for boards and shareholders alike. This depiction broadly reflects the archetypal U.K. public company as well, with legal and market structures resembling those in the United States, although

66 *See* BRUNER, *supra* note 62, at 97–107; Christopher M. Bruner, *Good Faith, State of Mind, and the Outer Boundaries of Director Liability in Corporate Law*, 41 WAKE FOREST L. REV. 1131 (2006).

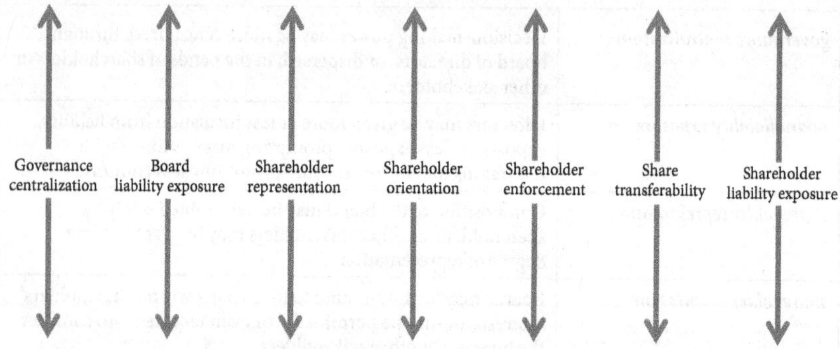

Figure 2 Corporate Technology

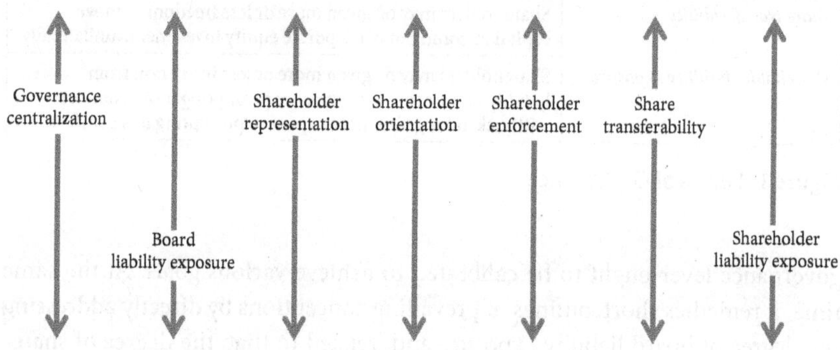

Figure 3 Archetypal U.S. Public Company

certain adjustments would be required in that setting. For example, in the archetypal U.K. public company, governance centralization would be somewhat lower (because U.K. shareholders are more powerful), shareholder orientation would be somewhat higher (because U.K. shareholder interests are expressly prioritized by statute), share transferability would be somewhat higher (because U.K. shareholders possess unfettered capacity to accept hostile takeover bids), and shareholder enforcement would be markedly lower (because mechanisms fostering U.S.-style shareholder litigation are largely absent).[67]

As Chapter 5 explores, this conception of the corporation—and this mode of representing the calibrations adopted in any given jurisdiction—offers substantial benefits. As a threshold matter, it invites critique and creative thought regarding how each lever ought to be set, and how calibrations of various

[67] For in-depth comparison of U.S. and U.K. shareholders' respective governance powers, see BRUNER, *supra* note 62, at 29–65.

governance levers might work together to facilitate the pursuit of various regulatory goals. It bears emphasizing that such possibilities are brought to light precisely because the false pretense of fixed and rigid characteristics has been jettisoned in favor of emphasizing the flexible capacities that together contribute to this dynamic legal technology. This conception likewise provides a straightforward means of depicting and comparing potential regulatory responses to governance-related problems, whether within a particular jurisdiction or across multiple jurisdictions.

The remainder of the book applies these insights, exploring how this conception of the corporation as a form of governance technology could open up new possibilities for responding to significant problems associated with current prevailing approaches to corporate governance. The discussion is rooted in the prevailing conception of sustainability, understood to mean development that "meets the needs of the present without compromising the ability of future generations to meet their own needs,"[68] and explores state-of-the-art approaches to corporate sustainability, understood to mean the promotion of corporate practices and governance structures contributing to—or at least not undermining—pursuit of environmental, social, and economic sustainability.[69] This approach in turn builds upon state-of-the-art approaches to sustainability more generally, which acknowledge the complexities and tensions already discussed through pursuit of practices that conform to planetary boundaries while at the same time ensuring a "social foundation" for all.[70]

To be sure, evidence suggesting that companies adopting more sustainable practices and policies deliver competitive financial returns—and may even prove to be more profitable in the long term—is good news to be welcomed.[71] However, it is critical to recognize that, from the sustainability perspective, those limited approaches that happen to be compatible with strong-form profit motive, while holding constant our current legal and market structures, are unlikely

[68] Report of the World Commission on Environment and Development: Our Common Future, ¶ 27 (1987). This Commission, established by the UN General Assembly and chaired by Gro Harlem Brundtland, was called upon to produce a "global agenda for change." *Id.*, Chairman's Foreword.

[69] *See* Beate Sjåfjell & Christopher M. Bruner, *Corporations and Sustainability*, *in* THE CAMBRIDGE HANDBOOK OF CORPORATE LAW, CORPORATE GOVERNANCE AND SUSTAINABILITY, *supra* note 41, at 1, 4.

[70] *See id.* at 7–11. Economist Kate Raworth's conception of "doughnut economics" reflects this pursuit of a "safe and just space for humanity" between the "ecological ceiling" established by planetary boundaries, on the one hand, and the "social foundation" established by universal human rights norms and sustainable development goals, on the other. *See generally* KATE RAWORTH, DOUGHNUT ECONOMICS: SEVEN WAYS TO THINK LIKE A 21ST CENTURY ECONOMIST (2017).

[71] *See, e.g.*, Robert G. Eccles et al., *The Impact of Corporate Sustainability on Organizational Processes and Performance*, 60 MGMT. SCI. 2835 (2014), https://ssrn.com/abstract=1964011 (working paper version); GEORGE SERAFEIM, TURNING A PROFIT WHILE DOING GOOD: ALIGNING SUSTAINABILITY WITH CORPORATE PERFORMANCE (Center for Effective Public Management, Brookings Institution, Dec. 2014).

to prove sufficient. The underlying environmental and social realities remain, and the long-term sustainability of a business practice or policy turns solely on whether it can actually be sustained over the long term by reference to those imperatives, regardless of whether it simultaneously maximizes short-term profitability or not.[72]

Drawing upon the growing literature in this field, I consider three of the most significant organizational and market pathologies inhibiting corporate sustainability today—financialization, excessive risk-taking, and cost externalization. Financialization refers to the increasing tendency over recent decades to prioritize generating returns for shareholders over all else—a complex phenomenon rooted in academic trends, capital market practices, and (depending on the jurisdiction) corporate law itself.[73] Excessive risk-taking and cost externalization, then, may be understood in balance sheet terms as efforts to increase revenues and reduce costs in order to boost profits available for distribution to shareholders; companies seek to increase revenues through greater entrepreneurial risk-taking, and conversely to reduce costs by off-loading as much of the downside as possible on non-shareholder constituencies and society generally.[74] Chapter 6 argues that financialization, excessive risk-taking, and cost externalization are closely related and mutually reinforcing phenomena associated with the calibration of governance levers in the archetypal U.S. public company, depicted in Figure 3 above. The chapter closes by assessing nascent efforts to develop impact-weighted forms of accounting, bringing such dynamics to bear on a corporation's financial statements and reported bottom line.[75] Such efforts provide a vivid reflection of the pervasiveness and complexity of these pathologies under current legal and market structures.

Chapter 7 proceeds to explore a variety of actual and potential re-calibrations of governance levers to respond to such problems in a variety of contexts. Industry-specific examples include the historical practice in various jurisdictions of constraining risk-taking in financial firms by adjusting upward the levers associated with board liability exposure and shareholder liability exposure—the former through a more demanding duty of care and the latter by imposing

[72] *See* Sjåfjell & Bruner, *supra* note 69, at 4, 7. *See also* BRITISH ACADEMY, PRINCIPLES FOR PURPOSEFUL BUSINESS: HOW TO DELIVER THE FRAMEWORK FOR THE FUTURE OF THE CORPORATION (2019) (calling for pursuit of profit to be subordinated to public purposes).

[73] *See* Geoffrey Wood & Mike Wright, *An Age of Corporate Governance Failure? Financialization and Its Limits*, *in* THE OXFORD HANDBOOK OF CORPORATE GOVERNANCE 703 (Mike Wright et al. eds., 2013); David Millon, *Radical Shareholder Primacy*, 10 U. ST. THOMAS L.J. 1013 (2013).

[74] Financial firms provide a vivid example, as the global financial crisis revealed. *See* Christopher M. Bruner, *Center-Left Politics and Corporate Governance: What Is the "Progressive" Agenda?*, 2018 BYU L. REV. 267, 277–78, 289, 304, 328 (2018); Christopher M. Bruner, *Corporate Governance Reform in a Time of Crisis*, 36 J. CORP. L. 309, 311–22 (2011).

[75] *See, e.g.*, GEORGE SERAFEIM ET AL., IMPACT-WEIGHTED FINANCIAL ACCOUNTS: THE MISSING PIECE FOR AN IMPACT ECONOMY (2019).

multiple liability rules upon shareholders in failed banks.[76] Contemporary calls to revive such structures in the wake of the financial crisis effectively advocate recalibrating these levers in major financial firms, which are increasingly thought to have engaged in excessive risk-taking precisely because their governance configuration has increasingly approximated the archetypal U.S. public company depicted in Figure 3 above.[77] Calls to diminish risk-taking in essential non-financial firms to prevent the need for crisis-driven bailouts,[78] and in various hazardous industries to prevent harms to consumers and society,[79] reflect a similar motivation and rationale.

Having addressed a range of calibrations of the levers of corporate governance in prior chapters, in a variety of legal, cultural, market, and historical contexts, Chapter 8 addresses an overarching issue looming in the background of the foregoing topics—the nature and scope of corporate accountability. Here, I explore further strategies for advancing corporate sustainability through various additional mechanisms. First, I assess the nature of a board's responsibilities through examination of the composition of the board itself, which naturally illuminates who a given society believes corporate decision-making ought to represent (even if directors' duties are formulated by reference to the entity itself). Here we find movement in a corporate governance lever held constant through many (though not all) of the foregoing discussions—the shareholder representation lever, which is calibrated quite differently in systems giving non-shareholders some degree of board representation.[80] At the same time, other ways of thinking about

[76] *See* Christopher M. Bruner, *Conceptions of Corporate Purpose in Post-Crisis Financial Firms*, 36 SEATTLE U. L. REV. 527, 533–41 (2013). *See also* Jonathan R. Macey & Geoffrey P. Miller, *Double Liability of Bank Shareholders: History and Implications*, 27 WAKE FOREST L. REV. 31 (1992); Patricia A. McCoy, *A Political Economy of the Business Judgment Rule in Banking: Implications for Corporate Law*, 47 CASE W. RES. L. REV. 1 (1996).

[77] *See* Bruner, *supra* note 76, at 553–61.

[78] *See, e.g.*, Shlomit Azgad-Tromer, *Too Important to Fail: Bankruptcy versus Bailout of Socially Important Non-Financial Institutions*, 7 HARV. BUS. L. REV. 159 (2017); Oscar Couwenberg & Stephen J. Lubben, *Not a Bank, Not a SIFI; Still Too Big to Fail*, 35 EMORY BANKR. DEV. J. 53 (2019). *See also* Henry Grabar, *Why Do the Airlines Need a Bailout?*, SLATE, Mar. 17, 2020, https://slate.com/business/2020/03/airlines-bailout-coronavirus.html; Kathryn Judge, *The Truth About the COVID-19 Bailouts*, FORBES, Apr. 15, 2020, https://www.forbes.com/sites/kathrynjudge/2020/04/15/the-covid-19-bailouts/; Stefan Redlich, *This Time It Is "Too Many to Fail" Rather Than "Too Big to Fail,"* SEEKING ALPHA, Mar. 20, 2020, https://seekingalpha.com/article/4333214-this-time-is-too-many-to-fail-rather-too-big-to-fail.

[79] *See* Henry Hansmann & Reinier Kraakman, *Toward Unlimited Shareholder Liability for Corporate Torts*, 100 YALE L.J. 1879 (1991).

[80] For example, German corporate governance—involving greater reliance on bank financing and substantial employee representation on the supervisory boards of large companies under the co-determination system—deviates from the archetypal U.S. public company depicted in Figure 3 principally by adjusting downward the shareholder representation, shareholder orientation, shareholder enforcement, and share transferability levers. This promotes employee interests, supporting social sustainability and a longer-term outlook—although this does not necessarily translate into environmental sustainability, as the Volkswagen emissions scandal vividly illustrated. *See, e.g.*, BRUNER, *supra* note 62, at 225–28; Matthew T. Bodie, *Worker Participation, Sustainability and the Puzzle of the Volkswagen Emissions Scandal*, *in* THE CAMBRIDGE HANDBOOK OF CORPORATE LAW, CORPORATE

how composition of the board of directors affects sustainability are assessed, including initiatives aimed at increasing the diversity of directors in publicly traded companies,[81] and increasing exploration of the potential for boards of directors to be augmented, or even replaced, by emerging technologies such as artificial intelligence—developments that could have profound consequences for corporate sustainability.[82]

Next, Chapter 8 considers another significant aspect of the nature and scope of corporate accountability—the degree to which responsibility for the impacts of global value chains ought to flow up to entities, and perhaps even management, at the top of those chains, whether organized through parent-subsidiary relationships or through nominally arms'-length contractual relationships.[83] In particular, I examine the apparent trend toward expanded responsibility along these lines and assess its potential to improve corporate sustainability in the multinational context.[84]

Finally, Chapter 8 assesses the nature and scope of corporate accountability through a striking national effort to re-imagine corporate governance along more sustainable lines, enlisting some (though by no means all) of the strategies discussed in this book—the corporate governance system of post-apartheid South Africa.[85] This provides a vivid case study through which to assess pitfalls

GOVERNANCE AND SUSTAINABILITY, *supra* note 41, at 246; Andreas Rühmkorf, *Stakeholder Value versus Corporate Sustainability: Company Law and Corporate Governance in Germany, in* THE CAMBRIDGE HANDBOOK OF CORPORATE LAW, CORPORATE GOVERNANCE AND SUSTAINABILITY, *supra* note 41, at 232.

[81] *See, e.g.*, BARNALI CHOUDHURY & MARTIN PETRIN, CORPORATE DUTIES TO THE PUBLIC 71–73 (2019); KENT GREENFIELD, THE FAILURE OF CORPORATE LAW: FUNDAMENTAL FLAWS AND PROGRESSIVE POSSIBILITIES 149–52 (2006); Darren Rosenblum & Daria Roithmayr, *More Than a Woman: Insights into Corporate Governance After the French Sex Quota*, 48 IND. L. REV. 889 (2015).

[82] *See, e.g.*, Christopher M. Bruner, *Distributed Ledgers, Artificial Intelligence and the Purpose of the Corporation*, 79 CAMBRIDGE L.J. 431 (2020).

[83] *See, e.g.*, Jaakko Salminen, *Sustainability and the Move from Corporate Governance to Governance through Contract, in* THE CAMBRIDGE HANDBOOK OF CORPORATE LAW, CORPORATE GOVERNANCE AND SUSTAINABILITY, *supra* note 41, at 57; Kishanthi Parella, *Protecting Third Parties in Contracts*, AM. BUS. L.J. (2021), https://ssrn.com/abstract=3697273.

[84] *See, e.g.*, Vivian Grosswald Curran, *Harmonizing Multinational Parent Company Liability for Foreign Subsidiary Human Rights Violations*, 17 CHI. J. INT'L L. 403 (2017). *See also* Blanaid Clarke & Linn Anker-Sørensen, *The EU as a Potential Norm Creator for Sustainable Corporate Groups, in* THE CAMBRIDGE HANDBOOK OF CORPORATE LAW, CORPORATE GOVERNANCE AND SUSTAINABILITY, *supra* note 41, at 190; Véronique Magnier, *Old-Fashioned Yet Innovative: Corporate Law, Corporate Governance and Sustainability in France, in* THE CAMBRIDGE HANDBOOK OF CORPORATE LAW, CORPORATE GOVERNANCE AND SUSTAINABILITY, *supra* note 41, at 276; Charlotte Villiers, *Global Supply Chains and Sustainability: The Role of Disclosure and Due Diligence Regulation, in* THE CAMBRIDGE HANDBOOK OF CORPORATE LAW, CORPORATE GOVERNANCE AND SUSTAINABILITY, *supra* note 41, at 551; Jingchen Zhao, *Extraterritorial Attempts at Addressing Challenges to Corporate Sustainability, in* THE CAMBRIDGE HANDBOOK OF CORPORATE LAW, CORPORATE GOVERNANCE AND SUSTAINABILITY, *supra* note 41, at 29.

[85] *See, e.g.*, Bonray Marsellus Botha, *Evaluating the Social and Ethics Committee: Is Labour the Missing Link?*, 79 J. CONTEMP. ROMAN-DUTCH L. 580 (2016) (part 1) and 80 J. CONTEMP. ROMAN-DUTCH L. 1 (2017) (part 2); Irene-marié Esser & Piet Delport, *The Protection of Stakeholders: The*

and opportunities that may arise in pursuing greater corporate sustainability through corporate governance.

Chapter 9 briefly concludes, emphasizing the degree to which some of the most pressing environmental, social, and economic problems that we face today are exacerbated by an unnecessarily static view of the corporate form and corporate law. The account of the corporation developed here opens up fresh theoretical perspectives on the corporate form, new avenues of critique in corporate law and governance, and a novel exploration of the corporation's potential to address a range of vexing sustainability-oriented problems. A host of potential solutions become available when we embrace the flexible capacities that the corporate technology provides.

Although his views on the corporation and corporate law are not endorsed here,[86] Milton Friedman was surely on to something when he observed that "[o]nly a crisis—actual or perceived—produces real change." Perceptively, he added that "[w]hen that crisis occurs, the actions that are taken depend on the ideas that are lying around." As to the role of scholars, then, "our basic function" is "to develop alternatives to existing policies, to keep them alive and available until the politically impossible becomes politically inevitable."[87] The overarching goal of this book is to ensure that the considerable range of potential calibrations for the corporation and corporate law remain "alive and available" to scholars, policymakers, and corporate stakeholders—that is, to everyone—as the environmental, social, and economic exigencies of our time become more fully apparent to all.

South African Social and Ethics Committee and the United Kingdom's Enlightened Shareholder Value Approach, 2017 DE JURE 97 (2017) (part 1) and 2017 DE JURE 221 (2017) (part 2); Michele Havenga, *The Social and Ethics Committee in South African Company Law*, 78 J. CONTEMP. ROMAN-DUTCH L. 285 (2015); H.J. Kloppers, *Driving Corporate Social Responsibility (CSR) through the* Companies Act: *An Overview of the Role of the Social and Ethics Committee*, 16 POTCHEFSTROOM ELECTRONIC L.J. 166 (2013); Tshepo H. Mongalo, *The Social and Ethics Committee: Innovating Corporate Governance in South Africa, in* THE CAMBRIDGE HANDBOOK OF CORPORATE LAW, CORPORATE GOVERNANCE AND SUSTAINABILITY, *supra* note 41, at 360.

[86] *See infra* Chapter 2.B.iii.

[87] MILTON FRIEDMAN, CAPITALISM AND FREEDOM ix (1982) (1962) (from the 1982 preface).

2
Defining the Corporation and Corporate Law

This book develops a new conception of the corporation, and associated rules of corporate law and governance, and then builds upon that framework to explore the corporation's potential to contribute to environmental, social, and economic sustainability. Accordingly, the starting point must be some account of why we need to re-conceptualize the corporation in the first place. Put differently, what is so bad about the status quo?

The short answer is that prevailing modes of defining the corporation, and by association corporate law and governance, either do not work as a theoretical matter, or produce bad outcomes as a practical matter. This chapter opens with a brief exploration of general challenges of legal taxonomy, focusing on the tension between internal and external views of law and the dynamic relationship between legal doctrine and social context, and then assesses three prevailing approaches to defining the domain of corporate law. While the question of what this conceptual vessel contains is seldom asked, let alone answered with any specificity,[1] discernible approaches have nevertheless emerged in the literature. These include frameworks emphasizing core constituencies, which describe corporate law as the body of law governing relations among constituencies thought to represent the central corporate actors; core features, which describe corporate law as the body of law providing features thought to be central to the corporate form's utility; and core theories, which describe corporate law as the body of law reflecting the central purposes and goals of corporate activity. In light of the inconsistencies and limitations revealed, the chapter closes with a brief discussion of the conceptual shift toward corporate governance as a predominant framing device, which I characterize as a trans-doctrinal lens through which to think about corporate power relations.

Ultimately, this analysis suggests that contextual and historical dynamics foreclose a single stable conception of corporate law's domain. This in turn suggests

[1] *See, e.g.*, John Armour et al., *What Is Corporate Law?*, *in* REINIER KRAAKMAN ET AL., THE ANATOMY OF CORPORATE LAW: A COMPARATIVE AND FUNCTIONAL APPROACH 1, 1 (3d ed. 2017); Stephen Bottomley, *What Is Corporate Law?: An Australian Perspective*, *in* ROUTLEDGE HANDBOOK OF CORPORATE LAW 49, 51 (Roman Tomasic ed., 2017).

The Corporation as Technology. Christopher M. Bruner, Oxford University Press. © Christopher M. Bruner 2022.
DOI: 10.1093/oso/9780197635179.003.0002

that, notwithstanding the universalizing thrust of much contemporary corporate law literature,[2] corporate law's fundamental contingency represents a feature rather than a bug—a capacity for adaptation that allows corporate law to respond to social and economic needs that may differ markedly from one jurisdiction to another and change over time.

A. Taxonomic Challenges

This part of the chapter provides a brief overview of two streams of discourse in the philosophy of law that condition how many have come to define legal fields and categorize legal problems—positivism and realism. Positivist approaches tend to emphasize lawmakers and doctrine while realist approaches tend to emphasize adjudicators and factual scenarios. Together, these differing postures reflect the inherent tension between internal and external views of law. Tellingly, however, when it comes to corporate law, positivists and realists express similar impatience with circular arguments that purport to deduce what a corporation can do from conclusory statements about what a corporation is, divorced from relevant contextual features—the legal landscape for the former, and the social and economic landscape for the latter. I argue that predominant approaches to defining the domain of corporate law have foundered precisely because they have failed to recognize these dynamics.

Positivism, a theory of law, is concerned principally with distinguishing legal from non-legal norms.[3] Central tenets of positivism include the "social thesis" that what a given society considers law "is fundamentally a matter of social fact," and the "separability thesis" that there is no necessary connection between morality and legal validity.[4] H.L.A. Hart, a major figure in this tradition, emphasizes the centrality of a "Rule of Recognition" to determine what counts as law.[5] As Hart expresses it, "nothing which legislators do makes law unless they comply with fundamental accepted rules specifying the essential law-making procedures," and these rules accordingly "lie at the root of a legal system."[6] Formalism, a theory of adjudication, is often associated with positivism due to the emphasis placed on how legal rules affect judicial decision-making. Formalism posits that

[2] *See* CHRISTOPHER M. BRUNER, CORPORATE GOVERNANCE IN THE COMMON-LAW WORLD: THE POLITICAL FOUNDATIONS OF SHAREHOLDER POWER 6 (2013).

[3] *See* Brian Leiter, *Positivism, Formalism, Realism*, 99 COLUM. L. REV. 1138, 1140–41 (1999) (reviewing ANTHONY SEBOK, LEGAL POSITIVISM IN AMERICAN JURISPRUDENCE (1998)).

[4] *See id.* at 1142–43; Jules L. Coleman & Brian Leiter, *Legal Positivism*, *in* A COMPANION TO PHILOSOPHY OF LAW AND LEGAL THEORY 241, 243 (Dennis Patterson ed., 1999).

[5] *See* Leiter, *supra* note 3, at 1143. *See also* Coleman & Leiter, *supra* note 4, at 241, 245.

[6] H.L.A. HART, *Positivism and the Separation of Law and Morals*, *in* ESSAYS IN JURISPRUDENCE AND PHILOSOPHY 49, 59 (1983)(essay published 1958).

"law is rationally determinate" and that "judging is mechanical" in the sense that "the class of legal reasons suffices to justify a unique outcome."[7] Positivism's preoccupation with the nature of law as such, however, distinguishes it from theories focusing on how judges resolve disputes, including formalism.

Realism, meanwhile, presents a strikingly divergent picture of adjudication, rejecting the formalist notion that doctrine alone can explain judicial outcomes. Judges, on the realist account, tend to "react primarily to the underlying facts of the case, rather than to applicable legal rules and reasons," which at most provide fodder for "post-hoc rationales."[8] Accordingly, realists have relied heavily on social sciences to develop accounts of patterned judicial decision-making rooted in judges' perceptions of contextual factors. Such accounts have gained particular purchase in the "commercial realm," where realists argue that judges typically "enforce the norms of the prevailing commercial culture," or simply do what they regard as "best socio-economically under the circumstances."[9] Felix Cohen, a major figure in this tradition,[10] declares that the U.S. legal system "is filled with supernatural concepts [that] cannot be defined in terms of experience," and urges legal scholars and practitioners "to admit that legal science necessarily involves us in psychology, economics, and political theory."[11]

Notwithstanding their differing emphases, a positivist view of law's fundamental nature does not inherently preclude a realist view of adjudication, or vice versa. Indeed, realists tacitly assume something like a positivist rule of recognition; arguing that "the class of legal reasons" is indeterminate, in the sense of justifying multiple potential outcomes, "presupposes some view about the boundaries of the class of legal reasons."[12] Conversely, positivists might reasonably adopt a realist account of adjudication, acknowledging a heavy dose of discretion in judicial decision-making, at least in difficult cases—as Hart himself does.[13] To the extent there is a fundamental tension here, it is perhaps not a matter of philosophical theory so much as an empirical disagreement about

[7] *See* Leiter, *supra* note 3, at 1145–46 (emphasis removed). *See also* Ernest J. Weinrib, *Legal Formalism*, *in* A COMPANION TO PHILOSOPHY OF LAW AND LEGAL THEORY, *supra* note 4, at 332, 339–40.

[8] Leiter, *supra* note 3, at 1148. *See also* David Cohen & Allan C. Hutchinson, *Of Persons and Property: The Politics of Legal Taxonomy*, 13 DALHOUSIE L.J. 20, 21 (1990); Andrew S. Gold & Henry E. Smith, *Sizing Up Private Law* 43–44 (Aug. 9, 2016), https://ssrn.com/abstract=2821354; Brian Leiter, *Legal Realism*, *in* A COMPANION TO PHILOSOPHY OF LAW AND LEGAL THEORY, *supra* note 4, at 261, 261, 276.

[9] Leiter, *supra* note 8, at 272. *See also* Leiter, *supra* note 3, at 1148–49.

[10] *See* Leiter, *supra* note 8, at 261.

[11] Felix S. Cohen, *Transcendental Nonsense and the Functional Approach*, 35 COLUM. L. REV. 809, 823, 834 (1935).

[12] Leiter, *supra* note 3, at 1154 (emphasis removed). *See also* Hanoch Dagan, *Legal Realism and the Taxonomy of Private Law* 2 (Oct. 30, 2006), https://ssrn.com/abstract=940913; Leiter, *supra* note 8, at 268–69.

[13] Leiter, *supra* note 3, at 1150. *See also* HART, *supra* note 6, at 64–72.

"how often rules do or do not matter (causally) in adjudication."[14] These differing perspectives interact in complex ways in legal taxonomy—including with respect to corporate law.

Legal taxonomy invites us to evaluate, and perhaps even clarify, the nature and aims of a given field[15]—an undertaking that lies close to the heart of legal reasoning itself.[16] It is a truism that the rule of law requires treating like cases alike,[17] challenging us to explore the psychological and philosophical underpinnings of analogical reasoning—notably, the criteria for identifying relevant similarity and difference.[18] Evaluating taxonomic choices may advance our understanding of these processes by revealing implicit value judgments and blind spots. If, as Jefferson White suggests, there is "no normatively independent way of counting similarities" for purposes of analogical reasoning,[19] then the same must be true of any taxonomic project. As Todd Aagaard observes, "the goal of legal taxonomy is to identify significant patterns in the law," and this will prove useful only "if the organizational framework reflects patterns that reveal something important to us about the materials being classified." In other words, the real work is done by the criteria allowing us to know "salient similarities and differences" when we see them.[20]

In devising taxonomies, much turns on who we envision using them, and how. Emily Sherwin observes that taxonomies vary considerably in their criteria, ranging from "formal" frameworks emphasizing "the logical relations among categories of law," to "function-based" frameworks classifying legal rules "according to the roles they perform within the legal system or society at large," to "reason-based" frameworks focusing on "higher-level reasons that explain or justify" legal rules.[21] Likewise, taxonomies differ in their intended audience and application.[22] The upshot is that "there may be multiple alternative frameworks that organize the field in a useful way,"[23] suggesting that contextual and perspectival contingency inherently condition legal taxonomy.

[14] Leiter, *supra* note 8, at 270–71.

[15] *See* Bottomley, *supra* note 1, at 50.

[16] *See* Todd S. Aagaard, *Environmental Law as a Legal Field: An Inquiry in Legal Taxonomy*, 95 CORNELL L. REV. 221, 224, 228 (2010); Dagan, *supra* note 12, at 6, 8–9; Stephanie Law, *Epistemological Considerations in Private Law: Exploring Taxonomical Structures in the Common Law, Civil Law and Beyond*, 18 MAASTRICHT J. EUR. & COMP. L. 454, 456 (2011); Emily Sherwin, *Legal Taxonomy*, 15 LEGAL THEORY 25, 25–26 (2009).

[17] *See* Jefferson White, *Analogical Reasoning*, *in* A COMPANION TO PHILOSOPHY OF LAW AND LEGAL THEORY, *supra* note 4, at 583, 583.

[18] *See id.* at 584–86, 589. *See also* BRUNER, *supra* note 2, at 18–20; Gold & Smith, *supra* note 8, at 34; Bayless Manning, *The Shareholder's Appraisal Remedy: An Essay for Frank Coker*, 72 YALE L.J. 223, 259 (1962).

[19] White, *supra* note 17, at 585.

[20] Aagaard, *supra* note 16, at 227–28. *See also* Law, *supra* note 16, at 457–58.

[21] Sherwin, *supra* note 16, at 31–39. *See also* Aagaard, *supra* note 16, at 240–41.

[22] Sherwin, *supra* note 16, at 39–50.

[23] Aagaard, *supra* note 16, at 249.

Such dynamics directly affect how various legal fields are defined, including corporate law. Peter Birks' effort to classify English private law[24] provides a striking example. Birks adopts a positivist perspective, developing a "formal classification" that aims to avoid overlaps among various fields of law.[25] Asserting that the "biggest problem facing the common law" is "information overload," Birks concludes that the solution is to impose "a structured overview of the law as a whole."[26] Following Blackstone's *Commentaries*, Birks aims to provide "a map of the law,"[27] contending that "no body of knowable data . . . can subsist as a jumble of mismatched categories."[28] Building on the Roman foundations of continental civil law, Birks' structure distinguishes "persons who can bear rights"; the "rights themselves" (divided into property and obligations); "the means by which the rights are realized in court"; and "sources of law."[29] Birks believes that the need for order is overwhelming and that this structure provides "the best software currently available" to sort legal data into useful knowledge.[30]

It is unsurprising that, in such a framework, providing a detailed account of any specific field takes a backseat to the larger task of mapping the broader terrain of private law. For Birks, corporate law simply represents a subset of the law of persons, and Charles Mitchell's contribution on this field accordingly focuses heavily on corporate personhood and various aspects of legal personality.[31] This presumably reflects the taxonomic aim of demonstrating where corporations reside within a much broader landscape, again following Blackstone's lead.[32]

In contrast with this form of top-down taxonomy, some proceed from the bottom up. For Aagaard, a coherent legal field exhibits four "constitutive dimensions," including "(1) a factual context that gives rise to (2) certain policy trade-offs, which are in turn resolved by (3) the application of values and interests to produce (4) legal doctrine."[33] The utility of a field, according to Aagaard, lies in its capacity to provide "a frame of reference for understanding the set of situations" encompassed by it, and this turns on the clarity and predominance of the "patterns" associated with it.[34] The imprecision and subjectivity of such criteria are apparent, suggesting that describing a legal field may easily blur into constructing it. In contrast with the more static positivist mapping approach,

24 *See* ENGLISH PRIVATE LAW (Peter Birks ed., 2000).
25 *See* Sherwin, *supra* note 16, at 26–27, 33–34.
26 Peter Birks, *Preface, in* 1 ENGLISH PRIVATE LAW, *supra* note 24, at xxix, xxix.
27 Peter Birks, *Introduction, in* 1 ENGLISH PRIVATE LAW, *supra* note 24, at xxxv, xlvii.
28 Birks, *supra* note 26, at xxxi–xxxii.
29 Birks, *supra* note 27, at xxxvi–xxxvii, xliv–xlv.
30 *Id.* at xlvi–xlvii.
31 *See* Charles Mitchell, *Companies and Other Associations, in* 1 ENGLISH PRIVATE LAW, *supra* note 24, at 133, 141–52.
32 *See* 1 WILLIAM BLACKSTONE, COMMENTARIES 455–56.
33 Aagaard, *supra* note 16, at 225.
34 *See id.* at 228–29.

realists emphasize the complexities that social and legal "dynamism" pose for the taxonomic project.[35] For realists, the risk is that taxonomy functions to generalize and distort, prospectively shaping the reality that it purports to describe[36]—particularly in private law, where private ordering "responds to these conceptual metaphors and reproduces itself in accordance with them."[37]

In this light, one might anticipate that realists would reject legal taxonomy outright. Approaching taxonomy with the foregoing dynamics in mind, however, may permit the project to neutralize its own negative tendencies—by serving as a means of developing "perspective and purchase on the 'fabricatedness' and 'non-naturalness'" of legal categories and fields.[38] Consistent with this view, as Aagaard suggests, even if coherence remains the emblem of a successful legal field, "incoherence is itself worthy of study."[39]

From this perspective, there is an intriguing commonality among realist and positivist critiques of analyses that assume a reified corporate form. Felix Cohen, in his discussion of the judicial tendency to "thingify" legal concepts, observes that the question "Where is a corporation?" cannot be answered empirically because there is no physical embodiment of a corporation; courts attaching real-world consequences to such questions effectively "create and distribute . . . economic wealth or power" without acknowledging what they are doing.[40] "Legal arguments couched in these terms," Cohen writes, "are necessarily circular, since these terms are themselves creations of law."[41] The realist Cohen's objection to the circularity of "thingifying" a legal concept like the corporation and then purporting to deduce its capacities from that reified legal construct—effectively burying the conclusion in the premise—resonates with the positivist Hart's objection to the same logical flaw in seeking to define the corporation as if it had a concrete referent from which corporate capacities could be deduced.[42] While Hart grapples with this by positing a new mode of legal definition emphasizing "the rules of a game"—urging us to define the term corporation solely by

[35] *See* Dagan, *supra* note 12, at 1, 7; Hanoch Dagan, *Doctrinal Categories, Legal Realism, and the Rule of Law*, 163 U. PA. L. REV. 1889, 1890–91, 1905–06 (2015). *See also* Cohen, *supra* note 11, at 833, 844–45.

[36] *See* Cohen & Hutchinson, *supra* note 8, at 24, 28–31. *See also* Aagaard, *supra* note 16, at 233–35; Dagan, *supra* note 12, at 2–6; Dagan, *supra* note 35, at 1906; Law, *supra* note 16, at 459–62.

[37] Cohen & Hutchinson, *supra* note 8, at 39. *See also* Dagan, *supra* note 12, at 7.

[38] Cohen & Hutchinson, *supra* note 8, at 53.

[39] Aagaard, *supra* note 16, at 236.

[40] Cohen, *supra* note 11, at 810–17. *See also* Dagan, *supra* note 12, at 7–8; John Dewey, *The Historic Background of Corporate Legal Personality*, 35 YALE L.J. 655, 665, 669–70 (1926).

[41] Cohen, *supra* note 11, at 820.

[42] *See* H.L.A. HART, *Definition and Theory in Jurisprudence*, *in* ESSAYS IN JURISPRUDENCE AND PHILOSOPHY, *supra* note 6, at 21, 23–26, 44–45 (essay published 1953). *See also* Christopher M. Bruner, *The Enduring Ambivalence of Corporate Law*, 59 ALA. L. REV. 1385, 1388 (2008); Dewey, *supra* note 40, at 657, 663–64; Manning, *supra* note 18, at 245–48; David Millon, *The Ambiguous Significance of Corporate Personhood*, 2 STAN. AGORA 39, 40–41, 56–58 (2001); Mitchell, *supra* note 31, at 147–49; *infra* Chapter 9.

reference to rule-based sentences in which the word is accurately used[43]—Hart's core concern is not materially different from Cohen's. Both object to purportedly deducing what a corporation can do from conclusory statements about what a corporation is, divorced from relevant contextual features.

For Hart and Cohen alike, legal taxonomy should prompt us to investigate contextual features that drive corporate law in a given society to tackle particular problems in particular ways. In this sense, they differ only in the types of contextual features that preoccupy them—the legal landscape giving rise to the corporation for Hart, and the social and economic landscape in which the corporation operates for Cohen. As we will see, predominant approaches to defining corporate law have foundered precisely because they have failed to grapple with these dynamics.

B. Predominant Frames of Reference

The foregoing taxonomic complexities shed light on why the domain of corporate law has proven so difficult to specify. Stephen Bottomley aptly describes the field as a "disciplinary chameleon,"[44] though one might rather describe it as a Rorschach inkblot—with varying accounts having as much to tell us about the frames through which we perceive the subject as they do about the subject itself.

Surprisingly little attention has been devoted to the specific contours of corporate law's domain,[45] but frameworks for thinking about the field's scope and content are often implicit within reference texts and other works. This section discusses prevailing approaches to defining the scope and content of corporate law, as well as the limitations of those approaches, focusing on corporations with securities trading in public markets—the context where the corporation is most sharply distinguished from other business entity forms.[46] For convenience, extant approaches discussed in this chapter are summarized in Figure 4. This section also considers the relationship between corporate law and the related though distinct corporate governance concept, arguing that increasing resort to the latter implicitly acknowledges the difficulties encountered in efforts to describe corporate power relations through static doctrinal frameworks.

[43] *See* HART, *supra* note 42, at 26–30, 39. *See also* Dewey, *supra* note 40, at 655–56, 661–62.
[44] Bottomley, *supra* note 1, at 61.
[45] *See supra* note 1 and accompanying text.
[46] *See, e.g.*, ROBERT A. RAGAZZO & FRANCES S. FENDLER, CLOSELY HELD BUSINESS ORGANIZATIONS: CASES, MATERIALS, AND PROBLEMS 1–6, 595–626 (2d ed. 2012).

core constituencies	law governing relations among constituencies thought to represent the central corporate actors
core features	law providing features thought to be central to the corporate form's utility
core theories	law reflecting purportedly central purposes and goals of corporate activity

Figure 4 Defining the Domain of Corporate Law: Extant Approaches

I. CORE CONSTITUENCIES

Many corporate law texts fall back on descriptive generalizations about the central actors and relationships involved in corporate activity, without any clear justification for limiting the scope of the field in that specific way. In such works the explanatory aims regarding corporate law's domain are typically modest, however, simply identifying predominant preoccupations of corporate law in an introductory spirit.

A prominent example is Melvin Eisenberg's declaration that "[c]orporate law is constitutional law," in that "its dominant function is to regulate the manner in which the corporate institution is constituted, to define the relative rights and duties of those participating in the institution, and to delimit the powers of the institution vis-à-vis the external world." This, Eisenberg suggests, boils down to relations among just a couple categories of central corporate actors—the board and the shareholders.[47] This sort of approach has been widely followed in the corporate law literature,[48] yet little explanation is provided for treating the field as if it were coextensive with these actors.[49] Eisenberg sidesteps this question by taking as his baseline partnership law's virtual equation of the business with the equity holders themselves, from which perspective the question becomes why even a second constituency (i.e., the board) enters the picture in a corporation.[50] The exclusion of all others, or even any regard for their interests, generally goes unexplored, limiting the explanatory utility of such an approach in terms of corporate purpose in U.S. jurisdictions—which in fact permit varying degrees of

[47] Melvin Aron Eisenberg, *The Legal Roles of Shareholders and Management in Modern Corporate Decisionmaking*, 57 CAL. L. REV. 1, 1–2 (1969).

[48] *See, e.g.*, Bernard S. Black, *Is Corporate Law Trivial?: A Political and Economic Analysis*, 84 NW. U.L. REV. 542, 546–47 (1990); D. Gordon Smith, *The Dystopian Potential of Corporate Law*, 57 EMORY L.J. 985, 990–91 (2008); Robert B. Thompson & Hillary A. Sale, *Securities Fraud as Corporate Governance: Reflections upon Federalism*, 56 VAND. L. REV. 859, 864 (2003); Harwell Wells, *"Corporation Law Is Dead": Heroic Managerialism, Legal Change, and the Puzzle of Corporation Law at the Height of the American Century*, 15 U. PA. J. BUS. L. 305, 308 & n.13 (2013).

[49] *See* Bottomley, *supra* note 1, at 51.

[50] *See* Eisenberg, *supra* note 47, at 5–6. *Compare* UNIF. P'SHIP ACT §§ 301(1), 401(h), (k) (amended 2013), *with* DEL. CODE ANN. tit. 8, § 141(a).

regard for other constituencies and interests (notably in takeovers and sometimes more generally)[51]—and in terms of corporate power in other jurisdictions, where employees enjoy greater recognition, as in co-determination systems.[52]

In other instances, not even this minimal degree of explanation is provided—typically because macro-level generalizations are offered in a purely introductory spirit. For example, Arthur Pinto and Douglas Branson simply state in their treatise that the shareholder-board relationship represents a "significant aspect" of the field.[53] Similarly, casebooks often focus on the shareholder-board relationship to give students some impression of what to expect. Accordingly, Charles O'Kelley and Robert Thompson describe this relationship as "the key recurring issue."[54] Alan Palmiter and Frank Partnoy, meanwhile, suggest that students approach the subject in terms of "the questions that you would ask if you were thinking of investing in a business," in light of which they assert that corporate law "is about investors and managers."[55]

A treatise aimed at practitioners may similarly employ such introductory generalizations, while directing attention to jurisdiction-specific dynamics. For example, in their introduction to the Balotti and Finkelstein treatise on the corporate law of Delaware—the leading U.S. state for incorporation of public companies[56]—Leo Herzel and Laura Richman present the shareholder-board relationship as an "important concern," while acknowledging the impact of factors that blur the boundaries between Delaware corporate law and other fields. Notably, they cite "populist" concerns regarding "the effects of the accumulation of wealth and power," responses to which "are usually federal."[57] In this light, Herzel and Richman describe Delaware corporate law's boundaries not by reference to intrinsic doctrinal features, but rather in negative terms. Various controversial issues have been "preempted by federal laws governing such matters as antitrust, bankruptcy, political corruption and pollution of the environment," rendering Delaware corporate law a sort of residual category. "What

[51] *See generally* BRUNER, *supra* note 2.

[52] *See, e.g.*, Thilo Kuntz, *German Corporate Law in the 20th Century*, *in* RESEARCH HANDBOOK ON THE HISTORY OF CORPORATE AND COMPANY LAW (Harwell Wells ed., 2018), https://ssrn.com/abstract=2930974 (working paper version).

[53] ARTHUR R. PINTO & DOUGLAS M. BRANSON, UNDERSTANDING CORPORATE LAW 2 (4th ed. 2013).

[54] CHARLES R.T. O'KELLEY & ROBERT B. THOMPSON, CORPORATIONS AND OTHER BUSINESS ASSOCIATIONS: CASES AND MATERIALS xxvi (7th ed. 2014).

[55] ALAN R. PALMITER & FRANK PARTNOY, CORPORATIONS: A CONTEMPORARY APPROACH iv, viii (2d ed. 2014)(emphasis removed).

[56] *See* State of Delaware, Division of Corporations, *Why Businesses Choose Delaware*, https://corplaw.delaware.gov/why-businesses-choose-delaware/ (reporting that "more than one million business entities have made Delaware their legal home" and that "more than 60 percent of the Fortune 500 companies are incorporated in Delaware").

[57] Leo Herzel & Laura D. Richman, *Foreword* to R. FRANKLIN BALOTTI & JESSE A. FINKELSTEIN, 1 THE DELAWARE LAW OF CORPORATIONS & BUSINESS ORGANIZATIONS F-1, F-7 (3d ed. 2016). *Cf.* Roman Tomasic, *Introduction: Corporate Law in Transition*, *in* ROUTLEDGE HANDBOOK OF CORPORATE LAW, *supra* note 1, at 1, 2.

remains are rules governing the relationships among stockholders, directors and management,"[58] a description reflecting the shortcomings already described while pointing toward the significance of contextual factors examined later in this book.

II. CORE FEATURES

Another common approach involves describing corporate law by reference to the distinctive features thought to give the corporate form special utility.[59] This approach accommodates a higher degree of variation across jurisdictions, but does so by retreating to a higher level of abstraction, where it becomes impossible to draw finer distinctions. More significantly, however, one finds that authoritative texts often do not agree on what the corporate form's critical features are—meaning that competing frameworks have very different ramifications regarding the domain of corporate law and the nature of the corporate form.

An influential framework of this sort appears in Robert Clark's treatise, which identifies four features to explain "the corporation's success as a form of organization"—limited liability, share transferability, "legal personality," and centralized management.[60] For Clark, corporate law represents "an attempt to synthesize" the benefits and costs of these features, the "major problem" being how to balance managers' discretionary powers with accountability—tackled principally through the fiduciary duty of loyalty.[61] Like the approaches already canvassed, however, Clark offers no clear explanation of why some problems related to corporate activity fall within corporate law while others do not. He observes that "traditionally, the subjects of corporation law and securities regulation are simply defined to deal only with relationships between shareholders and managers,"[62] without clarifying how we ought to think about the relationship between corporate law and securities regulation as distinct fields, let alone explaining the exclusive focus on these particular sets of actors. He then catalogs various other fields considered "not within conventional corporate law's jurisdiction"—notably fields relating to other constituencies and interests, such as commercial law, labor law, bankruptcy law, antitrust law, and environmental law. Clark obliquely acknowledges the difficult line-drawing problems, concluding that his "brief listing will drive home the point that knowing corporate law is not enough to make you a good general corporate counsel nor to give you a full sense

[58] Herzel & Richman, *supra* note 57, at F-17–F-18.
[59] *See* Bottomley, *supra* note 1, at 51.
[60] ROBERT CHARLES CLARK, CORPORATE LAW 2 (1986).
[61] *Id.* at 4, 32–34.
[62] *Id.* at 30.

of how the legal system shapes corporate activities."[63] This candid acknowledgment gestures toward acute taxonomic challenges.

Others have followed a similar approach, citing similar lists of attributes based on similar rationales. For example, in their casebook, Jesse Choper, John Coffee, and Ronald Gilson cite four features—limited liability, "perpetual existence," share transferability, and centralized management. Like Clark, they suggest that these features "provide a roadmap of much of the substantive content of corporate law"—the "master problem" again being "how to control management discretion . . . without chilling the efficiency and entrepreneurial style of the corporate form."[64] William Allen and Reinier Kraakman likewise list five features in their casebook (citing Clark's "similar list")—"legal personality," limited liability, share transferability, centralized management, and board appointment by equity holders—and suggest that these features respond to the correlative "weaknesses" of the partnership form.[65] They conclude that the "major problems in corporate law deal with the relations between 'outside' investors, who lack power, and 'insiders,' who control the company's assets,"[66] once again directing attention to the shareholder-manager relationship. Corporate law's linkage with securities regulation, meanwhile, is addressed historically; securities regulation, they explain, represents a reaction to the shift from mandatory to "enabling" corporate statutes in the late nineteenth century, a distinction suggesting that the line between these fields cannot be drawn by reference to intrinsic subject matter.[67]

Others similarly invoke purportedly intrinsic corporate features, while acknowledging that they do not specify the boundaries of corporate law in a comprehensive way. Melvin Eisenberg and James Cox, for example, cite five features in their casebook—limited liability, share transferability, "continuity of existence," centralized management, and "entity status."[68] While state law provides these corporate "endowments," however, federal law regulates certain important "functions" associated with them, and Eisenberg and Cox accordingly include this as one of four "modules" of corporate law, along with state statutes, state case law, and "soft law" (e.g. stock exchange rules).[69] In so doing, they essentially resort to a functional approach. "Any body of rules that addresses one or more of" certain enumerated "functions" related to shareholders and managers,

[63] *Id.* at 30–32.

[64] JESSE H. CHOPER ET AL., CASES AND MATERIALS ON CORPORATIONS 1–4 (8th ed. 2013).

[65] WILLIAM T. ALLEN & REINIER KRAAKMAN, COMMENTARIES AND CASES ON THE LAW OF BUSINESS ORGANIZATION 75 (5th ed. 2016).

[66] *Id.* at 77.

[67] *Id.* at 80–82. *See also* PINTO & BRANSON, *supra* note 53, at 5–6; Adam Winkler, *Corporate Law or the Law of Business?: Stakeholders and Corporate Governance at the End of History*, 67 L. CONTEMP. PROB. 109, 112–15 (2004).

[68] MELVIN ARON EISENBERG & JAMES D. COX, CORPORATIONS AND OTHER BUSINESS ORGANIZATIONS: CASES AND MATERIALS 191–92 (10th ed. 2011)(emphasis removed).

[69] *Id.* at 192–93.

they conclude, ought to be treated as part of the field.[70] This posture abandons any pretense of illuminating the boundaries of corporate law as such, gesturing toward the broader corporate governance framing discussed later in the chapter.

Paul Davies and Sarah Worthington adopt a similar approach in their treatise on company law in the United Kingdom, where a field that used to be contained to distinct "company" legislation has been reallocated over recent decades. Like those discussed before, Davies and Worthington cite a list of features said to distinguish the corporation from other forms of business organization—including a distinct legal entity (the "fundamental attribute"), limited liability, share transferability, and centralized management[71]—and take these as a framework to discuss "advantages and disadvantages of incorporation,"[72] along the lines that Clark does. They add, however, that U.K. company law's precise boundaries have become less clear due to statutory fragmentation; "the whole of the law relevant to companies has ceased to be contained in companies legislation," with insolvency and financial services being "hived off" in 1986—developments that highlighted "perennial problems of classification."[73] Presumably increasing complexity has been a driver of such statutory fragmentation—notably, the Companies Act 2006 involved "the most comprehensive review of the area since company law's inception," and the legislation that resulted was "said to be the longest ever to be passed by Parliament."[74] Like others, Davies and Worthington bracket these thorny questions by resort to a functional approach. "Whatever the decisions taken by Government," they conclude, "functionally, important parts of the law relating to companies are not to be found in Acts which contain the word 'company' in their title."[75]

Such a functional approach has proven attractive in comparative studies, where substantial variations in regulatory structures are often confronted. *The Anatomy of Corporate Law*[76] similarly highlights five features—"legal personality," limited liability, share transferability, centralized management, and "investor ownership"—and posits that "corporate law must, of necessity, provide for them." On this basis, the authors argue that "a principal function of corporate law is to provide business enterprises with a legal form that possesses these five core attributes," and they conclude that "[m]ost of corporate law can be understood as responding to" the problems that these attributes raise—notably "agency

[70] *Id.* at 192.
[71] PAUL L. DAVIES & SARAH WORTHINGTON, GOWER & DAVIES PRINCIPLES OF MODERN COMPANY LAW 35–53 (9th ed. 2012). They also note capacity to own property, to sue and be sued, to borrow, and to be taxed, *id.*, which are corollaries of a distinct legal entity.
[72] *Id.* at 35 (emphasis removed).
[73] *Id.* at 59.
[74] *Id.* at 57–58. *Cf.* Andrew Hutchinson & Iain Smedley, *The Juggernaut Comes to Grief*, LAW SOC. GAZ., Feb. 17, 1993.
[75] DAVIES & WORTHINGTON, *supra* note 71, at 59. *Cf.* Tomasic, *supra* note 57, at 1.
[76] *See* KRAAKMAN ET AL., *supra* note 1.

problems"[77] of the sort emphasized by financial economists and law-and-economics scholars.[78] Their approach is expressly "functional," a methodological choice that they root in the project's comparative and taxonomic nature. The aim of *The Anatomy* is "to give a highly integrated view of the role and structure of corporate law that provides a clear framework within which to organize an understanding of individual systems, both alone and in comparison with each other."[79]

This naturally raises acute line-drawing concerns, to which *The Anatomy* responds that any statute or case law beyond the "core statute" that are "nonetheless instrumental to the functioning of the five core characteristics of the corporate form" are viewed "functionally as part of corporate law."[80] While including literally any form of law that affects the aforementioned attributes would embrace an extraordinary regulatory terrain, the limiting principle appears to be whether or not the regulatory "objective" of a given legal field is to affect a central corporate feature. Thus, Germany's law of corporate groups and the co-determination system are considered part of corporate law, as are "supplemental sources" of governance and disclosure rules from securities regulation and stock exchange rules. Areas like bankruptcy, tax, and labor law, however, are not considered part of corporate law because they are "designed to serve objectives that are, in general, independent of the form taken by the organizations they affect."[81]

German co-determination nicely illustrates the tensions, and even contradictions, that plague comparative efforts to define corporate law and to describe the corporation in such universal terms. The co-determination system mandates substantial labor representation on the supervisory boards of large German companies.[82] This is treated as part of corporate law in *The Anatomy*, yet labor law generally is not[83]—even though German law doctrinally categorizes co-determination as an element of labor law.[84] While German corporate law

[77] *See* Armour et al., *supra* note 1, at 1–2, 5–15.

[78] *See* MARC MOORE & MARTIN PETRIN, CORPORATE GOVERNANCE: LAW, REGULATION AND THEORY 29–37 (2017).

[79] Armour et al., *supra* note 1, at 3.

[80] *Id.* at 15–16.

[81] *Id.* at 16–17.

[82] *See* Kuntz, *supra* note 52, at 17–30. In the German system, distinct management and supervisory boards create "a formal separation between the management and monitoring functions." John Armour et al., *The Basic Governance Structure: The Interests of Shareholders as a Class*, *in* KRAAKMAN ET AL., *supra* note 1, at 49, 50.

[83] *See* Armour et al., *supra* note 1, at 16–17.

[84] *See generally* FEDERAL MINISTRY OF LABOUR AND SOCIAL AFFAIRS, CO-DETERMINATION 2018 (Mar. 2018) [hereinafter CO-DETERMINATION]. *See also* Federal Ministry of Labour and Social Affairs, *Organisational Chart*, https://www.bmas.de/SharedDocs/Downloads/EN/organigramm-bmas-en.pdf?__blob=publicationFile&v=5 (updated Sept. 1, 2020).

does reference the co-determination system, it does so to incorporate by reference other laws that expressly govern the relevant aspects of board structure.[85]

Workers have substantial participation rights under German law, generally taking two forms—works councils at the establishment level and co-determination at the supervisory board level.[86] The Works Constitution Act requires works councils at companies with five or more employees, giving them extensive approval rights relating to "social welfare, personnel and economic matters."[87] For companies with over 2,000 employees, the "company's supervisory board must be made up of employee and shareholder representatives in equal measure," with the tie-breaking chairperson generally being elected by the shareholders.[88] For other companies with over 500 employees, the employees "have to make up one third of the membership."[89] In the coal, iron, and steel industries, meanwhile—where co-determination originated—employees make up half of the supervisory board in companies with over 1,000 employees and, in addition to the other half comprised of shareholder representatives, the board "includes one additional, 'neutral' member."[90] While some suggest that supervisory boards are deliberately kept poorly informed to limit labor's involvement,[91] *The Anatomy* itself acknowledges that German employees in co-determined companies "retain considerable power, formally through a statutory right to veto nominees to the management

[85] *See* Aktiengesetz [AktG] [Stock Corporation Act], Sept. 6, 1965, *last amended* July 17, 2017, arts. 95–116 (Ger.), https://www.gesetze-im-internet.de/englisch_aktg/englisch_aktg.html (translation by Samson Übersetzungen GmbH, Dr. Carmen von Schöning, published by the Federal Ministry of Justice and Consumer Protection).

[86] *See* CO-DETERMINATION, *supra* note 84, at 4. Co-determination rights are "usually thought only to cover workers in Germany." Ewan McGaughey, *Good for Governance: Erzberger v TUI AG and the Codetermination Bargains*, OXFORD BUSINESS LAW BLOG, Aug. 18, 2017, https://www.law.ox.ac.uk/business-law-blog/blog/2017/08/good-governance-erzberger-v-tui-ag-and-codetermination-bargains. *See also* Carsten Gerner-Beuerle & Edmund Schuster, *The Costs of Separation: Friction Between Company and Insolvency Law in the Single Market*, 14 J. CORP. L. STUD. 287, 298 (2014).

[87] *See* CO-DETERMINATION, *supra* note 84, at 4–9. *See also* Betriebsverfassungsgesetz [BetrVG] [Works Constitution Act], Sept. 25, 2001, *last amended* July 17, 2017 (Ger.), *translated in id.* at 17–71. Regarding EU-level rules on works councils, see Europäische Betriebsräte-Gesetz [EBRG] [Act on European Works Councils], Dec. 7, 2011, *last amended* July 17, 2017 (Ger.), *translated in id.* at 72–87; *id.* at 9–10.

[88] *See* CO-DETERMINATION, *supra* note 84, at 11–12. *See also* Mitbestimmungsgesetz [MitbestG] [Co-determination Act], May 4, 1976, *last amended* Apr. 24, 2015, arts. 1, 6–7, 27, 29 (Ger.), *translated in id.* at 88–102.

[89] *See* CO-DETERMINATION, *supra* note 84, at 12. *See also* Drittelbeteiligungsgesetz [DrittelbG] [Law on One-Third Employee Representation in the Supervisory Board], May 18, 2004, *last amended* Apr. 24, 2015, arts. 1, 4 (Ger.), *translated in id.* at 103–06.

[90] *See* CO-DETERMINATION, *supra* note 84, at 12. *See also* GRANT M. HAYDEN & MATTHEW T. BODIE, RECONSTRUCTING THE CORPORATION: FROM SHAREHOLDER PRIMACY TO SHARED GOVERNANCE 173–74 (2020). Regarding application to EU companies, see CO-DETERMINATION, *supra* note 84, at 13–14. *See also* SE-Beteiligungsgesetz [SEBG] [Act on the Involvement of Employees in a European Company], Dec. 22, 2004 (Ger.), *translated in id.* at 107–26. On the history of co-determination in Germany, see Ewan McGaughey, *The Codetermination Bargains: The History of German Corporate and Labor Law*, 23 COLUM. J. EUR. L. 135 (2016).

[91] *See, e.g.*, MARK J. ROE, POLITICAL DETERMINANTS OF CORPORATE GOVERNANCE: POLITICAL CONTEXT, CORPORATE IMPACT 73–76 (2003).

board, and informally, because they are in a position to disrupt the proceedings." Indeed, supervisory board representation further gives labor "power to withhold consent from contentious company decisions."[92]

Numerous other jurisdictions similarly give employees substantial governance roles. As of 2015, a majority of the members of the European Union provided some degree of board-level participation rights for employees,[93] and such structures have been adopted in other parts of the world as well. For example, many Chinese companies are required to have a two-tier structure "very similar to the German corporate governance model."[94] This corporate governance role for labor, as *The Anatomy* concedes, "deviates from the assumption of investor ownership"[95] that the project's overarching framework characterizes as a "necessity" of the corporate form.[96]

Beyond the foregoing taxonomic difficulties, however, authorities differ significantly regarding what the core features of the corporate form are—even within a given jurisdiction. For example, in contrast with the works cited earlier, Stephen Bainbridge's treatise cites six core features—"formal creation as prescribed by state law; legal personality; separation of ownership and control; freely alienable ownership interests; indefinite duration; and limited liability."[97] The key difference is that while others emphasize shareholder power to elect the board as a form of managerial accountability, Bainbridge suggests precisely the opposite in listing "separation of ownership and control" as a defining feature of the corporate form—the point being to underscore the board's structural insulation from meaningful shareholder influence, at least in widely held public companies.[98] While Bainbridge agrees that fiduciary constraints represent an important category of corporate law's content,[99] he clearly sees shareholders inhabiting a marginal governance role, pointing to broader theoretical divergences.[100]

[92] Luca Enriques et al., *The Basic Governance Structure: Minority Shareholders and Non-Shareholder Constituencies*, *in* KRAAKMAN ET AL., *supra* note 1, at 79, 90–91. *See also id.* at 105; CO-DETERMINATION, *supra* note 84, at 11–12. For a review of the mixed empirical results regarding the effects of co-determination, see Jens Dammann & Horst Eidenmüller, *Codetermination: A Poor Fit for U.S. Corporations*, 3 COLUM. BUS. L. REV. 870, 889–900 (2020).

[93] *See* HANS BÖCKLER STIFTUNG, WHY CO-DETERMINATION? A COLLECTION OF GOOD ARGUMENTS FOR STRONG WORKERS' VOICE (2019), slide 10, https://www.boeckler.de/pdf/mbf_praes_arguments_co_determination.pdf. *See also* Enriques et al., *supra* note 92, at 90.

[94] JINGCHEN ZHAO, CORPORATE SOCIAL RESPONSIBILITY IN CONTEMPORARY CHINA 96–98 (2014). *See also* Deloitte China Centre for Corporate Governance, *Board of Supervisors and Stakeholders*, https://www2.deloitte.com/cn/en/pages/risk/solutions/cg-supervisory-committee-and-shareholders.html.

[95] Armour et al., *supra* note 1, at 14.

[96] *Id.* at 1.

[97] STEPHEN M. BAINBRIDGE, CORPORATE LAW 1 (2d ed. 2009).

[98] *Id.* at 3–5.

[99] *Id.* at 3–4.

[100] *See* Christopher M. Bruner, *The Corporation's Intrinsic Attributes*, *in* UNDERSTANDING THE COMPANY: CORPORATE GOVERNANCE AND THEORY 60, 68 (Barnali Choudhury & Martin Petrin eds., 2017).

Meanwhile William Klein, John Coffee, and Frank Partnoy cite seven features—"separate entity," "divisible ownership," "assets separated from shareholders," "limited liability," "indefinite duration," "transferable and tradable shares and debt obligations," and "centralized control and separation of ownership and control."[101] Here, again, the "separation of ownership and control" in public companies tends to de-emphasize shareholder voting as a disciplinary mechanism. Yet Klein, Coffee, and Partnoy further deviate from the foregoing accounts by placing greater emphasis on debt financing—pointing toward creditors, and creditor protection, as central features of the corporate form and critical concerns for corporate law.[102] Such markedly differing views on what the core corporate features are clearly reflect divergent views on the domain of corporate law and the nature of the corporate form itself.[103]

To be sure, there is substantial agreement across these frameworks regarding the centrality of at least one corporate feature—a distinct legal entity. For example, Davies and Worthington identify "a legal entity distinct from its members" as "the fundamental attribute . . . from which indeed all the other consequences flow."[104] Likewise *The Anatomy* characterizes "legal personality" as the "first and most important contribution of corporate law."[105] In a similar spirit, Klein, Coffee, and Partnoy list a "separate entity" as the first corporate feature, and then link this expressly to other features relevant to creditor protection.[106]

Each of the foregoing authorities emphasizes the capacity of a distinct legal entity to provide "asset partitioning,"[107] a concept described by Henry Hansmann,

[101] WILLIAM A. KLEIN ET AL., BUSINESS ORGANIZATION AND FINANCE: LEGAL AND ECONOMIC PRINCIPLES 108–10 (11th ed. 2010)(emphasis removed).

[102] *See* Bruner, *supra* note 100, at 68–69.

[103] *Id.* at 69–70.

[104] DAVIES & WORTHINGTON, *supra* note 71, at 35.

[105] Armour et al., *supra* note 1, at 5.

[106] KLEIN ET AL., *supra* note 101, at 108–10. Conversely, in legal contexts where the corporate structure is considered problematic—notably under Islamic law—it is precisely due to objections regarding the desirability of a legal entity distinct from the business participants themselves. *See* RAJ BHALA, UNDERSTANDING ISLAMIC LAW (SHARĪ'A) 596 (2011); TIMUR KURAN, THE LONG DIVERGENCE: HOW ISLAMIC LAW HELD BACK THE MIDDLE EAST 97–142 (2011); Timur Kuran, *The Absence of the Corporation in Islamic Law: Origins and Persistence*, 53 AM. J. COMP. L. 785 (2005). There is considerable variation in the degree to which Muslim-majority jurisdictions have sought to conform corporate and financial law to Islamic law principles. *See, e.g.*, CHRISTOPHER M. BRUNER, RE-IMAGINING OFFSHORE FINANCE: MARKET-DOMINANT SMALL JURISDICTIONS IN A GLOBALIZING FINANCIAL WORLD 69–109 (2016) (discussing Islamic finance in Dubai); MOHAMAD TALAAT ET AL., DOING BUSINESS IN EGYPT 2 (2016) (Baker & McKenzie report) (observing that although "Egypt's legal system is based on Islamic law . . . and Napoleanic codes" and "there have been moves to consolidate the influence of the Shari'ah," Egypt's "commercial law remains based on modern commercial practice"); Abdul Karim Aldohni, *Islamic Financial Institutions and Corporate Sustainability: A Study of Oman, Dubai and Malaysia, in* THE CAMBRIDGE HANDBOOK OF CORPORATE LAW, CORPORATE GOVERNANCE AND SUSTAINABILITY 490 (Beate Sjåfjell & Christopher M. Bruner eds., 2019).

[107] *See* DAVIES & WORTHINGTON, *supra* note 71, at 42–43; KLEIN ET AL., *supra* note 101, at 108; Armour et al., *supra* note 1, at 5–7. *See also* Ofer Eldar & Andrew Verstein, *The Enduring Distinction between Business Entities and Security Interests*, 92 S. CAL. L. REV. 213, 220–24 (2019).

Reinier Kraakman, and Richard Squire as involving rules that clarify "which entities bond which contracts, and which assets belong to which entities."[108] The broader concept of asset partitioning includes both "entity shielding," which "protect[s] a firm's assets from the personal creditors of its owners," and "owner shielding," which "protect[s] the personal assets of a firm's owners from the firm's creditors"—the former arising from a distinct legal entity and the latter arising from limited liability.[109] Unlike owner shielding via limited liability, which could potentially "be achieved through contract," entity shielding via a distinct legal entity "clearly requires special rules of law." Accordingly, this represents "the primary virtue of legal entities" and a key to understanding "the policy tradeoffs that organizational law presents today."[110] Note, however, that this point of commonality among the frameworks canvassed earlier simply retreats to a higher level of abstraction; focusing on the core or foundation of a field may prove illuminating, yet it leaves to the side a full account of the field's content and boundaries, the specifics of which clearly cannot be deduced from this single elemental feature.

III. CORE THEORIES

Another approach involves sketching out the implications of a theory. The aim of such an effort is to articulate a theoretical framework that illuminates corporate law's fundamental social purpose and/or regulatory strategy, and then to support that claim through a mixed normative and positive argument that corporate law ought to, and in fact generally does, contain the mix of rules and standards that the theory would lead one to expect. Three prevailing theories of modern corporate law—nexus of contracts theory, team production theory, and shareholder primacy theory—advance competing normative and positive frameworks along these lines.[111] None of them, however, compellingly specifies the domain of corporate law or the nature of the corporate form in the comprehensive manner typically claimed.

The nexus of contracts theory, elaborated by Frank Easterbrook and Daniel Fischel, aims "to understand the logic of corporate law,"[112] advancing the mixed normative and positive claim that their framework reflects how corporate law "should" work and that corporate law "almost always conforms" to their account.[113] Noting that modern corporate law includes few mandatory rules,[114]

108 Henry Hansmann et al., *Law and the Rise of the Firm*, 119 HARV. L. REV. 1333, 1337 (2006).

109 *Id.* at 1337–39.

110 *Id.* at 1340–43.

111 *See generally* Bruner, *supra* note 42. *See also* BRUNER, *supra* note 2, at 53–65.

112 FRANK H. EASTERBROOK & DANIEL R. FISCHEL, THE ECONOMIC STRUCTURE OF CORPORATE LAW vii (1991).

113 *Id.* at 15.

114 *See id.* at 2–3.

and then loosely characterizing choices made available to business participants as "contractual" in nature,[115] Easterbrook and Fischel downplay the significance of the sorts of core features discussed earlier. The true heart of the field, in their view, is capacity to tailor the entity as one likes—hence their description of the corporation as a "nexus of contracts."[116]

For Easterbrook and Fischel, much turns on attracting capital providers through financial and governance structures that shareholders—characterized as the sole residual claimants—would find attractive.[117] Based on this premise, corporate law exists solely to reduce transaction costs through majoritarian default rules, combined with gap-filling devices—the sole purpose of fiduciary duty in the nexus of contracts corporation.[118] As to the substantive law, their claim is that capital providers will favor default rules that effectively reduce "agency costs" otherwise arising from misalignment between managers' incentives and their own.[119] This features exclusive shareholder power to elect the board and directors' duties focused exclusively on shareholder interests[120]—a structure that gains additional normative appeal, Easterbrook and Fischel argue, based on the purportedly unique homogeneity of shareholder interests, lending greater coherence and stability to shareholder-centric corporate governance.[121]

To say that this account presents a narrow domain for corporate law would be an understatement. Indeed, Bernard Black, taking an approach largely compatible with this contractarian framework,[122] concludes that U.S. corporate law is substantively "trivial" in the sense that it prohibits nothing of significance.[123] Reduction of corporate law to bilateral deal-making effectively assumes away corporate law as a coherent, conventional field of law; on this account, corporate law is essentially a branch of contract law.

While resembling the realist perspective in its focus on extralegal determinants of regulation, law-and-economics literature differs markedly in its general disregard of social context[124]—a tendency clearly reflected in associated corporate law scholarship, which correlatively falls short of a compelling descriptive account of the field. Easterbrook and Fischel's account relies on controversial empirical assumptions, including that (1) the market is highly efficient, which permits styling virtually all corporate activity as a matter of choice and facilitates

115 *See id.* at 14.
116 *See id.* at 11–12, 15.
117 *See id.* at 10–11, 35–39, 90–93.
118 *See id.* at 15, 34.
119 *See id.* at 10, 14.
120 *See id.* at 35–39, 90–93.
121 *See id.* at 23, 69–70.
122 *See* Black, *supra* note 48, at 546–51.
123 *See id.* at 544, 593. *See also* Daniel J.H. Greenwood, *Introduction to the Metaphors of Corporate Law*, 4 SEATTLE J. SOC. JUST. 273, 285–86 (2005).
124 *See* MOORE & PETRIN, *supra* note 78, at 36–37; Gold & Smith, *supra* note 8, at 9–10.

a race-to-the-top depiction of charter competition;[125] (2) shareholders homogeneously favor wealth maximization and are homogeneous in their preferences regarding its attainment;[126] (3) there are no externalities borne by "strangers to the contracts," which permits characterizing prevailing market practice as socially optimal and accordingly tends to blur normative and positive claims;[127] and (4) other constituencies, such as employees, can be fully protected through (real) contracts and extra-corporate regulation, which elides concerns about the social desirability of strong-form shareholder-centrism.[128] Only by making these problematic assumptions[129] can substantive corporate law be reduced to just two constituencies—managers and the capital they "hire"[130]—with little room for regulation of third-party effects, and even less for mandatory intrusions upon "intra-corporate affairs" otherwise left to private ordering.[131] Even if one were willing to accept such dubious assumptions, the gaps in this descriptive account remain substantial—perhaps the most glaring being U.S. law on hostile takeovers, where shareholder power and shareholder interests alike have been substantially subordinated, including by reference to vulnerabilities faced by other corporate constituencies.[132] Should these assumptions be relaxed or rejected outright, however, then that might lead one to predict coalescence around a very different set of default rules, reflecting a broader conception of whose welfare ought to be weighed in the balance in corporate decision-making,[133] and/or who ought to have corporate governance power.[134] It might even prompt outright abandonment of the enabling approach on a given subject in favor of mandatory rules better aligned with society's broader priorities.[135]

[125] *See* EASTERBROOK & FISCHEL, *supra* note 112, at 4–6, 19, 24.

[126] *See id.* at 23, 69–70.

[127] *See id.* at 6–7, 15–17. *See also* Margaret M. Blair, *On Models, Metaphors, Rhetoric, and the Law*, 41 TULSA L. REV. 513, 514–16 (2006); Millon, *supra* note 42, at 53–56. *Cf.* Gold & Smith, *supra* note 8, at 16–17.

[128] *See* EASTERBROOK & FISCHEL, *supra* note 112, at 24, 35–39.

[129] "Progressive" corporate scholarship coalesced around rejection of such contractarian assumptions. *See generally* PROGRESSIVE CORPORATE LAW (Lawrence E. Mitchell ed., 1995); Christopher M. Bruner, *Center-Left Politics and Corporate Governance: What Is the "Progressive" Agenda?*, 2018 BYU L. REV. 267 (2018).

[130] *See* EASTERBROOK & FISCHEL, *supra* note 112, at 10–11.

[131] *See id.* at 23.

[132] *See, e.g.*, IND. CODE § 23-1-35-1(d); Unocal Corp. v. Mesa Petroleum Co., 493 A.2d 946, 955 (Del. 1985); Revlon, Inc. v. MacAndrews & Forbes Holdings, Inc., 506 A.2d 173, 182 (Del. 1986). *See also* BRUNER, *supra* note 2, at 42–44, 53–57, 171–73.

[133] *See, e.g.*, KENT GREENFIELD, THE FAILURE OF CORPORATE LAW: FUNDAMENTAL FLAWS AND PROGRESSIVE POSSIBILITIES 14–19 (2006); Greenwood, *supra* note 123, at 287.

[134] *See* HAYDEN & BODIE, *supra* note 90, at 68–87, 145–60 (rejecting characterization of shareholders as uniquely homogeneous and arguing in favor of board representation for employees).

[135] Cass Sunstein, for example, argues that the "preferred approach" to establishing a default rule is to select the rule reflecting "what most people would choose if they were adequately informed." Cass R. Sunstein, *Deciding by Default*, 162 U. PENN. L. REV. 1, 31 (2013) (emphasis removed). Where there are "third-party effects," however, the matter "is no longer limited to the welfare of choosers," and selection of the default rule should therefore "be based on an analysis of all relevant benefits and costs (capaciously understood), and choice architects should select the approach that maximizes net

The most significant competing conception of the corporation and corporate law is the team production theory. As elaborated by Margaret Blair and Lynn Stout, team production theory likewise purports to present "a solid theoretical foundation for the basic structure of public corporation law," including "both positive and normative components,"[136] and their claim is that this framework "is more consistent with the way a corporation actually works than are prominent contractarian interpretations of corporate law that focus on the principal-agent problem."[137] Blair and Stout conclude that the purpose of the corporation and corporate law is to provide a "mediating hierarchy" that promotes firm-specific investment by all the stakeholders contributing to corporate production.[138] Observing that the board's power under corporate law is "virtually absolute,"[139] they argue that the core regulatory strategy is "to protect the enterprise-specific investments of all the members of the corporate 'team,' including shareholders, managers, rank and file employees, and possibly other groups, such as creditors"—all of whom are styled as residual claimants.[140]

Team production theory is not an inherently progressive or communitarian theory. Rather, it is a variant of nexus theory focused on inducing all the various stakeholders to contribute to corporate production. Blair and Stout style the corporation "not as a nexus of implicit or explicit contracts, but as a nexus of firm-specific investments made by many and varied individuals who give up control over those resources to a decisionmaking process in hopes of sharing in the benefits that can flow from team production."[141] As a substantive matter, the core claim is that public corporations depend critically on an all-powerful board. An "overlooked 'contract' fundamental to the nature of public corporations," they argue, "is the '*pactum subjectionis*' under which shareholders, managers, employees, and other groups that make firm-specific investments yield control over both those investments and the resulting output to the corporation's internal governing hierarchy."[142]

Descriptively, team production theory is at its strongest precisely where nexus of contracts theory falters, including capacity to deviate from shareholder

benefits (understood to include the range of ingredients in social welfare)." Indeed, "if third-party effects are large, we might not be in the domain of mere default rules" at all, as mandatory rules may be required to prevent "the imposition of serious costs on third parties." *Id.* at 35–36.

[136] Margaret M. Blair & Lynn A. Stout, *A Team Production Theory of Corporate Law*, 85 VA. L. REV. 247, 289 (1999).
[137] *Id.* at 254.
[138] *See id.* at 250–51, 288–89.
[139] *Id.* at 251.
[140] *Id.* at 253, 280–81 (emphasis removed). *See also* HAYDEN & BODIE, *supra* note 90, at 96–102 (arguing that employees ought to be regarded as residual claimants).
[141] Blair & Stout, *supra* note 136, at 253–54, 285 (emphasis removed).
[142] *Id.* at 320.

preferences under the law of hostile takeovers.[143] Conversely, however, the claim that the board serves as a "mediating hierarch" consisting of directors charged to act as "trustees for the corporation itself"[144] renders it difficult to account for those corporate law structures that really do favor shareholders—including voting power and standing to bring fiduciary duty claims.[145] Indeed, the lack of a general stakeholder mandate is itself problematic for a theory premised on the mediating hierarch conception of the board. "The very discretion that allows corporate boards to pay attention to nonshareholder as well as shareholder interests," David Millon observes, "also allows them to pursue shareholder value with relentless disregard for social costs."[146] This renders it all the more surprising that team production theory remains content with the exclusive shareholder franchise—an awkward posture apparently reflecting acceptance of the widespread, yet likely flawed, assumption that shareholders' interests are uniquely homogeneous.[147] Ultimately, team production theory fares no better than nexus of contracts theory in terms of providing a compelling holistic account of corporate law and the nature of the corporate form.

Strict shareholder primacy, meanwhile, appears the weakest of the three—certainly in the U.S. context, where its description of the shareholder-manager relationship is fundamentally at odds with basic principles of corporate law. The shareholder primacy theory posits that shareholders own the corporation, and that managers work for them in a straightforward principal-agent relationship. As Milton Friedman expressed it in an influential statement of this view:

> In a free-enterprise, private-property system, a corporate executive is an employe [sic] of the owners of the business. He has direct responsibility to his employers. That responsibility is to conduct the business in accordance with their desires, which generally will be to make as much money as possible while conforming to the basic rules of the society....[148]

Lest there be any doubt about the lens through which Friedman views internal corporate affairs, he adds that the "whole justification for permitting the corporate executive to be selected by the stockholders is that the executive is an agent serving the interests of his principal."[149]

[143] *See* BRUNER, *supra* note 2, at 58–60.

[144] Blair & Stout, *supra* note 136, at 280–81 (emphasis removed).

[145] *See* BRUNER, *supra* note 2, at 59–60.

[146] David Millon, *New Game Plan or Business as Usual? A Critique of the Team Production Model of Corporate Law*, 86 VA. L. REV. 1001, 1022 (2000).

[147] *See* HAYDEN & BODIE, *supra* note 90, at 132–34.

[148] Milton Friedman, *A Friedman Doctrine—The Social Responsibility of Business Is to Increase Profits*, N.Y. TIMES MAG., Sept. 13, 1970, at 33. *See also* MILTON FRIEDMAN, CAPITALISM AND FREEDOM 133–36 (1982)(1962).

[149] Friedman, *supra* note 148, at 122.

This characterization is easily dispensed with; it is plainly incorrect as a legal matter. Whatever descriptive purchase such a shareholder-focused depiction might have in (say) the United Kingdom—where a board's power is literally delegated by the shareholders via the articles, where shareholders retain extraordinary governance powers, and where corporate fiduciaries are expressly duty bound by statute to prioritize shareholder interests[150]—U.S. boards occupy a different position. The governance powers of a Delaware board, once elected, flow from the statute itself,[151] and neither officers nor directors are considered legal agents of the shareholders; officers are agents of the corporation, and directors are not agents at all (though they are most assuredly fiduciaries).[152] As Jonathan Macey observes, the notion that shareholders "own" the corporation is undercut by the fact that shareholders "do not enjoy any of the indicia or hallmarks of ownership," rendering this characterization a "myth."[153] Overall, U.S. boards are largely insulated from shareholder override, and possess substantial capacity to consider non-shareholder interests (minimally in hostile takeovers, and more generally in some states)—realities entirely at odds with the depiction offered by Friedman.[154]

While more sophisticated arguments have been made along such lines, they are expressly normative, conceding that U.S. corporate law does not in fact reflect the strict shareholder primacy model. Lucian Bebchuk, for example, strenuously advocates profit maximization and greater managerial accountability to shareholders, while acknowledging that the shareholder franchise itself remains a "myth" as a practical matter.[155] The key premise of Bebchuk's normative argument is that this approach is not currently reflected in U.S. corporate law.

[150] *See* BRUNER, *supra* note 2, at 29–35.

[151] DEL. CODE ANN. tit. 8, § 141(a).

[152] *See* ALLEN & KRAAKMAN, *supra* note 65, at 97–101; Christopher M. Bruner, *Opting Out of Fiduciary Duties and Liabilities in U.S. and U.K. Business Entities*, *in* RESEARCH HANDBOOK ON FIDUCIARY LAW 285, 287 (D. Gordon Smith & Andrew S. Gold eds., 2018); Greenwood, *supra* note 123, at 288. *See also* MOORE & PETRIN, *supra* note 78, at 72–74 (observing that, notwithstanding U.K. shareholders' substantial governance powers, U.K. directors are not technically the shareholders' agents either); Lynn Stout et al., *The Modern Corporation Statement on Company Law* 2 (2016), https://ssrn.com/abstract=2848833.

[153] Jonathan R. Macey, *Corporate Law as Myth*, 93 S. CAL. L. REV. 923, 934–37 (2020). *See also* Stout et al., *supra* note 152, at 1–2.

[154] *See* BRUNER, *supra* note 2, at 60–64.

[155] *See generally* Lucian A. Bebchuk, *The Myth of the Shareholder Franchise*, 93 VA. L. REV. 675 (2007). *See also* Lucian A. Bebchuk & Roberto Tallarita, *The Illusory Promise of Stakeholder Governance*, 106 CORNELL L. REV. 91 (2020).

IV. CORPORATE LAW VERSUS CORPORATE GOVERNANCE

Ultimately, none of the foregoing accounts compellingly illuminate the substance and scope of corporate law or the nature of the corporate form.[156] This, I argue, is the key to understanding why many have turned to corporate governance as a trans-doctrinal lens through which to think about corporate power relations. Critically, corporate governance framing avoids having to grapple directly with the persistent uncertainties and blurriness regarding corporate law's domain.

While defined in a variety of ways, corporate governance broadly reflects a focus on "the system by which companies are directed and controlled."[157] As such, the term draws particular attention to "the relative allocation of power,"[158] which involves a wide array of legal inputs.[159] As Marc Moore and Martin Petrin observe in their study of U.K. corporate governance, while a "contested term of reference," corporate governance "is concerned—first and foremost—with the problem of power," representing "an enquiry into the causes and consequences of the allocation of decision-making power within large, socially significant business organizations."[160]

While corporate governance is sometimes described as a broader concept than corporate law for this reason,[161] it is more accurate to describe them as "two overlapping circles."[162] This sort of framing is particularly attractive in comparative studies, precisely because it sidesteps doctrinal and theoretical inconsistencies through terminology designed to transcend corporate law itself. For example, in his work on the United States and Germany, John Cioffi describes corporate governance as "a juridical nexus of securities, company, and labor relations law that structurally allocates power among managers, shareholders, and employees within the corporation"—a formulation permitting employees, favored through German co-determination, to be included as corporate "insiders."[163] Other stakeholders, meanwhile, are said to remain "outside the firm's boundaries," and other areas of law that affect corporate activity are similarly omitted because they do not "regulate or modify the firm's internal governance relationships."[164] This

[156] *See* BRUNER, *supra* note 2, at 141–42; Bruner, *supra* note 42, at 1395–1408.

[157] ROBERT P. AUSTIN & IAN M. RAMSAY, FORD, AUSTIN & RAMSAY'S PRINCIPLES OF CORPORATIONS LAW 405 (17th ed. 2018).

[158] Thompson & Sale, *supra* note 48, at 864.

[159] *See, e.g.*, AUSTIN & RAMSAY, *supra* note 157, at 407–10.

[160] MOORE & PETRIN, *supra* note 78, at 3–4 (emphasis removed).

[161] *See, e.g.*, Bottomley, *supra* note 1, at 59; Winkler, *supra* note 67, at 128–29.

[162] Mathias Siems & David Cabrelli, *Form, Style and Substance in Comparative Company Law*, *in* COMPARATIVE COMPANY LAW: A CASE-BASED APPROACH 363, 365–66 (Mathias Siems & David Cabrelli eds., 2013).

[163] JOHN W. CIOFFI, PUBLIC LAW AND PRIVATE POWER: CORPORATE GOVERNANCE REFORM IN THE AGE OF FINANCE CAPITALISM 38–39 (2010).

[164] *Id.* at 38–40.

illustrates the capacity of the corporate governance concept to permit the framework for analysis to be re-drawn, presumably with less resistance than might have been encountered if the same effort had been directed at corporate law itself.

Ronald Gilson suggests as much in his historical treatment of the concept, arguing that this term allows one to grapple more directly with contextual dynamism. Gilson notes concern among academic lawyers and financial economists alike in the 1960s and 1970s that corporate law as such "no longer was enough to understand what really mattered: how the corporation performed."[165] The shift in conceptual framing and perspective toward corporate governance, then, correlated with the emergence of a spirit of renewed vigor in corporate studies.[166]

This approach, Gilson argues, is more inherently interdisciplinary and directs attention to the need for "contextual specificity"[167] to grapple with "factors such as culture, politics, or geography," as well as "the role of complementarities" among "governance elements that create value because they make the existing system work better as a whole."[168] Highlighting examples such as lifetime employment in Japan—more a cultural practice and a market norm than a legal mandate, yet profoundly impacting the role of employees in corporate affairs[169]—Gilson concludes that the governance of large corporations is highly context-driven and dynamic, eluding prevailing theories of corporate law precisely because they are "largely static."[170]

Gilson's analysis further exposes the shortcomings canvassed in this chapter among various efforts to describe the domain of corporate law. While the effort to link up legal and non-legal determinants of corporate power is a fascinating and important project in its own right, however, the increasing prevalence of corporate governance as a conceptual frame also reflects growing impatience with hidebound approaches to corporate law, which routinely fail to acknowledge the broader contextual determinants of the law itself. There is an acute need to account for differing contexts between jurisdictions, and within a given jurisdiction over time, if we are to understand the drivers that impact corporate law's domain and the nature of the corporate form.

[165] Ronald J. Gilson, *From Corporate Law to Corporate Governance*, *in* THE OXFORD HANDBOOK OF CORPORATE LAW AND GOVERNANCE 3, 3 (Jeffrey N. Gordon & Wolf-Georg Ringe eds., 2018). *See also* Wells, *supra* note 48, at 306–07.

[166] Gilson, *supra* note 165, at 4–8.

[167] *See id.* at 6.

[168] *Id.* at 9.

[169] *See id.* at 10–12. *See also* Peter Matanle & Kenji Matsui, *Lifetime Employment in 21st Century Japan: Stability and Resilience Under Pressure in the Japanese Management System*, *in* EMERGING PERSPECTIVES IN JAPANESE HUMAN RESOURCE MANAGEMENT (Sierk A. Horn ed., 2011), https://ssrn.com/abstract=1971825 (working paper version).

[170] Gilson, *supra* note 165, at 14–25.

3

Contextual Drivers of Difference

As the analyses provided in Chapter 2 suggest, context often complicates efforts to define the nature of the corporation and the domain of corporate law. Among other things, divergences driven by politics, a jurisdiction's state of economic development, the degree of share ownership concentration, and prevailing social and cultural values[1] can affect not only how a particular doctrinal subject is addressed, but even whether that subject is conceptualized as a matter of corporate law at all. Consequently, it appears that the question of corporate law's domain is amenable to "no single answer"[2]—a reality that even the authors of *The Anatomy*, committed as they are to identifying universal functional similarities, must concede.[3]

Ultimately, the project of describing the corporation and corporate law's domain becomes a matter of describing drivers of difference around the world.[4] Toward that end, this chapter explores various forms of legal, cultural, market, and historical dynamics that have led to substantial divergences in terms of how the corporation is conceptualized, and how corporate law's domain is defined, across jurisdictions and over time.

The aim at this stage is not to provide a comprehensive account of these drivers of difference. Rather, the more modest goal at this stage is simply to identify a set of core contextual dynamics that are critical to the more flexible framework developed later in the book,[5] and that help to illuminate the underlying forces at work in the various comparative analyses that subsequently build upon that framework.[6]

[1] *See* Roman Tomasic, *Introduction: Corporate Law in Transition*, *in* ROUTLEDGE HANDBOOK OF CORPORATE LAW 1, 1–2 (Roman Tomasic ed., 2017).

[2] *See* Stephen Bottomley, *What Is Corporate Law?: An Australian Perspective*, *in* ROUTLEDGE HANDBOOK OF CORPORATE LAW, *supra* note 1, at 49, 50.

[3] *See* John Armour et al., *What Is Corporate Law?*, *in* REINIER KRAAKMAN ET AL., THE ANATOMY OF CORPORATE LAW: A COMPARATIVE AND FUNCTIONAL APPROACH 1, 4 (3d ed. 2017).

[4] *Cf.* Pierre Legrand, *The Same and the Different*, *in* COMPARATIVE LEGAL STUDIES: TRADITIONS AND TRANSITIONS 240, 287–88 (Pierre Legrand & Roderick Munday eds., 2003).

[5] *See infra* Part Two.

[6] *See infra* Part Three.

The Corporation as Technology. Christopher M. Bruner, Oxford University Press. © Christopher M. Bruner 2022.
DOI: 10.1093/oso/9780197635179.003.0003

A. Law

The taxonomic question of corporate law's scope and boundaries may become bound up with constitutional idiosyncrasies that impact the division of regulatory competence, affecting who gets to say what a corporation consists of in a given jurisdiction—a factor that can operate quite differently across jurisdictions, even among those with closely related legal systems. Consider, for example, the major common law jurisdictions. Corporate law regulatory competence in the United States has defaulted to individual states subject to federal override, whereas in Australia the states possess clear corporate law regulatory competence but have chosen to refer it to the Australian government to permit an integrated national corporate legal system. In Canada, meanwhile, both the provinces and the Canadian government possess simultaneous corporate law regulatory competence, yet securities regulation has (unusually) been reserved solely to the provinces.[7] Such distinctions can impact how the field of corporate law is defined and how doctrinal issues and practical problems are conceptualized and addressed.

From the founding era, defining the scope and boundaries of U.S. corporate law has been closely bound up with issues of federalism. During the Constitutional Convention, James Madison proposed that Congress be given power "To grant charters of incorporation in cases where the public good may require them, and the authority of a single State may be incompetent," but this was not adopted.[8] Consequently, the states are said to have "reserved the power to form corporations," subject to Congress' ability to do so where "necessary and proper to accomplish some expressly granted power."[9] Additionally, Congress possesses broad power to "regulate Commerce . . . among the several States,"[10] permitting federal intervention into internal corporate affairs on numerous occasions—typically in the wake of crises such as the Great Depression, precipitating federal securities regulation; the Enron and WorldCom scandals, precipitating the Sarbanes-Oxley Act of 2002; and the global financial crisis, precipitating the Dodd-Frank Act of 2010.[11] While targeted to date, there is little question—even in Delaware—that Congress' interstate commerce authority would permit the

[7] *See* CHRISTOPHER M. BRUNER, CORPORATE GOVERNANCE IN THE COMMON-LAW WORLD: THE POLITICAL FOUNDATIONS OF SHAREHOLDER POWER 37–38, 66–67, 77–80 (2013).

[8] *See* JAMES MADISON, DEBATES IN THE FEDERAL CONVENTION OF 1787, at 420, 564 (Gaillard Hunt & James Brown Scott eds., Prometheus Books 1987); 1 1787: DRAFTING THE U.S. CONSTITUTION 904–05, 934–36 (Wilbourn E. Benton ed., Texas A&M University Press 1986).

[9] *See* WILLIAM T. ALLEN & REINIER KRAAKMAN, COMMENTARIES AND CASES ON THE LAW OF BUSINESS ORGANIZATION 79 n.6 (5th ed. 2016). *See also* U.S. CONST. art. I, § 8, cl. 18; McCulloch v. Maryland, 17 U.S. 316, 406–09, 422–25 (1819).

[10] U.S. CONST. art. I, § 8, cl. 3.

[11] *See* BRUNER, *supra* note 7, at 37–38.

federal government to take over corporate law entirely as it pertains to publicly traded companies.[12]

On the whole, however, U.S. corporate law has largely been left to individual states, as reflected in a unique choice of law rule called the "internal affairs doctrine." The "internal affairs" of a corporation are generally governed by the state of incorporation, regardless of where the company is headquartered and operates.[13] A comment to the Restatement (Second) of Conflict of Laws defines "internal affairs" as "the relations inter se of the corporation, its shareholders, directors, officers or agents,"[14] and rationales for the internal affairs doctrine are said to include "the needs of the interstate and international systems, certainty, predictability and uniformity of result, protection of the justified expectations of the parties and ease in the application of the law to be applied."[15] The internal affairs doctrine has been recognized by the U.S. Supreme Court,[16] and embraced by the predominant models for U.S. corporate law—Delaware, and the Model Business Corporation Act.[17]

This constitutional context has prompted what many regard as a unique hallmark of U.S. corporate law—charter competition.[18] States are motivated to supply attractive corporate laws "to obtain local incorporation fees"—a substantial proportion of Delaware's state budget—and states tending to lose incorporations have capitulated for fear that companies operating there might otherwise relocate production.[19] Delaware has been the clear winner due not only to the flexibility of its corporate law, but also to various institutional features—including a service-oriented Division of Corporations, an expert bar and judiciary applying highly developed case law, and a responsive legislature focused on preserving corporate franchise fees.[20]

In their introduction to the Balotti and Finkelstein treatise, Herzel and Richman acknowledge "Delaware's public policy to foster a favorable climate for corporations,"[21] explaining that Delaware must balance the preferences

[12] *See* Leo E. Strine, Jr., *Breaking the Corporate Governance Logjam in Washington: Some Constructive Thoughts on a Responsible Path Forward*, 63 BUS. LAW. 1079, 1084 (2008).

[13] *See* RESTATEMENT (SECOND) OF CONFLICT OF LAWS §§ 302(2), 304 (1971).

[14] *Id.* § 302 cmt. a. *See also id.* § 302 cmt. g.

[15] *Id.* § 302 cmt. e.

[16] *See* CTS Corp. v. Dynamics Corp. of Am., 481 U.S. 69, 88–91 (1987).

[17] *See* VantagePoint Venture Partners 1996 v. Examen, Inc., 871 A.2d 1108, 1113–16 (Del. 2005); MODEL BUSINESS CORPORATION ACT §§ 1.40, 2.08, 8.40 cmt, 15.01 (rev. 2016). *But see* ERIN A. O'HARA & LARRY E. RIBSTEIN, THE LAW MARKET 126 (2009).

[18] *See, e.g.*, O'HARA & RIBSTEIN, *supra* note 17, ch. 6.

[19] *See id.* at 109–17.

[20] *See* CHRISTOPHER M. BRUNER, RE-IMAGINING OFFSHORE FINANCE: MARKET-DOMINANT SMALL JURISDICTIONS IN A GLOBALIZING FINANCIAL WORLD 179–87 (2016). *See also* O'HARA & RIBSTEIN, *supra* note 17, at 110–11; Christopher M. Bruner, *Leveraging Corporate Law: A Broader Account of Delaware's Competition*, 80 MD. L. REV. 72 (2020); Leo Herzel & Laura D. Richman, *Foreword* to R. FRANKLIN BALOTTI & JESSE A. FINKELSTEIN, 1 THE DELAWARE LAW OF CORPORATIONS & BUSINESS ORGANIZATIONS F-16–F-17 (3d ed. 2016).

[21] Herzel & Richman, *supra* note 20, at F-2.

of management and shareholders, and that both the federal government's and other states' actions impact Delaware corporate law.[22] In addition to "populist" constraints imposed through federal legislation,[23] other states have forced Delaware's hand in controversial areas such as takeovers, where managers' and shareholders' preferences cannot be straightforwardly reconciled.[24]

This indicates that the practical insulation of state-level prerogative is not so complete as the internal affairs doctrine might lead one to expect—because, as a taxonomic matter, "contentious issues, such as bankruptcy, securities, [and] antitrust" can be removed from its reach by simply defining them out of corporate law.[25] In the context of U.S. federalism, much comes down to how the line is drawn between corporate law, left to the states, and securities regulation, predominantly promulgated at the federal level—and this line is notoriously difficult to draw. As noted earlier, the federal government often subsumes important aspects of corporate governance following crises, and federal securities regulation now substantially regulates significant internal affairs of public companies including proxy voting, tender offers,[26] and aspects of board structure.[27] More generally, Robert Thompson and Hillary Sale have found that federal disclosure rules have, via securities fraud class actions, stepped in where state corporate law has traditionally eschewed robust enforcement—notably the duty of care (blunted at the state level by the business judgment rule and statutory liability shields), and exercise of jurisdiction over officers.[28]

Efforts have been made to substantively distinguish state corporate law and federal securities regulation, but none are wholly satisfactory. The "rough division between internal and external affairs" may serve "as a rhetorical boundary," yet the internal affairs doctrine remains "too vaguely defined to separate corporate and securities law," and "fails to provide a compelling reason for limiting federal regulation of internal affairs."[29] Likewise, the distinction between substantive rules and disclosure-based investor protection[30] fails because securities

[22] *Id.* at F-5.

[23] *See id.* at F-7–F-10. *See also* Mark J. Roe, *Delaware's Competition*, 117 HARV. L. REV. 588 (2003); Mark J. Roe, *Delaware and Washington as Corporate Lawmakers*, 34 DEL. J. CORP. L. 1 (2009).

[24] Herzel & Richman, *supra* note 20, at F-12–F-13. *See also* BRUNER, *supra* note 7, at 42–52.

[25] O'HARA & RIBSTEIN, *supra* note 17, at 115–16. *See also* Adam Winkler, *Corporate Law or the Law of Business?: Stakeholders and Corporate Governance at the End of History*, 67 L. CONTEMP. PROB. 109, 111, 130–31 (2004).

[26] *See* 15 U.S.C. § 78m–n.

[27] *See* Sarbanes-Oxley Act of 2002, H.R. 3763, 107th Cong. (2002), § 301; Dodd-Frank Wall Street Reform and Consumer Protection Act, H.R. 4173, 111th Cong. (2010), §§ 165(h), 951, 953–54, 956, 971. *See also* BRUNER, *supra* note 7, at 258–86; Robert B. Thompson & Hillary A. Sale, *Securities Fraud as Corporate Governance: Reflections upon Federalism*, 56 VAND. L. REV. 859, 869–86 (2003).

[28] *See* Thompson & Sale, *supra* note 27, at 892–99, 906–07.

[29] James J. Park, *Reassessing the Distinction between Corporate and Securities Law*, 64 UCLA L. REV. 116, 132–33 (2017).

[30] *See, e.g.*, ARTHUR R. PINTO & DOUGLAS M. BRANSON, UNDERSTANDING CORPORATE LAW 4 (4th ed. 2013). *See also* STEPHEN M. BAINBRIDGE, CORPORATE LAW 8–11 (2d ed. 2009).

regulation "often goes beyond disclosure," while state corporate law "often sets forth significant disclosure requirements."[31] James Park has advanced an intriguing alternative, arguing that "securities law protects the investor while he is a trader, and corporate law protects the investor while he is an owner"[32]—the former facilitating "the process of valuation" while the latter "seeks to prevent corporate misconduct that diminishes the value of a shareholder-owner's investment."[33] This is arguably a coherent normative distinction,[34] but it cannot provide a full descriptive account, as Park's critique of more or less appropriate examples of "federal regulation of corporate law" implicitly acknowledges.[35]

The principal upshot is that the domain of corporate law and the nature of the corporation in the United States have shifted over time in response to a constitutional context and associated politics and market dynamics that are idiosyncratic to this country.[36] The substantial impact that the allocation of doctrinal issues can have on their resolution is demonstrated by contrast with systems where the constitutional allocation of regulatory competence, and prevailing approaches to such taxonomic challenges, have differed. For example, in the United States we can readily see in retrospect that our treatment of hostile takeovers was impacted by the federal decision to focus on regulation of mechanics and disclosure,[37] leaving it to state corporate law to work out the balance of power in differing local contexts[38]—and in ways that appear substantially less shareholder-centric than one might have expected if these issues had been approached through an investor protection-oriented federal regime.[39] Conversely, in Canada, the degree of capacity for target boards to deploy defenses—and thus the overall degree of shareholder-centrism in Canadian takeover law—is expected to be driven primarily by whether these matters are viewed through the lens of federal corporate law, which tends to be more stakeholder-oriented, or provincial securities regulation, which tends to be more shareholder-oriented. The latter appears likely

31 Park, *supra* note 29, at 134–37. *See also* ALLEN & KRAAKMAN, *supra* note 9, at 226–27.

32 Park, *supra* note 29, at 120.

33 *Id.* at 143.

34 *See, e.g.*, *id.* at 122, 155.

35 *See id.* at 180.

36 Although Canadian businesses similarly have a menu of provincial and national options, Canada has not seen substantial charter competition. Generally, smaller companies incorporate in their home province while public companies incorporate federally. *See* CHRISTOPHER C. NICHOLLS, MERGERS, ACQUISITIONS, AND OTHER CHANGES OF CORPORATE CONTROL 27 (2007); Taylor R. Gray, *A Corporate Geography of Canada: Insights into a Multi-Jurisdictional Model of Corporate Governance*, 41 GROWTH & CHANGE 467, 480–86 (2010).

37 *See* ALLEN & KRAAKMAN, *supra* note 9, at 450–56. *See also* CTS Corp. v. Dynamics Corp. of Am., 481 U.S. 69, 79–87 (1987).

38 *See* Lyman Johnson & David Millon, *Misreading the Williams Act*, 87 MICH. L. REV. 1862, 1918–19 (1989).

39 *See* BRUNER, *supra* note 7, at 40–44, 166–76; Christopher M. Bruner, *Center-Left Politics and Corporate Governance: What Is the "Progressive" Agenda?*, 2018 BYU L. REV. 267, 291–93 (2018).

(though this is not a certainty).[40] This contrast illustrates how idiosyncrasies of constitutional context, resulting regulatory structures, and categorization of doctrinal problems can drive the formation and definition of corporate law, as well as substantive aspects of how a corporation in a given jurisdiction functions.[41]

B. Culture

Just as the legal context can affect corporate law's domain and the manner in which the corporation is conceptualized in a given jurisdiction, so can the cultural context. The impact of culture has been vividly illustrated by the failure of efforts to create a harmonized corporate law across Europe as a part of the European Union's common market project.

Notwithstanding the ambition to forge a European common market, the only way to enact a takeover directive "after fourteen years of negotiations" was through "the radical compromise of making its two most important provisions optional."[42] Article 9 of the 2004 Takeover Directive requires shareholder authorization before a target board may pursue "any action, other than seeking alternative bids, which may result in the frustration of the bid"—preventing target boards from implementing defenses without shareholder approval.[43] Article 11 creates a "breakthrough" rule, making it easier for a successful bidder to remove the board, notwithstanding charter restrictions on voting and transfer of securities.[44] However, Article 12 guts these nominal requirements, providing that "Member States may reserve the right not to require companies . . . to apply Article 9(2) and (3) and/or Article 11."[45] This invitation has been accepted by significant economies across Europe, with Germany and the Netherlands opting out of Article 9 and most Member States—including France, Germany, Italy, the Netherlands, Spain, and the United Kingdom (then a member)—opting out of Article 11.[46]

Functional analyses suggest that we should expect substantial convergence in the field of corporate law over time.[47] If this is true, however, then "why is it," as

[40] *See* NICHOLLS, *supra* note 36, at 202; Jeffrey G. MacIntosh, BCE *and the Peoples' Corporate Law: Learning to Live on Quicksand*, 48 CAN. BUS. L.J. 255, 270–71 (2009). *See also* BRUNER, *supra* note 7, at 94–97.

[41] South Africa provides another vivid example. *See infra* Chapter 8.C.

[42] ALLEN & KRAAKMAN, *supra* note 9, at 583.

[43] Directive 2004/25/EC of the European Parliament and of the Council of 21 April 2004 on Takeover Bids, 2004 O.J. (L 142/12), arts. 9(2)–(3).

[44] *See id.*, art. 11.

[45] *Id.*, art. 12(1).

[46] *See* ALLEN & KRAAKMAN, *supra* note 9, at 583. *See also* Andrew Johnston, *The European Takeover Directive: Ruined by Protectionism or Respecting Diversity?*, 25 COMPANY LAWYER 270, 275–76 (2004).

[47] *See* BRUNER, *supra* note 7, at 14–16, 112–15.

Jeffrey Gordon asks, "that the corporate governance regimes of the EU Member States still exhibit significant divergence?"[48] Gordon emphasizes not only economic and legal factors, but cultural factors as well. In addition to "diverse initial conditions" including differing levels of share ownership concentration, " 'bottom up' harmonization in which companies could choose the corporate governance model most suited to their objectives would upset national decisions about the balance of power between shareholders and employees"—notably, the strong commitment to employee participation reflected in German-style co-determination.[49] More fundamentally, however, Gordon emphasizes "the profound ambivalence about the project of transnational economic and political integration" at the heart of the European Union and the common market, citing the Takeover Directive as a case in point. "Strong form convergence, which truly would have brought about free mobility of capital, people, and products—genuine transnational economic integration—was actually not what the Member States wanted." He concludes that the "strength of national identity and the comparative weakness of European identity is the ultimate hindrance to corporate law convergence in the EU."[50]

Even where harmonization has been imposed from the top, national prerogatives may be reasserted by other means—including through strategic redefinition of what constitutes corporate law, and specifically whether a given type of problem ought to be analyzed through that lens or some other legal lens. In a series of rulings following the 1999 *Centros* decision, the European Court of Justice determined that the right of establishment[51] requires recognition of a corporation formed in another member state, and that the corporation's internal affairs be governed according to the corporate law of the member state where it was formed.[52] This amounts to rejecting the formerly widespread "real seat" doctrine—requiring incorporation in the jurisdiction of the principal place of business—and facilitates charter competition akin to that in the United States.[53] These developments prompted some continental businesses to incorporate in the United Kingdom, notably to avoid minimum capital requirements intended to protect creditors.[54] One response, however, was simply to redefine various

[48] Jeffrey N. Gordon, *Convergence and Persistence in Corporate Law and Governance*, *in* THE OXFORD HANDBOOK OF CORPORATE LAW AND GOVERNANCE 28, 32 (Jeffrey N. Gordon & Wolf-Georg Ringe eds., 2018).

[49] *Id.* at 51–52 (emphasis removed).

[50] *Id.* at 52–53.

[51] *See* Treaty on the Functioning of the European Union, 2012 O.J. (C326/47), arts. 49, 54.

[52] *See* Case C-212/97, Centros Ltd v. Erhvervs-og Selskabsstyrelsen, 1999 E.C.R. I-1484; Case C-208/00, Überseering BV v. Nordic Construction Company Baumanagement GmbH (NCC), 2002 E.C.R. I-9943; Case C-167/01, Kamer van Koophandel en Frabriken voor Amsterdam v. Inspire Art Ltd, 2003 E.C.R. I-10195.

[53] *See* O'HARA & RIBSTEIN, *supra* note 17, at 121–23; Armour et al., *supra* note 3, at 21.

[54] *See* Luca Enriques & Martin Gelter, *How the Old World Encountered the New One: Regulatory Competition and Cooperation in European Corporate and Bankruptcy Law*, 81 TUL. L. REV. 577, 580,

creditor protections out of corporate law and into insolvency law, where choice of law rules more closely resemble the real seat doctrine—a move that Luca Enriques and Martin Gelter term "insolvencification."[55] "Whether something is considered corporate or insolvency law is largely an issue of the national conception of these fields," they explain, and "Member States may even 'relabel' rules as insolvency law if it serves the purpose of being able to apply their own law."[56]

Substantial harmonization of EU company law has proven controversial because the respective national polities face persistent differences in their social and economic realities.[57] This dynamic is hardly unique to Europe, of course. Closely related common law legal systems vary substantially in their degrees of shareholder-centrism, reflecting variations in the robustness of external regulatory structures affecting the welfare of other stakeholders.[58] Meanwhile, the United States itself reflects a patchwork of local approaches to contentious issues such as hostile takeovers, varying in their degrees of deference to target boards.[59] Looking globally, then, Gordon identifies a trend toward "divergence within convergence," referring to "formal similarities that mask important functional differences."[60] For example, there is widespread rhetorical embrace of director independence, but actual practice nevertheless diverges considerably across jurisdictions due to differences in ratios and definitions of independence, degrees of power that nominally independent directors might be given to review various forms of transactions, who appoints them, and so on.[61] Overall, the persistence of such divergences contradicts the functionalist claim that the world's major economies are steadily converging upon a single optimal approach to corporate governance, a shared vision of corporate law's domain, and/or a single optimal conception of the corporate form.

600–02 (2007). *See also* Carsten Gerner-Beuerle et al., *Why Do Businesses Incorporate in Other EU Member States? An Empirical Analysis of the Role of Conflict of Laws Rules*, 56 INT'L REV. L. ECON. 14, 17–19 (2018). The impact of Brexit remains to be seen, but is expected to undermine the United Kingdom's attractiveness as a jurisdiction of incorporation for European businesses. *See, e.g.*, Macfarlanes LLP, *In Corporate Law, It's Beginning to Look a Lot Like Brexit*, LEXOLOGY, Nov. 8, 2018, https://www.lexology.com/library/detail.aspx?g=89904578-dde5-4dc4-8428-62191f12d04b.

[55] *See generally* Enriques & Gelter, *supra* note 54.

[56] *Id.* at 593–94. *See also* Case C-594/14, Kornhaas v. Dithmar, ELCI:EU:C:2015:806; Carsten Gerner-Beuerle & Edmund Schuster, *The Costs of Separation: Friction between Company and Insolvency Law in the Single Market*, 14 J. CORP. L. STUD. 287 (2014); Wolf-Georg Ringe, *Kornhaas and the Limits of Corporate Establishment*, OXFORD BUS. L. BLOG, May 25, 2016, https://www.law.ox.ac.uk/business-law-blog/blog/2016/05/kornhaas-and-limits-corporate-establishment.

[57] *Cf.* Luca Enriques, *A Harmonized European Company Law: Are We There Already?*, 66 INT'L & COMP. L. Q. 763, pt. III (2017).

[58] *See generally* BRUNER, *supra* note 7.

[59] *See id.* at 43–44, 171–72.

[60] Gordon, *supra* note 48, at 32–33.

[61] *Id.* at 41–44.

C. Markets

The structure of commercial and capital markets can also impact how a jurisdiction defines corporate law, and how responsibilities and relationships among various corporate constituencies are conceptualized. As already discussed,[62] many authorities characterize the domain of corporate law primarily by reference to shareholders, suggesting that fundamental concerns of corporate law include balancing managerial authority and accountability, and reducing managers' and controlling shareholders' capacity to abuse minority shareholders. As a consequence, policing conflicts of interest is widely regarded as lying close to the heart of corporate law—indeed, for many it represents the field's central concern. William Allen and Reinier Kraakman, for example, explain in their casebook that "corporate law in every jurisdiction imposes specific controls" on conflicted transactions, and they observe that in the United States such transactions are "regulated first and foremost by the fiduciary duty of loyalty."[63]

It has long been recognized, however, that even financial conflicts of interest might be addressed through other areas of law, depending on how market conditions lead authorities to conceptualize the problem and, relatedly, how they conceptualize a corporate actor's core responsibilities.[64] This dynamic is vividly illustrated by South Korea's response to "tunneling," a term that refers to "extraction of wealth from the firm by its controlling shareholders."[65] While most jurisdictions would view this, first and foremost, as a harm to minority shareholders to be addressed through corporate law, South Korea has taken a strikingly different approach, viewing this primarily as a harm to consumers—outsiders to the corporation itself—and thus a matter to be addressed through antitrust law.[66]

The Monopoly Regulation and Fair Trade Act—which aims "to promote fair and free competition" and "to protect consumers"[67]—prohibits transactions that are "likely to hinder fair trade," including those providing benefits to "a related party or other company" on "substantially advantageous terms," and those where

[62] *See supra* Chapter 2.

[63] ALLEN & KRAAKMAN, *supra* note 9, at 283.

[64] *Cf.* LOUIS D. BRANDEIS, OTHER PEOPLE'S MONEY AND HOW THE BANKERS USE IT 51, 61–62 (1914) (observing that the "practice of interlocking directorates" both "tends to the suppression of competition" and "tends to disloyalty and to violation of the fundamental law that no man can serve two masters").

[65] *See* Yong Lim & Geeyoung Min, *Competition and Corporate Governance: Teaming Up to Police Tunneling*, 36 NW. J. INT'L L. & BUS. 267, 269 (2016).

[66] *See id.* at 270–71, 295–301.

[67] Dokjeom-Gyuje Mit Gongjeong-Georae-e Gwanhan Beobryul [Monopoly Regulation and Fair Trade Act], Act. No. 4198, Jan. 13, 1990, *last amended by* Act No. 14127, Mar. 29, 2016, art. 1 (S. Kor.), https://elaw.klri.re.kr/eng_service/lawView.do?hseq=41658&lang=ENG (translation by Korea Legislation Research Institute).

such an entity is "an intermediary . . . that does not play a practical role."[68] The Act likewise prohibits various transactions among affiliated companies,[69] and reaches counterparties to such transactions, not just the controller.[70] The Fair Trade Commission, South Korea's antitrust regulator,[71] possesses extensive enforcement authority.[72]

Why would South Korea categorize related-party conflicts of interest—regarded by many as a central preoccupation of corporate law and a reflection of intra-corporate agency costs—as a matter to be addressed by antitrust law? The answer, as Yong Lim and Geeyoung Min explain, is that this move was driven by South Korea's market context. South Korea's highly concentrated share ownership market is dominated by "chaebols," which are "large family-controlled conglomerates."[73] While these groups "were instrumental in implementing industrial policy during Korea's post-war development," by 1980 "the share of the top thirty chaebols amounted to 36% of the national economy," and this degree of economic concentration came to be "perceived as a threat to the sustainable and balanced development of the nation's market economy." Various responses to check their dominance failed, and by 1997—when the foregoing rules took effect—"one could find at least one of the top thirty chaebols among the top three competitors in 83.4% of the product markets where they were active."[74] Against this backdrop, the "primary legislative goal" of the rules described "was to control economic concentration." While the "ramifications for corporate governance" were recognized, this was not the primary concern for lawmakers at the time, and accordingly was not the conceptual lens through which they initially viewed the problem.[75] While other jurisdictions tend to see it otherwise for comprehensible reasons, in South Korea, policing corporate conflicts of interest represented an extra-corporate problem of market regulation and consumer protection, logically falling within the ambit of antitrust law.

Over time, these rules did come to be viewed "as a part of the corporate governance toolkit" as new circumstances presented new problems in a differing market context. Following the East Asian financial crisis, South Korean authorities focused on "a slew of problems with the management and corporate governance of chaebols," and the Fair Trade Commission's "regulation of undue support among chaebol affiliates became an integral part of the Korean government's post-crisis

[68] *Id.*, art. 23(1)(7). *See also* Lim & Min, *supra* note 65, at 272–74.
[69] Monopoly Regulation and Fair Trade Act, *supra* note 67, art. 23–2(1).
[70] *See id.*, arts. 23(2), 23–2(3).
[71] *See* Korea Fair Trade Commission, *About KFTC: Who We Are,* https://www.ftc.go.kr/eng/contents.do?key=493.
[72] *See* Monopoly Regulation and Fair Trade Act, *supra* note 67, arts. 24, 24–2.
[73] Lim & Min, *supra* note 65, at 273.
[74] *See id.* at 274–76 (emphasis removed).
[75] *See id.* at 276–77.

corporate restructuring and reform program."[76] This shift illustrates not only the relevance of market context to the conceptualization of legal problems, but also the fact that prevailing views on these matters can evolve in response to dynamic circumstances.

D. History

Just as differing legal, cultural, and market contexts may result in differing conceptions of corporate law's domain and the corporation itself, so these understandings may change over time as ideas and background conditions evolve. This is vividly illustrated by the U.S. experience since the modern business corporation emerged in the late nineteenth century.[77]

Historical analysis demonstrates that the "public/private distinction" has been a significant driver of prevailing conceptions of U.S. corporate law's scope and content over time. "Under the first view," David Millon explains, "corporate law takes on an external perspective, paying explicit regard to the relations between the corporation and the rest of society," whereas the "opposing view conceives of corporate law's focus as internal," leaving "to other bodies of law . . . the task of regulating the corporation's external relationships."[78] In the late nineteenth century the corporation was widely viewed as "an artificial entity," placing emphasis on "the state's constitutive role" and promoting "a public law approach to corporate law" characterized by mandatory rules "designed to address important public concerns."[79] Over time, however, corporations came to be viewed increasingly as "a natural creation of private initiative and market forces," displacing the public-oriented conception of corporate law in favor of a "private law, anti-regulatory, shareholder-centered program."[80]

By the 1930s share ownership had dispersed to the point that retail shareholders could not realistically be expected to participate meaningfully in corporate affairs,[81] raising the "problem of managerial discretion and

[76] *Id.* at 277.

[77] The emergence of the modern public corporation in the United Kingdom and the United States is explored more fully later in the book. *See infra* Chapter 4.A.

[78] *See* David Millon, *Theories of the Corporation*, 1990 DUKE L.J. 201, 201–02 (1990).

[79] *Id.* at 202. *See also id.* at 205–11.

[80] *Id.* at 202–03. *See also id.* at 211–16; Eric C. Chaffee, *The Origins of Corporate Social Responsibility*, 85 U. CINCINNATI L. REV. 347, 355–62 (2017); Harwell Wells, *"Corporation Law Is Dead": Heroic Managerialism, Legal Change, and the Puzzle of Corporation Law at the Height of the American Century*, 15 U. PA. J. BUS. L. 305, 313–14 (2013).

[81] *See* ADOLPH A. BERLE, JR. & GARDINER C. MEANS, THE MODERN CORPORATION AND PRIVATE PROPERTY 47–65 (1932). *See also* BRANDEIS, *supra* note 64, at 7 (observing that, as of 1914, U.S. stocks were "owned, in large part, by small investors, who do not participate in the management of the company").

accountability to shareholders."[82] Some favored accountability to the entity itself as a means of promoting "corporate social responsibility," while others favored accountability to the shareholders as a more realistic and efficient form of constraint[83]—competing positions that would each hold sway at various points in the twentieth century as times and circumstances evolved.

Until the mid-1970s, expansive managerial authority was tolerated without substantial controversy, in part because the postwar decades were "an economic golden age" when "new wealth was spread widely" and "wage inequality fell sharply."[84] Although "corporations were perceived as more powerful than ever," their collective standing had been bolstered by their contributions to the war effort and their status as exemplars of American capitalism in the Cold War era. At the same time, their economic power was effectively balanced by a robust labor movement and the government itself—coordinating agents of consensus-based politics in a time of growing prosperity. The large American corporation was seen less as "an economic entity" and increasingly as a "social institution,"[85] ushering in a period of what Harwell Wells calls "heroic managerialism," when "corporate leaders were increasingly depicted as taking responsibility to multiple constituencies."[86] The legal impacts included a more expansive conception of corporate purpose, expanded judicial deference under the business judgment rule, and diminished capacity for shareholders to bring derivative suits.[87]

It is critical to recognize the contingent and "transitory nature" of these developments. "The product of a particular moment, the long 1950s," this conception of heroic managerialism could not outlast "the larger societal and economic presuppositions on which it rested." By the mid-1970s, "corporate management was no longer seen as heroic," and large conglomerates foundering in radically different socioeconomic circumstances were no longer predominantly viewed as "social institutions." This created a conceptual vacuum that would be filled by entirely different conceptions of corporate law and governance rooted in financial economics, placing shareholders and their interests at center stage.[88] By the 1990s, the prevailing conception of corporate law's scope and content had become firmly rooted in what Millon terms the "private" paradigm—notably through the nexus of contracts theory, focused intently on the

[82] Millon, *supra* note 78, at 222.

[83] *See id.* at 216–25.

[84] *See* Wells, *supra* note 80, at 316.

[85] *See id.* at 319–22. *See also* Anna Stansbury & Lawrence H. Summers, *The Declining Worker Power Hypothesis: An Explanation for the Recent Evolution of the American Economy* 9 (NBER Working Paper No. 27193, 2020), https://www.nber.org/system/files/working_papers/w27193/w27193.pdf (observing that private sector union membership in the United States reached "a peak of around one third in the 1950s").

[86] Wells, *supra* note 80, at 326–27.

[87] *See id.* at 331–47.

[88] *See id.* at 351–54.

shareholder-management relationship.[89] At the same time, however, the aggregate view of the corporation reflected in the atomistic nexus conception bore "contrary implications," depending on how one defined the relevant aggregate—a nod to the advent of hostile takeovers, which problematized the highly shareholder-centric and privately oriented conception of corporate law's content embraced by scholars rooted in the law-and-economics tradition.[90]

In light of the various forms of contingency discussed in this chapter, it is unsurprising that historical study would lead Millon to advocate attention to context in the spirit of the "legal realists." Observing that "so-called private activity always takes place within a framework of legal rules justified by their social, public utility," he notes that the very "decision to treat particular conduct as private . . . is, of course, a public policy determination"[91] that might be discarded tomorrow as readily as it is accepted today. Similarly, in his study of hostile takeover law, Lyman Johnson has observed that while some "will draw on formalist legal theory to contend that it is wholly illicit for judges to consider social norms" in evaluating such transactions, this argument ignores the fact that "shareholder primacy" itself "is inescapably grounded in larger social norms."[92] Corporate law is inevitably "bound in time and place,"[93] and no single vision of the field's scope and content is any less contingent than the rest. As Wells expresses it, "ideas of corporate law" will "inevitably change as the legal and economic contexts change, and ideas and theories that seemed plausible and even welcome in one era can baffle the next."[94]

E. The Dynamism of the Corporation and Corporate Law

As legal, cultural, market, and historical contexts evolve, so do prevailing conceptions of corporate law's domain and the nature of the corporation as an entity. In light of this reality, we ought to acknowledge the contingency of our own prevailing views on the matter, and closely scrutinize arguments about the scope of potential corporate legal responses to governance-related problems that purport to be deducible from contestable premises that we need not accept.

Corporate law's potential for adaptation suggests that it pays to remain flexible, to accept that yesterday's views on what the corporation "is" may not serve us

[89] *See* Millon, *supra* note 78, at 228–31. *See also* Lyman Johnson, *The Delaware Judiciary and the Meaning of Corporate Life and Corporate Law*, 68 TEX. L. REV. 865, 875–80 (1990)

[90] *See* Millon, *supra* note 78, at 236, 258–59. *See also* Johnson, *supra* note 89, at 878–80.

[91] Millon, *supra* note 78, at 261.

[92] Johnson, *supra* note 89, at 889–90.

[93] *Id.* at 935.

[94] Wells, *supra* note 80, at 355.

well today, and to anticipate that today's views may not serve us well tomorrow.[95] To the extent they prove incompatible with broader social and economic needs, prevailing conceptions of corporate law's domain and the nature of the corporate form need not bind us. We wrote the rules, and they remain ours to revise as new times and circumstances present new problems to solve.

From this perspective, the question becomes what an alternative vision—one that acknowledges the inevitable contingency of the corporate form—might look like. The next part of the book takes up this question, detailing the flux and dynamism reflected in the emergence of the archetypal public company, exploring the fundamental controversies that continue to characterize the field of corporate law today, and re-conceptualizing the corporation in a manner that embraces the flexibility and dynamism offered by this pervasive form of human organization.

[95] *Cf.* Christopher M. Bruner, *Conceptions of Corporate Purpose in Post-Crisis Financial Firms*, 36 SEATTLE U. L. REV. 527, 559 (2013).

PART TWO

RE-CONCEPTUALIZING THE CORPORATION

4

Enduring Controversies in Corporate Law

Predominant frames of reference for conceptualizing the corporate form and corporate law have foundered principally because they are static, each positing a singular and fixed conception that fails to account for the dynamism of this form of organization. Such frameworks cannot account for the contextual realities leading the corporation to function differently from one jurisdiction to another—notably, the legal, cultural, market, and historical contexts that impact how we approach the corporate form and corporate law. This part of the book takes up the task of re-conceptualizing the corporation toward the aim of more fully and accurately describing its fundamental features and governance capacities, focusing on publicly traded corporations due to the significance of their impacts, and the associated vigor of contemporary debates regarding their nature and purposes.[1]

This chapter sets the stage by exploring the emergence of the modern public corporation in the United Kingdom and the United States. As discussed earlier and analyzed in considerable depth throughout the remainder of the book,[2] Anglo-American scholars, in particular, often approach this topic with a singular archetype in mind—widely dispersed ownership of freely transferable stock by passive investors; highly centralized management through a powerful board of directors; fiduciary obligations strongly emphasizing shareholders' interests; and substantial insulation from liability exposure for boards and shareholders alike. My analysis, however, emphasizes the flux and dynamism that in fact characterized the historical emergence of the modern public corporation, indicating that the attributes of the corporate form are less static and rigid than contemporary accounts suggest. I then turn to long-standing controversies in corporate governance that remain hotly contested today—notably, who ought to have the last word in corporate decision-making, whose interests ought to guide corporate

[1] *See generally* CHRISTOPHER M. BRUNER, CORPORATE GOVERNANCE IN THE COMMON-LAW WORLD: THE POLITICAL FOUNDATIONS OF SHAREHOLDER POWER (2013). *See also* WILLIAM T. ALLEN & REINIER KRAAKMAN, COMMENTARIES AND CASES ON THE LAW OF BUSINESS ORGANIZATION 284 (5th ed. 2016); MARC MOORE & MARTIN PETRIN, CORPORATE GOVERNANCE: LAW, REGULATION AND THEORY 10–16 (2017) (focusing on publicly traded corporations "due to the especially vexing governance challenges" they raise, "the general . . . synonymy of 'public' and 'largeness' when it comes to correlating companies by status and relative size," and their "unique capacity . . . to attract capital from the many notionally 'passive' investors").

[2] *See supra* Chapter 1, *infra* Part Three.

The Corporation as Technology. Christopher M. Bruner, Oxford University Press. © Christopher M. Bruner 2022.
DOI: 10.1093/oso/9780197635179.003.0004

decision-making, and how much risk-taking is desirable. The fact that such fundamental issues remain unsettled today underscores the need for a re-conceptualization of the corporate form and corporate law.

A. Emergence of the Modern Public Corporation

From our present vantage point, the corporate form is widely thought to represent "a superior structure for capitalizing large firms that require capital contributions from many individuals" because "the corporation's legal characteristics have strongly complementary qualities." For example, as William Allen and Reinier Kraakman observe, limited liability for shareholders "makes free transferability more valuable by reducing the costs associated with transfers of interest," in so far as it renders share value independent of the financial wherewithal of the shareholders themselves. Free transferability, in turn, "permits the development of large capital (equity or stock) markets, which are also advanced by the presence of centralized management."[3] Moreover, limited liability simultaneously tends to "encourage risk-averse shareholders to invest in risky ventures" by assuring them that they cannot generally lose more than they initially invested, while at the same time making diversification available as a means of further buffering downside risks.[4] For such reasons, limited liability often takes centerstage in retrospectively constructed accounts of the widely held public corporation,[5] some going so far as to suggest that the significance of limited liability in our economic history exceeds that of the steam engine, or even electricity.[6]

The interactions among various aspects of the corporate form are addressed in some depth,[7] but as a threshold matter it is critical to understand that the widely held public corporation was not in fact a holistically conceived creation; it did not simply appear one day in its present form. Rather, it gradually took shape over the course of centuries, reflecting a series of policy decisions made in response to evolving legal, cultural, and market contexts. This section briefly canvasses that history in the United Kingdom and the United States, the aim

[3] ALLEN & KRAAKMAN, *supra* note 1, at 75.

[4] *Id.* at 86–89.

[5] *See, e.g.*, FRANK H. EASTERBROOK & DANIEL R. FISCHEL, THE ECONOMIC STRUCTURE OF CORPORATE LAW 40 (1991) ("Limited liability is a distinguishing feature of corporate law—perhaps *the* distinguishing feature."); Frank H. Easterbrook & Daniel R. Fischel, *Limited Liability and the Corporation*, 52 U. CHI. L. REV. 89, 93–97 (1985). *See also* Ron Harris, *A New Understanding of the History of Limited Liability: An Invitation for Theoretical Reframing*, 16 J. INSTITUTIONAL ECON. 643, 659–60 (2020)(observing this tendency in retrospective theoretical accounts).

[6] *See, e.g.*, DAVID A. MOSS, WHEN ALL ELSE FAILS: GOVERNMENT AS THE ULTIMATE RISK MANAGER 53 (2002)(quoting Nicholas Murray Butler to this effect).

[7] *See infra* Chapter 5.

being not to provide a comprehensive historical account but rather to emphasize the dynamism of the process and the contingency of some significant choices made along the way.

While accounts of the corporation's early origins differ, "it is clear that the idea of a corporate body endowed with a separate legal personality and its own pool of assets is distinctly European." By medieval times, the corporate form was widely employed by "religious orders, abbeys, monasteries, cathedral chapters, boroughs, towns, guilds, charities, and universities,"[8] and the most obvious attraction was continuity—a straightforward artifact of a distinct, collective legal personality "defined without reference to specific individuals" and therefore able to "survive changes in organizational membership."[9] More subtly, the fact that the corporation could itself own a distinct pool of assets provided what has come to be called "entity shielding," meaning "rules that protect a firm's assets from the personal creditors of its owners." Henry Hansmann, Reinier Kraakman, and Richard Squire describe this as the "sine qua non of the legal entity," demarcating a distinct pool of assets associated with a given undertaking to which contractual counterparties could look in assessing creditworthiness.[10] This contrasts with "owner shielding" provided by limited liability, meaning "rules that protect the personal assets of a firm's owners from the firm's creditors."[11] Critically, although both of these forms of asset partitioning are "important for understanding the pattern of creditors' rights in modern business firms" today, "only entity shielding clearly requires special rules of law," whereas owner shielding through limited liability "can often be achieved through contract."[12] Accordingly, although businesses "can prosper without limited liability, . . . significant enterprises lacking entity shielding are largely unknown in modern times."[13]

The manner in which the modern corporation took shape over the course of centuries generally supports this claim. By the turn of the seventeenth century the corporate form had been adapted for use in substantial commercial ventures such as the East India Company (established in 1600) and the Dutch East India Company (established in 1602).[14] These entities were rendered more stable through "joint stock" investment, under which "shareholders lost their power to withdraw at will," but "were compensated with a new right to sell their shares without the consent of other owners, a compromise that reconciled a company's

[8] David Gindis, *Conceptualizing the Business Corporation: Insights from History*, 16 J. INSTITUTIONAL ECON. 569, 570 (2020).

[9] *Id.* at 3. *See also* Christopher M. Bruner, *The Enduring Ambivalence of Corporate Law*, 59 ALA. L. REV. 1385, 1387–88 (2008).

[10] Henry Hansmann et al., *Law and the Rise of the Firm*, 119 HARV. L. REV. 1333, 1336–38 (2006). *See also* Gindis, *supra* note 8, at 570; Harris, *supra* note 5, at 645.

[11] Hansmann et al., *supra* note 10, at 1339–40.

[12] *Id.* at 1340.

[13] *Id.* at 1336.

[14] *See* Harris, *supra* note 5, at 645.

need for fixed capital with a shareholders' need for liquidity."[15] Limited liability for shareholders did not figure prominently at this time, however, and would not become a widely adopted corporate feature for centuries to come. Ron Harris observes that just as limited liability had been irrelevant to earlier corporations because they were essentially nonprofit undertakings without equity investors, the subject largely remained irrelevant for these early business corporations. Both the East India Company and the Dutch East India Company were initially capitalized principally with equity, such that "there was no significant conflict between shareholders and creditors"—and while each later resorted to longer-term debt financing, Harris argues that insolvency was not a practical possibility due to (de facto or express) public backing.[16]

From the late seventeenth century through the eighteenth century, "numerous additional business corporations were created by Royal Charter," generally endowed with features expressly created through their individual charters. In some cases these included "limitations on the personal liability of shareholders to creditors,"[17] but in others they did not—suggesting that "limited liability is not a prerequisite of tradable shares."[18] Indeed, even for those providing some measure of limited liability, the practical relevance of such provisions remains open to question, given the limited resort to debt financing during this period.[19] This may explain why prominent eighteenth-century legal texts do not refer to limited liability as a significant corporate feature,[20] focusing rather on the nature and utility of a legal entity distinct from the business participants themselves.[21]

In light of the foregoing, the fundamental questions are when limited liability for investors came to be associated with the preexisting corporate form, and how this ultimately related to the emergence of the widely held public corporation as we know it today. In both the United Kingdom and the United States, the course of relevant events was episodic and contested. There was no single "watershed" moment when limited liability appeared on the scene, further suggesting that perhaps "this attribute was not essential for the spread of widely-held and publicly-traded corporations, or for the unfolding of the industrial revolution."[22] Harris argues that, as a practical matter, limitation of shareholders' liability vis-à-vis creditors became an issue only with the advent of corporate bankruptcy

[15] Hansmann et al., *supra* note 10, at 1376–77.

[16] *See* Harris, *supra* note 5, at 645–47.

[17] BRIAN R. CHEFFINS, CORPORATE OWNERSHIP AND CONTROL: BRITISH BUSINESS TRANSFORMED 134 (2008).

[18] Hansmann et al., *supra* note 10, at 1378.

[19] *See* Harris, *supra* note 5, at 647–48.

[20] *See id.* at 648–49.

[21] *See* Christopher M. Bruner, *The Corporation's Intrinsic Attributes*, *in* UNDERSTANDING THE COMPANY: CORPORATE GOVERNANCE AND THEORY 60, 61–63 (Barnali Choudhury & Martin Petrin eds., 2017).

[22] Harris, *supra* note 5, at 644–45.

procedures, which arose in both the United Kingdom and the United States in the nineteenth century[23]—the period when limited liability became a widespread concern in both countries.

Although England's Bubble Act, from its enactment in 1720 to its repeal in 1825, "explicitly prohibit[ed] undertakings lacking authorization from a Royal Charter or an Act of Parliament from acting as a corporate body or raising capital by the issuance of transferable shares,"[24] the Act was not meaningfully enforced. This period witnessed a proliferation of so-called unincorporated joint stock companies—essentially partnerships with assets "held in trust for the partners by trustees whom the partners had themselves selected," permitting business participants to "mimic the chartered company" during a period of acute "charter shortage."[25] Drafters sometimes endeavored to imbue these unincorporated joint stock companies with limited liability by contract,[26] but this proved challenging in undertakings that remained, in essence, partnerships.[27] The Joint Stock Companies Act 1844 made general incorporation by registration available, but did not provide limited liability[28]—and this, paired with enactment of a statutory means for creditors to petition a court to dissolve insolvent companies, effectively "brought the question of the shareholders' limited liability regime to the centre stage."[29] Limited liability for U.K. companies first received clear statutory endorsement through the Limited Liability Act 1855.[30]

In the United States, the relevant history unfolded somewhat differently—principally because "American states were less stingy than Parliament in granting charters," and because "they were also quicker to enact general incorporation statutes."[31] The U.S. experience does, however, reinforce the conclusion that fully limited liability is not an inevitable incident of formal entity status. While limited liability for shareholders accompanied general incorporation in the first such U.S. statute, enacted in New York in 1811,[32] limited liability would only emerge in other states sporadically, and over the course of several decades. "New Hampshire, Connecticut, and Vermont had begun granting limited liability on a regular basis to their incorporated manufacturers in the late 1810s; and Maine,

[23] *See id.* at 649.
[24] CHEFFINS, *supra* note 17, at 139.
[25] Hansmann et al., *supra* note 10, at 1383–86. *See also* CHEFFINS, *supra* note 17, at 149–50.
[26] *See* Gindis, *supra* note 8, at 573–74.
[27] *See* CHEFFINS, *supra* note 17, at 149; Hansmann et al., *supra* note 10, at 1384; Harris, *supra* note 5, at 651. *See also* JOHN MAIR, BOOK-KEEPING METHODIZ'D: OR, A METHODICAL TREATISE OF MERCHANT-ACCOMPTS, ACCORDING TO THE ITALIAN FORM 17 (7th ed. 1763)(explaining that the personal assets of merchants in this period would customarily appear on their books)
[28] *See* CHEFFINS, *supra* note 17, at 164–65.
[29] Harris, *supra* note 5, at 653. *See also* Gindis, *supra* note 8, at 573–74.
[30] *See* CHEFFINS, *supra* note 17, at 164–65; Gindis, *supra* note 8, at 574.
[31] Hansmann et al., *supra* note 10, at 1394.
[32] *See* MOSS, *supra* note 6, at 55–58.

just recently separated from Massachusetts in 1820, enacted a broad rule of limited liability for its manufacturing corporations in 1823."[33] Massachusetts would itself provide limited liability for shareholders in manufacturing corporations in 1830.[34] As in the United Kingdom, concerns regarding U.S. shareholders' liability exposure became particularly acute once a corporate insolvency regime took shape through the Bankruptcy Act of 1867, which set the stage for corporate insolvencies to become "a major issue in the 1870s, during a wave of railroad companies' failures."[35] Limited liability could not be regarded as a consistent U.S. approach, however, until the twentieth century. Indeed, California did not provide fully limited liability until 1931.[36]

Intriguingly, just as limited liability would gain traction at different times across jurisdictions, so it took different forms. While often described in "binary" terms, as if shareholders are either to be fully exposed or fully shielded, the historical experience reveals that, in fact, there was a "continuum" of approaches.[37] In the United Kingdom, the Limited Liability Act 1855 did not establish fully limited liability as a default rule, but rather "allowed incorporators to decide how much shareholders would personally owe creditors by determining how much of the nominal capital was not to be paid up initially."[38] As Brian Cheffins explains, this was widespread among nineteenth-century British industrial companies, for which it was "standard practice . . . to incorporate with shares having a sizeable nominal capital . . . and only requiring subscribers to pay a small portion upon issuance (30 per cent on average), with the remainder being available for the company to call." This effectively exposed shareholders in such companies to a capped, though nontrivial, "residual liability" that "gave them a financial incentive to be vigilant."[39] Such a structure functions much like a multiple liability regime, and this means of protecting creditors survived into the twentieth century.[40]

In the United States, meanwhile, a number of distinct regimes long coexisted across the states. New York's 1811 general incorporation statute was interpreted as providing double liability, meaning that shareholders of a failed corporation

[33] *Id.* at 61.

[34] *Id.* at 68.

[35] *See* Harris, *supra* note 5, at 653.

[36] MOSS, *supra* note 6, at 68–69. *See also* ALLEN & KRAAKMAN, *supra* note 1, at 86. Harris speculates that the equitable doctrine of piercing the corporate veil, which arose in the early twentieth century, may have represented "a response or a partial offset to the uniform application of full limited liability." *See* Harris, *supra* note 5, at 658 n.24. This doctrine generally applies exclusively in the context of closely held corporations and parent-subsidiary relationships, however, where the rationale for limited liability is weaker. *See* Easterbrook & Fischel, *supra* note 5, at 109–11.

[37] *See* Harris, *supra* note 5, at 651. *See also* MOSS, *supra* note 6, at 68–69.

[38] Harris, *supra* note 5, at 655. *See also* Gindis, *supra* note 8, at 574; Hansmann et al., *supra* note 10, at 1387.

[39] CHEFFINS, *supra* note 17, at 171–74.

[40] *See* Harris, *supra* note 5, at 658.

not only stood to lose what they had initially paid for their stock, but could be assessed again for that amount to the extent necessary to pay the corporation's debts at the time of dissolution.[41] Massachusetts, by contrast, maintained an unlimited liability regime until 1830,[42] apparently without hindering the state's industrial development.[43] California, for its part, maintained a regime of pro rata unlimited liability for shareholders well into the twentieth century, and this likewise "did not prevent California from achieving a greater growth rate than most other US states."[44] As David Moss concludes, it remains "difficult to demonstrate a clear connection between limited liability and economic performance," as "there is no definitive evidence demonstrating that states which adopted limited liability first consistently outperformed their economic rivals."[45]

In addition to differing general approaches to shareholder liability, there were also sectoral and industry-specific approaches. As already discussed, U.K. industrial companies in the nineteenth century customarily required those subscribing for shares only to pay 30 percent of the nominal capital on average, creating a potentially significant "residual liability" moving forward that functioned much like a multiple liability regime.[46] In finance, meanwhile, multiple liability regimes were often required industry-wide. These regimes, and their potential today, will be assessed in greater depth,[47] but it is telling that multiple liability regimes were common in banking on both sides of the Atlantic, and indeed in various common law jurisdictions, for much of the late nineteenth and early twentieth centuries.[48] Following the Companies Act 1879, British banks "that wanted to convert to limited liability could divide any unpaid capital on issued shares into an amount callable at the discretion of the directors and a remainder callable only in the event of the winding up of the bank," and the "credit standing of banks with this sort of 'reserved' liability was well regarded," reflecting the relatively greater creditor protection provided.[49] In the United States, meanwhile, double liability was required for national banks from the 1860s until the 1930s,

[41] *See* MOSS, *supra* note 6, at 57–58; Harris, *supra* note 5, at 652.

[42] *See* MOSS, *supra* note 6, at 58–68.

[43] *See* Harris, *supra* note 5, at 655.

[44] *Id.* at 658. *See also* Bruner, *supra* note 21, at 64–65; Henry Hansmann & Reinier Kraakman, *Toward Unlimited Shareholder Liability for Corporate Torts*, 100 YALE L.J. 1879, 1924 (1991).

[45] MOSS, *supra* note 6, at 69.

[46] *See supra* notes 38–40 and accompanying text.

[47] *See infra* Chapter 4.B.iii, Chapter 7.A.

[48] *See* Christopher M. Bruner, *Conceptions of Corporate Purpose in Post-Crisis Financial Firms*, 36 SEATTLE U. L. REV. 527, 540, 546–48 (2013).

[49] CHEFFINS, *supra* note 17, at 233. *See also* Harris, *supra* note 5, at 656. For additional background on use of multiple liability rules in Australia, Canada, and the United Kingdom, see Lewis T. Evans & Neil C. Quigley, *Shareholder Liability Regimes, Principal-Agent Relationships, and Banking Industry Performance*, 38 J. L. & ECON. 497 (1995); John D. Turner, *"The Last Acre and Sixpence": Views on Bank Liability Regimes in Nineteenth-Century Britain*, 16 FIN. HIST. REV. 111 (2009).

and was similarly required for most state banks as well[50]—a policy aimed at protecting depositors, a category of creditors, from the excessive risk-taking that shareholders might otherwise have favored if they had been protected by fully limited liability.[51] As Jonathan Macey and Geoffrey Miller found in their U.S. historical study, such rules "fostered cautious banking practices on the part of bank managers who were either themselves shareholders and always were subject to monitoring by shareholders anxious to avoid the specter of assessment."[52] Fully limited liability took hold in commercial banking later than in other sectors,[53] yet the approach of constraining risk through liability exposure for equity holders persisted even longer in investment banking, where the partnership organizational form prevailed until the 1980s.[54]

In much the same way that corporate legal history reveals a more dynamic and contested landscape than contemporary accounts generally recognize in terms of desirable levels of shareholder liability exposure, so one finds substantial variability when it comes to directors' exposure in the context of corporate decision-making. Doctrines that insulate directors from liability for breach of the duty of care, based on ex post second-guessing, are long-standing in both countries. In the United States, the historical roots of the business judgment rule date back at least to the early nineteenth century,[55] meaning that this doctrinal structure evolved over roughly the same time frame that the shareholder liability rules already discussed did. Under current Delaware law, the business judgment rule takes the form of "a presumption that in making a business decision the directors of a corporation acted on an informed basis, in good faith and in the honest belief that the action taken was in the best interests of the company," and the practical upshot of this presumption is that directors will not be held personally liable for care breaches unless the plaintiff can show "gross negligence" in the board's decision-making process.[56] The insulation provided is quite substantial,

[50] *See* Jonathan R. Macey & Geoffrey P. Miller, *Double Liability of Bank Shareholders: History and Implications*, 27 WAKE FOREST L. REV. 31, 35–39 (1992).

[51] *See* MOSS, *supra* note 6, at 93, 97–100, 115; Peter Conti-Brown, *Elective Shareholder Liability*, 64 STAN. L. REV. 409, 458–59 (2012); Bruner, *supra* note 48, at 546–48.

[52] Macey & Miller, *supra* note 50, at 33. For additional discussion, see Howell E. Jackson, *Losses from National Bank Failures during the Great Depression: A Response to Professors Macey and Miller*, 28 WAKE FOREST L. REV. 919, 921 (1993) (arguing that "losses imposed on depositors in national banks that failed during the 1930–34 period were much higher than those reported by Macey and Miller"); Jonathan R. Macey & Geoffrey P. Miller, *Double Liability of Bank Shareholders: A Look at the New Data*, 28 WAKE FOREST L. REV. 933 (1993) (responding that "the conclusion that *depositors would have been worse off without double liability* seems impossible to refute").

[53] *See* Gindis, *supra* note 8, at 574.

[54] *See* Bruner, *supra* note 48, at 541; Conti-Brown, *supra* note 51, at 459–60; Claire Hill & Richard Painter, *Berle's Vision Beyond Shareholder Interests: Why Investment Bankers Should Have (Some) Personal Liability*, 33 SEATTLE U. L. REV. 1173, 1179–81 (2010).

[55] *See* S. Samuel Arsht, *The Business Judgment Rule Revisited*, 8 HOFSTRA L. REV. 93, 97–100 (1979). *See also* ALLEN & KRAAKMAN, *supra* note 1, at 239–40.

[56] Aronson v. Lewis, 473 A.2d 805, 812 (Del. 1984).

and various statutory structures provide further insulation, including exculpatory charter provisions, indemnification, and insurance.[57]

In the United Kingdom, meanwhile, such protections for directors are less complete, reflecting shareholders' clearer statutory priority in the corporation, the styling of directors' governance powers as a direct delegation from shareholders, and the greater residual governance powers that shareholders retain.[58] Although U.K. company law permits insurance, exculpation and indemnification are not permitted.[59] U.K. directors do receive substantial protection against judicial second-guessing, however, from the internal management doctrine, which "dictates that where the corporate contract vests sovereignty (in the sense of supreme governance power) in a particular organ, that organ consequently has the power to determine . . . what conduct does and does not constitute a legally cognisable harm to the company." This styling of governance power has "enabled courts to adopt a liberal and non-interventionist stance" akin to that promoted by the U.S. business judgment rule.[60]

Robust insulating doctrines like these are widely understood today as means of aligning directors' risk-taking incentives with those of shareholders, who generally favor greater risk—because they capture the upside but, with limited liability protection, need not fear the downside.[61] However, just as limited liability for shareholders was historically carved back in banks through double liability rules, so these sorts of insulating doctrines were carved back for bank directors. These regimes, and their significance for us today, will be likewise assessed in greater depth,[62] but it is similarly significant that some U.S. courts historically held that bank directors owe fiduciary duties directly to bank depositors—a category of creditors[63]—and applied a more rigorous standard of conduct to bank

[57] *See* DEL. CODE ANN. tit. 8, §§ 102(b)(7), 145. *See also* Christopher M. Bruner, *Good Faith, State of Mind, and the Outer Boundaries of Director Liability in Corporate Law*, 41 WAKE FOREST L. REV. 1131 (2006); Christopher M. Bruner, *Is the Corporate Director's Duty of Care a "Fiduciary" Duty? Does It Matter?*, 48 WAKE FOREST L. REV. 1027 (2013).

[58] For in-depth comparison of the U.K. and U.S. corporate governance systems in these respects, see BRUNER, *supra* note 1, at 29–65.

[59] *See* Companies Act 2006, c. 46, §§ 232–33 (U.K.) (generally prohibiting exculpation and indemnification but permitting insurance). *See also* MARC T. MOORE, CORPORATE GOVERNANCE IN THE SHADOW OF THE STATE 157–63 (2013).

[60] MOORE, *supra* note 59, at 144–49. *See also* John Armour et al., *The Basic Governance Structure: The Interests of Shareholders as a Class*, *in* REINIER KRAAKMAN ET AL., THE ANATOMY OF CORPORATE LAW: A COMPARATIVE AND FUNCTIONAL APPROACH 49, 69–71 (3d ed. 2017); Christopher M. Bruner, *Opting Out of Fiduciary Duties and Liabilities in U.S. and U.K. Business Entities*, *in* RESEARCH HANDBOOK ON FIDUCIARY LAW 285 (D. Gordon Smith & Andrew S. Gold eds., 2018).

[61] *See* ALLEN & KRAAKMAN, *supra* note 1, at 230–32.

[62] *See infra* Chapter 4.B.iii, Chapter 7.A.

[63] *See* Patricia A. McCoy, *A Political Economy of the Business Judgment Rule in Banking: Implications for Corporate Law*, 47 CASE W. RES. L. REV. 1, 38–39 (1996). *See also* Bruner, *supra* note 48, at 536–38, 544–48. I have argued elsewhere that the duty of care is not properly conceptualized as fiduciary in nature, but U.S. corporate governance literature routinely refers to duties of loyalty and care as "fiduciary duties" (plural). For consistency and ease of reference, I follow that convention here. *See generally* Bruner, *Is the Corporate Director's Duty of Care a "Fiduciary" Duty?*, *supra* note 57.

directors, whether taking the form of a higher standard of care or diminished business judgment rule protection.[64] Accordingly, doctrines insulating directors from liability exposure have likewise evolved over time and differed from one context to another, reflecting the same sorts of concerns that drove the divergent approaches to shareholder liability exposure described earlier.

It is widely acknowledged that the entity shielding capacities of a distinct corporate entity, combined with the trend toward greater liability insulation for shareholders and boards of directors alike that took shape over the nineteenth and early twentieth centuries, facilitated industrialization and the development of deep, liquid capital markets, paving the way toward widely held U.K. and U.S. public companies as we know them today. Cheffins observes that U.K. statutory reforms of the mid-nineteenth century gave "those operating businesses a straightforward and reliable procedure to incorporate a company with full legal personality, transferable shares, limited liability," and other now-common attributes.[65] Railways represented "mid-19th-century forerunners" of the widely held British corporation, requiring capital exceeding what even the most affluent investors could provide alone, and prompting sufficient trading to support the development of organized stock markets across the country.[66] Over the latter decades of the nineteenth century and the early decades of the twentieth century, then, founders of companies across various industries increasingly sought exits on stock markets, unwinding their exclusive control, and investors were increasingly willing to buy shares as minority shareholder protections took shape and the financial information environment improved—developments that eventually culminated in substantial dispersal of shares in British companies following World War II.[67]

Meanwhile, railroads and continental-scale communications networks similarly became "the first modern business enterprises to appear in the United States."[68] These entities catalyzed the development of American capital markets,[69] and provided administrative models and infrastructure for the expansion and development of other industries.[70] "By the early twentieth century," Alfred

[64] *See* McCoy, *supra* note 63, at 35–55. *See also* Bruner, *supra* note 48, at 538–40.

[65] CHEFFINS, *supra* note 17, at 164.

[66] *Id.* at 147, 157–64.

[67] *See id.* chapters 6–10. In the United Kingdom and the United States alike, share ownership dispersal responded initially to minority shareholder protections developed in the marketplace (e.g., by stock exchanges and financial firms), which were only later incorporated into law. *See* BRUNER, *supra* note 1, at 117. *See also* Brian R. Cheffins, *Does Law Matter? The Separation of Ownership and Control in the United Kingdom*, 30 J. LEGAL STUD. 459 (2001); John C. Coffee, Jr., *The Rise of Dispersed Ownership: The Roles of Law and the State in the Separation of Ownership and Control*, 111 YALE L.J. 1 (2001).

[68] ALFRED D. CHANDLER, JR., THE VISIBLE HAND: THE MANAGERIAL REVOLUTION IN AMERICAN BUSINESS 79 (1977).

[69] *See id.* at 92.

[70] *See id.* part two.

Chandler concludes, "modern business enterprise, with its large staff of salaried managers and its clear separation of ownership and control, completely dominated the American transportation and communications networks," supporting "the coming of mass production and mass distribution and . . . the rise of modern business enterprise in other sectors of the economy."[71] In the United States, this involved widespread consolidation of mass production and distribution capacities,[72] facilitated by corporate law reforms that encouraged large-scale capital raising and more complex corporate structures—notably, allowing corporations to amend their own charters; to hold stock in other corporations without express legislative authorization, permitting holding company structures to develop; and to engage in merger transactions.[73] By the early 1930s, Adolf Berle and Gardiner Means could marshal considerable evidence that "a large measure of separation of ownership and control" had come to characterize American business.[74]

Although hardly a comprehensive historical account, this overview is sufficient to convey that the conception of the widely held public corporation that prevails in contemporary Anglo-American scholarship is neither inevitable nor derivable from fundamental laws of economic science.[75] Beyond the bedrock capacity of a distinct legal entity to provide continuity and to partition and insulate a set of business-specific assets, the corporate form embraces considerable variation in its other characteristics, even in terms of liability exposure for shareholders and directors—contradicting contemporary claims that near-total insulation is intrinsic to the form and essential to its utility. As the foregoing analysis demonstrates, the emergence of the modern public corporation is a dynamic story, revealing that the attributes of the corporate form are neither static nor rigid. Indeed, to the extent there is a constant, it is that the corporate form's deployment has consistently turned on the prevailing legal, cultural, market, and historical context.

Various calibrations of shareholder liability, director liability, and other corporate features have always reflected policy choices that have differed across jurisdictions, across industry contexts, and over time. Although perhaps comprehensible by reference to context, those choices remain entirely "contingent and contestable"[76]—realities that help illuminate why, despite having hundreds of years of legal history and market experience to draw upon, some of

[71] *Id.* at 80.

[72] *See id.* part four.

[73] *See* ALLEN & KRAAKMAN, *supra* note 1, at 80–82; CHANDLER, *supra* note 68, at 315–44.

[74] *See* ADOLF A. BERLE & GARDINER C. MEANS, THE MODERN CORPORATION AND PRIVATE PROPERTY 3–10 (1932). *See also* LOUIS D. BRANDEIS, OTHER PEOPLE'S MONEY AND HOW THE BANKERS USE IT 7 (1914) (observing that, as of 1914, U.S. stocks were "owned, in large part, by small investors, who do not participate in the management of the company").

[75] *Cf.* BRUNER, *supra* note 1, at 6 (noting "the scientific pretensions of the 'law and economics' movement").

[76] *Id.* at 291. *See also* Bruner, *supra* note 21, at 65; Harris, *supra* note 5, at 660–61.

power	Who ought to have the last word in corporate decision-making?
purpose	Whose interests, and what values, ought to guide corporate decision-making?
risk	How much risk-taking is desirable—either generally, or in any particular business context?

Figure 5 Enduring Controversies: Power, Purpose, and Risk

the most fundamental issues of corporate law and governance remain so hotly contested today.

B. Enduring Controversies: Power, Purpose, and Risk

In light of the flux and dynamism that characterized the emergence of the modern public corporation in the United Kingdom and the United States alike, it is unsurprising that questions relating to the core mechanics and aims of corporate governance continue to elude singular answers. These include the fundamental issues of power, purpose, and risk, and this chapter concludes with a discussion of various ways in which we continue to grapple with them. For convenience, the core corporate issues discussed are summarized in Figure 5.

1. WHO HAS THE LAST WORD?

A considerable range of views has been vigorously advocated regarding who, precisely, ought to possess ultimate governance authority in a corporation. This is readily apparent not only in global-level divergences among national systems, but also the surprising degree of divergence to be found within categories of jurisdictions that share close legal and market linkages—subjects addressed briefly here, and taken up more fully later in the book.[77] Indeed, normative disagreements and uncertainties regarding who ought to have the last word continue to unfold within many jurisdictions.

The debate regarding who ought to possess ultimate corporate governance authority is typically framed in terms of whether we should favor the efficiency of centralized board authority, or accountability to some particular constituency—in most accounts, the shareholders (naturally raising the related issue of corporate purpose, addressed immediately below).[78] Stephen Bainbridge's "director

[77] *See infra* Chapters 7–8.

[78] *See, e.g.*, Armour et al., *supra* note 60, at 51–53.

primacy" theory, for example, cites shareholder heterogeneity and rational apathy in arguing against substantial shareholder involvement in corporate governance.[79] In Bainbridge's view, the board of directors represents the true heart of the corporation, serving as "a sort of Platonic guardian" deriving its legitimacy not from shareholder endorsement but rather by virtue of its status as the corporation's true organizational nexus.[80] This approach is grounded in Ronald Coase's conception of firm efficiency as a function of the capacity of "command-and-control" governance to eliminate costs of bargaining in external markets, and Kenneth Arrow's argument that authority-based decision-making is superior to consensus-based decision-making where stakeholders have differing information and interests.[81] Lucian Bebchuk counters, however, that courts' substantial deference to the board—generally under the business judgment rule, and particularly in defending against hostile takeover bids and initiating other fundamental transactions—has generally been predicated upon the shareholders' practical ability to "replace the board." Accordingly, Bebchuk calls for reforms to corporate law and federal securities regulation to bolster the shareholder franchise as a disciplinary mechanism.[82]

This authority-versus-accountability framing provides a coherent way into certain dimensions of the issue of ultimate corporate governance authority, but there are limitations. Notably, these analyses tend to assume a binary relationship between an economic (if not legal) principal (the shareholders) and agent (the board), ignoring the potential for broader participation in governance. At the same time, they tend to argue in the abstract, with insufficient regard for contextual drivers that might point toward differing balances in various settings. The reality is that the divergences across jurisdictions are so substantial as to suggest that there must be more to it than this simplistic binary framework suggests.

Clearly there are substantial macro-level divergences, the most striking among them being the distinction between two-tier co-determined boards—widely embraced in Europe, but also in other parts of the world, including China—and one-tier boards elected by shareholders.[83] Plainly the direct involvement of employees in board-level governance defies frameworks focused exclusively on

[79] *See* Stephen M. Bainbridge, *The Case for Limited Shareholder Voting Rights*, 53 UCLA L. REV. 601, 607, 623 (2006). He further notes that ability to sell stock into liquid capital markets gives shareholders some capacity to exert discipline upon managers by creating a "market for corporate control." *Id.* at 614. *See also* EASTERBROOK & FISCHEL, *supra* note 5, at 70–72.

[80] *See* Stephen M. Bainbridge, *Director Primacy: The Means and Ends of Corporate Governance*, 97 NW. U. L. REV. 547, 560 (2003).

[81] *See id.* at 554–59; Stephen M. Bainbridge, Unocal *at 20: Director Primacy in Corporate Takeovers*, 31 DEL. J. CORP. L. 769, 779–84 (2006). *See also* KENNETH J. ARROW, THE LIMITS OF ORGANIZATION (1974); R.H. Coase, *The Nature of the Firm*, 4 ECONOMICA 386 (1937).

[82] *See* Lucian A. Bebchuk, *The Myth of the Shareholder Franchise*, 93 VA. L. REV. 675, 680–711 (2007).

[83] *See supra* Chapter 2.B.ii. *See also* BRUNER, *supra* note 1, at 225–27.

accountability to equity holders,[84] suggesting to some that more fundamental divergences are at work. For example, the "Varieties of Capitalism" literature sharply distinguishes "coordinated market economies" such as Germany, where companies rely heavily on cooperative "non-market" coordinating mechanisms to promote stable, long-term, firm-specific investment by employees and others, from "liberal market economies" like the United States and the United Kingdom, where companies alternatively rely on "competitive" market-based exchange, prioritizing shareholders' interests and seeking labor market flexibility.[85] At the same time, however, intriguing new structures have been developed to promote employee interests in systems historically rooted in Anglo-American corporate governance frameworks, suggesting that this sort of binary may itself prove too simplistic—a topic taken up later in the book.[86] Other systems, meanwhile, simply defy straightforward categorization in such terms; although beyond the scope of this work, it bears noting that so-called "state capitalism," where the government is directly involved in large companies as a significant equity holder, might be viewed either as shareholder-centric due to the state's structural governance power or as stakeholder-centric due to the state's interest in matters ranging well beyond financial performance.[87]

Global divergences like this are certainly striking, but it is arguably more illuminating that jurisdictions sharing common legal and market traditions themselves differ significantly in terms of how they conceptualize corporate governance power and who ultimately has the last word. Among common law jurisdictions (tracing their legal origins to English judge-made case law), the U.K. and Australian systems most clearly style shareholders as the ultimate source of corporate governance power. In each of these jurisdictions, the core governance document is treated as a form of contract, and the board's governance power is said to be granted to them by the shareholders, through a sort of contractual delegation—meaning that the shareholders themselves are considered the ultimate and original source of governance power in each of these systems.[88] This is generally consistent with shareholder-centric theories of

[84] *Cf.* John Armour et al., *What Is Corporate Law?*, *in* KRAAKMAN ET AL., *supra* note 60, at 1, 14.

[85] *See* Peter A. Hall & David Soskice, *An Introduction to Varieties of Capitalism*, *in* VARIETIES OF CAPITALISM: THE INSTITUTIONAL FOUNDATIONS OF COMPARATIVE ADVANTAGE 1, 8–10, 17–33 (Peter A. Hall & David Soskice eds., 2001).

[86] *See infra* Chapter 8.C (discussing South Africa).

[87] Prominent examples include China and Russia. *See, e.g.*, JINGCHEN ZHAO, CORPORATE SOCIAL RESPONSIBILITY IN CONTEMPORARY CHINA 91–96 (2014); Merritt B. Fox, *Ongoing Issues in Russian Corporate Governance*, 52 COLUM. J. TRANSNAT'L L. 435 (2014). *See also* Mariana Pargendler, *State Ownership and Corporate Governance*, 80 FORDHAM L. REV. 2917 (2012).

[88] *See* Companies Act 2006, c. 46, § 33(1) (U.K.); Model Articles for Public Companies, art. 3 (U.K.) (applicable to companies incorporated on or after Apr. 28, 2013) [hereinafter U.K. Model Articles]; Corporations Act 2001 (Cth) §§ 140(1), 198A (Austl.). For discussion, see BRUNER, *supra* note 1, at 35–36, 68–69.

corporate governance, which tend to describe the shareholder-board relationship in economic principal-agent terms (even if this depiction is not strictly accurate as a legal matter).[89] In the United States, Canada, and South Africa, however, the board's power is styled very differently. Once elected, the board's governance power is said to flow from the statute itself,[90] and in that sense to be "original and undelegated."[91]

Given how differently they style the fundamental nature of corporate governance power, it is unsurprising that these jurisdictions differ considerably in terms of how much raw power they give shareholders to intervene unilaterally in corporate affairs. As I have explored elsewhere,[92] U.K. shareholders have substantial unilateral capacity to call special meetings and remove directors without cause;[93] to initiate charter amendments;[94] to approve takeover defenses and accept hostile takeover bids;[95] and even to compel board action or inaction.[96] Australian shareholders possess substantially similar governance powers, except that they cannot direct the directors to take or refrain from taking any particular action.[97] The predominant U.S. approach reflected in Delaware law, meanwhile, gives shareholders no such default powers;[98] the only unilateral action available to Delaware shareholders is to amend the bylaws[99]—a power of uncertain extent, and to be discussed. Canada, for its part, falls closer to the U.K. and Australian

[89] *See supra* Chapter 2.B.iii. *See also* MOORE & PETRIN, *supra* note 1, at 72–74 (observing that, notwithstanding U.K. shareholders' substantial governance powers, U.K. directors are not technically the shareholders' agents).

[90] *See* DEL. CODE ANN. tit. 8, § 141(a); Canada Business Corporations Act, R.S.C. 1985, c. C-44, § 102(1); Companies Act 71 of 2008 § 66(1) (S. Afr.). For additional background, see BRUNER, *supra* note 1, at 38–39, 82–83; Tshepo H. Mongalo, *The Social and Ethics Committee: Innovating Corporate Governance in South Africa, in* THE CAMBRIDGE HANDBOOK OF CORPORATE LAW, CORPORATE GOVERNANCE AND SUSTAINABILITY 360, 367–68 (Beate Sjåfjell & Christopher M. Bruner eds., 2019).

[91] Manson v. Curtis, 119 N.E. 559, 562 (N.Y. 1918). *See also* STEPHEN M. BAINBRIDGE, CORPORATE LAW 74–75 (2d ed. 2009).

[92] *See* BRUNER, *supra* note 1, at 28–107.

[93] *See* Companies Act 2006, c. 46, §§ 168–69, 282, 303–04 (U.K.).

[94] *See id.* §§ 19–21, 283.

[95] PANEL ON TAKEOVERS AND MERGERS, THE TAKEOVER CODE, General Principles 1, 3; Rule 21.1(a) (12th ed. 2016).

[96] *See* U.K. Model Articles, *supra* note 88, art. 4(1).

[97] *See* Corporations Act 2001 (Cth) §§ 203D(1)–249D(1), 249F (calling special meetings and removing directors), §§ 9, 136(2) (initiating charter amendments) (Austl.); Takeovers Panel, Commonwealth of Australia, Guidance Note 12—Frustrating Action (Dec. 1, 2016) (approving takeover defenses and accepting hostile takeover bids). On Australian shareholders' inability to direct the directors, see ROBERT P. AUSTIN & IAN M. RAMSAY, FORD, AUSTIN AND RAMSAY'S PRINCIPLES OF CORPORATIONS LAW 403 (17th ed. 2018).

[98] *See* DEL. CODE ANN. tit. 8, §§ 141(d), (k), 211(d) (providing no default power for shareholders to call special meetings and requiring cause for removal of directors from a staggered board unless the charter says otherwise), § 242(b) (giving boards exclusive power to initiate charter amendments); Moran v. Household Int'l, Inc., 500 A.2d 1346, 1350–54 (Del. 1985) (endorsing poison pills adopted preemptively). On U.S. shareholders' inability to direct the directors, see ALLEN & KRAAKMAN, *supra* note 1, at 92.

[99] *See* DEL. CODE ANN. tit. 8, § 109(a).

end of the spectrum, with strong shareholder governance powers, although with somewhat less capacity to unilaterally accept hostile takeovers.[100] By the same token, other jurisdictions historically building their company laws on English models have diverged markedly in more stakeholder-oriented directions—South Africa representing a striking example discussed later in the book.[101]

To be clear, none of this is to say that the United States does not strongly favor shareholders—U.S. corporate law plainly places them in a strong position relative to other corporate constituencies,[102] and the larger regulatory system tends to reinforce this. Among other things, U.S. shareholders have greater practical ability to bring both corporate and securities lawsuits advancing their own interests;[103] federal laws regulating securities markets and pension fund managers strongly emphasize shareholder interests;[104] and shareholder-centric norms are widely embraced in U.S. academia, business, and financial markets.[105] As a matter of corporate law, however, the bottom line is that U.S. shareholders remain structurally weak relative to their counterparts in other common law jurisdictions, consistent with the differing ways in which corporate power has been conceptualized from one country to another.

At the same time, recalling the degree to which views can differ regarding the nature, utility, and aims of the corporate form,[106] it should come as no surprise that substantial divergences can arise within a given country—perhaps most vividly in federal systems that include numerous potential jurisdictions of incorporation, such as the United States.[107] I have focused on Delaware due to its

[100] *See* Canada Business Corporations Act, R.S.C. 1985, c. C-44, §§ 109(1), 143(1) (calling special meetings and removing directors), §§ 2(1), 173 (initiating charter amendments); Ontario Securities Commission, Notice of National Policy 62-202 and Rescission of National Policy Statement No. 38: Take-Over Bids—Defensive Tactics (July 4, 1997) (providing limited capacity for boards to deploy defenses "in a genuine attempt to obtain a better bid"). On Canadian shareholders' inability to direct the directors, see BRUCE WELLING, CORPORATE LAW IN CANADA: THE GOVERNING PRINCIPLES 298–99 (3rd ed. 2006).

[101] *See infra* Chapter 8.C.

[102] *See supra* Chapter 2.B.iii.

[103] *See, e.g.*, Robert B. Thompson & Hillary A. Sale, *Securities Fraud as Corporate Governance: Reflections upon Federalism*, 56 VAND. L. REV. 859, 892–99, 906–907 (2003) (finding that securities fraud suits implicate "care-based concerns" regarding managerial performance, and tend to focus on officers to a greater extent than Delaware corporate suits do). The practical significance of such lawsuits as a means of shoring up weak governance powers, however, may be overstated. *See* BRUNER, *supra* note 1, at 97–107. *See also* John Armour et al., *Private Enforcement of Corporate Law: An Empirical Comparison of the UK and US*, 6 J. EMPIRICAL LEGAL STUD. 687, 690, 706, 709–10 (2009)(finding that although U.S. public company directors are more likely to be sued than their U.K. counterparts, the chances of a U.S. director facing out-of-pocket liability are very low).

[104] *See* Christopher M. Bruner, *Center-Left Politics and Corporate Governance: What Is the "Progressive" Agenda?*, 2018 BYU L. REV. 267, 291–93, 303–14 (2018).

[105] *See, e.g.*, Lyman P.Q. Johnson, *The Social Responsibility of Corporate Law Professors*, 76 TUL. L. REV. 1483, 1487–93 (2002); David Millon, *Radical Shareholder Primacy*, 10 U. ST. THOMAS L.J. 1013, 1025–42 (2013). *See also* Christopher M. Bruner, *The Fiduciary Enterprise of Corporate Law*, 74 WASH. & LEE L. REV. 791, 795–96, 804–05 (2017).

[106] *See supra* Chapter 2.

[107] *See* BRUNER, *supra* note 1, at 40–45, 63.

prominence as a jurisdiction of incorporation for public companies,[108] but various states have taken divergent approaches to some of the most controversial issues in corporate law and governance, including hostile takeovers. Although Delaware case law largely defers to boards of directors—giving them substantial unilateral discretion to maintain strong defenses against takeovers in order to pursue preexisting corporate policies over a time frame of the board's own choosing, and to consider other constituencies' interests where rationally connected with the shareholders' interests[109]—the board does formally bear the burden of establishing that defensive measures represent a proportionate response to the threat,[110] and defenses must be removed to facilitate an auction if the target board has itself determined that there will be a sale, breakup, or change of control, in which case their singular duty becomes maximizing price for the shareholders.[111] Other states, however, deviate markedly from the Delaware approach. Over thirty states have enacted constituency statutes, generally giving boards unfettered latitude to maintain defenses, granting them open-ended discretion to decide what is in the corporation's best interests and, in so doing, to consider other corporate stakeholders, without necessarily prioritizing the shareholders.[112] North Dakota, meanwhile, departs from the Delaware approach in the opposite direction, reining in the duration of poison pills in a manner resembling the other common law jurisdictions described earlier.[113]

At the same time, one encounters substantial uncertainty regarding how much power shareholders ought to have within particular jurisdictions. A vivid example arises in the context of shareholders' unilateral authority to adopt, amend, and repeal bylaws in Delaware, as the statute places no express limits on the reach of this power, yet likewise provides no means of reconciling it with

[108] *See* State of Delaware, Division of Corporations, *Why Businesses Choose Delaware*, https://corplaw.delaware.gov/why-businesses-choose-delaware/ (reporting that "more than one million business entities have made Delaware their legal home" and that "more than 60 percent of the Fortune 500 companies are incorporated in Delaware").

[109] *See* Moran v. Household Int'l, Inc., 500 A.2d 1346, 1350–54 (Del. 1985); Paramount Commc'ns v. Time Inc., 571 A.2d 1140, 1152–54 (Del. 1990).

[110] *See* Unocal Corp. v. Mesa Petroleum Co., 493 A.2d 946, 954–55 (Del. 1985).

[111] *See* Revlon, Inc. v. MacAndrews & Forbes Holdings, Inc., 506 A.2d 173, 182 (Del. 1986).

[112] *See, e.g.*, CONN. GEN. STAT. § 33–756(g) (applying such latitude for public companies contemplating various fundamental transactions); IND. CODE § 23-1–35-1(d)-(g) (applying such latitude generally). As of 2019, thirty-two constituency statutes were in force across the United States. All of them reference employees and customers; most reference suppliers; over half reference creditors and local communities; some reference society, the economy and/or the environment; and "almost half . . . include an explicit catch-all phrase that permits directors to consider any other (unidentified) groups or factors not listed in the statute." *See* Lucian A. Bebchuk & Roberto Tallarita, *The Illusory Promise of Stakeholder Governance*, 106 CORNELL L. REV. 91, 116–18 (2020).

[113] *See* N.D. CENT. CODE § 10-35-22–10-35-26. This is one of a number of shareholder-centric reforms adopted as part of the "North Dakota Publicly Traded Corporations Act," at the behest of activist investor Carl Icahn. *See* BRUNER, *supra* note 1, at 62–64.

the board's own statutory governance authority.[114] The Delaware Supreme Court has only begun to work out how these competing forms of authority relate to one another, declining to provide a "bright line"; the court has simply indicated that shareholders cannot dictate substantive decisions, but generally have more latitude with bylaws that are genuinely procedurally oriented.[115] Considerable uncertainty remains, however, regarding the potential for shareholder-initiated incursions into the board's management prerogative via bylaws nominally governing procedure. As I have argued elsewhere, this reflects fundamental ambivalence in Delaware regarding how much power shareholders ought to have to prioritize their own interests, presenting courts with the thorny problem of striking a balance on their own with no meaningful guidance from the legislature. This closely resembles the quandary the Delaware judiciary has faced in grappling with hostile takeovers.[116]

II. WHOSE INTERESTS MATTER?

The foregoing discussion underscores that who ought to possess ultimate corporate governance power is closely bound up with a related question—what is the ultimate corporate objective? As the authors of *The Anatomy* observe, "the overall objective of corporate law—as of any branch of law—is presumably to serve the interests of society as a whole," and this "may be compatible with different immediate goals for corporate law."[117] So, whose interests ought to be prioritized in corporate decision-making?

It is hornbook corporate law that directors, as fiduciaries, possess decision-making power to advance the interests of the corporation, not themselves—hence the intense focus on conflicts of interest in case law addressing the duty of loyalty.[118] Even when directors are unconflicted, however, and act in perfect good faith, thorny questions remain regarding whose interests ought to prevail among various corporate constituencies when they come into conflict. This issue is typically phrased in terms of whether boards of directors should prioritize shareholders alone, or some broader group of corporate stakeholders.[119]

[114] *Compare* DEL. CODE ANN. tit. 8, § 109(a) (establishing shareholders' bylaw authority) *with* § 141(a) (establishing the board's management authority).

[115] *See* CA, Inc. v. AFSCME Emp. Pension Plan, 953 A.2d 227, 234–36 (Del. 2008).

[116] *See* BRUNER, *supra* note 1, at 48–52; Bruner, *supra* note 21, at 70–72; Christopher M. Bruner, *Managing Corporate Federalism: The Least-Bad Approach to the Shareholder Bylaw Debate*, 36 DEL. J. CORP. L. 1 (2011).

[117] Armour et al., *supra* note 84, at 22–23.

[118] *See, e.g.*, ALLEN & KRAAKMAN, *supra* note 1, at 292 (observing that "'related-party' transactions offer the paradigmatic circumstance in which courts are required to assess compliance with the duty of loyalty").

[119] *See id.* at 284.

To the extent a jurisdiction aims to advance the interests of a given stakeholder group—say, employees—this could, in theory, be accomplished by imposing a duty on the board of directors to focus on their interests or, as we have seen, by simply giving the employees some measure of governance power, as co-determination systems do.[120] It is important to recognize, however, that questions of power and purpose, respectively, are not identical and need not be answered in the same way. Bainbridge, for example, argues strenuously that shareholder interests ought to represent the ultimate objective for boards of directors, yet that boards ought to be substantially insulated from direct shareholder influence—in other words, that we ought to favor a highly shareholder-centric conception of corporate purpose, yet a highly board-centric conception of corporate power, each purportedly in the name of overall organizational efficiency.[121] As a descriptive matter, such an account has trouble making sense of even minimal shareholder voting rights or capacity for unilateral shareholder action, let alone anti-takeover laws accommodating other interests.[122] As a normative matter, however, the key point is simply that one need not necessarily answer questions of power and purpose by reference to the same constituencies.

Much debate over recent decades regarding whose interests matter in corporate law has taken the form of "contractualist" argument and "progressive" counterargument. In their influential volume titled *The Economic Structure of Corporate Law,* Easterbrook and Fischel take the position that a shareholder-centric default rule is most efficient because "the expectation is that the residual risk bearers have contracted for a promise to maximize long-run profits of the firm," while other corporate stakeholders "contract for fixed payouts." Any additional protections for these non-shareholder stakeholders, they argue, are most efficiently provided through external regulation, rather than muddying the purported clarity of a shareholder-focused corporate objective.[123] Progressive corporate scholars respond, however, that employees generally cannot effectively negotiate for adequate protections and that external regulation cannot effectively force businesses to internalize environmental and other externalities—empirical concerns leading these scholars to conclude that corporate governance must itself give boards some leeway to advance interests beyond profit maximization.[124]

[120] *See supra* Chapter 2.B.ii.

[121] *See generally* Bainbridge, *supra* note 80.

[122] *See* BRUNER, *supra* note 1, at 55–57.

[123] *See* EASTERBROOK & FISCHEL, *supra* note 5, at 35–39.

[124] *See, e.g.*, KENT GREENFIELD, THE FAILURE OF CORPORATE LAW: FUNDAMENTAL FLAWS AND PROGRESSIVE POSSIBILITIES 14–19 (2006); David Millon, *Communitarianism in Corporate Law: Foundations and Law Reform Strategies, in* PROGRESSIVE CORPORATE LAW 1, 1–2 (Lawrence E. Mitchell ed., 1995); David Millon, *Communitarians, Contractarians, and the Crisis in Corporate Law,* 50 WASH. & LEE L. REV. 1373, 1381–86 (1993). Note that I speak here of progressive views regarding state corporate law. The matter becomes more complicated at the federal level, where securities regulation and pension fund managers' duties strongly favor shareholders, and where Democratic Party

As to the contractarian claim that shareholder primacy offers an attractive singularity of purpose, then, many have responded that this is in fact illusory, as shareholders themselves are quite heterogeneous.[125]

This shareholder-versus-stakeholder debate has preoccupied scholars at least since the advent of the modern widely held public corporation,[126] and the underlying issues continue to defy tidy resolution. In August 2019, the Business Roundtable revised its "Statement on the Purpose of a Corporation" to express "a fundamental commitment to all of our stakeholders," including customers, employees, suppliers, communities, and shareholders. The statement further commits signatories to "deliver value to all of them, for the future success of our companies, our communities and our country," without prioritizing the interests of shareholders over others.[127] This met with an immediate response from the Council of Institutional Investors, expressing concern that the statement "undercuts notions of managerial accountability to shareholders" without proposing alternative accountability mechanisms. "If 'stakeholder governance' and 'sustainability' become hiding places for poor management," the Council argues, then "the economy more generally will lose out."[128] Lucian Bebchuk, a vocal advocate for greater accountability to shareholders, in a 2020 article co-authored with Roberto Tallarita, similarly characterized the Business Roundtable Statement as part of a broader managerial effort to consolidate discretionary power, undermining shareholder accountability without acknowledging the difficult "trade-offs" that a stakeholder-oriented approach to corporate governance generates.[129] To this, Colin Mayer responded that shareholders are themselves hardly homogeneous, "differ[ing] according to their degree of risk aversion and preferences, their time horizons and discounting of future returns, their assessments of future

politics have produced a coalition heavily favoring finance. For additional background, see Bruner, *supra* note 104.

[125] *See, e.g.*, GRANT M. HAYDEN & MATTHEW T. BODIE, RECONSTRUCTING THE CORPORATION: FROM SHAREHOLDER PRIMACY TO SHARED GOVERNANCE 68–87 (2020); LYNN STOUT, THE SHAREHOLDER VALUE MYTH: HOW PUTTING SHAREHOLDERS FIRST HARMS INVESTORS, CORPORATIONS, AND THE PUBLIC 63–94 (2012); Iman Anabtawi, *Some Skepticism about Increasing Shareholder Power*, 53 UCLA L. REV. 561, 577–93 (2006).

[126] *See, e.g.*, E. Merrick Dodd, Jr., *For Whom Are Corporate Managers Trustees?*, 45 HARV. L. REV. 1145, 1161–63 (1932) (arguing that fiduciary duties should flow to the corporate entity rather than the shareholders to permit broader "social responsibility"); A.A. Berle, Jr., *For Whom Corporate Managers Are Trustees*, 45 HARV. L. REV. 1365, 1368–72 (1932)(responding to Dodd that more broadly conceived fiduciary duties would undercut accountability).

[127] Business Roundtable, *Statement on the Purpose of a Corporation* (Aug. 19, 2019), https://www.businessroundtable.org/business-roundtable-redefines-the-purpose-of-a-corporation-to-promote-an-economy-that-serves-all-americans (emphasis removed).

[128] Council of Institutional Investors, *Council of Institutional Investors Responds to Business Roundtable Statement on Corporate Purpose* (Aug. 19, 2019), https://www.cii.org/aug19_brt_response.

[129] Bebchuk & Tallarita, *supra* note 112, at 121–39.

earnings and investment analyses, and their views about relevant risk classes and unquantifiable uncertainties"—meaning that "[t]rade-offs and judgments are indeed ubiquitous" whether corporate law focuses on shareholders or some broader set of stakeholders.[130] "The issue is not therefore whether trade-offs and judgments should be made," Mayer concludes, "but what purposes and values should underpin them, and who should determine and implement them."[131]

As with the related issue of who has the last word, when it comes to whose interests matter, one encounters such a high degree of global variation—among well-performing legal systems and economies—that more must be going on than simple failure of some to recognize and pursue the singular, optimal approach. In Germany, for example, directors on the management boards of large companies—appointed by their co-determined supervisory boards to manage their respective companies—are duty-bound to focus on "the interest of the company," generally understood to mean that "the interests of all groups affected by a company (e.g., employees, shareholders, but also creditors and local communities) are to be taken into account by the board in its decisions."[132] In contrast with this stakeholder-oriented approach to the corporate objective, common law jurisdictions focus quite a bit more intently on shareholders[133]—although here we again find considerable divergences regarding commitment to shareholder interests, just we did regarding shareholder power. In the United Kingdom, shareholders are expressly prioritized by statute, with other stakeholders' interests and other issues of social significance representing, at most, means to that end.[134] Although a more robustly "pluralist" approach was advocated by some during the consultations that led to the Companies Act 2006, they ultimately had to settled for the so-called "enlightened shareholder value" approach, which effectively amounts to shareholder primacy with a nod to others' interests.[135] To be sure, the statute leaves it to a director's subjective judgment to "act in the way he considers, in good faith, would be most likely to promote" the shareholders' interests, but

130 Colin Mayer, *Shareholderism versus Stakeholderism—A Misconceived Contradiction* 5–6 (ECGI Law Working Paper No. 522/2020), https://ssrn.com/abstract=3617847 (commenting on Bebchuk & Tallarita).

131 *Id.* at 6.

132 Andreas Rühmkorf, *Stakeholder Value versus Corporate Sustainability: Company Law and Corporate Governance in Germany, in* THE CAMBRIDGE HANDBOOK OF CORPORATE LAW, CORPORATE GOVERNANCE AND SUSTAINABILITY, *supra* note 90, at 232, 233–36.

133 *See* BRUNER, *supra* note 1, at 3–4 (describing this generalization).

134 *See* Companies Act 2006, c. 46, § 172(1) (U.K.).

135 *See* COMPANY LAW REVIEW STEERING GROUP, MODERN COMPANY LAW FOR A COMPETITIVE ECONOMY: THE STRATEGIC FRAMEWORK 37–39, 44 (1999). *See also* BRUNER, *supra* note 1, at 34–35, 161–66; PAUL L. DAVIES & SARAH WORTHINGTON, GOWER & DAVIES PRINCIPLES OF MODERN COMPANY LAW 540–43 (9th ed. 2012); Andrew Johnston, *Market-Led Sustainability through Information Disclosure: The UK Approach, in* THE CAMBRIDGE HANDBOOK OF CORPORATE LAW, CORPORATE GOVERNANCE AND SUSTAINABILITY, *supra* note 90, at 204, 208–10.

the formal prioritization of shareholders could not be more clear.[136] This express focus of corporate decision-making on the shareholders' interests similarly characterizes the company law of several other finance-oriented common law jurisdictions historically linked with the United Kingdom.[137] In some common law jurisdictions, however, things appear less straightforward. Canadian law, for example, gives shareholders strong governance powers and includes shareholder-centric aspects of provincial securities regulation governing hostile takeovers,[138] yet at the same time includes more stakeholder-friendly elements of corporate law. These include an oppression remedy broadly available to various corporate constituencies,[139] and corporate case law that, over recent decades, has increasingly tended to subordinate shareholder interests to a broader conception of "the best interests of the corporation."[140]

In the United States, meanwhile, one encounters a complex posture regarding corporate purpose that I have described as a fundamental ambivalence regarding the degree to which shareholder interests proxy for the larger social good. In Delaware, this takes the form of a vague formulation of fiduciary loyalty owed to "the corporation and its stockholders," simultaneously;[141] structurally weak shareholders;[142] and takeover law that acknowledges the interests and vulnerabilities of non-shareholders to a greater extent than one finds in other common law jurisdictions.[143] William Allen and Reinier Kraakman aptly describe shareholder primacy as "an important theme of U.S. corporate law," acknowledging that beyond the simple fact of the shareholder franchise, "exactly what additional weight the norm of shareholder primacy carries in litigation is not always clear." They conclude that "shareholder priority more closely resembles a deep

[136] *See* Companies Act 2006, c. 46, § 172(1) (U.K.). *See also* DAVIES & WORTHINGTON, *supra* note 135, at 544–45.

[137] *See, e.g.*, BRUNER, *supra* note 1, at 73–77 (regarding Australia); Victoria Schnure Baumfield, *The Australian Paradox: Conservative Corporate Law in a Progressive Culture*, *in* THE CAMBRIDGE HANDBOOK OF CORPORATE LAW, CORPORATE GOVERNANCE AND SUSTAINABILITY, *supra* note 90, at 161, 162–66; Christopher M. Bruner, *Leaders or Laggards? Corporate Sustainability in Hong Kong and Singapore*, *in* THE CAMBRIDGE HANDBOOK OF CORPORATE LAW, CORPORATE GOVERNANCE AND SUSTAINABILITY, *supra* note 90, at 504, 510–11, 513–14 (regarding Hong Kong and Singapore).

[138] *See supra* Chapter 3.A, Chapter 4.B.i.

[139] *See* Canada Business Corporations Act, R.S.C. 1985, c. C-44, §§ 238, 241 (providing that a "complainant" could include "any . . . person who, in the discretion of a court, is a proper person to make an application").

[140] *See, e.g.*, BCE Inc. v. 1976 Debentureholders, [2008] 3 S.C.R. 560, paras. 37–40 (Can.). For additional background, see BRUNER, *supra* note 1, at 85–97; Poonam Puri, *Green but Not Enough: Sustainability in Canadian Corporate Governance*, *in* THE CAMBRIDGE HANDBOOK OF CORPORATE LAW, CORPORATE GOVERNANCE AND SUSTAINABILITY, *supra* note 90, at 146, 148–53.

[141] Guth v. Loft, 5 A.2d 503, 510 (Del. 1939). *See also* N. Am. Catholic Educ. Programming Found., Inc. v. Gheewalla, 930 A.2d 92, 99 (Del. 2007).

[142] *See supra* Chapter 4.B.i.

[143] *See supra* Chapter 2.B.iii, Chapter 4.B.i. For additional background, see BRUNER, *supra* note 1, at 42–53. *See also generally* STOUT, *supra* note 125; Bruner, *supra* note 9; Einer Elhauge, *Sacrificing Corporate Profits in the Public Interest*, 80 N.Y.U. L. REV. 733 (2005); Lyman Johnson, *The Delaware Judiciary and the Meaning of Corporate Life and Corporate Law*, 68 TEX. L. REV. 865 (1990).

but implicit value in American corporate law than a legal rule in any normal sense."[144] Delaware's corporate law statute provides no clear statement of corporate purpose and no clear resolution to straightforward collisions of board and shareholder powers.[145]

The limited Delaware case law expressly favoring shareholders' interests has involved idiosyncratic circumstances arising in the closely held context,[146] creditors opportunistically seeking protections against adverse transactions after the fact,[147] or final-period scenarios requiring maximization of the price received in the narrow circumstance where the target board has itself already decided that there is to be a sale, breakup, or change of control.[148] Tellingly, those who locate strong commitment to shareholder primacy in such cases generally acknowledge that the handful of judicial expressions to this effect themselves cite no authority.[149] In fact, "directors essentially can do whatever they want" as long as they "refrain from actively damaging shareholders' interests by stealing from them or destroying corporate assets indiscriminately." As Jonathan Macey explains, "the business judgment rule is the key to understanding why the notion of shareholder wealth maximization is a norm and not an enforceable legal principle," even in Delaware. "Judges go to such great lengths to defer to directors' decisions that the shareholder wealth maximization norm is for all intents and purposes a complete nullity."[150] Meanwhile, many states provide straightforward statutory discretion for boards of directors to consider a wide range of corporate constituencies and interests without necessarily prioritizing shareholders, clearly reflecting a stakeholder-oriented conception of corporate purpose.[151]

[144] ALLEN & KRAAKMAN, *supra* note 1, at 284–86.

[145] *See* Bruner, *supra* note 104, at 281.

[146] *See* eBay Domestic Holdings, Inc. v. Newmark, 16 A.3d 1 (Del. Ch. 2010) (rejecting use of a poison pill by controlling shareholders of closely held Craigslist to protect the company's "corporate culture," which openly disavowed "revenue maximization").

[147] *See* Katz v. Oak Indus., Inc. 508 A.2d 873 (Del. Ch. 1986).

[148] *See* Revlon, Inc. v. MacAndrews & Forbes Holdings, Inc., 506 A.2d 173 (Del. 1986).

[149] *See, e.g.*, Leo E. Strine, Jr., *The Dangers of Denial: The Need for a Clear-Eyed Understanding of the Power and Accountability Structure Established by the Delaware General Corporation Law*, 50 WAKE FOREST L. REV. 761, 772–77 (2015); David G. Yosifon, *The Law of Corporate Purpose*, 10 BERKELEY BUS. L.J. 181, 190–94, 223–24 (2014). To this point, another recent Court of Chancery opinion endorsing shareholder primacy in dicta (offered for context in analyzing the limited partnership duties at issue) relies heavily on *eBay* and law review articles by former Delaware Chief Justice Strine. *See* Bandera Master Fund LP v. Boardwalk Pipeline Partners, LP, C.A. No. 2018-0372-JTL, at 29–31 (Del. Ch. Oct. 7, 2019). For additional historical background, see Judd F. Sneirson, *The History of Shareholder Primacy, from Adam Smith through the Rise of Financialism, in* THE CAMBRIDGE HANDBOOK OF CORPORATE LAW, CORPORATE GOVERNANCE AND SUSTAINABILITY, *supra* note 90, at 73, 74–77.

[150] Jonathan R. Macey, *Corporate Law as Myth*, 93 S. CAL. L. REV. 923, 950 (2020). *See also* Bruner, *supra* note 9, at 1417–18; Lynn Stout et al., *The Modern Corporation Statement on Company Law* 2 (2016), https://ssrn.com/abstract=2848833.

[151] *See supra* Chapter 4.B.i.

Ultimately, various jurisdictions—and various authorities within a given jurisdiction—may break quite differently on the fundamental issue of whose interests matter, for a variety of reasons that are considered later in the book. The political economy that corporate law inhabits turns out to be quite central in understanding these dynamics; simply put, differing legal, cultural, market, and historical contexts require these entities to operate differently from one jurisdiction to another, to perform different types of social and economic work, and therefore to be conceptualized and regulated in different ways.[152]

III. HOW MUCH RISK IS TOO MUCH?

Closely bound up with all of the differing views regarding who ought to have the last word in corporate decision-making, and whose interests ought to be prioritized, are differing views about the degree to which various actors' interests and incentives—notably, those of shareholders—are compatible with the interests of society generally.[153] Adam Smith's "invisible hand" metaphor reflects an influential view on this, essentially equating pursuit of profit for the benefit of equity owners with the broader social good.[154] Many increasingly respond, however, that while shareholder primacy may have made investors a lot of money, it has imposed wide-ranging social harms as well.[155]

As we saw earlier, several developments in the historical emergence of the modern public corporation had to do with risk—most vividly, the capacity of limited liability to make shareholders more comfortable investing in large industrial undertakings, and the capacity of the business judgment rule and other protections to make managers more comfortable undertaking the risks that shareholders with limited liability generally prefer.[156] However, that history at the same time conveys ambivalence regarding whether we really want as much risk-taking as these structures tend to promote. Responses such as multiple liability for bank shareholders and more demanding care standards for bank directors quite clearly aimed, as we saw, to reduce risk-taking in this vital industry—and there is growing evidence that abandoning these structures has contributed to dangerous levels of risk in the financial system, fueling recurrent crises.[157] At the same time, by a similar rationale, some have asked whether we

[152] *See supra* Chapter 3, *infra* Chapter 8.
[153] *See, e.g.*, Armour et al., *supra* note 84, at 23–24; Bruner, *supra* note 9, at 1421–32.
[154] *See* Sneirson, *supra* note 149, at 77–79.
[155] *See* Christopher M. Bruner & Beate Sjåfjell, *Corporate Law, Corporate Governance and the Pursuit of Sustainability*, *in* THE CAMBRIDGE HANDBOOK OF CORPORATE LAW, CORPORATE GOVERNANCE AND SUSTAINABILITY, *supra* note 90, at 713, 715–16. *See also infra* Chapter 6.
[156] *See supra* Chapter 4.A.
[157] *See infra* Chapter 7.A. *See also* Bruner, *supra* note 48; Christopher M. Bruner, *Corporate Governance Reform in Post-Crisis Financial Firms: Two Fundamental Tensions*, 60 ARIZ. L. REV. 959

might benefit from carving back risk in other industry contexts[158] through these or other governance structures—say, by extending board representation to corporate constituencies favoring long-term stability over risk-driven pursuit of short-term gains.[159]

The significance of these matters today, and the range of choices available to us, are investigated more fully later in the book,[160] but for the moment the critical point is simply to observe that calibrating risk incentives in this manner is fundamental to the corporate form and corporate law. As the history recounted here suggests, there is no intrinsically right answer; optimally calibrating risk-taking incentives remains a context-driven project that cannot be dealt with in a singular and stable way for all places, industry settings, and times, any more than the related questions of corporate power and corporate purpose can. Differing approaches persist regarding the structure and operation of the board and the allocation of governance powers among various corporate stakeholders, the appropriate aims of corporate decision-making, and exposure to potential liability for corporate decision-making—because differing views persist regarding who should have the last word, whose interests matter, and how much risk is too much. The next chapter sets out a framework for thinking through the range of choices available to us as we seek to calibrate corporate governance.

(2018); Christopher M. Bruner, *Corporate Governance Reform in a Time of Crisis*, 36 J. CORP. L. 309 (2011).

158 *See* Bruner, *supra* note 21, at 74–77; Hansmann & Kraakman, *supra* note 44.
159 *See infra* Chapter 8.A.
160 *See infra* Chapter 7.

5
The Corporation as Technology

This chapter takes up the task of re-conceptualizing the corporation. I argue that we should think about the corporate form not as a set of fixed, rigid legal characteristics, but rather as a dynamic legal technology that can be calibrated and re-calibrated, in varying contexts and over time, in response to a dynamic contextual landscape.

The corporation has occasionally been described as a form of legal or social "technology," typically to emphasize the corporate form's failure to achieve desired social goals or to perform desirable social functions.[1] While I consider this appraisal of the status quo to be amply justified in light of the scale and scope of environmental, social, and economic crises to which the corporate form has contributed[2] and the pathologies associated with our present use of this technology,[3] I nevertheless take up the technology descriptor in a more hopeful spirit, arguing that the corporate form's flexible capabilities could be directed in more beneficial ways and contribute to a more sustainable balance across environmental, social, and economic domains. In this respect, my conceptualization lies closer to the view of Lynn Stout, who has suggested that the corporation might be conceptualized as "a multifunction tool" that performs "something like a Swiss army knife," which "can be employed by different people to serve different purposes."[4] While I prefer a conceptualization that emphasizes flexible capacities rather than a multiplicity of rigid ones, I am nevertheless on the same page. The same corporate form that has exacerbated so many problems could, differently calibrated, help us retain the core benefits of the form while mitigating its costs.

To be sure, there is already considerable legal capacity under corporate law to address a wide range of associated issues on a firm-by-firm basis, notably through tailored organizational documents[5] or statutory election to be treated as a "benefit corporation"—an option now available in over thirty U.S. states,

[1] *See, e.g.*, L. Metcalf & S. Benn, *The Corporation Is Ailing Social Technology: Creating a "Fit for Purpose" Design for Sustainability*, 11 J. BUS. ETHICS 195, 197 (2012); Benjamin K. Sovacool, *Broken by Design: The Corporation as a Failed Technology*, 15 SCI., TECH. & SOC'Y 1, 2 (2010).

[2] *See supra* Chapter 1.

[3] *See infra* Chapter 6.B.

[4] Lynn Stout, *The Troubling Question of Corporate Purpose*, 3 ACCT. ECON. & L. 61, 65 (2013).

[5] *See, e.g.*, DEL. CODE ANN. tit. 8, § 102(a)(3), (b)(1) (requiring the charter to include the "nature of the business or purposes to be conducted or promoted," and permitting it to include "[a]ny provision for the management of the business and for the conduct of the affairs of the corporation"); Companies Act 2006, c. 46, § 172(2) (U.K.) ("Where or to the extent that the purposes of the company consist of or include purposes other than the benefit of its members, subsection (1) has effect

The Corporation as Technology. Christopher M. Bruner, Oxford University Press.
DOI: 10.1093/oso/9780197635179.003.0005

including Delaware.[6] However, the former long-standing capacities have plainly been insufficient to stem the crises that we now face, and the latter capacities have not made a dent in the problem. Indeed, there are only about 3,000 benefit corporations in the entire United States,[7] compared with over 1 million business entities organized in tiny Delaware alone.[8] Significantly, almost none of those benefit corporations are publicly traded,[9] and the handful that are typically have controllers—meaning that they do not actually rely on benefit corporation status to insulate pursuit of their distinctive purposes.[10] In this light, the advent of benefit corporations may represent a step backward; take-up remains meager, yet their very existence suggests, by negative implication, that standard corporate law is more fixed on shareholder primacy than it in fact is.[11]

Accordingly, I focus here on fostering capacity to think critically and creatively about the structure of the standard corporate form and the regulatory content of corporate law,[12] which requires a clearer and fuller picture of what the

as if the reference to promoting the success of the company for the benefit of its members were to achieving those purposes.").

[6] *See* Paul C. de Bernier et al., *A Primer on Public Benefit-Focused Corporate Models in California and Beyond*, MAYER BROWN (June 10, 2020), https://www.mayerbrown.com/en/perspectives-events/publications/2020/06/the-benefit-corporation-a-primer; Urban Sustainability Directors Network, *B Corps and Benefit Corporations*, https://sustainableconsumption.usdn.org/initiatives-list/b-corps-and-benefit-corporations. In Delaware this takes the form of a subchapter of the General Corporation Law. *See* DEL. CODE ANN. tit. 8, §§ 361–68 ("Subchapter XV. Public Benefit Corporations").

[7] *See* Urban Sustainability Directors Network, *supra* note 6.

[8] *See* State of Delaware, Division of Corporations, *Why Businesses Choose Delaware*, https://corplaw.delaware.gov/why-businesses-choose-delaware/.

[9] Bernier et al., *supra* note 6 (observing that "many publicly traded companies embrace the benefit corporation concept through their subsidiaries," but that there are "few US publicly traded benefit corporations"). Etsy presents a vivid example of the incompatibility of this form with the expectations of public equity markets. *See* David Gelles, *Inside the Revolution at Etsy*, N.Y. TIMES, Nov. 25, 2017, https://www.nytimes.com/2017/11/25/business/etsy-josh-silverman.html (describing how Etsy declined to become a Delaware public benefit corporation and dropped its certified B Corp status after going public and undergoing a management shake-up at the behest of hedge fund and private equity investors).

[10] *See* Ann Lipton, *Benefit Corporations Go Public*, BUSINESS LAW PROF BLOG, July 18, 2020, https://lawprofessors.typepad.com/business_law/2020/07/benefit-corporations-go-public.html.

[11] *See, e.g.*, CHRISTOPHER M. BRUNER, CORPORATE GOVERNANCE IN THE COMMON-LAW WORLD: THE POLITICAL FOUNDATIONS OF SHAREHOLDER POWER 45 n.95 (2013); Carol Liao, *Social Enterprise Law: Friend or Foe to Corporate Sustainability?*, *in* THE CAMBRIDGE HANDBOOK OF CORPORATE LAW, CORPORATE GOVERNANCE AND SUSTAINABILITY 655, 667 (Beate Sjåfjell & Christopher M. Bruner eds., 2019). *See also* WILLIAM T. ALLEN & REINIER KRAAKMAN, COMMENTARIES AND CASES ON THE LAW OF BUSINESS ORGANIZATION 291 (5th ed. 2016) (observing that "mission-driven business" could already be pursued by tailoring charters in standard corporations). Meanwhile, certification schemes raise distinct though related concerns, creating a potentially perverse incentive to paint all corporate law as highly shareholder-centric, regardless of doctrinal realities, in order for certifiers to more effectively market and sell their antidote. *See* Liao, *supra*, at 667–68. *See also* Urban Sustainability Directors Network, *supra* note 6 (observing that "B Lab certification costs range from $500–$50,000/year, based on annual revenues").

[12] I focus specifically on the corporate form, rather than unincorporated hybrid entities such as the U.S. limited liability company, as the latter appeal principally to those engaged in smaller, closely held, and/or early-stage businesses in which investors themselves typically engage directly in

corporate form can actually do. This chapter provides a general framework for thinking about the considerable flexibilities offered by the corporate technology, and the correlative range of policy options available to us.

A. Levers of Governance

What sort of technology does the corporation represent? I suggest that the corporate form is best conceptualized as a dynamic governance technology, and that its flexible capacities are themselves best conceptualized as a series of governance levers that can be calibrated in myriad ways, both individually and in various workable combinations.[13] This approach responds to the prevailing static conceptions of the corporate form described earlier[14] by focusing on governance-related attributes and then re-conceptualizing each as a spectrum, inviting critical thought about how each ought to be calibrated—and how calibrations of multiple levers might act in tandem—to achieve various goals.[15] This section describes various significant governance levers, and then the next section presents them as an integrated framework, analyzing how they interact.

For convenience, the corporate governance levers described are summarized in tabular form in Figure 6.

I. GOVERNANCE CENTRALIZATION

> Decision-making power may be more centralized, through a board of directors, or dispersed, in the hands of shareholders or other stakeholders.

The authority-versus-accountability framework through which many assess the core issue of corporate governance power—that is, who has the last word—essentially reflects the fact that a wide range of balances might be struck regarding

management, and to those organizing investment funds. *See* ALLEN & KRAAKMAN, *supra* note 11, at 63–73. *See also* Christopher M. Bruner, *Opting Out of Fiduciary Duties and Liabilities in U.S. and U.K. Business Entities*, *in* RESEARCH HANDBOOK ON FIDUCIARY LAW 285 (D. Gordon Smith & Andrew S. Gold eds., 2018).

[13] For preliminary analysis along these lines, see Christopher M. Bruner, *The Corporation's Intrinsic Attributes*, *in* UNDERSTANDING THE COMPANY: CORPORATE GOVERNANCE AND THEORY 60 (Barnali Choudhury & Martin Petrin eds., 2017). *Cf.* Stout, *supra* note 4, at 63, 67 (arguing that a "multifunction theory" of corporate purpose could represent a superior alternative to shareholder primacy).

[14] *See supra* Chapter 2.B.ii.

[15] This framework also remedies shortcomings of prevailing static conceptions by addressing important governance determinants that they ignore, notably board liability and shareholder enforcement. *See supra* Chapter 4.

governance centralization	Decision-making power may be more centralized, through a board of directors, or dispersed, in the hands of shareholders or other stakeholders.
board liability exposure	Directors may be given more or less insulation from liability exposure—less exposure prompting more comfort with risk-taking and more exposure prompting less comfort.
shareholder representation	Composition of the board may be determined solely by shareholders, or other stakeholders may be granted some degree of representation.
shareholder orientation	Boards may be duty-bound to focus narrowly on shareholders' interests, or may be permitted—or even required—to consider the interests of other stakeholders.
shareholder enforcement	Shareholders may be given more or less capacity to advance their own interests through lawsuits, either exclusively or in common with other stakeholders.
share transferability	Shareholders may be given more or less freedom to move capital into and out of corporate equity investments unilaterally.
shareholder liability exposure	Shareholders may be given more or less insulation from liability exposure—less exposure prompting more comfort with risk-taking and more exposure prompting less comfort.

Figure 6 Levers of Governance

the degree to which decision-making power is centralized through a board of directors, as opposed to being directly exercised by shareholders or, conceivably, other stakeholders. Recall that Stephen Bainbridge's director primacy theory cites public company shareholders' heterogeneity and rational apathy as evidence that we are better off deferring to boards of directors, and correlatively avoiding substantial shareholder involvement in corporate governance.[16] The

[16] *See* Stephen M. Bainbridge, *The Case for Limited Shareholder Voting Rights*, 53 UCLA L. REV. 601, 607, 623 (2006).

board, from Bainbridge's perspective, ought to be viewed as "a sort of Platonic guardian,"[17] an approach grounded in Coase's conception of firm efficiency as a function of the capacity of "command-and-control" governance to reduce transaction costs, and Arrow's argument that authority-based decision-making outperforms consensus-based approaches where various stakeholders' information and interests differ.[18] All of this, for Bainbridge, points toward a highly centralized decision-making structure through a strong board of directors, and structurally weak shareholders. At least at the macro level, this is often what we find in U.S. corporate law.[19]

In evaluating such arguments, it is important to observe how much turns on empirical claims regarding market structures and the capacities of relatively dispersed stakeholders—most obviously the shareholders, although one could imagine similar problems arising with other stakeholders to the extent they are given a direct governance role.[20] As a generalization, one tends to find stronger shareholder rights—and correlatively less governance centralization—in countries where controlling shareholders predominate, perhaps because concerns regarding heterogeneous interests and rational apathy loom less large where there is a substantial shareholder with the resources and incentive to keep informed about corporate affairs.[21] By the same token, however, one might imagine a given jurisdiction deciding to try to overcome the empirical problems associated with dispersed stock ownership by creating structures prompting engagement and facilitating collective decision-making, as various jurisdictions have sought to do.[22]

Given the centrality of empirical questions here, one could imagine perceptions regarding the optimal balance varying considerably from one jurisdiction to another, and evolving over time within a given jurisdiction as shareholding patterns change and technologies that affect coordinating capacities evolve. Naturally, one would envision the analysis being impacted by who the shareholders are and how shares are held, which likely will continue to change—a vivid example being the increasing prevalence of indirect investing through large institutions with sophistication and capacities far exceeding those of the

[17] *See* Stephen M. Bainbridge, *Director Primacy: The Means and Ends of Corporate Governance*, 97 NW. U. L. REV. 547, 560 (2003).

[18] *See id.* at 554–59; Stephen M. Bainbridge, Unocal *at 20: Director Primacy in Corporate Takeovers*, 31 DEL. J. CORP. L. 769, 779–84 (2006). *See also* KENNETH J. ARROW, THE LIMITS OF ORGANIZATION (1974); R.H. Coase, *The Nature of the Firm*, 4 ECONOMICA 386 (1937).

[19] *See supra* Chapter 4.B.i.

[20] *See* Luca Enriques et al., *The Basic Governance Structure: Minority Shareholders and Non-Shareholder Constituencies*, *in* REINIER KRAAKMAN ET AL., THE ANATOMY OF CORPORATE LAW: A COMPARATIVE AND FUNCTIONAL APPROACH 79, 95–97 (3d ed. 2017).

[21] *See* John Armour et al., *The Basic Governance Structure: The Interests of Shareholders as a Class*, *in* KRAAKMAN ET AL., *supra* note 20, at 49, 49.

[22] *See id.* at 58–59.

average retail investor.[23] Today, the market is increasingly dominated by enormous institutions—notably BlackRock with assets under management (AUM) in 2021 of $9 trillion and Vanguard with AUM of $7.2 trillion.[24] Accordingly, there is a growing literature investigating the complex incentives of such investment funds, which are certainly sophisticated enough to digest governance-relevant corporate information, yet often pursue passive investment strategies by design.[25] The global proliferation of stewardship codes may encourage large institutions to take up the governance powers afforded them in any given jurisdiction, although whether they will do so, and if so to what ends, remains to be seen.[26] In any event, hedge fund activism has become a major preoccupation in corporate governance (with widely varying views on its desirability), and sometimes these funds are able to amplify pressure on managers by enlisting support from larger, and otherwise passive, institutions.[27] The U.S. debate regarding the degree to which the shareholders' statutory bylaw authority can be used to carve back at the board's statutory governance authority reflects deep uncertainty regarding what sort of balance ought to be struck between centralized decision-making and unilateral interventions by investors.[28]

Meanwhile, technological developments offering the potential to increase shareholders' capacity to coordinate and participate in governance, and/or to reduce reliance on human management, may alter perceptions regarding the desirable balance moving forward. For example, distributed ledgers and blockchain technology are prompting experiments with more decentralized modes of decision-making, while advances in artificial intelligence lead some to predict growing reliance on algorithmic decision-making—operationally and perhaps even strategically.[29] While such possibilities are often exaggerated, in that they simultaneously overstate the near-term potential of such technologies and understate our residual policy

[23] *See id.* at 59–62. *See also* Christopher M. Bruner, *The Enduring Ambivalence of Corporate Law*, 59 ALA. L. REV. 1385, 1432–35 (2008).

[24] *See* Michael Mackenzie, *BlackRock Assets Under Management Surge to Record $9tn*, FIN. TIMES, Apr. 15, 2021, https://www.ft.com/content/e49180b1-2158-4adf-85d6-0eb4766f4d5f; Vanguard, *Fast Facts About Vanguard*, https://about.vanguard.com/who-we-are/fast-facts/. *See also* Christopher M. Bruner, *Corporate Governance Reform in Post-Crisis Financial Firms: Two Fundamental Tensions*, 60 ARIZ. L. REV. 959, 970–74 (2018).

[25] *See generally, e.g.*, Lucian Bebchuk et al., *The Agency Problems of Institutional Investors*, 31 J. ECON. PERSPECTIVES 89 (2017); Dorothy S. Lund, *The Case Against Passive Shareholder Voting*, 43 J. CORP. L. 493 (2018); John D. Morley, *Too Big to Be Activist*, 92 S. CAL. L. REV. 1407 (2019); Yesha Yadav, *Too-Big-to-Fail Shareholders*, 103 MINN. L. REV. 587 (2018).

[26] *See generally* Dionysia Katelouzou, *Shareholder Stewardship: A Case of (Re)Embedding the Institutional Investors and the Corporation?*, *in* THE CAMBRIDGE HANDBOOK OF CORPORATE LAW, CORPORATE GOVERNANCE AND SUSTAINABILITY, *supra* note 11, at 581. *See also* BRUNER, *supra* note 11, at 265–67, 271–74.

[27] *See* Armour et al., *supra* note 21, at 52–53.

[28] *See supra* Chapter 4.B.i.

[29] *See generally* Christopher M. Bruner, *Distributed Ledgers, Artificial Intelligence and the Purpose of the Corporation*, 79 CAMBRIDGE L.J. 431 (2020).

autonomy (regardless of what the technology might enable), there is no gainsaying that such technologies could prompt new governance debates, or reinvigorate old ones, by expanding the realm of the possible along such lines.[30]

At the same time, it is critical to recognize that constituencies other than shareholders can be given direct corporate governance powers as well—notably, employees. While it is common to generalize that "corporate laws never confer direct decision-making rights on workers," this is plainly incorrect because, as we have already seen, German laws "permit works councils to co-decide (with management) on a number of employee-sensitive matters."[31] Indeed, the Works Constitution Act requires works councils at companies with five or more employees, giving workers extensive approval rights relating to "social welfare, personnel and economic matters."[32] This demonstrates that there is no inherent structural barrier to providing direct corporate governance powers to non-shareholder constituencies, and that doing so is not incompatible with maintaining a well-functioning corporate legal system.

II. BOARD LIABILITY EXPOSURE

> Directors may be given more or less insulation from liability exposure—less exposure prompting more comfort with risk-taking and more exposure prompting less comfort.

We have already seen that board liability exposure became a live issue in the nineteenth century—particularly with the advent of industrialization—and

[30] *See id.*; *infra* Chapter 8.A. For additional background on these technologies and their potential impacts, see NIKITA AGGARWAL ET AL., AUTONOMOUS SYSTEMS AND THE LAW (2019); Luca Enriques & Dirk A. Zetzsche, *Corporate Technologies and the Tech Nirvana Fallacy*, 72 HASTINGS L.J. 55 (2020); George S. Geis, *Traceable Shares and Corporate Law*, 113 NW. U. L. REV. 227 (2018); Akshaya Kamalnath, *The Perennial Quest for Board Independence: Artificial Intelligence to the Rescue?*, 83 ALB. L. REV. 43 (2019/2020); Anne Lafarre & Christoph Van der Elst, *Blockchain Technology for Corporate Governance and Shareholder Activism* (Tilburg Law School Legal Studies Research Paper No. 07/2018), https://ssrn.com/abstract=3135209; Martin Petrin, *Corporate Management in the Age of AI*, 2019 COLUM. BUS. L. REV. 965 (2019); Carla L. Reyes et al., *Distributed Governance*, 59 WM. & MARY L. REV. ONLINE (2017), https://scholarship.law.wm.edu/wmlronline/vol59/iss1/1/; Usha R. Rodrigues, *Law and the Blockchain*, 104 IOWA L. REV. 679 (2019); Sergio Alberto Gramitto Ricci, *Artificial Agents in Corporate Boardrooms*, 105 CORNELL L. REV. 869 (2020); David Yermack, *Corporate Governance and Blockchains*, 21 REV. FIN. 7 (2017).

[31] Enriques et al., *supra* note 20, at 91.

[32] *See* FEDERAL MINISTRY OF LABOUR AND SOCIAL AFFAIRS, CO-DETERMINATION 2018 (Mar. 2018), at 4–9. *See also* Betriebsverfassungsgesetz [BetrVG] [Works Constitution Act], Sept. 25, 2001, *last amended* July 17, 2017 (Ger.), *translated in id.* at 17–71. Works councils are recognized in other countries as well, although they typically receive only information and consultation rights. Regarding EU-level rules on works councils, see Europäische Betriebsräte-Gesetz [EBRG] [Act on European Works Councils], Dec. 7, 2011, *last amended* July 17, 2017 (Ger.), *translated in id.* at 72–87; *id.* at 9–10. *See also* Enriques et al., *supra* note 20, at 91, 102.

that the general trend has been toward board insulation to promote entrepreneurial risk-taking.[33] At the same time, however, we have also seen that in at least one industry setting where a high degree of risk-taking was not considered desirable—banking—directors were exposed to a higher degree of potential liability.[34] This suggests that director liability exposure relates closely to achieving desirable levels of entrepreneurial risk, and that the appropriate level of exposure for directors may vary from one context to another, a topic explored in greater depth later in the book.[35]

Corporate law (in contrast with the law of unincorporated entities) has generally insisted on a relatively higher degree of exposure for breaches of the duty of loyalty, so when we speak of calibrating directors' liability exposure, this effectively focuses on the duty of care[36] and causes of action that might implicate similar concerns, notably securities fraud suits.[37] To be sure, there are institutional dynamics that reasonably leave many skeptical about the wisdom of inviting substantial judicial scrutiny for potential breaches of the duty of care. To some degree, the business judgment rule and related doctrines reflect recognition that, "as human beings, directors are not infallible and are not able to please all of the stockholders all of the time," as well as "the need to foster both business and judicial economy."[38] At the same time, the business judgment rule reflects judicial humility regarding judges' own capacity to assess the substantive wisdom of highly complex business decisions that are often made under extreme time pressure and in conditions of substantial uncertainty, creating a high risk of hindsight bias—that is, a greater likelihood of perceiving negligence after the fact, simply because the outcome was bad, even though the decision may have been a reasonable one under the circumstances at the time.[39]

33 *See supra* Chapter 4.A.

34 *See id.; supra* Chapter 4.B.iii. *See also* Patricia A. McCoy, *A Political Economy of the Business Judgment Rule in Banking: Implications for Corporate Law*, 47 CASE W. RES. L. REV. 1, 35–55 (1996).

35 *See infra* Chapter 7.

36 *Cf.* Bruner, *supra* note 12, at 287–90, 293–96 (addressing the limited capacity to contractually carve back at the duty of loyalty in U.S. and U.K. corporate law, respectively). The limited means of reducing liability exposure for loyalty breaches include renouncing corporate opportunities and insulating conflicted transactions from judicial scrutiny through disclosure and disinterested approval. *See, e.g.*, DEL. CODE ANN. tit. 8, §§ 122(17), 144(a).

37 *See* Robert B. Thompson & Hillary A. Sale, *Securities Fraud as Corporate Governance: Reflections upon Federalism*, 56 VAND. L. REV. 859, 892–99, 906–07 (2003) (finding that securities fraud suits implicate "care-based concerns" regarding managerial performance, and tend to focus on officers to a greater extent than Delaware corporate suits do).

38 S. Samuel Arsht, *The Business Judgment Rule Revisited*, 8 HOFSTRA L. REV. 93, 95 (1979).

39 *See* Armour et al., *supra* note 21, at 70. The one area where Delaware judges are affirmatively invited to exercise their own independent business judgment is in evaluating the decision of a "special litigation committee" of the board to request dismissal of ongoing derivative litigation, but this has itself prompted some exasperation from the Chancery court. *See, e.g.*, In re Oracle Corp. Deriv. Litig., 824 A.2d 917, 928 (Del. Ch. 2003) (then-Vice Chancellor Strine describing this as an invitation to exercise "my oxymoronic judicial 'business judgment' ").

Perhaps more significantly, however, directors' care liability has traditionally been limited in order to promote comfort with entrepreneurial risk. As William Allen and Reinier Kraakman express it, "there is an important policy reason why a business loss cannot be analogized to a traffic accident or a slip on a banana peel"—namely, "corporate directors and officers invest other people's money." As a consequence, these fiduciaries would "bear the full costs of any personal liability," but would "receive only a small fraction of the gains from a risky decision." Under such circumstances, simple negligence liability "would predictably discourage officers and directors from undertaking valuable but risky projects."[40] As Allen himself explained in an opinion written during his time as Delaware's Chancellor, shareholders capable of diversifying risks on their own should favor a rule encouraging directors "to accept in rank order all positive net present value investment projects available to the corporation," and correlatively disfavor doctrinal structures that impede this by prompting risk aversion. If directors "were to be found liable for a corporate loss from a risky project on the ground that the investment was too risky (foolishly risky! stupidly risk! egregiously risky!—you supply the adverb), their liability would be joint and several for the whole loss." Recalling their limited share of the upside and the magnitude of public company operations, virtually any degree of exposure for simple negligence would lead directors to avoid any substantial risks, undercutting shareholders' own returns. "Obviously, it is in the shareholders' economic interest to offer sufficient protection to directors from liability for negligence"—hence the business judgment rule and other structures that aim to limit or preclude such liability exposure.[41] Depending on the jurisdiction, such protections might include some form of business judgment rule, directors' and officers' (D&O) liability insurance, indemnification, and/or exculpation.[42] Delaware's experience suggests that perceived stinginess with such protections can impact director risk tolerance, the clearest example being adoption of statutory exculpation in response to perceived shortcomings of Delaware's judge-made business judgment rule.[43]

For present purposes, however, the critical point is to observe the converse of all this. To the extent that additional entrepreneurial risk-taking is strongly

[40] *See* ALLEN & KRAAKMAN, *supra* note 11, at 231.

[41] Gagliardi v. Trifoods International, Inc., 683 A.2d 1049, 1052 (Del. Ch. 1996).

[42] *See id.* at 1052–53. *See also supra* Chapter 4.A.

[43] This transpired following the Delaware Supreme Court's imposition of care liability upon disinterested directors found to have approved a merger in a grossly negligent manner, overcoming Delaware's business judgment rule. *See* Smith v. Van Gorkom, 488 A.2d 858, 873–93 (Del. 1985). This surprised the marketplace and led directly to Delaware's statutory exculpation regime the following year. *See* DEL. CODE ANN. tit. 8, § 102(b)(7). On the market's reaction and the legislative response, see Christopher M. Bruner, *Good Faith, State of Mind, and the Outer Boundaries of Director Liability in Corporate Law*, 41 WAKE FOREST L. REV. 1131, 1139–47 (2006).

disfavored in a given context, liability exposure may be augmented to curtail directors' appetite to pursue risky projects. In this light, it is important to observe that discussions on this topic often proceed in a relatively crude manner, in so far as director liability is presented as an on-off switch, leaving one to imagine that we only have two options—either directors are either fully insulated, or they are fully exposed. In reality, there are various ways in which personal liability exposure for directors might be more finely calibrated—say, through proportionate liability rules and liability caps.[44] Such approaches can be implemented in various ways, including in combination with market-based mechanisms—as in Germany, where exculpation is not available, and D&O insurance must impose "a deductible of at least 10% of the loss up to 1.5 times the fixed annual remuneration" for management board members,[45] creating a form of capped liability. In the United States, meanwhile, existing statutory protections against care liability exposure are relatively flexible, permitting varying degrees of protection on a firm-by-firm basis.[46]

A more realistic appraisal opens up the possibility of rethinking what the ideal degree of exposure for directors might look like. This analysis would ideally be keyed to how much risk-taking we want to promote in particular fields such as banking, essential non-financial firms, and hazardous industries, but more concerted thought should also be given to whether we have struck the right balance more generally.[47]

III. SHAREHOLDER REPRESENTATION

> Composition of the board may be determined solely by shareholders, or other stakeholders may be granted some degree of representation.

Prevailing corporate theories generally presume that directors are to be elected by the equity holders—the shareholders.[48] However, this need not be the case.

[44] *See* BRUNER, *supra* note 11, at 101; Bruner, *supra* note 43, at 1143–44.

[45] Christoph H. Seibt & Sabrina Kulenkamp, *Corporate Governance and Directors' Duties in Germany: Overview*, THOMSON REUTERS PRAC. L., June 1, 2020, at 17–18. "The board members can get insurance coverage for that deductible," but only "on their own cost." *Id.* at 18. *See also* Aktiengesetz [AktG] [Stock Corporation Act], Sept. 6, 1965, *last amended* July 17, 2017, arts. 93, 116 (Ger.), https://www.gesetze-im-internet.de/englisch_aktg/englisch_aktg.html (translation by Samson Übersetzungen GmbH, Dr. Carmen von Schöning, published by the Federal Ministry of Justice and Consumer Protection).

[46] *See, e.g.*, DEL. CODE ANN. tit. 8, §§ 102(b)(7) (permitting charter provisions "eliminating or limiting" directors' monetary liability for care breaches), 145(a)–(c) (requiring indemnification where a director or officer was "successful on the merits or otherwise," but providing more open-ended corporate "power" to indemnify in other circumstances), 145(g) (similarly providing corporate "power" to insure).

[47] *See infra* Chapter 7.

[48] *See supra* Chapter 2.B.

Most vividly, German-style co-determination gives employees substantial supervisory board representation, which plainly contradicts the notion that companies cannot work effectively without limiting the franchise solely to shareholders.[49] According to the European Trade Union Institute, a "majority of the 28 states of the [European Union] plus Norway provide for employee representation at board level," sometimes varying across categories of companies. In six countries—the Czech Republic, Greece, Ireland, Poland, Portugal, and Spain—board representation for employees "is limited to some state-owned or municipally-owned companies." In thirteen countries, meanwhile—Austria, Croatia, Denmark, Finland, France, Germany, Hungary, Luxembourg, the Netherlands, Norway, Slovakia, Slovenia, and Sweden—"employee representation at board level extends to private companies."[50] As these systems are "always embedded in the wider context of the national industrial relations system," they also vary in terms of the number of employees required to trigger such representation; the proportion of seats held by employee representatives; whether they sit on the supervisory board of a two-tier structure, or a unitary board otherwise; how they are appointed; and their specific powers—notably, whether they are permitted to "deal with collective bargaining issues."[51]

At the same time, some have called for greater attention to the more general de facto heterogeneity of boards of directors, beyond shareholder and employee representatives. Although board appointment rights are generally limited to shareholders and, in some cases, employees as a matter of corporate law,[52] in practice boards of directors often find themselves grappling with the viewpoints of numerous distinct constituencies that are represented in one way or another on the board. Martin Gelter and Geneviève Helleringer observe that directors' duties are typically formulated by reference to a "uniform goal," yet in reality boards are often comprised of "constituency" directors "formally or informally selected by specific shareholders (such as a venture capitalist or an important shareholder) or other stakeholders of the corporation (such as creditors or employees), or they are elected to represent specific types of shareholders (e.g., minority investors)."[53] In light of the widespread de facto heterogeneity of boards of directors, Gelter and Helleringer conclude that the relative laxity as to the articulation and enforcement of a singular corporate purpose that one

[49] *See supra* Chapter 2.B.ii.

[50] European Trade Union Institute, *Board-Level Representation*, https://www.worker-participation.eu/National-Industrial-Relations/Across-Europe/Board-level-Representation2.

[51] *See id.*

[52] *See* Enriques et al., *supra* note 20, at 95.

[53] Martin Gelter & Geneviève Helleringer, *Lift Not the Painted Veil! To Whom Are Directors' Duties Really Owed?*, 2015 ILL. L. REV. 1069, 1069 (2015) (emphasis removed). *See also id.* at 1076–87 (describing examples including representatives of labor, various categories of shareholders and creditors, governments, and minority shareholders).

finds in many jurisdictions[54] may in fact perform the pragmatic function of building in the required flexibility to allow various constituencies to bring their differing interests and incentives to bear upon the corporation's overall decision-making. The result, they observe, may be decision-making processes that vary "depending on which groups are represented on the board and that may, at times, look more like negotiation between different groups than deliberation for a common purpose."[55]

Such balancing of varying interests and incentives is clearly widespread in corporate governance, in one form or another—de jure in co-determination systems, and de facto elsewhere. This indicates that accommodating non-shareholder interests through board representation is hardly in tension with the core logic of the corporate form, or inherently inefficient, as advocates of shareholder primacy often claim.[56]

IV. SHAREHOLDER ORIENTATION

> Boards may be duty-bound to focus narrowly on shareholders' interests, or may be permitted—or even required—to consider the interests of other stakeholders.

Notwithstanding the prevalence of corporate theories strongly emphasizing shareholder interests and placing equity investment at the heart of the corporate enterprise,[57] there is in fact a wide range of approaches to articulating the corporate objective, ranging from highly shareholder-focused to more stakeholder-focused.[58] Likewise, varying approaches have historically been adopted in industry-specific settings, the most significant example being banking, where some U.S. courts historically held that directors owe fiduciary duties directly to bank depositors—a category of creditors[59]—and applied a more rigorous standard of conduct to bank directors.[60]

[54] *See id.* at 1088–1117. *Cf.* Bruner, *supra* note 23, at 1448–49 (concluding that corporate law's "ambivalence" regarding whether corporate interests ought to be equated with shareholder interests reflects a pragmatic need for balancing).

[55] *See* Gelter & Helleringer, *supra* note 53, at 1117–18.

[56] *See, e.g.*, FRANK H. EASTERBROOK & DANIEL R. FISCHEL, THE ECONOMIC STRUCTURE OF CORPORATE LAW 67–70 (1991) (asserting, incorrectly, that "voting rights are universally held by shareholders" because they are the "residual claimants to the firm's income").

[57] *See supra* Chapter 2.B.

[58] *See supra* Chapter 4.B.ii.

[59] *See* McCoy, *supra* note 34, at 38–39.

[60] *See id.* at 35–55. *See also supra* Chapter 4.A, Chapter 4.B.iii.

As we have likewise seen, vibrant normative debates on this subject continue, some arguing that we need accountability to a narrow set of actors and interests while others respond that we need flexibility to balance the needs of all those who participate in corporate production.[61] As discussed earlier, prominent theoretical accounts of corporate law advocate designing default rules by reference to shareholders' interests and incentives on the assumption that external contracts and regulation can be counted on to sufficiently constrain negative externalities, while critiques of those accounts question this assumption and argue that default rules accordingly should be set by reference to a broader range of concerns (with mandatory rules perhaps being required in some instances).[62]

Setting aside the normative merits of this debate for the moment, there is a strong case to be made that boards of directors will, as a practical matter, be called upon to balance a wide range of interests and issues in any event—not merely due to the heterogeneity of all the various corporate stakeholders, but also due to the heterogeneity of shareholders themselves. As Lynn Stout observes, "shareholders with different investing time horizons have conflicting interests," prompting "a dilemma for the standard shareholder-oriented model." Specifically: "*Toward which shareholders is it oriented*?"[63] The upshot is that "trade-offs and judgments" become unavoidable, in which case, as Colin Mayer points out, the real issue becomes "what purposes and values should underpin them."[64] In this light, we should not be surprised by Gelter and Helleringer's conclusion that a vaguely defined corporate objective already facilitates this sort of balancing function through the board of directors in many jurisdictions[65]—a dynamic that arguably

[61] *Compare* Lucian A. Bebchuk & Roberto Tallarita, *The Illusory Promise of Stakeholder Governance*, 106 CORNELL L. REV. 91, 121–23 (2020) (arguing that stakeholder orientation undermines accountability that a singular focus on shareholders would otherwise deliver), *with* Colin Mayer, *Shareholderism versus Stakeholderism—A Misconceived Contradiction* 5–6 (ECGI Law Working Paper No. 522/2020), https://ssrn.com/abstract=3617847 (arguing in response that "trade-offs and judgments" are "ubiquitous" in board decision-making, and that the real issue is therefore "what purposes and values should underpin them"); *compare* Business Roundtable, *Statement on the Purpose of a Corporation* (Aug. 19, 2019), https://www.businessroundtable.org/business-roundtable-redefines-the-purpose-of-a-corporation-to-promote-an-economy-that-serves-all-americans (conveying signatories' commitment to stakeholder orientation) *with* Council of Institutional Investors, *Council of Institutional Investors Responds to Business Roundtable Statement on Corporate Purpose* (Aug. 19, 2019), https://www.cii.org/aug19_brt_response (arguing that this will undermine accountability).

[62] *See supra* Chapter 2.B.iii.

[63] LYNN STOUT, THE SHAREHOLDER VALUE MYTH: HOW PUTTING SHAREHOLDERS FIRST HARMS INVESTORS, CORPORATIONS, AND THE PUBLIC 69–71 (2012). For additional background, see GRANT M. HAYDEN & MATTHEW T. BODIE, RECONSTRUCTING THE CORPORATION: FROM SHAREHOLDER PRIMACY TO SHARED GOVERNANCE 68–87 (2020); STOUT, *supra*, at 63–94 (2012); Iman Anabtawi, *Some Skepticism about Increasing Shareholder Power*, 53 UCLA L. REV. 561, 577–93 (2006).

[64] Mayer, *supra* note 61, at 6.

[65] *See* Gelter & Helleringer, *supra* note 53, at 1117–18.

even characterizes the United States itself, with constituency statutes defining the corporate objective in stakeholder-centric terms in the majority of states, and an "ambivalent" fiduciary duty framework in Delaware giving most public company directors substantial room to maneuver.[66]

Even in jurisdictions expressing a clear, singular focus, a substantial measure of flexibility can be restored through subjective framing of the duty. For example, the U.K. Companies Act 2006 requires directors to "promote the success of the company for the benefit of its members as a whole," meaning the shareholders collectively.[67] However, this duty is not assessed against an objective standard, but rather by reference to what the director subjectively "considers, in good faith, would be most likely" to benefit shareholders. The statute further expands the director's discretion, then, by requiring some "regard," as means to that end, for various other constituencies and interests, including "consequences of any decision in the long term."[68] To be sure, shareholders have substantial capacity in the less centralized U.K. corporate governance system to advance their own interests through unilateral action,[69] but the subjective framing of this core duty undoubtedly takes some of the edge off of the strong-form shareholder-centrism otherwise reflected in the framing of U.K. directors' duties.

As the foregoing example illustrates, it is important to bear in mind that the overall degree of flexibility to bring non-shareholder interests to bear on board decision-making is not exclusively a function of the core duty itself. In its application, this will also turn on whose interpretation of that duty will be regarded as authoritative—and if this is left to directors themselves, then it effectively restores a substantial measure of capacity to engage in the sort of balancing that Stout, Mayer, and others regard as inevitable, without fearing adverse consequences for their good faith judgments on the matter.[70]

[66] *See generally* Bruner, *supra* note 23. *See also* William T. Allen, *Our Schizophrenic Conception of the Business Corporation*, 14 CARDOZO L. REV. 261 (1992); Margaret M. Blair & Lynn A. Stout, *A Team Production Theory of Corporate Law*, 85 VA. L. REV. 247 (1999); Einer Elhauge, *Sacrificing Corporate Profits in the Public Interest*, 80 N.Y.U. L. REV. 733 (2005); Lyman Johnson, *The Delaware Judiciary and the Meaning of Corporate Life and Corporate Law*, 68 TEX. L. REV. 865 (1990).

[67] Companies Act 2006, c. 46, § 172(1) (U.K.).

[68] *Id. See also* PAUL L. DAVIES & SARAH WORTHINGTON, GOWER & DAVIES PRINCIPLES OF MODERN COMPANY LAW 544–45 (9th ed. 2012).

[69] *See supra* Chapter 4.B.i.

[70] *Cf.* Andrew Johnston, *Market-Led Sustainability through Information Disclosure: The UK Approach, in* THE CAMBRIDGE HANDBOOK OF CORPORATE LAW, CORPORATE GOVERNANCE AND SUSTAINABILITY, *supra* note 11, at 204, 209–10 ("In more than a decade since its introduction, [§ 172] has . . . had little impact in terms of litigation in the courts.").

V. SHAREHOLDER ENFORCEMENT

> Shareholders may be given more or less capacity to advance their own interests through lawsuits, either exclusively or in common with other stakeholders.

Another mechanism through which shareholders might exert themselves upon governance is by threatening lawsuits if the board acts contrary to their wishes. Generally speaking, although U.S. shareholders remain structurally weak, various aspects of the U.S. litigation environment make it much easier for shareholders to bring corporate derivative suits and, relatedly, securities fraud suits. This contrasts sharply with other jurisdictions—including other common law jurisdictions—where such suits are considerably more difficult to pursue as a practical matter. The main features of U.S. law and procedure that facilitate such suits include fee rules generally requiring each side in the litigation to bear their own costs, contingency fee arrangements under which an entrepreneurial plaintiffs bar generally finances litigation, opt-out class actions, and relaxed requirements for establishing fraud in the securities context.[71] While I have argued elsewhere that ex post capacity to sue cannot reasonably be expected to raise overall shareholder orientation to the level exhibited by jurisdictions that give shareholders strong ex ante governance powers, there is certainly reason to believe that strong capacity to sue will tend to focus the minds of directors and officers on shareholders to a greater extent.[72]

Just as the impact of corporate litigation on governance can vary considerably across jurisdictions based on the ease or difficulty for shareholders, in particular, to launch and proceed with such actions, so the impact of litigation on corporate governance can vary based on whether or not other corporate stakeholders are permitted to bring such lawsuits. In the United States, non-shareholder constituencies generally cannot bring corporate lawsuits, as such; they are left, at most, to seek judicial enforcement of their contracts with the corporation.[73] Other

[71] *See* BRUNER, *supra* note 11, at 97–107. *See also* ALLEN & KRAAKMAN, *supra* note 11, at 379, 383–85, 670–71; John Armour et al., *Private Enforcement of Corporate Law: An Empirical Comparison of the UK and US*, 6 J. EMPIRICAL LEGAL STUD. 687, 692 (2009); Johnston, *supra* note 70, at 209–10 (noting the "significant procedural barriers to shareholders bringing claims against directors for breach of duty" in the U.K. context).

[72] *See* BRUNER, *supra* note 11, at 97–107 (discussing these dynamics while acknowledging that this is "inevitably a matter of speculation" due to the difficulty of empirically studying the deterrent effects of shareholder lawsuits).

[73] *See, e.g.*, Katz v. Oak Indus., Inc. 508 A.2d 873, 875–79 (Del. Ch. 1986) (holding that creditors' relationship with the corporation is "contractual in nature," not fiduciary, such that the creditors could not challenge an adverse reorganization and recapitalization on that basis); N. Am. Catholic Educ. Programming Found., Inc. v. Gheewalla, 930 A.2d 92, 99–103 (Del. 2007) (holding that although creditors have derivative standing if the corporation is literally insolvent, having become "the residual beneficiaries of any increase in value," creditors cannot sue derivatively while the corporation remains solvent and never have direct standing to sue for breach of fiduciary duty).

jurisdictions, however, have made various statutory remedies available for non-shareholders through their corporate laws. For example, Canada makes a broad oppression remedy available to various corporate constituencies, including not just shareholders, but also directors, officers, and "any . . . person who, in the discretion of a court, is a proper person to make an application"—potentially including employees, creditors, and other non-shareholders.[74] More dramatically, South African company law makes available a range of structures facilitating non-shareholder corporate lawsuits. Under the Companies Act 2008, while core corporate governance structures generally remain shareholder-focused,[75] the statutory derivative action has been expanded to include not just shareholders, but also directors, officers, employee representatives (e.g., trade unions), and anyone else "granted leave of the court to do so" where the court determines that it is "necessary or expedient . . . to protect a legal right of that other person."[76] Giving employee representatives derivative standing is regarded as "striking," and thought to be "unique to South African law."[77] At the same time, the South African statute makes available a more open-ended action permitting shareholders, directors, officers, and trade union representatives to "take proceedings to restrain the company from doing anything inconsistent with this Act,"[78] and further provides that "[a]ny person who contravenes any provision of this Act is liable to any other person for any loss or damage suffered by that person as a result of that contravention."[79]

These and other distinctive innovations are examined later in the book.[80] For present purposes, however, it suffices to observe that, to the degree other stakeholders take up these powers, or negotiate to advance their interests in the

[74] *See* Canada Business Corporations Act, R.S.C. 1985, c. C-44, §§ 238, 241. *See also* BRUNER, *supra* note 11, at 92–93; Poonam Puri, *Green but Not Enough: Sustainability in Canadian Corporate Governance, in* THE CAMBRIDGE HANDBOOK OF CORPORATE LAW, CORPORATE GOVERNANCE AND SUSTAINABILITY, *supra* note 11, at 146, 152–53.

[75] *See, e.g.*, Companies Act 71 of 2008 §§ 68 (election by shareholders), 71 (removal by shareholders), 76(3) (directors' duty to promote "the best interests of the company") (S. Afr.); 1 J.L. YEATS ET AL., COMMENTARY ON THE COMPANIES ACT OF 2008, at 2-1280–2-1281 (2018) (observing that "some decisions have equated the interests of the company with the interests of the shareholders as a general body").

[76] Companies Act 71 of 2008 § 165(2) (S. Afr.).

[77] MALEKA FEMIDA CASSIM, THE NEW DERIVATIVE ACTION UNDER THE COMPANIES ACT: GUIDELINES FOR JUDICIAL DISCRETION 14–15 (2016). *See also* HENOCHSBERG ON THE COMPANIES ACT 71 OF 2008, at 594–95 (P.A. Delport ed., updated May 2019); 2 J.L. YEATS ET AL., COMMENTARY ON THE COMPANIES ACT OF 2008, at 7-30–7-31 (2018).

[78] Companies Act 71 of 2008 § 20(4) (S. Afr.). *See also* DENNIS DAVIS ET AL., COMPANIES AND OTHER BUSINESS STRUCTURES 12 (4th ed. 2019) (observing that this provision makes it "clear that a trade union representing employees now has rights in terms of the Act, and can play an important part in the governance of companies").

[79] Companies Act 71 of 2008 § 218(2) (S. Afr.). *See also* CASSIM, *supra* note 77, at 86; DAVIS ET AL., *supra* note 78, at 12–13; HENOCHSBERG ON THE COMPANIES ACT 71 OF 2008, *supra* note 77, at 641–43; YEATS ET AL., *supra* note 77, at 9–5.

[80] *See infra* Chapter 8.C.

shadow of such powers,[81] they could dilute the effect that shareholder litigation might otherwise have as a means of focusing corporate decision-making more intently on the shareholders' interests. Put differently, the impact of corporate litigation on the degree of shareholder-centrism exhibited by a given corporate governance system reflects not only the degree to which shareholder litigation is facilitated, but also the degree to which corporate litigation by other stakeholders is facilitated as well.

VI. SHARE TRANSFERABILITY

> Shareholders may be given more or less freedom to move capital into and out of corporate equity investments unilaterally.

In contrast with a primary market transaction, through which a corporation sells stock to investors and receives proceeds (less underwriting fees and other transaction costs), in a secondary market transaction among investors themselves—typically intermediated through brokers and exchanges (imposing their own transaction costs)—no money enters or leaves the corporation itself.[82] This does not, however, mean that a corporation, its management, and its other stakeholders remain unaffected by secondary market trading. Substantial stock sales—perhaps prompted by dissatisfaction with management's stewardship of the business—will drive down the stock price, diminishing the value of equity-based executive compensation, impairing managers' future opportunities, and perhaps attracting hostile takeover bids.[83] For such reasons, the relative ease with which shareholders can liquidate their investments through secondary market transactions has substantial (if indirect) impacts on the management of public corporations, with follow-on consequences for all concerned.

Secondary market liquidity is largely a function of legal and market structures that facilitate disclosure of corporate information and execution of securities trades—notably through securities regulation, stock exchange rules, and the development of intermediary structures and technologies that increase the speed and reduce the costs of trading.[84] While generally thought to improve the

[81] *Cf.* BRUNER, *supra* note 11, at 101–02 (noting that, even in the U.S. context, "the inherent challenges involved with empirically studying the deterrent value of litigation in the corporate governance context are presumably heightened" by the fact that non-shareholders could bring contract claims to advance their interests).

[82] *See* STEPHEN J. CHOI & A.C. PRITCHARD, SECURITIES REGULATION: CASES AND ANALYSIS 1–2 (4th ed. 2015); STEPHEN J. LUBBEN, CORPORATE FINANCE 160–61 (2d ed. 2017).

[83] *See* ALLEN & KRAAKMAN, *supra* note 11, at 344–55, 531; EASTERBROOK & FISCHEL, *supra* note 56, at 95–97.

[84] *See* CHOI & PRITCHARD, *supra* note 82, at 1–45; LUBBEN, *supra* note 82, at 160–61.

accuracy of prices and overall market efficiency, it is also important to recognize how such developments may impact time horizons for investors, and accordingly for managers. For example, Stout observes that while share turnover for New York Stock Exchange listed companies was 12 percent annually in 1960, as of 1987 "this figure had risen to 73 percent," and as of 2010 "the average annual turnover for equities listed on U.S. exchanges reached an astonishing 300 percent annually, implying an average holding period of only four months." Such short holding periods prompt institutional pressure on corporate managers "to pursue myopic business strategies that don't add lasting value," reflecting a fundamental mismatch between institutional investors' strategies and the interests of long-term savers whose funds they invest. Indeed, "some funds specialize in computerized 'flash trading' strategies in which shares are bought and held for mere seconds before being sold again."[85]

Hostile takeovers present the most vivid example of the implications of stockholder liquidity for corporate governance, and perspectives on their costs and benefits, and legal approaches to their regulation, vary enormously.[86] Hostile takeovers have become a major issue primarily in the few jurisdictions with widely dispersed stock; elsewhere, major shareholders able to dictate board composition can simply decide not to transfer control.[87] Dispersed stock ownership has mainly arisen among common law jurisdictions, and regulatory approaches range from those, like the United Kingdom, giving shareholders unfettered control over the decision to accept or reject a hostile bid,[88] to those, like the United States, giving incumbent boards substantial power to impede such transactions through powerful defenses including poison pills.[89]

[85] STOUT, *supra* note 63, at 66–71.

[86] *See supra* Chapter 2.B.iii, Chapter 3.A–B, Chapter 4.B.i–ii.

[87] *See* Paul Davies et al., *Control Transactions, in* KRAAKMAN ET AL., *supra* note 20, at 205, 206–08, 238–39. By the same token, hostile takeovers can quickly become an issue to the extent that a historically concentrated market begins to disperse, as Japan's did in the mid-1990s with the unwinding of keiretsu cross-shareholdings. *See id.* at 238.

[88] *See, e.g.*, PANEL ON TAKEOVERS AND MERGERS, THE TAKEOVER CODE, General Principles 1, 3, Rule 21.1(a) (12th ed. 2016) (U.K.); Takeovers Panel, Commonwealth of Australia, Guidance Note 12—Frustrating Action (Dec. 1, 2016); Hong Kong Securities and Futures Commission, The Codes on Takeovers and Mergers and Share Buy-Backs (July 2018), general principle 9; The Singapore Code on Take-Overs and Mergers (January 24, 2019), general principle 7. *See also* Ontario Securities Commission, Notice of National Policy 62-202 and Rescission of National Policy Statement No. 38: Take-Over Bids—Defensive Tactics (July 4, 1997) (providing limited capacity for boards to deploy defenses "in a genuine attempt to obtain a better bid"). For additional background on Hong Kong and Singapore, see Christopher M. Bruner, *Leaders or Laggards? Corporate Sustainability in Hong Kong and Singapore, in* THE CAMBRIDGE HANDBOOK OF CORPORATE LAW, CORPORATE GOVERNANCE AND SUSTAINABILITY, *supra* note 11, at 504, 510–11, 513–14.

[89] *See, e.g.*, CONN. GEN. STAT. § 33-756(g); IND. CODE § 23-1-35-1(d)–(g). For Delaware case law to similar effect, see Moran v. Household Int'l, Inc., 500 A.2d 1346, 1350–54 (Del. 1985); Unocal Corp. v. Mesa Petroleum Co., 493 A.2d 946, 954–55 (Del. 1985); Revlon, Inc. v. MacAndrews & Forbes Holdings, Inc., 506 A.2d 173, 182 (Del. 1986); Paramount Commc'ns v. Time Inc., 571 A.2d 1140, 1152–54 (Del. 1990). Japan, faced with the emergence of hostile takeovers following the unwinding of cross-shareholdings, has adopted an approach more closely resembling the U.S. approach.

Varying approaches to hostile takeovers reflect fundamental policy choices rooted in distinctive national contexts that are impacted by legal, cultural, market, and historical forces conditioning the political economy that public corporations inhabit.[90] Collectively, however, they demonstrate that there is considerable room for variation in terms of how much capacity shareholders have to liquidate corporate investments, and that these choices have significant implications for corporate governance and society generally.

VII. SHAREHOLDER LIABILITY EXPOSURE

> Shareholders may be given more or less insulation from liability exposure—less exposure prompting more comfort with risk-taking and more exposure prompting less comfort.

The centrality of fully limited liability for shareholders in prevailing accounts of the corporate form[91] leads many to assume that this must represent a critical and immutable element of modern corporate law.[92] We have seen that limiting shareholders' liability exposure facilitated marshaling substantial investment capital for large industrial undertakings starting in the nineteenth century, yet we have also seen that the emergence of limited liability as a component of the modern public corporation in the United Kingdom and the United States alike was episodic and contested. Limited liability took a wide range of forms and evolved over a long period of time, with fully limited liability establishing itself as the predominant approach only in the late nineteenth and early twentieth centuries.[93]

At the same time, while the value of limited liability as a means of promoting comfort with entrepreneurial risk-taking in major industrial undertakings gained broader recognition, its tendency to generate too much risk—at least in certain contexts—was well recognized. Hence the very different balance struck in banking in the nineteenth and early twentieth centuries, when risk-taking was constrained not only by more robust standards of care and liability exposure for directors, but also by greater liability exposure for shareholders themselves through multiple liability

See BRUNER, *supra* note 11, at 233–36; PEPPER D. CULPEPPER, QUIET POLITICS AND BUSINESS POWER: CORPORATE CONTROL IN EUROPE AND JAPAN 44–46, 116–19, 134–38 (2011).

[90] *See* BRUNER, *supra* note 11, ch. 5.

[91] *See, e.g.*, EASTERBROOK & FISCHEL, *supra* note 56, at 40 ("Limited liability is a distinguishing feature of corporate law—perhaps *the* distinguishing feature.").

[92] *See supra* Chapter 2.B.ii.

[93] *See supra* Chapter 4.A.

rules.[94] Recall also the widespread nineteenth-century practice among British industrial companies of incorporating "with shares having a sizeable nominal capital . . . and only requiring subscribers to pay a small portion upon issuance (30 per cent on average), with the remainder being available for the company to call"—a practice that similarly exposed shareholders in such companies to a capped though nontrivial "residual liability," giving them "a financial incentive to be vigilant."[95]

The variation that has occurred across jurisdictions—in terms of limited liability's emergence and coalescence, the general forms of liability limitation adopted, and the tailoring of shareholders' liability exposure in particular industry contexts—clearly reflects that there is nothing inevitable about fully limited liability. There are choices to be made, as with the governance levers described here, and there is a much wider array of options available to policymakers than contemporary corporate governance literature typically acknowledges. By the same token, the fact that limited liability's development mapped onto similar developments related to directors' liability, as well as the emergence of deep, liquid capital markets, further suggests that attention needs to be paid to how various levers of governance interact.

B. Calibrating the Levers

Taken together, the levers of corporate governance described in this chapter can readily be depicted visually in a way that conveys their individual and collective dynamics.

Figure 7 effectively represents a blank slate, summarizing a range of important choices that all jurisdictions face in calibrating their respective corporate governance systems—and, correlatively, a range of opportunities for re-calibrating them as circumstances, needs, and goals evolve over time. Critically, this requires evaluating not solely how each lever ought to be calibrated in isolation, but also how various calibrations of multiple levers might interact and work in tandem.

I have argued in prior chapters that economic analyses have erred by suggesting that corporate characteristics, priorities, and governance structures

[94] *See* Lewis T. Evans & Neil C. Quigley, *Shareholder Liability Regimes, Principal-Agent Relationships, and Banking Industry Performance*, 38 J. L. & ECON. 497 (1995); Jonathan R. Macey & Geoffrey P. Miller, *Double Liability of Bank Shareholders: History and Implications*, 27 WAKE FOREST L. REV. 31 (1992); Jonathan R. Macey & Geoffrey P. Miller, *Double Liability of Bank Shareholders: A Look at the New Data*, 28 WAKE FOREST L. REV. 933 (1993); John D. Turner, *'The Last Acre and Sixpence': Views on Bank Liability Regimes in Nineteenth-Century Britain*, 16 FIN. HIST. REV. 111 (2009). *See also supra* Chapter 4.A, Chapter 4.B.iii.

[95] BRIAN R. CHEFFINS, CORPORATE OWNERSHIP AND CONTROL: BRITISH BUSINESS TRANSFORMED 171–74 (2008).

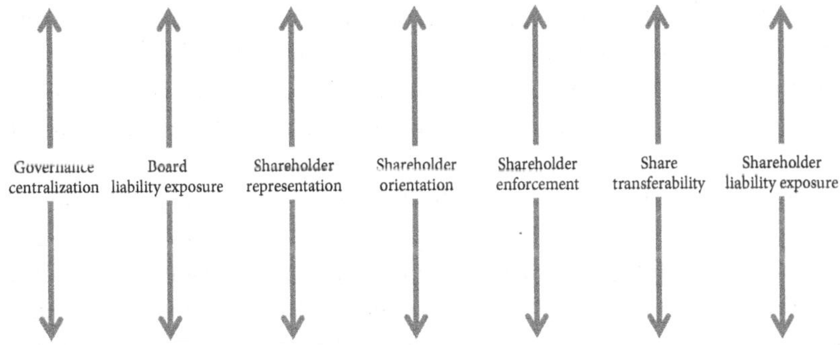

Figure 7 Corporate Technology

favored today are somehow inevitable, or deducible from universally applicable premises. Such claims do not bear moderate scrutiny; they are plainly contradicted by comparative analyses that reveal substantial variation in response to legal, cultural, market, and historical contexts. Work in this vein has, however, generated valuable insights regarding how various aspects of the corporate form and corporate law interact to facilitate a range of corporate capacities and market structures. In this section I build on their insights yet arrive at exactly the opposite conclusion; rather than suggesting that there is a single optimal configuration of the corporate form, the interactions that these analyses highlight suggest that various levers of corporate governance may be calibrated in different ways to facilitate a range of outcomes, depending on a given jurisdiction's needs and goals.

In a 1985 article titled "Limited Liability and the Corporation,"[96] Easterbrook and Fischel provide a discussion of the "rationale" for fully limited liability, exploring its broader facilitative capacities and how it relates to other corporate and market structures. Observing that public corporations "typically dominate other organizational forms when the technology of production requires firms to combine both the specialized skills of multiple agents and large amounts of capital," they emphasize the "division of labor" between "workers who lack capital" and "owners of funds who lack specialized production skills."[97] Consistent with their later work, Easterbrook and Fischel argue that limited liability principally "reduces the costs of this separation and specialization," and provide an account in which facilitating and channeling risk plays a central role.[98] First, limited liability "decreases the need to monitor" management because shareholders bear

[96] Frank H. Easterbrook & Daniel R. Fischel, *Limited Liability and the Corporation*, 52 U. CHI. L. REV. 89 (1985).

[97] *Id.* at 93–94.

[98] For the following account, see *id.* at 94–97.

less downside risk, rendering "passivity a more rational strategy." Second, limited liability "reduces the costs of monitoring other shareholders" because, unlike in a joint-and-several liability regime, other investors' lack of financial wherewithal no longer generates additional exposure for affluent investors; with limited liability, one's exposure is generally limited to the amount of one's own upfront investment, rendering others' wealth (or lack thereof) irrelevant. Third, limited liability promotes "free transfer of shares" because, having rendered the identity of other investors financially irrelevant, a single trading price for shares emerges, reflecting solely "the present value of the income stream generated by a firm's assets"—a clearer signal of managerial quality that in turn exposes managers to the discipline of a market for corporate control through takeovers. Fourth, by making it "possible for market prices to impound additional information about the value of firms" along the foregoing lines, limited liability eliminates wasteful research by investors, who can more comfortably rely on market prices. Fifth, limited liability opens up diversification as a means of reducing idiosyncratic risks because, rather than multiplying risks as they would if each investment involved an additional source of joint-and-several liability exposure, an investor's overall exposure from multiple investments in a limited liability regime generally remains capped at the aggregate amount invested across all of them. Sixth, limited liability "facilitates optimal investment decisions" in the sense that shareholders who are protected on the downside in this manner, and further able to manage their risk exposure through diversification, will tend to leave managers free to accept higher-risk-higher-reward ventures.

I have no fundamental qualms with the foregoing analysis, so far as it goes. In fact, this provides a nuanced and helpful account of how a range of common corporate features and market structures interact. I part ways with Easterbrook and Fischel, however, regarding their further assumption that this particular configuration necessarily maximizes benefits for society by reducing the cost of pursuing riskier corporate ventures.[99] Based on their assumption, it would seem that fully limited liability and the suite of other corporate features and market structures that it facilitates represent an optimal end state for corporate law. As we have seen, however, and as the remainder of the book will further explore, there are good reasons to reject this assumption—if not universally, then certainly in a number of contexts.

Indeed, if we set this assumption aside, then Easterbrook and Fischel's analysis actually yields some important corollary insights. Phrased by reference to the levers of corporate governance described in this chapter, they essentially observe that lower shareholder liability exposure prompts greater governance centralization and more risk-taking—because shareholders with downside

[99] *See id.* at 97.

insulation will be more likely to remain passive, leaving governance entirely to professional managers, and will favor riskier projects with higher net present values. Implicitly, this further suggests that shareholders should be comfortable giving boards greater insulation from care liability in order to incentivize the risk-taking that those shareholders, granted fully limited liability protection, will naturally prefer.[100] Limited liability in turn facilitates greater share transferability and a market for corporate control by promoting a single market trading price keyed more directly to the business itself, which in turn reinforces—and is reinforced by—normative commitment to greater shareholder orientation. From this perspective, Easterbrook and Fischel's analysis likewise goes hand in hand with other calibrations favoring greater shareholder representation and enforcement.[101]

As Easterbrook and Fischel acknowledge, however, things could be otherwise. For example, they recognize that greater liability exposure for shareholders would correlatively reduce governance centralization, because "[t]he more risk they bear, the more they will monitor" management.[102] Indeed, this is precisely the mechanism through which multiple liability regimes in banks, and partially paid-up shares in industrial companies, historically functioned to reduce risk.[103] Likewise, this further suggests that shareholders themselves would be less comfortable giving boards—even those acting in perfect good faith—substantial insulation from care liability, precisely because shareholders facing greater liability exposure themselves no longer favor heightened risk-taking.[104] By the same token, the greater liability exposure involved with equity investments would presumably impair share transferability and make less capital available for highly risky companies, because shareholders would rationally demand a price discount to be induced to accept that exposure. As Easterbrook and Fischel observe, "[t]he price they are willing to pay for shares will reflect the risk,"[105] and "[t]he more risk comes with an equity investment, the less the investor will pay."[106] Of course, unlike Easterbrook and Fischel, those viewing this from a differing normative perspective might regard these consequences positively, in so far as they amount to forcing the business to internalize the costs associated with risky projects generating harms exceeding the value of the business itself.[107] At the

[100] *See supra* Chapter 5.A.ii. *See also* Gagliardi v. Trifoods International, Inc., 683 A.2d 1049, 1052–53 (Del. Ch. 1996).

[101] *See supra* Chapter 2.B.iii.

[102] Easterbrook & Fischel, *supra* note 96, at 94.

[103] *See, e.g.*, CHEFFINS, *supra* note 95, at 171–74; Macey & Miller, *Double Liability of Bank Shareholders: History and Implications*, *supra* note 94, at 33.

[104] *See, e.g.*, McCoy, *supra* note 34, at 35–55.

[105] Easterbrook & Fischel, *supra* note 96, at 94.

[106] *Id.* at 97.

[107] *Cf.* Henry Hansmann & Reinier Kraakman, *Toward Unlimited Shareholder Liability for Corporate Torts*, 100 YALE L.J. 1879, 1880–85, 1892–94, 1933 (1991) (advocating unlimited pro rata shareholder liability in tort per a similar rationale).

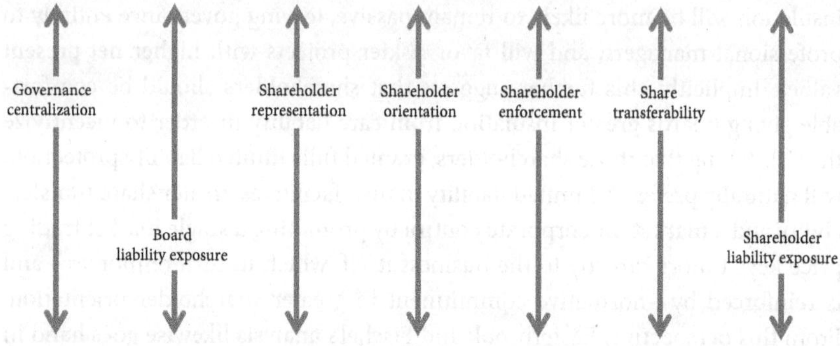

Figure 8 Archetypal U.S. Public Company

same time, from this perspective, one might have considerable doubts about the wisdom of calibrating other levers to strongly favor shareholders.

In light of all this, consider again the archetypal U.S. public company, expressed visually in terms of the calibration of governance levers that it embodies.

In Figure 8, the various levers of corporate governance are set to reflect what we have come to expect of U.S. public companies with widely dispersed stock ownership—strong boards elected solely by shareholders; greater emphasis on generating financial returns for shareholders, who possess substantial capacity to further focus governance on their own interests through corporate derivative suits and securities fraud suits; a high degree of investment liquidity; and limited liability exposure for boards and shareholders alike.[108]

As we have already seen, however, the corporate form need not be calibrated in this manner. The remainder of the book will further investigate alternative calibrations of various sorts, but to illustrate the degree of variation that is possible, consider corporate governance in banks, as it was typically structured back in the nineteenth and early twentieth centuries, with heightened exposure for boards and shareholders alike.[109] Expressed by reference to the calibration of corporate governance levers, that historical approach cuts a very different figure indeed.

[108] As discussed earlier, this depiction broadly resembles the archetypal U.K. public company as well, although adjustments would be required for a fully accurate depiction. Notably, governance centralization would be somewhat lower, because U.K. shareholders have more governance power; shareholder orientation would be somewhat higher, because U.K. shareholder interests are clearly and expressly prioritized by statute; share transferability would be somewhat higher, because U.K. shareholders possess unfettered capacity to accept hostile takeover bids; and shareholder enforcement would be markedly lower, because mechanisms fostering U.S.-style shareholder litigation are largely absent. *See supra* Chapter 1, Chapter 4.

[109] *See supra* Chapter 4.A.

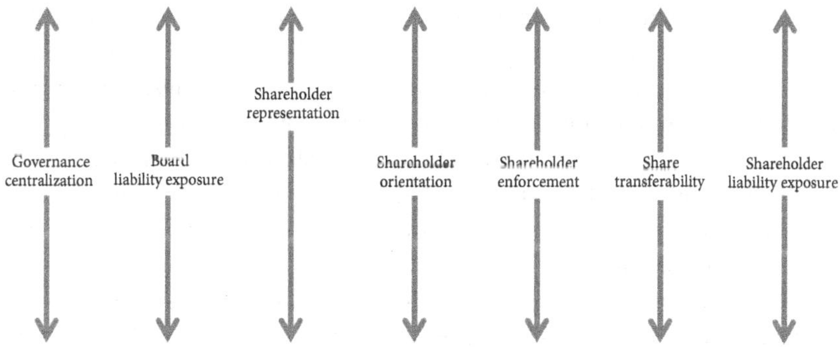

Figure 9 Banks (Historical)

The configuration of corporate governance levers historically adopted in banking, illustrated in Figure 9, represents a dramatic departure from what we now regard as the norm in public companies—and it further illustrates the degree of interconnection among the various levers. If both board and shareholder liability exposure are increased and duties are extended to depositors, then we should further expect reduced governance centralization, because shareholders facing greater liability exposure will monitor the board more closely; reduced shareholder orientation, because recognizing depositors as beneficiaries of directors' duties deviates from strict shareholder-centrism; reduced shareholder enforcement, because depositors become an additional constituency that can pursue distinct interests through litigation; and reduced share transferability, because shareholders' greater potential exposure would be priced into the shares, leading investors to demand a discount. Taken together, this mode of representing the distinctive configuration of corporate governance levers in banks vividly conveys the moderating effect of these policies; while they lasted, these rules helped to keep the banking business safe and boring—and of course that was the point.[110] Indeed, as discussed later in the book,[111] their abandonment—and the increasing tendency over recent decades to apply to financial firms a governance model more closely approximating that reflected in the archetypal U.S. public company depicted in Figure 8 above—correlated with a dramatic and destabilizing build-up of risk in the financial system that contributed to the global financial crisis.[112]

[110] *See, e.g.*, Macey & Miller, *Double Liability of Bank Shareholders: A Look at the New Data*, *supra* note 94 (finding that "the conclusion that *depositors would have been worse off without double liability* seems impossible to refute").

[111] *See infra* Chapter 7.A.

[112] *See, e.g.*, Christopher M. Bruner, *Conceptions of Corporate Purpose in Post-Crisis Financial Firms*, 36 SEATTLE U. L. REV. 527 (2013); Bruner, *supra* note 24; Christopher M. Bruner, *Corporate Governance Reform in a Time of Crisis*, 36 J. CORP. L. 309 (2011).

In the comparative realm, then, we can readily imagine how differing corporate governance systems around the world reflect differing choices along these lines. The only lever that has not yet moved in the foregoing illustrations is the shareholder representation lever, reflecting the common law norm that the shareholders alone elect the board of directors. Looking further afield, however, it is not difficult to identify contrary examples—the most obvious being co-determination systems, which straightforwardly lower the shareholder representation lever by giving employees some degree of board representation.[113]

Moving forward, we will consider some of the most significant problems associated with the configuration of corporate governance levers reflected in the archetypal U.S. public corporation,[114] and then examine several alternatives (extant or proposed) that are specific to an industry context[115] or generalized across an entire corporate governance system.[116] As Part Three of the book explores, the considerable flexibilities of the corporate form—if thoughtfully harnessed—offer great potential to respond to many of our most pressing environmental, social, and economic challenges.

113 *See infra* Chapter 8.A.
114 *See infra* Chapter 6.
115 *See infra* Chapter 7.
116 *See infra* Chapter 8.

PART THREE

HARNESSING THE CORPORATION

6
Corporate Pathologies and Corporate Sustainability

Contemporary corporate governance literature exhibits adherence to a conception of the corporate form defined by reference to a handful of purportedly fixed, intrinsic characteristics—notably legal personality, limited liability, freely transferable shares, centralized management, and shareholder election of directors.[1] These features relate closely to the characteristics and practices generally associated with the archetypal U.S. public company today—notably strong boards elected by shareholders, strong emphasis on generating financial returns for shareholders, substantial capacity for shareholders to further prioritize their own interests through lawsuits, a high degree of investment liquidity, and limited liability exposure for boards and shareholders alike. While retrospective theoretical accounts often present this conception of the corporate form—and, by association, the archetypal U.S. public company—as an economically deducible optimum,[2] this is a contestable view. Among other things, it effectively ignores the manner in which the modern public corporation historically took shape in the United Kingdom and the United States—involving far greater flux, dynamism, and diversity than prevailing accounts suggest[3]—and likewise fails to acknowledge, let alone explain, the extraordinary global diversity of the corporate form.[4]

As the last chapter described, the corporate form is better conceptualized as a flexible legal technology that can be calibrated and re-calibrated, in varying contexts and over time, in response to a dynamic contextual landscape. Subsequent chapters will explore several alternative calibrations, some specific to particular industry contexts while others are embraced more generally. To that end, this chapter establishes some baselines for evaluating those alternative calibrations of the corporate form. First, it explores the concept of sustainability—increasingly regarded as a literal imperative for our long-term survival—and assesses the merits of sustainability as a normative metric relative to alternative

[1] *See supra* Chapter 2.B.ii.
[2] *See supra* Chapter 5.B.
[3] *See supra* Chapter 4.A.
[4] *See supra* Chapter 2.B, Chapter 3, Chapter 4.B, Chapter 5.

The Corporation as Technology. Christopher M. Bruner, Oxford University Press. © Christopher M. Bruner 2022.
DOI: 10.1093/oso/9780197635179.003.0006

concepts that emphasize corporate responsibility. Second, it explores some of the principal corporate pathologies that have impeded the achievement of corporate sustainability, further informing assessment of how and when alternative calibrations of the corporate technology might prove advantageous. Finally, it explores the potential for disclosure strategies and novel accounting systems to reflect the impacts of corporate production more fully, whether through narrative supplements or by bringing them directly to bear upon a corporation's financial statements. If it proved possible, the latter in particular could have far-reaching consequences for debates regarding corporate sustainability, including what the appropriate role of corporate governance reforms might be in achieving it. For the reasons discussed below, however, extant disclosure strategies and nascent efforts to develop a workable mode of impact-weighted accounting appear incapable of delivering corporate sustainability on their own.

A. What Does Corporate Sustainability Mean?

The global community faces a complex array of extraordinary and interconnected crises—environmental, social, and economic[5]—and the conception of the corporate form as a flexible governance technology could open up new possibilities for rendering corporate production more sustainable. Assessing these possibilities, however, requires a clearer impression of what the sustainability concept entails, both generally and as applied to corporate entities.

In 1983, the UN Secretary-General, on behalf of the General Assembly, asked Gro Harlem Brundtland to establish an independent commission with the charge to develop a "global agenda for change," and specifically to propose "long-term environmental strategies" and means of fostering international cooperation toward that end.[6] With degrees in medicine and public health, having served as Norway's Minister of the Environment, and more recently having become Norway's youngest and first female Prime Minister,[7] Brundtland was well positioned to perceive and communicate how environmental problems were intrinsically bound up with pervasive social and economic challenges—linkages emphasized in the work of what came to be called the Brundtland Commission.[8] Indeed, the Commission quite deliberately avoided treating environmental,

[5] *See supra* Chapter 1.

[6] Report of the World Commission on Environment and Development: Our Common Future, Chairman's Foreword (1987) [hereinafter Brundtland Report].

[7] Brundtland served as Norway's Prime Minister in 1981, and then again from 1986–89 and 1990–96. Subsequently, she served as Director-General of the World Health Organization from 1998–2003. *See* UN Foundation, *Gro Harlem Brundtland (Norway)*, https://unfoundation.org/who-we-are/our-board/gro-harlem-brundtland-norway-vice-chair/.

[8] Brundtland Report, *supra* note 6, Chairman's Foreword; UN Foundation, *supra* note 7.

social, and economic issues independently from one another. "The environment does not exist as a sphere separate from human actions, ambitions, and needs," rendering alternative modes of analytical framing too narrow. As Brundtland explained in her preface to the Commission's 1987 report to the General Assembly, titled *Our Common Future*, "attempts to defend it in isolation from human concerns have given the very word 'environment' a connotation of naivety in some political circles," while the "word 'development' has also been narrowed by some into a very limited focus, along the lines of 'what poor nations should do to become richer', and thus again is automatically dismissed by many in the international arena as being a concern of specialists." She emphasized, however, that "the 'environment' is where we all live; and 'development' is what we all do in attempting to improve our lot within that abode. The two are inseparable."[9] Consequently, the Brundtland Commission focused more broadly on "sustainable development," embracing environmental, social, and economic concerns.[10] According to their report, "sustainable development" aims to ensure that humanity "meets the needs of the present without compromising the ability of future generations to meet their own needs," a challenge involving interrelated environmental, social, and economic dimensions.[11]

This approach continues to frame the pursuit of sustainability today,[12] and has become highly influential both generally[13] and in the corporate context, where it has increasingly displaced alternative conceptions that resemble the siloed analytical approaches rejected by the Brundtland Commission. Concepts such as "corporate social responsibility" generally focus on "discussing the 'business case' for sustainability," implicitly holding constant the prioritization of financial returns—an approach fairly described as "weak sustainability," in so far as it subordinates sustainability-related aims to what can be achieved within the constraints of existing legal and market structures. By contrast, "strong" sustainability means "actual sustainability." It relaxes the assumption that existing legal and market structures are immutable and reverses the analytical approach, critiquing those structures by reference to their compatibility with sustainability imperatives.[14] This analytical posture is exemplified by Kate Raworth's

[9] Brundtland Report, *supra* note 6, Chairman's Foreword.

[10] *Id.* paras. 5–26.

[11] *Id.* para. 27.

[12] *See, e.g.*, United Nations, *Transforming Our World: The 2030 Agenda for Sustainable Development*, Preamble, ¶¶ 2, 54–59, U.N. Doc. A/RES/70/1 (Sept. 25, 2015).

[13] *See* Beate Sjåfjell & Christopher M. Bruner, *Corporations and Sustainability*, *in* THE CAMBRIDGE HANDBOOK OF CORPORATE LAW, CORPORATE GOVERNANCE AND SUSTAINABILITY 3, 7–11 (Beate Sjåfjell & Christopher M. Bruner eds., 2019).

[14] *See id.* In some jurisdictions, the term "corporate social responsibility" has effectively become synonymous with formalized philanthropy. *See, e.g.*, Afra Afsharipour, *Corporate Social Responsibility and the Corporate Board: Assessing the Indian Experiment*, *in* GLOBALISATION OF CORPORATE SOCIAL RESPONSIBILITY AND ITS IMPACT ON CORPORATE GOVERNANCE (Jean J. du Plessis et al. eds., 2018), https://ssrn.com/abstract=3355808 (working paper version); Harpreet Kaur, *Achieving*

"doughnut" metaphor, depicting "a sweet spot . . . that is both an ecologically safe and socially just space for humanity" between an environmental ceiling and a social floor—an approach that requires an alternative maximand, "shift[ing] the image of economic progress from endless GDP growth to thriving-in-balance" within that safe and just space.[15]

Regardless of where one might stand on core issues of corporate power, corporate purpose, and risk-taking,[16] the concept of sustainability—in contrast with narrower alternatives—offers the benefit of a clear long-term policy benchmark that is more directly keyed to broader human interests. Whatever one's prior normative commitments on corporate legal issues may be, all should minimally be interested in knowing whether present approaches to these issues in a given jurisdiction can be expected to perform sustainably in the future. In this light, corporate sustainability as such means "business and finance creating value in a manner that is (a) *environmentally* sustainable, in that it ensures the long-term stability and resilience of the ecosystems that support human life; (b) *socially* sustainable, in that it facilitates the achievement of human rights and other basic social rights, as well as good governance; and (c) *economically* sustainable in that it satisfies the economic needs necessary for stable and resilient societies."[17] Implicit within this formulation of corporate sustainability, as an evaluative benchmark, is the notion that the environmental capacity of the Earth system effectively imposes a ceiling, and that basic social rights impose a floor, for the sustainable pursuit of economic goals—including through corporate financing and production.[18] Accordingly, it further embeds within it a precautionary posture toward the very incentive structures that corporate law and governance foster, given the degree of uncertainty regarding what the planet and any given society can bear; the complexity of the interactions among environmental, social, and

Sustainable Development Goals in India, in THE CAMBRIDGE HANDBOOK OF CORPORATE LAW, CORPORATE GOVERNANCE AND SUSTAINABILITY, *supra* note 13, at 460, 464–65; Renginee G. Pillay et al., *Enlightenment or Resistance? Promoting Sustainability through Corporate Law and Governance in Mauritius, in* THE CAMBRIDGE HANDBOOK OF CORPORATE LAW, CORPORATE GOVERNANCE AND SUSTAINABILITY, *supra* note 13, at 387, 394–97.

[15] KATE RAWORTH, DOUGHNUT ECONOMICS: SEVEN WAYS TO THINK LIKE A 21ST CENTURY ECONOMIST 37–51 (2017). *See also id.* chapters 5–7. The argument that GDP growth can "continue indefinitely," despite ecological limits, rests on the claim that technological developments will permit "decoupling" of "economic value" from "material throughput" due to "more efficient processes, lighter and less polluting products, or a structural shift from materially intensive goods to materially light services." Given the degree of reduction in carbon emissions thought necessary to achieve sustainability, however, the plausibility of this claim remains doubtful. *See* Tim Jackson & Peter A. Victor, *Unraveling the Claims for (and against) Green Growth*, SCIENCE, Nov. 22, 2019, at 950–51.

[16] *See supra* Chapter 4.B.

[17] *See* Sjåfjell & Bruner, *supra* note 13, at 11.

[18] *See* RAWORTH, *supra* note 15, at 74–76, 197–201. *See also supra* Chapter 1.

economic phenomena; and the potentially catastrophic consequences of getting it wrong.[19]

Pursuit of corporate sustainability as an overarching policy goal could lead us in any of a number of directions in terms of structural initiatives in corporate governance, for at least two reasons. First, in employing corporate sustainability as a benchmark, we measure such initiatives against a widely desired outcome that is increasingly acknowledged and (at least nominally) prioritized by powerful corporate actors in the abstract, although they may differ on the best means to that end.[20] Second, how a given structural initiative in corporate governance actually performs will be heavily impacted by legal, cultural, market, and historical contexts, meaning that an approach that performs well in one place and time may or may not perform well in another.[21] At a mid-level of abstraction, however, there are a number of fundamental issues and dynamics in corporate law and governance that are attracting particular attention from a sustainability perspective, including the mismatch between global markets and domestic regulation; widespread normative commitment to shareholder wealth maximization; various trends in the organization of firms, markets, and financial systems; and various innovations in corporate governance systems around the world.[22] A number of corporate governance structures and calibrations of the corporate

[19] *See* Sjåfjell & Bruner, *supra* note 13, at 8. The precautionary principle calls for preventive action where the threat of harms is uncertain, meaning that stable probabilities cannot be assigned to potential outcomes, and incommensurate, meaning that potential harms cannot be measured by reference to the same scale as potential outcomes associated with another course of action. *See generally* Jonathan Aldred, *Justifying Precautionary Policies: Incommensurability and Uncertainty*, 96 ECOLOGICAL ECON. 132 (2013). Climate change exemplifies these conditions because scientific understanding of the range of potential outcomes is constantly evolving, and because the potentially catastrophic losses differ in kind from any gains that declining to mitigate climate change might offer (e.g., marginally greater near-term economic growth). *See id.* at 132, 136–38. The "planetary boundaries" project reflects such an approach. *See* Johan Rockström et al., *Planetary Boundaries: Exploring the Safe Operating Space for Humanity*, 14 ECOLOGY & SOC'Y, article 32 (2009), at 2–6; Will Steffen et al., *Planetary Boundaries: Guiding Human Development on a Changing Planet*, 347 SCIENCE 1259855 (2015), at 1–2.

[20] *See, e.g.*, Business Roundtable, *Statement on the Purpose of a Corporation* (Aug. 19, 2019), https://www.businessroundtable.org/business-roundtable-redefines-the-purpose-of-a-corporation-to-promote-an-economy-that-serves-all-americans (statement by 181 CEOs, departing from strict "shareholder primacy" in favor of "a fundamental commitment to all of our stakeholders" and to "protect the environment by embracing sustainable practices across our businesses"); Larry Fink, *A Fundamental Reshaping of Finance* (Jan. 14, 2020), https://www.blackrock.com/us/individual/larry-fink-ceo-letter#:~:text=A%20Fundamental%20Reshaping%20of%20Finance&text=It%20belongs%20to%20people%20in,to%20promote%20long%2Dterm%20value. (letter from BlackRock CEO to corporate CEOs, similarly emphasizing the importance of "considering the needs of a broad range of stakeholders" and addressing climate risks, but justifying this as a shareholder-centric means to "achieve long-term profits" and "attract investment," and citing shareholder voting power as a means of enforcing shareholder preferences).

[21] *See supra* Chapter 3.

[22] *See* Sjåfjell & Bruner, *supra* note 13, at 11–12; Christopher M. Bruner & Beate Sjåfjell, *Corporate Law, Corporate Governance and the Pursuit of Sustainability*, *in* THE CAMBRIDGE HANDBOOK OF CORPORATE LAW, CORPORATE GOVERNANCE AND SUSTAINABILITY, *supra* note 13, at 713, 715–19.

financialization	increasingly orienting corporate decision-making toward financial market considerations
excessive risk	aiming to boost revenues available for distribution to shareholders through socially harmful risk-taking
cost externalization	aiming to reduce costs borne by shareholders by off-loading them onto other stakeholders

Figure 10 Corporate Pathologies: Financialization, Excessive Risk, and Cost Externalization

form are explored in subsequent chapters through the lens of corporate sustainability, with particular sensitivity to how contextual features impact their performance in particular jurisdictions.

B. Enduring Pathologies: Financialization, Excessive Risk, and Cost Externalization

At various points I have already alluded to some fundamental pathologies that continue to inhibit the pursuit of corporate sustainability today. These include financialization, excessive risk, and externalization of costs associated with corporate production. In the corporate governance context, financialization contributes to the increasing tendency to prioritize shareholder returns over all else—a complex phenomenon that emanates from academic trends, capital market practices, and (in varying measures) corporate law itself. Excessive risk-taking and cost externalization, then, are essentially corollaries of shareholder primacy that can be understood in simple balance sheet terms; companies aim to boost revenues available for distribution to shareholders by taking greater risks, and conversely to reduce costs by off-loading as much of the downside as possible onto other stakeholders. In this sense, financialization, excessive risk, and cost externalization are closely related and mutually reinforcing phenomena. For convenience, these corporate pathologies are summarized in Figure 10.

The term financialization refers to the "historical trend since the late twentieth century in which finance and financial considerations became increasingly central to the workings of the economy."[23] Dating to the 1970s, this trend is observable at industry, firm, and household levels,[24] and in the corporate context "implies the growing orientation of corporations toward financial markets, with

[23] Gerald F. Davis & Suntae Kim, *Financialization of the Economy*, 41 ANN. REV. SOCIOLOGY 203, 205 (2015).

[24] *See id.* at 204–05.

changes in corporate governance favouring shareholder value as a central characteristic."[25] Explanations for these complex developments have included deregulatory moves in the face of crises undertaken by governments hoping to avoid "difficult decisions on prioritizing diverse social needs"; efforts by "the rentier class . . . to maintain the existing rate of wealth accumulation" in the face of economic stagnation through a shift away from industrial capitalism and toward finance capitalism; and, most pertinently for the corporate context, the market impacts of hostile takeovers. As Gerald Davis and Suntae Kim observe, the emergence of hostile takeovers in the 1980s largely reflected "disappointing corporate performance in the 1970s, deregulations of the financial industry by the Reagan administration, and a series of financial innovations such as junk bonds." These developments catalyzed a range of consequences including the breakup of diversified conglomerates; greater reliance on equity-based executive compensation; a shift toward defined contribution pensions heavily invested in stocks; and widespread re-concentration of corporate equity in the hands of prominent institutions that "encouraged corporations to spin off inefficient parts, lay off employees, and engage in corporate restructuring, all in the name of maximizing shareholder value."[26]

Macro- and micro-level factors have closely interacted in prompting this historical trend, both generally and in the corporate context. While technological developments clearly promoted financialization through improved capacity to value and trade complex securities at higher speed and lower cost,[27] broader historical, economic, and market forces were strongly incentivizing greater reliance on financial institutions and techniques at the same time. As Ronald Gilson and Charles Whitehead explain, the emergence of new financial and risk management techniques reflected, among other things, the collapse of the Bretton Woods regime of fixed exchange rates and the OPEC oil embargo, which "subjected peacetime businesses to new, and potentially catastrophic, exchange rate and energy cost volatility." There being only limited capacity to insure against such risks, "capital markets quickly responded" because financial institutions perceived "an

[25] Stefanie Hiss, *The Politics of the Financialization of Sustainability*, 17 COMPETITION & CHANGE 234, 239 (2013).

[26] Davis & Kim, *supra* note 23, at 206–09. *See also* Gerald F. Davis, *After the Corporation*, 4 POLITICS & SOC'Y 283, 285–90 (2013). For an overview of the literature on financialization, see generally Geoffrey Wood & Mike Wright, *An Age of Corporate Governance Failure? Financialization and its Limits*, *in* THE OXFORD HANDBOOK OF CORPORATE GOVERNANCE 703 (Mike Wright et al. eds., 2013). On the transition to defined contribution pensions and the rise of institutional shareholders more generally, see WILLIAM A. BIRDTHISTLE, EMPIRE OF THE FUND: THE WAY WE SAVE NOW (2016); Christopher M. Bruner, *Center-Left Politics and Corporate Governance: What Is the "Progressive" Agenda?*, 2018 BYU L. REV. 267, 295–314 (2018); Christopher M. Bruner, *The Enduring Ambivalence of Corporate Law*, 59 ALA. L. REV. 1385, 1432–35 (2008); Martin Gelter, *The Pension System and the Rise of Shareholder Primacy*, 43 SETON HALL L. REV. 909 (2013).

[27] *See* Davis & Kim, *supra* note 23, at 207–08.

opportunity to profit from the creation and trading of new financial instruments that responded to client demands to improve risk sharing"—aims achieved most directly through expansion of derivatives markets.[28] This permitted companies "to reduce cash flow volatility," thereby allowing them "to free up capital they would otherwise set aside against the risk of a future drop in revenues," which in turn permitted reduced reliance on equity financing to the extent that these new financial techniques function to preserve internal financing capacity and improve borrowing capacity.[29] Such dynamics would appear to have been operative in the wave of leveraged buyouts in the 1980s, in which public shareholders received premium prices for their stock as publicly traded equity was effectively swapped out for debt financing.[30] As Gilson and Whitehead acknowledge, however, while the cost-benefit analysis may have shifted regarding various financing strategies, this does not mean that no benefits to going public remain. Public sales of stock may remain attractive, for example, to generate currency for acquisitions, to facilitate equity-based compensation, to invite market feedback on strategy, to maintain publicity, and to provide an exit for investors.[31]

Such manifestations of financialization in corporate governance and financial markets have all reinforced the coalescing norm of shareholder primacy (of which more below), with profound consequences for the economy and society. In addition to catalyzing the further pathologies discussed below, increasing financialization over recent decades has been closely associated with growing inequality.[32] Boards and CEOs have gradually reoriented corporate strategy toward appealing to financial markets, which strongly incentivizes maximizing profits relative to assets. From this perspective, the overarching aim becomes "to be as small as feasible, maintaining the lightest possible base of assets and employment through spin-offs and layoffs," which results in widespread outsourcing, offshoring, and reliance on contractors for production and distribution—a strategy that Davis has termed "Nikefication" after "the firm that pioneered this approach." This strategy "has spread widely across the economy, not just in clothing and consumer packaged goods but in electronics and pharmaceuticals" as well. In such cases "the top-selling brands are managed by corporations that

[28] *See* Ronald J. Gilson & Charles K. Whitehead, *Deconstructing Equity: Public Ownership, Agency Costs, and Complete Capital Markets*, 108 COLUM. L. REV. 231, 243–47 (2008).

[29] *See id.* at 247–51.

[30] *See id.* at 251–53.

[31] *See id.* at 254–62.

[32] *See generally* Zohar Goshen & Doron Levit, *Common Ownership and the Decline of the American Worker* (ECGI Law Working Paper No. 584/2021), https://ssrn.com/abstract=3832069; Anna Stansbury & Lawrence H. Summers, *The Declining Worker Power Hypothesis: An Explanation for the Recent Evolution of the American Economy* (NBER Working Paper No. 27193, 2020), https://www.nber.org/system/files/working_papers/w27193/w27193.pdf. *See also* GRANT M. HAYDEN & MATTHEW T. BODIE, RECONSTRUCTING THE CORPORATION: FROM SHAREHOLDER PRIMACY TO SHARED GOVERNANCE 184–85 (2020).

do little or no production themselves and employ relatively few people directly," essentially functioning as corporate containers for intellectual property, marketing, and management. Compensation for corporate executives and financiers has grown substantially while workers' wages and benefits have stagnated, and "laborers whose employment and work schedules are uncertain and variable from week to week because of these corporate practices have come to be called the precariat."[33] Meanwhile, such an approach to production results in complex value chains that are inherently difficult to monitor, and which have been associated with environmental and social harms in jurisdictions where production actually occurs.[34] Although the United States "clearly stands out as the most financialized economy," such policies have been promoted around the world by development agencies and others, and while formal convergence appears unlikely, financialization clearly represents a global trend.[35]

In light of all this, it is important to understand how shareholder primacy, in particular, has attracted such widespread normative support. Shareholder primacy has been reinforced, and promoted as a norm, through a host of interrelated channels. As discussed,[36] this conception of corporate purpose and power relations has derived substantial force from the rise of the law and economics movement starting in the 1970s, generally depicting the corporation in simple principal-agent terms—from which perspective the main focus of corporate law

[33] *See* Davis & Kim, *supra* note 23, at 209–13. *See also* Davis, *supra* note 26, at 287–95; Goshen & Levit, *supra* note 32; Stansbury & Summers, *supra* note 32. For additional background, see GERALD F. DAVIS, THE VANISHING AMERICAN CORPORATION: NAVIGATING THE HAZARDS OF A NEW ECONOMY 69–94, 115–37 (2016); RANA FOROOHAR, MAKERS AND TAKERS: THE RISE OF FINANCE AND THE FALL OF AMERICAN BUSINESS 13–21, 152–78 (2016). *Cf.* CHRISTOPHER M. BRUNER, CORPORATE GOVERNANCE IN THE COMMON-LAW WORLD: THE POLITICAL FOUNDATIONS OF SHAREHOLDER POWER 166–76 (2013) (arguing that threats to the capacity of public company employers to provide social welfare benefits have prompted counter-reactions against shareholder-centric policies, notably in the context of hostile takeovers). On rising inequality more generally, see THOMAS PIKETTY, CAPITAL IN THE TWENTY-FIRST CENTURY 23–27 (Arthur Goldhammer trans., 2014) (arguing that high rates of inequality have resulted from the rate of return on capital exceeding the growth rate of the economy); RAWORTH, *supra* note 15, at 139–73 ("Rather than accept growing inequality as a law of economic development, an inevitability that must be endured, twenty-first-century economists will regard it as a failure of economic design and will seek to make economies far more distributive of the value that they generate.").

[34] *See, e.g.*, Jaakko Salminen, *Sustainability and the Move from Corporate Governance to Governance through Contract, in* THE CAMBRIDGE HANDBOOK OF CORPORATE LAW, CORPORATE GOVERNANCE AND SUSTAINABILITY, *supra* note 13, at 57; Charlotte Villiers, *Global Supply Chains and Sustainability: The Role of Disclosure and Due Diligence Regulation, in* THE CAMBRIDGE HANDBOOK OF CORPORATE LAW, CORPORATE GOVERNANCE AND SUSTAINABILITY, *supra* note 13, at 551; Jingchen Zhao, *Extraterritorial Attempts at Addressing Challenges to Corporate Sustainability, in* THE CAMBRIDGE HANDBOOK OF CORPORATE LAW, CORPORATE GOVERNANCE AND SUSTAINABILITY, *supra* note 13, at 29. *See also infra* Chapter 8.B.

[35] *See* Davis & Kim, *supra* note 23, at 216–17. *See also* CHRISTOPHER M. BRUNER, RE-IMAGINING OFFSHORE FINANCE: MARKET-DOMINANT SMALL JURISDICTIONS IN A GLOBALIZING FINANCIAL WORLD 30–38 (2016) (discussing capital mobility and regulatory competition); *supra* Chapter 3 (exploring contextual drivers of difference).

[36] *See supra* Chapter 2.B, Chapter 4.B.

and governance ought to be limiting agency costs that might arise from misalignment of shareholders' and managers' incentives.[37] The shift over recent decades toward what David Millon calls "radical shareholder primacy" largely tracks the ascendance of the nexus of contracts view of the corporation, itself rooted in these intellectual currents, and has gained currency as promoters of this conception in legal and business academia and the business press have increasingly influenced corporate counsel, corporate management, and major investors.[38]

As Lyman Johnson observes in an article titled "The Social Responsibility of Corporate Law Professors," corporate executives are advised by corporate lawyers, and "[t]he people who introduce them to the language of corporate law are law professors."[39] Accordingly, if corporate law professors default to the prevailing nexus conception of the corporation, then this will have straightforward downstream consequences for the practice of corporate law and the management of corporations.[40] As Millon concludes, radical shareholder primacy in law schools is fundamentally bound up with "a larger ideological, economic, and socio-political phenomenon that now shapes and legitimates business practice in powerful ways."[41] Students of this field, he explains, "need to understand that non-legal values and incentives—including political commitment, social norms, compensation arrangements, pressure from institutional shareholders, to name a few—can lead corporate management to prioritize current share price maximization over long-term strategic investment and cultivation of the well-being of key nonshareholder constituencies."[42]

These views and practices are amplified by institutions with their own distinct market and legal imperatives to generate short-term returns, leading them to impose substantial pressure on investee companies to do so themselves. For example, "[t]o meet their current obligations, public pension funds have

[37] *See, e.g.*, FRANK H. EASTERBROOK & DANIEL R. FISCHEL, THE ECONOMIC STRUCTURE OF CORPORATE LAW (1991); Michael C. Jensen & William H. Meckling, *Theory of the Firm: Managerial Behavior, Agency Costs and Ownership Structure*, 3 J. FIN. ECON. 305 (1976); Milton Friedman, *A Friedman Doctrine—The Social Responsibility of Business Is to Increase Profits*, N.Y. TIMES MAG., Sept. 13, 1970, at 33, 122.

[38] *See* David Millon, *Radical Shareholder Primacy*, 10 U. ST. THOMAS L.J. 1013, 1018–42 (2013). *See also* Dorothy S. Lund & Elizabeth Pollman, *The Corporate Governance Machine*, 121 COLUM. L. REV., at 27–29 (forthcoming 2021), https://ssrn.com/abstract=3775846; David Millon, *Shareholder Primacy in the Classroom After the Financial Crisis*, 8 J. BUS. & TECH. L. 191, 191–92 (2013). On the increasingly financialized approach to business education, see FOROOHAR, *supra* note 33, at 90–120.

[39] *See* Lyman P.Q. Johnson, *The Social Responsibility of Corporate Law Professors*, 76 TUL. L. REV. 1483, 1493 (2002).

[40] *See id.* at 1487–90. *See also* Lyman Johnson, *Corporate Law Professors as Gatekeepers*, 6 U. ST. THOMAS L.J. 447, 447 (2009); Millon, *Shareholder Primacy in the Classroom After the Financial Crisis*, *supra* note 38, at 193–95.

[41] Millon, *Radical Shareholder Primacy*, *supra* note 38, at 1042.

[42] Millon, *Shareholder Primacy in the Classroom After the Financial Crisis*, *supra* note 38, at 195. *See also* Christopher M. Bruner, *The Fiduciary Enterprise of Corporate Law*, 74 WASH. & LEE L. REV. 791, 796–97, 804–06 (2017).

historically assumed an annual rate of return of 8%," leading such funds in the wake of the financial crisis to "focus on short-term stock price performance" and to shift toward trading strategies that involve "high turnover rates," exerting correlative pressures on corporate management.[43] At the same time, pension fund managers' legal duties prompt intense focus on profit maximization by investee corporations in order to maximize returns to the fund, and such duties may even be interpreted to require concerted activism toward this end.[44] Notably, the U.S. Department of Labor (DOL) requires employee benefit plans subject to the Employee Retirement Income Security Act (ERISA) to focus their investment and voting decisions exclusively on "pecuniary" factors, defined to mean those factors "expected to have a material effect on the risk and/or return of an investment." Consideration of "non-pecuniary" factors is permitted only in narrow tie-breaker scenarios where the choice between competing investment alternatives cannot be made "on the basis of pecuniary factors alone."[45] Statements describing these requirements clearly convey the DOL's skepticism regarding "so-called ESG investments" and their impact on "the rigor of the prudence and loyalty analysis by some participating in the ESG investment marketplace,"[46] and have widely been interpreted as reflecting hostility toward sustainability-related investment initiatives.[47] It remains to be seen whether this posture will meaningfully change following President Biden's election.[48]

[43] David Millon, *Shareholder Social Responsibility*, 36 SEATTLE U. L. REV. 911, 930–32 (2013). *See also* Bruner, *Center-Left Politics and Corporate Governance*, *supra* note 26, at 299–301.

[44] *See* Bruner, *Center-Left Politics and Corporate Governance*, *supra* note 26, at 303–14 (discussing pension fund fiduciary duties under the Employee Retirement Income Security Act (ERISA) and interpretations of those duties issued by the U.S. Department of Labor).

[45] *See* 29 C.F.R. § 2550.404a-1(c), (e)(2)(ii), (f)(3). *See also* Fifth Third Bancorp v. Dudenhoeffer, 134 S. Ct. 2459, 2468 (2014) (interpreting the term "benefits" in ERISA to mean "*financial* benefits").

[46] *See* Press Release, U.S. Department of Labor, U.S. Department of Labor Announces Final Rule to Protect Americans' Retirement Investments (Oct. 30, 2020). *See also* U.S. Department of Labor, Financial Factors in Selecting Plan Investments, 85 Fed. Reg. 72846, 72848, 72859–62, 72875 (Nov. 13, 2020); U.S. Department of Labor, Fiduciary Duties Regarding Proxy Voting and Shareholder Rights, 85 Fed. Reg. 81658, 81665–67, 81681–85 (Dec. 16, 2020); Press Release, U.S. Department of Labor, U.S. Department of Labor Issues Final Rule on Proxy Voting and Shareholder Rights by Employee Benefit Plans (Dec. 11, 2020).

[47] *See, e.g.*, Brian Croce, *DOL Finalizes Rule on Proxy Voting*, PENSIONS & INV., Dec. 11, 2020, https://www.pionline.com/regulation/dol-finalizes-rule-proxy-voting; Joseph A. Lifsics, *The Department of Labor's ESG-less Final ESG Rule*, MAYER BROWN BENEFITS & COMPENSATION BLOG, Nov. 11, 2020, https://www.usbenefits.law/2020/11/the-dol-final-esg-rule/; Brian Menickella, *DOL Not Socially Aware*, FORBES, Nov. 24, 2020, https://www.forbes.com/sites/brianmenickella/2020/11/24/dol-not-socially-aware/; Sarah Min, *DOL Eases Overly Prescriptive Stance in Final Proxy Voting Rule*, CHIEF INV. OFFICER, Dec. 14, 2020, https://www.ai-cio.com/news/dol-eases-overly-prescriptive-stance-final-proxy-voting-rule/; Kristina M. Zanotti & Robert L. Sichel, *DOL Issues Final "ESG" Rule; Focuses on "Pecuniary" Factors*, NAT'L L. REV., Nov. 12, 2020, https://www.natlawreview.com/article/dol-issues-final-esg-rule-focuses-pecuniary-factors.

[48] *See* Press Release, Biden-Harris Transition, Fact Sheet: List of Agency Actions for Review (Jan. 20, 2021) (including this regulation in "a non-exclusive list of agency actions that heads of the relevant agencies will review"); Press Release, U.S. Department of Labor, U.S. Department of Labor Statement Regarding Enforcement of Its Final Rules on ESG Investments and Proxy Voting by Employee Benefit Plans (Mar. 10, 2021) (indicating that these rules will not be enforced until the

Meanwhile, a shift toward securities regulation and exchange listing requirements as sources of corporate governance rules tends to reinforce the elevation of investor preferences and interests above those of other stakeholders—a shift that is particularly noteworthy in the U.S. legal system, where state corporate law has historically permitted greater regard for other constituencies.[49] These policy preferences and legal constraints are naturally transmitted through various other actors in financial markets that service major investors or are otherwise influenced by them, contributing to what Dorothy Lund and Elizabeth Pollman call the "corporate governance machine"—a constellation of actors mutually reinforcing a market-wide focus on shareholder interests above all else. This includes (among others) the exchanges, stock indices, proxy advisors, rating agencies, and major investors themselves, as well as associations of various market actors.[50] Meanwhile, actual beneficial investors—typically long-term investors, such as households saving for retirement or the education of their children—may be lost in the shuffle to the extent that the short-term interests and incentives of institutional intermediaries deviate from their own.[51] By the same token, beneficial investors are certainly distanced psychologically from the consequences of investment decisions ostensibly taken on their behalf by multiple layers of intermediary fiduciaries.[52]

Shareholder primacy—the principal manifestation of financialization in the corporate governance context—strongly emphasizes maximizing profits in order to have more distributable returns for shareholders, raising the corollary concerns of excessive risk and cost externalization. These additional corporate pathologies are best understood in simple balance sheet terms. It is elemental to financial accounting that a corporation's equity amounts to whatever is left once liabilities are subtracted from assets. Indeed, it is equity's residual status that balances a corporation's balance sheet (with assets on the left side and liabilities plus

Department of Labor "publishes further guidance"). *See also* Jason Bisnoff, *Why Socially Responsible Investing Is Likely to Gain Momentum Under Biden*, FORBES, Dec. 14, 2020, https://www.forbes.com/sites/jasonbisnoff/2020/12/14/esg-investing-a-sizzling-sector-that-will-get-even--hotter-under-president-biden/.

[49] *See* Bruner, *Center-Left Politics and Corporate Governance*, *supra* note 26, at 284–93, 314–26 (contrasting the ambivalence of state corporate law with the more decided focus on investor interests under federal securities regulation, and observing the increasingly shareholder-centric nature of federal corporate governance reforms). *See also* U.S. Securities and Exchange Commission, *What We Do*, https://www.sec.gov/Article/whatwedo.html ("The mission of the U.S. Securities and Exchange Commission is to protect investors, maintain fair, orderly, and efficient markets, and facilitate capital formation.").

[50] *See* Lund & Pollman, *supra* note 38, at 17–27. They also emphasize legal and cultural factors reinforcing shareholder primacy. *See id.* at 10–32.

[51] *See* Leo E. Strine, Jr., *Toward Common Sense and Common Ground? Reflections on the Shared Interests of Managers and Labor in a More Rational System of Corporate Governance*, 33 J. CORP. L. 1, 10, 15 (2007).

[52] *See* Bruner, *The Enduring Ambivalence of Corporate Law*, *supra* note 26, at 1432–35.

stockholders' equity on the right).[53] Accordingly, shareholders straightforwardly benefit from increases in assets and decreases in liabilities because, by definition, they increase the shareholders' equity on the balance sheet. Corporate actions that enrich the shareholders in this manner could plausibly be compatible with the interests of other stakeholders and society generally, to the extent that there is "a direct pecuniary interest in making sure that corporate transactions are beneficial . . . to all parties who deal with the firm,"[54] but of course such accounting results might be brought about in other ways. In the extreme, management might engage in various forms of fraud in order to overstate revenues and/or understate liabilities, with the aim of boosting stockholders' equity, reported profits, and the company's stock price in public markets.[55]

Less nefariously—but no more desirably in the long-run—management might pursue indiscriminate measures to boost risk-taking and/or cut costs in order to achieve the same ends over short time frames.[56] In this light, it is critical to recall that the scope of what financial statements reflect is in fact quite narrow. As Kent Greenfield emphasizes, "company financial reports do not indicate the value of the company to its workers or to the communities in which it does business," nor do they reflect "environmental costs of the company's products or services" or "whether the company has been complicit in human rights violations." Overall, "there is no general obligation on the part of companies to gather information about, much less publicly report on, the true costs and benefits of their activities."[57] Although inherently difficult to quantify precisely—either in the aggregate or at the firm level[58]—the costs to society omitted from corporate balance sheets are enormous by any coherent reckoning,[59] and constitute a de facto

[53] *See, e.g.*, WILLIAM T. ALLEN & REINIER KRAAKMAN, COMMENTARIES AND CASES ON THE LAW OF BUSINESS ORGANIZATION 105–09 (5th ed. 2016); STEPHEN J. LUBBEN, CORPORATE FINANCE 3–9 (2d ed. 2017).

[54] John Armour et al., *What Is Corporate Law?*, *in* REINIER KRAAKMAN ET AL., THE ANATOMY OF CORPORATE LAW: A COMPARATIVE AND FUNCTIONAL APPROACH 1, 23 (3d ed. 2017).

[55] *See, e.g.*, LYNN STOUT, THE SHAREHOLDER VALUE MYTH: HOW PUTTING SHAREHOLDERS FIRST HARMS INVESTORS, CORPORATIONS, AND THE PUBLIC 67–69 (2012). Regulatory responses include antifraud liability and regulation of various "gatekeeper" professionals, notably auditors. *See, e.g.*, STEPHEN J. CHOI & A.C. PRITCHARD, SECURITIES REGULATION: CASES AND ANALYSIS 1, 10–11, 265–83, 476, 736–39 (4th ed. 2015); John Armour et al., *Transactions with Creditors*, *in* KRAAKMAN ET AL., *supra* note 54, at 109, 122–23.

[56] *See, e.g.*, ALLEN & KRAAKMAN, *supra* note 53, at 112–14; STOUT, *supra* note 55, at 67.

[57] KENT GREENFIELD, THE FAILURE OF CORPORATE LAW: FUNDAMENTAL FLAWS AND PROGRESSIVE POSSIBILITIES 129 (2006). *See also* Jeremy Andrew Nicholls, *Integrating Financial, Social and Environmental Accounting*, SUSTAINABILITY ACCT., MGMT. & POL'Y J., Jan. 30, 2020, at 3. Potential responses to such shortcomings will be examined. *See infra* Chapter 6.C, Chapter 8.

[58] *See infra* Chapter 6.C.

[59] For example, Ralph Estes, writing in the 1990s, compiled various estimates of costs externalized to workers, customers, communities, and the nation "to develop a perspective on the total social costs of business enterprise in the United States." He acknowledges that a "degree of double-counting is probably inevitable," yet concludes that the estimates are likely "conservative" because "only those costs that are directly identifiable have been estimated," and "other social costs, as well as secondary and multiplier effects, have generally been omitted." Estes arrives at an annual total exceeding $2.6

public subsidy that straightforwardly distorts the market's allocation of resources to the extent that costs are not fully brought to bear on prices.[60]

Viewed through the lens of these fundamental dynamics of financial accounting, the pathologies of excessive risk and cost externalization quickly come into focus. As discussed earlier, shareholders with limited liability generally favor more entrepreneurial risk-taking because they are protected on the downside, yet fully capture the upside[61]—an incentive structure that can readily result in the externalization of costs, to the extent that harms imposed on others through such risk-taking ultimately exceed the value of the company's assets.[62] Prominent reflections of these dynamics include undercapitalization, including through subsidiaries in corporate groups; profit-seeking activities that may impose substantial losses or other harms on unsecured creditors, including tort creditors afforded no ex ante opportunities to assess those risks or to negotiate contractual protections; and bet-the-farm decision-making when a company is struggling.[63] Such concerns are only heightened, meanwhile, in fields where risk-taking is exacerbated by explicit or implicit public guarantees, as with financial firms.[64] To be sure, corporate law reflects some limited recognition of these dynamics, but the creditor protections made available in response—notably distribution constraints, minimum capital requirements, and equitable doctrines such as subordination and veil piercing—are typically weak, reactive, and/or unpredictable, and are widely regarded as ineffective.[65]

trillion in 1994 dollars. RALPH ESTES, TYRANNY OF THE BOTTOM LINE: WHY CORPORATIONS MAKE GOOD PEOPLE DO BAD THINGS 171–78 (1996). This would equate to over $4.7 trillion in 2021 dollars. U.S. Bureau of Labor Statistics, CPI Inflation Calculator, https://data.bls.gov/cgi-bin/cpicalc.pl (reflecting buying power of December 1994 dollars in June 2021). *See also* Michael Simkovic, *Limited Liability and the Known Unknown*, 68 DUKE L.J. 275, 304–06 (2018) (observing that "Estes's study remains one of the most comprehensive and widely cited studies of aggregate externalization costs"). *Cf.* Walter H. Corson, *Recognizing Hidden Environmental and Social Costs and Reducing Ecological and Societal Damage through Tax, Price, and Subsidy Reform*, 22 ENVIRONMENTALIST 67, 67–72 (2002) (citing "published estimates for the United States of annual environmental, economic, and social costs of various human activities" from between 1990 and 1995 totaling $5.1 trillion, and acknowledging "duplication and overlap" but concluding that this provides a sense of "general magnitude").

60 *See* DAVID. C. KORTEN, THE POST-CORPORATE WORLD: LIFE AFTER CAPITALISM 46–48 (1999).

61 *See supra* Chapter 4.B.iii, Chapter 5.

62 *See* GREENFIELD, *supra* note 57, at 14–21.

63 *See* ALLEN & KRAAKMAN, *supra* note 53, at 103–04, 112–14, 131–41; Armour et al., *supra* note 55, at 111–16; Frank H. Easterbrook & Daniel R. Fischel, *Limited Liability and the Corporation*, 52 U. CHI. L. REV. 89, 109–13 (1985).

64 *See, e.g.*, Christopher M. Bruner, *Corporate Governance Reform in a Time of Crisis*, 36 J. CORP. L. 309, 311–16 (2011) (describing moral hazard concerns arising from deposit insurance and the "too big to fail" problem). *See also infra* Chapter 7.A-B.

65 *See* ALLEN & KRAAKMAN, *supra* note 53, at 104, 109–12, 116–38 (discussing corporate law's "limited efforts to protect creditors" and describing sophisticated creditors' reliance on contractual protections); Easterbrook & Fischel, *supra* note 63, at 103, 109–17. Belgian law takes a unique approach, requiring that a plan be filed with a notary detailing the sufficiency of the company's initial "equity" for a two-year period and then imposing liability on the founders if the company goes bankrupt within three years and a judge decides upon review that the "initial capital" was "obviously

As discussed, economically oriented theories of corporate law and governance that strongly favor shareholders generally assume the sufficiency of external contracts and regulation to contain risk-taking and to force companies to internalize the full costs of production. There is growing skepticism, however, regarding their adequacy—particularly in light of the confluence of interconnected environmental, social, and economic challenges that we now face.[66] Indeed, as Raworth observes, "many economic effects that were treated as 'externalities' in twentieth-century theory have turned into defining social and ecological crises in the twenty-first century."[67] To be sure, external regulatory reforms will likewise prove critical, particularly to the degree that other areas of law further incentivize excessive risk-taking and externalization of costs, and/or function in ways that impede pursuit of more sustainable corporate operations.[68] There is growing acknowledgment, however, that to the extent external regulatory mechanisms for containing corporate risk and cost externalization fail to perform, there may be no alternative but to revisit those features of the corporate form and corporate governance that most directly generate these harmful incentives in the first place.[69]

In this respect, we can fairly characterize financialization, excessive risk, and cost externalization as three enduring and interrelated pathologies that inhibit the pursuit of corporate sustainability. Likewise, they cast considerable doubt on the desirability of corporate structures that are widely (and incorrectly) presumed to be intrinsic to the corporate form. The upshot is that the sustainability concept, on the one hand, and these pathologies associated with the status quo, on the other, respectively provide positive and negative metrics against which to assess the alternative structures discussed in the remaining chapters of the book.

insufficient." *See* Code des sociétés et des associations [Code of Companies and Associations] of Mar. 23, 2019, arts. 5:3–5:4, 5:16 (Belg.) (translation by Thomson Reuters, RIA Worldwide Tax & Commercial Law, last reviewed Feb. 23, 2021). However, this approach similarly relies on ex post judicial application of a vague standard. For additional background, see Alessio Bartolacelli, *Capital Requirements and the Abuse of Companies*, *in* ABUSE OF COMPANIES 179, 181, 200 (Hanne S. Birkmose et al. eds., 2019); Christoph Van der Elst, *21st Century Company Law in Belgium*, 17 EUR. COMPANY L.J. 25, 28 (2020).

[66] *See supra* Chapter 1, Chapter 2.B, Chapter 4.B, Chapter 5.B. *See also* Nicholls, *supra* note 57, at 15.

[67] RAWORTH, *supra* note 15, at 123.

[68] Noteworthy examples include antitrust and bankruptcy. *See, e.g.*, Paul Balmer, *Colluding to Save the World: How Antitrust Laws Discourage Corporations from Taking Action on Climate Change*, 47 ECOLOGY L. CURRENTS 219 (2020); Vincent S.J. Buccola & Joshua C. Macey, *Claim Durability and Bankruptcy's Tort Problem*, 38 YALE J. ON REG. 766 (2021); Joshua Macey & Jackson Salovaara, *Bankruptcy as Bailout: Coal Company Insolvency and the Erosion of Federal Law*, 71 STAN. L. REV. 879 (2019).

[69] *See, e.g.*, John Armour et al., *Beyond the Anatomy*, *in* KRAAKMAN ET AL., *supra* note 54, at 267, 271–72; Leo E. Strine, Jr., & Nicholas Walter, *Conservative Collision Course?: The Tension between Conservative Corporate Law Theory and* Citizens United, 100 CORNELL L. REV. 335, 342–46, 350–59, 363–65, 381–90 (2015).

C. Disclosure, Impact-Weighted Accounting, and Sustainability

Before turning to alternative calibrations of the corporate technology in subsequent chapters, it is important to consider the extent to which disclosure might provide a means of achieving sustainability while holding constant the prevailing corporate structure. In addition to non-financial reporting regimes and so-called integrated reporting—which combines financial and non-financial means of analyzing corporate performance—increasing attention has been directed toward the potential for novel accounting systems to quantify impacts of corporate production more fully and to bring a range of environmental, social, and economic factors directly to bear upon a corporation's financial statements. To the degree this proves possible, it could have far-reaching consequences for debates regarding corporate sustainability and what the appropriate role of corporate governance reforms might be in achieving it. For the reasons discussed below, however, extant disclosure strategies and nascent efforts to develop a workable mode of impact-weighted accounting appear incapable of delivering corporate sustainability on their own.

Much research on the environmental and social impacts of corporate production has been framed by reference to "corporate social responsibility" (CSR) or, more recently, "environmental, social, and governance" (ESG) factors. CSR arose in the corporate governance context in the mid-twentieth century to refer to more socially oriented conceptions of corporate purpose, whereas ESG arose in the capital market context in the late twentieth century "as a portfolio risk management concept linked to financial performance."[70] Today, however, both concepts have come to reflect a widespread motivation to make a "business case" for sustainability-oriented efforts by reference to normative commitments already prevailing in corporate governance and capital markets—notably to establish that such initiatives generally represent a win-win, even if shareholder primacy is held constant, in so far as they actually benefit shareholders.[71] For example, Ethisphere gives awards to what it deems "the World's Most Ethical Companies," premised on the notion that "conducting ethical business is the key to maximizing profits."[72] They cite research indicating that "ethics and

[70] Iain MacNeil & Irene-marié Esser, *From a Financial to an Entity Model of ESG*, EUR. BUS. ORG. L. REV., at 4–8 (forthcoming 2021), https://ssrn.com/abstract=3834529.

[71] *See* Bruner & Sjåfjell, *supra* note 22, at 718; Sjåfjell & Bruner, *supra* note 13, at 4, 7. *See also* MacNeil & Esser, *supra* note 70, at 7–12.

[72] Ethisphere, *Ethisphere Announces the 2020 World's Most Ethical Companies*, Feb. 25, 2020, https://ethisphere.com/ethisphere-announces-the-2020-worlds-most-ethical-companies/ (quoting Ethisphere CEO Timothy Erblich). These determinations are based on their "proprietary Ethics Quotient," which "includes more than 200 data points on culture, environmental and social practices, ethics and compliance activities, governance, diversity and initiatives to support a strong value chain." *Id.*

financial performance go hand-in-hand," and indicate that their honorees have "outperformed the large cap sector over five years by 13.5 percent"—an "Ethics Premium" that "forms the basis upon which companies can correlate responsible behavior with shareholder value."[73]

This sort of approach effectively subordinates sustainability-related concerns to financial concerns, implicitly cabining potential reforms by holding constant the prevailing structures of corporate law and governance.[74] For example, former Delaware Chief Justice Leo Strine and co-authors frame the challenge as being "to situate" ESG considerations within existing corporate governance parameters.[75] Their solution is simply to annex these matters to the compliance function.[76] Framed in this manner, ESG considerations might at most help justify corporate decisions that err on the side of caution when the company is operating in a legal "grey zone,"[77] and militate toward a revised board committee structure that unifies compliance and ESG responsibilities.[78] However, it remains unclear how—if at all—such measures would actively promote more sustainable corporate conduct, given that extant normative commitments and incentive structures would remain untouched.[79]

To be sure, to the extent it proves possible to have our cake and eat it too—generating greater profits through adoption of policies compatible with long-term sustainability—that is to the good. Profit-driven motivations for adopting sustainability-oriented initiatives are thought to include advancing "management's private interests and values"; responding to pressures exerted by socially responsible investment (SRI) strategies; gaining "leverage in connecting,

[73] *Id. See also* Ethisphere, *Five-Year Ethics Premium: 13.5%*, Jan. 2020, https://www.worldsmostethicalcompanies.com/wp-content/uploads/2020-5-Year-Ethics-Premium-Chart-2.png.

[74] *Cf.* Sjåfjell & Bruner, *supra* note 13, at 4 (distinguishing "strong" and "weak" sustainability efforts along such lines).

[75] Leo E. Strine, Jr., et al., Caremark *and ESG, Perfect Together: A Practical Approach to Implementing an Integrated, Efficient, and Effective* Caremark *and EESG Strategy*, 106 IOWA L. REV. 1885, 1887–88 (2021).

[76] *See id.* at 1905–10.

[77] *See id.* at 1910.

[78] *See id.* at 1910–21 (observing that public companies typically assign compliance and risk management responsibilities to the audit committee, while ESG responsibilities are typically assigned to the nominating and corporate governance committee).

[79] *See, e.g., id.* at 1910–11 (focusing on compliance with external regulation and assuming that ESG concerns "will tend to track" external regulatory concerns). *See also generally* Stavros Gadinis & Amelia Miazad, *Corporate Law and Social Risk*, 73 VAND. L. REV. 1401 (2020) (distinguishing the "ESG" approach as broader and more proactive than legal compliance and advocating a board-level duty to establish a distinct "ESG process" to gather information from corporate stakeholders); *Cf.* INTERNATIONAL MONETARY FUND, GLOBAL FINANCIAL STABILITY REPORT: LOWER FOR LONGER X, 81 (2019) (describing ESG as a means of risk mitigation); Lund & Pollman, *supra* note 38, at 34–36 (describing how ESG is widely regarded as a means toward the end of shareholder value); Brett McDonnell et al., *Green Boardrooms?*, 53 CONN. L. REV. 335, 344–45 (2021) (same). Innovative committee structures will be discussed below, but in those cases such structures aim to operationalize more ambitious reforms to corporate law and governance—South Africa representing a vivid example. *See infra* Chapter 8.C.

recruiting, and motivating employees' performance"; sending "a signal for the company's virtuous social identity, aiming consumers to attribute virtue to their brands"; and pursuing a regulatory strategy—for example, preempting regulation of a corporation's own conduct and/or "attempting to raise rivals' costs by encouraging environmental, labor, or safety regulations that will particularly handicap competitors."[80] Such initiatives may also permit companies to "identify and manage social risks to their business."[81] Empirical results on the financial impacts of sustainability-oriented corporate policies are mixed,[82] but there is evidence suggesting that adoption of certain sustainability-oriented policies can redound to a corporation's long-term financial benefit. For example, Robert Eccles, Ioannis Ioannou, and George Serafeim have found that U.S. companies adopting such policies by the early 1990s were, by the late 2010s, more likely to have board-level responsibility for sustainability and executive compensation linked to sustainability-related metrics. Additionally, they were more likely "to have established processes for stakeholder engagement, to be more long-term oriented, and to exhibit higher measurement and disclosure of nonfinancial information." They further found evidence that such companies "significantly outperform their counterparts over the long-term, both in terms of stock market as well as accounting performance."[83] These findings are consistent with evidence suggesting that sustainability-oriented practices genuinely brought to bear on a company's strategy offer potential to improve both financial and non-financial performance to a degree that more superficial and conformity-oriented gestures do not.[84]

As discussed earlier, however, such weak sustainability initiatives clearly have not proven sufficient to stem the crises we now face, particularly given the

[80] Shlomit Azgad-Tromer, *The Virtuous Corporation: On Corporate Social Motivation and Law*, 19 U. PENN. J. BUS. L. 341, 349–59 (2017). *See also* Silda Wall Spitzer & John Mandyck, *What Boards Need to Know About Sustainability Ratings*, HARV. BUS. REV., Reprint H04Z5P, May 30, 2019, at 3–4.

[81] *See* Gadinis & Miazad, *supra* note 79, at 1410.

[82] *See, e.g.*, INTERNATIONAL MONETARY FUND, *supra* note 79, at 85–87; Robert G. Eccles et al., *The Impact of Corporate Sustainability on Organizational Processes and Performance*, 60 MGMT. SCI. 2835 (2014), https://ssrn.com/abstract=1964011 (working paper version), at 17–18; GEORGE SERAFEIM, TURNING A PROFIT WHILE DOING GOOD: ALIGNING SUSTAINABILITY WITH CORPORATE PERFORMANCE (Center for Effective Public Management, Brookings Institution, Dec. 2014), at 6–8.

[83] *See* Eccles et al., *supra* note 82, at 1. *See also* BRITISH ACADEMY, PRINCIPLES FOR PURPOSEFUL BUSINESS: HOW TO DELIVER THE FRAMEWORK FOR THE FUTURE OF THE CORPORATION 12–14 (2019); SERAFEIM, *supra* note 82, at 8–10.

[84] *See generally* Ioannis Ioannou & George Serafeim, *Corporate Sustainability: A Strategy?* (Harvard Business School Working Paper 19-065, 2019); Nurlan Orazalin, *Do Board Sustainability Committees Contribute to Corporate Environmental and Social Performance? The Mediating Role of Corporate Social Responsibility Strategy*, 29 BUS. STRATEGY 140 (2019). *See also* Pascual Berrone, *Owners, Boards & Managers: Aligning Governance Interests for the Long Haul*, IESE INSIGHT, IIR046, First Quarter 2011, at 36, 37–38 (arguing that "merely paying lip service to social and environmental concerns"—that is, greenwashing—"is a risky strategy" because "symbolic actions have become so much the norm as to be virtually meaningless," and "may be perceived as deceitful").

weakness of external regulatory strategies.[85] Critically, if corporate incentives to adopt sustainability-oriented policies are left to rest entirely on their capacity to produce further profits, then companies will presumably pursue sustainability initiatives where they improve profitability and avoid them where they impair profitability. The reality, as Serafeim observes, is that, "in some cases, with the current regulations, market logics, processes, products and business models, economic returns and better performance on some environmental or social issue are at odds"—notably where the corporation benefits from a negative externality, or cannot benefit from a positive externality.[86] Serafeim concludes that "many companies have already plucked the low-hanging fruit," and that further improvement "typically requires innovation—sometimes at a major scale—in processes, products, and business models," which in turn "will largely depend on the corporate governance model that prevails."[87]

Much turns on public perceptions, which affect the degree to which commercial, labor, and investment markets punish companies for ignoring sustainability concerns.[88] Yet, corporate strategies are ultimately determined by boards of directors—and the conflicting signals they receive on these issues appear to net out, from their perspective, in favor of a strong default toward shareholder primacy. While awareness is certainly increasing, "many companies have not expected, nor have their directors felt required, to understand sustainability and ESG or to provide board education in that area,"[89] and prevailing degrees of board-level engagement are generally regarded as insufficient.[90] For example, Craig Smith and Ron Soonieus "interviewed nonexecutive directors representing 50 large, well-known European companies." These directors reported that, "while boards are increasingly conscious about the need to incorporate sustainability into broader business practice," as a practical matter "many fellow board members and corporate executives don't take sustainability all that seriously." One candidly related that sustainability at his company had been characterized as "the last wagon in the train," while another "summed up his company's 'technocratic approach,' saying, 'We are listed much higher on the Dow Jones Sustainability Index than we think we should be. Apparently, we have become very skilled in filling out their 300-page questionnaire.' "[91]

85 *See supra* Chapter 1, Chapter 6.B.

86 SERAFEIM, *supra* note 82, at 4–6. *See also* Azgad-Tromer, *supra* note 80, at 366–67 (observing that "the social priorities of the corporation may differ from those of the public").

87 SERAFEIM, *supra* note 82, at 15–16.

88 *See id.* at 15.

89 Spitzer & Mandyck, *supra* note 80, at 3.

90 *See* Lynn S. Paine, *Sustainability in the Boardroom*, HARV. BUS. REV., Reprint R1407G, July–Aug 2014, at 4 (observing that "no more than 10% of U.S. public company boards have a committee dedicated solely to corporate responsibility or sustainability").

91 *See* N. Craig Smith, *How Corporate Boards Can Get Serious about Sustainability Issues*, WALL ST. J., June 24, 2019, https://www.wsj.com/articles/how-corporate-boards-can-get-serious-about-sustainability-issues-11561379882. *See also* N. Craig Smith & Ron Soonieus, *How Board Members Really*

This "technocratic" response to sustainability poignantly highlights a major shortcoming in the prevailing approach, which relies heavily on disclosure-based regimes that in fact require little substantive engagement. The theory behind a disclosure-based strategy is that if a business "is not meeting societal expectations of responsible behavior, then market or nonmarket-based pressure from stakeholders may provide incentives for the company to reform its behavior."[92] In the corporate sustainability context, however, such regimes "are plagued by greenwashing and a magnetic draw toward generic boilerplate," and effectively reinforce shareholder primacy and the pathologies of financialization to the extent they are "presented as a reflection of (and cabined by reference to) the need for investors to assess these considerations as a distinctive basket of investment risks, without direct regard for the broader significance and impacts of the corporate production practices at issue."[93] Although sustainability-oriented disclosures may be "a necessary step to incentivize firms to change," as an IMF analysis explains, "generally this does not yet seem to be sufficient for adequate differentiation." Further action is still required "to incentivize firms to carry out investment or make other changes in their business practices that would help reduce negative externalities, especially from climate-change-related risks."[94]

Numerous practical challenges have arisen with disclosure-based sustainability regimes that tend to limit their effectiveness. These include a proliferation of voluntary standards for sustainability-related reporting, effectively undermining comparability of resulting disclosures, and a tendency to cabin such disclosures—either by focusing on their materiality to investors, which effectively marginalizes other concerns, or by presenting them in the form of a self-standing report, which hives these matters off from the company's financial reports.[95]

Feel about ESG, from Deniers to True Believers, HARV. BUS. REV., Apr. 19, 2019, https://hbr.org/2019/04/how-board-members-really-feel-about-esg-from-deniers-to-true-believers.

92 David Hess, *The Transparency Trap: Non-Financial Disclosure and the Responsibility of Business to Respect Human Rights*, 56 AM. BUS. L.J. 5, 16 (2019).

93 Bruner & Sjåfjell, *supra* note 22, at 718. *See also* Jay Cullen & Jukka Mähönen, *Taming Unsustainable Finance: The Perils of Modern Risk Management*, *in* THE CAMBRIDGE HANDBOOK OF CORPORATE LAW, CORPORATE GOVERNANCE AND SUSTAINABILITY, *supra* note 13, at 100, 102; Hess, *supra* note 92, at 10, 41–42; McDonnell et al., *supra* note 79, at 364. For broader discussion of disclosure-based approaches, see generally Iris H.-Y. Chiu, *Disclosure Regulation and Sustainability: Legislation and Governance Implications*, *in* THE CAMBRIDGE HANDBOOK OF CORPORATE LAW, CORPORATE GOVERNANCE AND SUSTAINABILITY, *supra* note 13, at 521; Villiers, *supra* note 34.

94 INTERNATIONAL MONETARY FUND, *supra* note 79, at 81. *See also* BARNALI CHOUDHURY & MARTIN PETRIN, CORPORATE DUTIES TO THE PUBLIC 85–88 (2019); Hess, *supra* note 92, at 27, 42; *infra* Chapter 8.B.

95 *See, e.g.*, INTERNATIONAL MONETARY FUND, *supra* note 79, at 82, 87–89; Hess, *supra* note 92, at 26–31; Virginia Harper Ho, *Non-Financial Reporting & Corporate Governance: Explaining American Divergence & Its Implications for Disclosure Reform*, 10 ACCT., ECON. & L.: A CONVIVIUM 1, 6 (2020); Virginia Harper Ho & Stephen Kim Park, *ESG Disclosure in Comparative Perspective: Optimizing*

The Global Reporting Initiative (GRI) Standards—which are "the world's most widely used standards for sustainability reporting"[96]—are flexible and voluntary, combining a few "universal" standards with "topic-specific" standards from which a company may choose "to report on its material topics."[97] Any given "requirements" apply only to the extent necessary to legitimate a company's own claims of compliance with the standards.[98] Materiality, for purposes of the GRI Standards, is defined broadly to "reflect an organization's significant economic, environmental and social impacts" and matters that "substantively influence the assessments and decisions of stakeholders,"[99] but the product is relatively circumscribed, essentially taking the form of a distinct non-financial report.[100]

The International Integrated Reporting Council (IIRC)[101] International Framework similarly provides a voluntary framework based upon "a principles-based approach" that aims to "strike an appropriate balance between flexibility and prescription," generating a "standalone" product.[102] Although the IIRC's framework provides a broader conceptualization of materiality keyed to "value creation" through various forms of capital—including not just financial capital, but also manufactured, intellectual, human, social and relationship, and natural capitals[103]—an integrated report nevertheless "aims to improve the quality of information available to providers of financial capital to enable a more efficient and productive allocation of capital," thereby remaining focused on financial investors as end users of the resulting disclosures.[104] As Jukka Mähönen concludes, this at most creates "the illusion that something is being

Private Ordering in Public Reporting, 41 U. PA. J. INT'L L. 249, 255, 266–67 (2019); McDonnell et al., *supra* note 79, at 363–71; Nicholls, *supra* note 57, at 7–10. *See also* LOWELL UNGAR & ANDREW WHITLOCK, ENERGY EFFICIENCY AND CORPORATE SUSTAINABILITY: SAVING MONEY WHILE MEETING CLIMATE GOALS 10 (2019) (observing that ESG ratings from Sustainalytics, MSCI, RobecoSAM, and others similarly "focus on financial risk and materiality").

[96] Global Reporting Initiative, *About GRI*, https://www.globalreporting.org/about-gri/. *See also* Global Reporting Initiative, *The Global Standards for Sustainability Reporting*, https://www.globalreporting.org/standards/.

[97] Global Reporting Initiative, *How to Use the GRI Standards: English*, https://www.globalreporting.org/how-to-use-the-gri-standards/gri-standards-english-language/.

[98] GLOBAL REPORTING INITIATIVE, GRI STANDARD 103: MANAGEMENT APPROACH (2016), Introduction.

[99] *Id.*, Disclosure 103-1. *See also id.*, Glossary (defining "impact" and "material topic").

[100] Global Reporting Initiative, *How to Use the GRI Standards*, https://www.globalreporting.org/how-to-use-the-gri-standards/. *See also* Jukka Mähönen, *Comprehensive Approach to Relevant and Reliable Reporting in Europe: A Dream Impossible?*, 12 SUSTAINABILITY 5277 (2020), at 1, 8–9.

[101] It has been announced that the IIRC will merge with the Sustainability Accounting Standards Board in 2021, forming the Value Reporting Foundation. *See* George S. Georgiev, *The Human Capital Management Movement in U.S. Corporate Law*, 95 TUL. L. REV. 639, 688–89 (2021).

[102] *See* INTERNATIONAL INTEGRATED REPORTING COUNCIL, THE INTERNATIONAL FRAMEWORK 4 (2013).

[103] *See id.* at 10–19.

[104] *Id.* at 4.

done to acknowledge stakeholders' interests," while in fact reinforcing shareholder primacy.[105]

Public disclosure regimes, meanwhile, are typically weak. In some jurisdictions, disclosure-based sustainability regimes remain predominantly voluntary—as in the United States,[106] where moves toward mandating greater social and environmental disclosures by public companies have been tentative and patchy. In 2020, the U.S. Securities and Exchange Commission (SEC) expanded on the prior requirement to disclose the number of people employed to require moving forward that public companies provide a more general description of "human capital resources."[107] Such disclosures remain cabined, however, by reference to financial materiality, and open-ended in so far as no particular disclosure standard is required.[108] Mandated disclosures regarding governmental proceedings under environmental laws were effectively carved back at the same time, in so far as the minimum dollar threshold for reporting was substantially increased.[109] Early indications suggest that "the quality of disclosure provided by firms has been low so far,"[110] and whether the SEC will require

[105] Mähönen, *supra* note 100, at 18. For additional background, see *id.* at 10–19. As discussed later, however, more robust approaches to integrated reporting are possible, and have been embraced in practice—notably in South Africa. *See infra* Chapter 8.C. *See also* INSTITUTE OF DIRECTORS SOUTHERN AFRICA, KING IV: REPORT ON CORPORATE GOVERNANCE FOR SOUTH AFRICA 25–26 (2016) (advocating "a stakeholder-inclusive approach" rather than "prioritising the interests of the providers of financial capital"); Mähönen, *supra* note 100, at 14–18 (emphasizing that South Africa's "unique conception of integrated thinking is an exception and brings hope to those seeing integrated thinking and reporting as a path to sustainable governance").

[106] *See* Harper Ho, *supra* note 95, at 9, 23–24 (observing that "the continued reliance of Congress and the SEC on voluntary regimes" for U.S. companies "is increasingly an outlier," but that there may be more potential for regulatory action at the state level).

[107] Modernization of Regulation S-K Items 101, 103, and 105, Securities Act Release No. 33-10825, Exchange Act Release No. 34-89670, File No. S7-11-19 (Aug. 26, 2020), at 45–54, 95–97, 125.

[108] *See id.* at 52–54, 96, 125. *See also* Georgiev, *supra* note 101, at 677–78, 682, 717–18. Similar limitations apply to sustainability-related disclosures in the insurance context, as the handful of states surveying insurers' responses to climate change require "a description of how they incorporate climate risks into their mitigation, risk-management and investment plans." *See* California Department of Insurance, *NAIC Climate Risk Disclosure Survey*, https://www.insurance.ca.gov/0250-insurers/0300-insurers/0100-applications/ClimateSurvey/index.cfm. *But see* Aaron Nicodemus, *Biden's SEC Set to Require Disclosure of ESG, Climate Change Risk*, COMPLIANCE WEEK, Dec. 3, 2020, https://www.complianceweek.com/regulatory-policy/bidens-sec-set-to-require-disclosure-of-esg-climate-change-risk/29788.article (reporting speculation that the SEC, with a Democratic majority following President Biden's election, may require more specific disclosures in this area).

[109] *See* Modernization of Regulation S-K Items 101, 103, and 105, *supra* note 107, at 61, 64–65, 102–04. For additional background, see Press Release, U.S. Securities and Exchange Commission, SEC Adopts Rule Amendments to Modernize Disclosures of Business, Legal Proceedings, and Risk Factors Under Regulation S-K (Aug. 26, 2020), https://www.sec.gov/news/press-release/2020-192; Andrew Ramonas, *Divided SEC Requires More Workforce Disclosures from Companies*, BLOOMBERG L. NEWS, Aug. 26, 2020 (reporting that Commissioners were "divided" on the amendments, with Democratic Commissioners calling for "more specific reporting about company workforces, as well as disclosures about climate change risk").

[110] Georgiev, *supra* note 101, at 718. *See also id.* at 682.

any significant climate-related disclosures remains to be seen.[111] Many other jurisdictions, meanwhile, impose more wide-ranging disclosure requirements, yet these likewise typically remain modest and highly flexible, leaving the core of the public company disclosure regime to focus almost exclusively on the interests of investors—notably shareholders.[112] Fundamentally, such disclosures "say nothing about what the company is not acting upon," give "no insight into what stakeholders' real concerns are," and typically describe the company's actions "without any basis on which to assess their adequacy."[113] As Barnali Choudhury and Martin Petrin conclude, non-financial disclosure regimes have had "limited or, in some cases, no effects at all," in which light growing reliance on this regulatory strategy suggests that "governments are more focused on giving the *appearance* that these types of problems are being addressed rather than working to eradicate the problem's root causes."[114]

[111] *See* Press Release, U.S. Securities and Exchange Commission, Statement of Acting Chair Allison Herren Lee on the Review of Climate-Related Disclosure (Feb. 24, 2021), https://www.sec.gov/news/public-statement/lee-statement-review-climate-related-disclosure. *See also Telling All: Regulators Want Firms to Own Up to Climate Risks*, ECONOMIST, Mar. 13, 2021, https://www.economist.com/business/2021/03/13/regulators-want-firms-to-own-up-to-climate-risks; Andrew Ramonas et al., *SEC Plans Rules on Climate Disclosures, Cyber Risks This Fall*, BLOOMBERG L. NEWS, June 11, 2021; Andrew Ramonas, *SEC "Mission Creep" on Climate Ups Republican Lawsuit Threats*, BLOOMBERG L. NEWS, June 29, 2021.

[112] *See, e.g.*, Christopher M. Bruner, *Leaders or Laggards? Corporate Sustainability in Hong Kong and Singapore, in* THE CAMBRIDGE HANDBOOK OF CORPORATE LAW, CORPORATE GOVERNANCE AND SUSTAINABILITY, *supra* note 13, at 504, 511–12, 514–15 (describing modest disclosure regimes in Singapore and Hong Kong, respectively); Chiu, *supra* note 93, at 523–26 (observing that EU and U.K. requirements for non-financial reporting remain directed toward shareholders); Hess, *supra* note 92, at 20–22 (observing the flexibility of EU requirements); Harper Ho & Park, *supra* note 95, at 288–316 (describing disclosure regimes in the United States, South Africa, Brazil, the European Union, the United Kingdom, Hong Kong, and China, and finding that "none of [them] attempts to preempt private ordering"); Mähönen, *supra* note 100, at 19–30 (discussing shortcomings of the EU reporting framework). *See also, e.g.*, Directive 2014/95/EU of the European Parliament and of the Council of 22 October 2014 amending Directive 2013/34/EU as regards disclosure of non-financial and diversity information by certain large undertakings and groups, 2014 O.J. (L 330/1), art. 1 (requiring certain large companies to "include in the management report a non-financial statement" addressing "environmental, social and employee matters, respect for human rights, anti-corruption and bribery matters"); Regulation (EU) 2019/2088 of the European Parliament and of the Council of 27 November 2019 on sustainability-related disclosures in the financial services sector, 2019 O.J. (L317/1), art. 3 (requiring "financial market participants" and "financial advisers" to "publish on their websites information about their policies on the integration of sustainability risks" in their investment decision-making and investment advice, respectively); European Commission, *Corporate Sustainability Reporting*, https://ec.europa.eu/info/business-economy-euro/company-reporting-and-auditing/company-reporting/corporate-sustainability-reporting_en; David M. Silk et al., *Wachtell Lipton Discusses UK and EU Regulators' Latest Moves on ESG*, CLS BLUE SKY BLOG, Apr. 16, 2020, https://clsbluesky.law.columbia.edu/2020/04/16/wachtell-lipton-discusses-uk-and-eu-regulators-latest-moves-on-esg/. More ambitious initiatives recently pursued elsewhere are discussed below. *See infra* Chapter 8.C.

[113] Gadinis & Miazad, *supra* note 79, at 1471. *See also* Hess, *supra* note 92, at 31–42 (reviewing empirical literature suggesting that "companies are producing low-quality, unbalanced reports").

[114] CHOUDHURY & PETRIN, *supra* note 94, at 91. *See also* Georgiev, *supra* note 101, at 702; Hess, *supra* note 92, at 7–9, 41.

Institutional investors, for their part, have adopted an equivocal posture regarding sustainability. The proximate impetus for "ESG-related policies and disclosures" at public companies is thought to be "shareholder driven,"[115] and activist investors have achieved some noteworthy victories, but such initiatives are often pitched in decidedly financial terms—as with the successful 2021 proxy battle electing three dissidents to Exxon's board, a campaign that focused on the "financial case" that "Exxon had generated poor returns . . . through years of wasteful energy-project spending and rising debt."[116] Meanwhile, it remains far from clear whether the largest institutions would—or even could—make consequential use of further sustainability disclosures. There is a growing literature investigating the complex incentives of major investment funds, which are certainly sophisticated enough to digest governance-relevant corporate information, yet often pursue low-cost, passive investment strategies by design.[117] For example, while BlackRock CEO Larry Fink has called for greater corporate action in response to climate change, this appears to have responded to protests "decrying BlackRock for inaction on global warming and other issues" itself, and it remains unclear what BlackRock can concretely do, with "more than two-thirds of its . . . assets in products linked to indexes."[118] While "the attitudinal shift should not be underestimated," the fact remains that, as of 2021, "BlackRock still has huge investments in coal and other fossil fuels,"[119] and a very small stewardship team.[120]

Although it is certainly plausible that the big index funds might pursue certain forms of sustainability-related initiatives to attract assets from millennial

[115] Cathy Hwang & Yaron Nili, *Shareholder-Driven Stakeholderism*, U. CHI. L. REV. ONLINE, Apr. 15, 2020, https://lawreviewblog.uchicago.edu/2020/04/15/shareholder-driven-stakeholderism-hwang-nili/ (reviewing "non-charter, non-bylaw governance documents . . . from the websites of all 1,500 of the large American companies listed in the Standard & Poor's Composite 1500 index," many of which "fall into the ESG category"). *See also* Harper Ho & Park, *supra* note 95, at 260–62.

[116] Saijel Kishan & Joe Carroll, *Exxon Activist Victory Marks Coming of Age for ESG Investing*, BLOOMBERG L. NEWS, June 9, 2021.

[117] *See* Christopher M. Bruner, *Corporate Governance Reform in Post-Crisis Financial Firms: Two Fundamental Tensions*, 60 ARIZ. L. REV. 959, 970–74 (2018). For additional background, see generally Lucian Bebchuk et al., *The Agency Problems of Institutional Investors*, 31 J. ECON. PERSPECTIVES 89 (2017); Dorothy S. Lund, *The Case Against Passive Shareholder Voting*, 43 J. CORP. L. 493 (2018); John D. Morley, *Too Big to Be Activist*, 92 S. CAL. L. REV. 1407 (2019); Yesha Yadav, *Too-Big-to-Fail Shareholders*, 103 MINN. L. REV. 587 (2018).

[118] Annie Massa, *BlackRock Puts Climate at Center of $7 Trillion Strategy*, BLOOMBERG L. NEWS, Jan. 14, 2020. *See also* Mark R. Kramer, *Larry Fink Isn't Going to Read Your Sustainability Report*, HARV. BUS. REV., Jan. 20, 2020, https://hbr.org/2020/01/larry-fink-isnt-going-to-read-your-sustainability-report; McDonnell et al., *supra* note 79, at 371–86; Sarah Min, *BlackRock to Double Down on Climate Offenders in 2021*, CHIEF INV. OFFICER, Dec. 11, 2020, https://www.ai-cio.com/news/blackrock-double-climate-offenders-2021/.

[119] Dominic Rushe, *"Reading the Writing on the Wall": Why Wall Street Is Acting on the Climate Crisis*, GUARDIAN, Mar. 16, 2021, https://www.theguardian.com/us-news/2021/mar/16/wall-street-climate-crisis-emissions.

[120] *See* Georgiev, *supra* note 101, at 712.

generation investors over coming decades,[121] the range of clients to whom they must simultaneously appeal may blunt such effects. "BlackRock's size puts it in a delicate position: operating in more than 30 countries, and as one of the biggest holders of most U.S. publicly traded companies, its clients include large sovereign wealth funds, state pension plans and financial advisers with viewpoints that don't necessarily align on what to do about climate change and social issues." Although BlackRock has joined Climate Action 100+, "a group of more than 370 investment managers with a combined $41 trillion in assets that pressures greenhouse gas emitters to reform," it remains striking that, as recently as the 2019 proxy season, BlackRock and Vanguard "voted against at least 16 climate-related shareholder proposals where their support could have given the measures majority support."[122] In this light, it is not surprising that major investors' interest in climate change has been described as "a strategic detour," and that environmental activists have responded to this new turn with caution.[123]

The explanation may simply be that climate change activism is more costly to these funds than other forms of sustainability-related initiatives. As Michal Barzuza, Quinn Curtis, and David Webber suggest, "fear of confronting management may explain index funds' more cautious approach to climate change so far." Whereas "millennials care about both diversity and climate, the gender composition of a corporate board is a far less sensitive issue for most firms than their carbon footprint." Accordingly, the index funds "intervene aggressively when the cost is low and tread lightly when it is not."[124] BlackRock, in particular, has called for companies to "disclose a plan for how their business model will be compatible with a low-carbon economy," and indicated that if corporate plans and/or disclosures are insufficient they "may vote against the directors we consider responsible for climate risk oversight" and "support shareholder proposals that we believe address gaps."[125] Critics observe, however, that "without the actual threat of exclusion, this policy update remains yet another paper tiger."[126] Whether reinforcement by bond investors might move the dial further remains to be seen.[127]

121 *See generally* Michal Barzuza et al., *Shareholder Value(s): Index Fund ESG Activism and the New Millennial Corporate Governance*, 93 S. CAL. L. REV. 1243 (2020). *See also* Gadinis & Miazad, *supra* note 79, at 1451; Rushe, *supra* note 119.

122 Massa, *supra* note 118.

123 Rushe, *supra* note 119.

124 Barzuza et al., *supra* note 121, at 1305–06.

125 BlackRock, *Investment Stewardship Commentary: Climate Risk and the Transition to a Low-Carbon Economy* 4–5 (Feb. 2021).

126 Akshat Rathi, *BlackRock's Latest Climate Instructions Come with a New Threat*, BLOOMBERG L. NEWS, Feb. 17, 2021 (quoting Katrin Ganswindt of Urgewald).

127 *See* Alice Gledhill, *Credit Market Throws Weight Behind Shareholder ESG Activism*, BLOOMBERG L. NEWS, Feb. 1, 2021. *See also* Stephen Kim Park, *Green Bonds and Beyond: Debt Financing as a Sustainability Driver*, *in* THE CAMBRIDGE HANDBOOK OF CORPORATE LAW, CORPORATE GOVERNANCE AND SUSTAINABILITY, *supra* note 13, at 596.

Given the insufficiency of extant disclosure strategies, there are at least a couple potential modes of response from the corporate governance perspective. One is to explore ways to re-calibrate various features of the corporate form itself in order to more effectively incentivize corporate conduct compatible with sustainability-related goals—the approach emphasized in this book, and further explored in subsequent chapters.[128] Another is to hold the corporate form constant, yet to try to change decision-making incentives by altering the way in which profit is calculated—specifically, to do so in a manner that more comprehensively forces companies to bring the full range of costs imposed on society and the planet to bear upon their own financial results.

Financial accounting remains decidedly focused on capital providers, ignoring externalities that do not directly impact the bottom line.[129] Accordingly, to the extent the problem is that a corporation's balance sheet does not actually capture the full range of corporate impacts, perhaps the solution might be to fix how we construct the balance sheet, and specifically to broaden what counts as a "cost" that is deemed "material" to a corporation's own financial condition.[130] Along these lines, it has been argued that "impact-weighted" accounting, assigning monetary values to environmental and social impacts of corporate conduct, "represents a critical next step in portfolio theory" that could "permit the development of effective risk-return-impact optimization tools and the identification of a new efficient investment frontier."[131] To the extent this proves feasible, it could bolster a range of regulatory and market-based disciplinary mechanisms. Governments could "tax companies directly for the harm they create," investors could "price the environmental and social impacts of companies into their investment analysis," and customers and workers could "align their purchasing and career choices with their values."[132]

Clearly there is force to the argument that we need a broader conception of costs that are material to investors, let alone society as a whole, as a

[128] *See infra* Chapter 7, Chapter 8.

[129] *See, e.g.*, FINANCIAL ACCOUNTING STANDARDS BOARD, CONCEPTUAL FRAMEWORK FOR FINANCIAL REPORTING 1–3 (Statement of Financial Accounting Concepts No. 8, amended Aug. 2018); INTERNATIONAL ACCOUNTING STANDARDS BOARD, CONCEPTUAL FRAMEWORK FOR FINANCIAL REPORTING A15–A17 (revised Mar. 2018). *See also* Financial Accounting Standards Board, *About the FASB*, https://www.fasb.org/facts/ (updated July 1, 2020); International Financial Reporting Standards Foundation, *Who We Are*, https://www.ifrs.org/about-us/who-we-are/.

[130] *See, e.g.*, BRITISH ACADEMY, *supra* note 83, at 26; ESTES, *supra* note 59, at 174; Kramer, *supra* note 118; Mähönen, *supra* note 100, at 3–6; Nicholls, *supra* note 57, at 1–3.

[131] GEORGE SERAFEIM ET AL., IMPACT-WEIGHTED FINANCIAL ACCOUNTS: THE MISSING PIECE FOR AN IMPACT ECONOMY 25 (2019). As already discussed, sustainability reporting and integrated reporting do not go this far. *See* INTERNATIONAL INTEGRATED REPORTING COUNCIL, *supra* note 102, at 8; Nicholls, *supra* note 57, at 8.

[132] *See* Ronald Cohen & George Serafeim, *How to Measure a Company's Real Impact*, HARV. BUS. REV., Sept. 3, 2020, https://hbr.org/2020/09/how-to-measure-a-companys-real-impact. *See also* Corson, *supra* note 59, at 73–79 (advocating tax reform as a response to corporate externalities).

purely financialized approach continues to hamstring efforts to adopt a more encompassing evaluative framework. Consider, for example, the State of New York's pursuit of securities litigation against Exxon, based on the claim "that investors were misled by Exxon applying one set of proxy greenhouse gas emissions costs—essentially, approximating the costs of a range of government-related climate change actions—to its business while using a second set of lower proxy costs in its internal business planning."[133] The litigation failed because the court found the matter immaterial to investors—evidenced by the fact that it had "no market impact and, based on the evidence presented, was essentially ignored by investors." There were no allegations of any negative impacts on the company's financial statements, or of any adverse impacts on Exxon's stock price, suggesting that the matter simply was not significant to investors, and thus provided no basis for a securities claim.[134] This clearly illustrates the limits of reliance upon a regulatory structure that remains focused on financial investment as a means of pursuing corporate sustainability—because that structure inherently subordinates all else to investor interests, with no regulatory imperative to look beyond financial returns.[135]

A prominent effort to develop a mode of impact-weighted accounting that would bring a substantial range of environmental and social matters directly to bear upon the corporation's financial statements has been led by George Serafeim at Harvard Business School. Observing that a shareholder-focused system of accounting results in a situation where "businesses deemed successful by owner-centric measures may destroy value for other stakeholders,"[136] Serafeim and his team argue that the "key to understanding the total value of a company is the ability to measure its impact along multiple dimensions using the same units." Accordingly, we "need an accounting system to convert impacts of diverse nature and origin into a common currency that can be evaluated alongside conventional financials and to determine how these can be meaningfully aggregated to inform decision making."[137] The core behavioral claim is essentially that monetary value is clear and comprehensible—it being "harder for people to wrap their minds around the value of something non-financial"—and that being able to express the full range of corporate impacts through a common metric will make it easier to inform all stakeholders more fully and thus "to create incentives

[133] Keith Goldberg, *Exxon Win Casts Doubt on Climate Securities Fraud Suits*, LAW360, Dec. 10, 2019.

[134] *See id. See also* Keith Goldberg, *Exxon Defeats NY Fraud Claims in Landmark Climate Trial*, LAW360, Dec. 10, 2019.

[135] *Cf.* Bruner, *Center-Left Politics and Corporate Governance*, *supra* note 26, at 285–86 (describing the focus of the U.S. Securities and Exchange Commission's mission on investor protection); Harper Ho, *supra* note 95, at 16–17 (describing the SEC's interpretation of its statutory mandate "in narrowly economic terms").

[136] SERAFEIM ET AL., *supra* note 131, at 10–12.

[137] *Id.* at 13.

for companies to improve their impact."[138] They recognize that this effort "is not without risks"—notably, that monetizing "a formerly 'priceless' social or environmental outcome runs the risk of capping its perceived value," or implying that it might be sold for the right price or legitimately netted against other forms of monetary gain. Yet, they argue in response that such risks "must be weighed against an arguably greater risk of maintaining the status quo in which social and environmental value is destroyed freely because we have no mechanism to price it."[139]

In evaluating such efforts, it must be acknowledged that it remains early days, and that the work is essentially just beginning in terms of grappling with difficult decisions regarding the stakeholders and forms of impact to include, as well as the "tradeoff between accuracy and generalizability of impact metrics."[140] Current efforts at producing such reports illustrate the challenges involved. It is now "highly customary for public corporations to disclose sustainability information," with over 6,000 now issuing sustainability reports and virtually all S&P 500 companies "having made a sustainability disclosure or linked financial performance with a sustainability initiative."[141] Far fewer, however, have actually endeavored to monetize their impacts. Serafeim and his team found just fifty-six companies that have "undergone some process to monetize an aspect of their business impacts," and those companies tend to be based in Europe, to have "focused primarily on monetizing inputs/activities," and only rarely to have measured product impacts.[142]

One such exceptional company is Kering SA, and their approach to monetizing non-financial impacts reflects both the potential and the limitations of this form of initiative. Kering is a Paris-headquartered multinational corporation describing itself as a "global Luxury group," with brands including Gucci, Saint Laurent, Bottega Veneta, Balenciaga, Alexander McQueen, Brioni, Boucheron, Pomellato, Dodo, Qeelin, Ulysse Nardin, Girard-Perregaux, and Kering Eyewear. Their stated "ambition" is "to be the world's most influential Luxury group in terms of creativity, sustainability, and economic performance."[143] They emphasize that the name is pronounced "caring," and that this "reflects how we think of and build our relationships with our Houses, employees, customers, and our stakeholders in general—as well as with the planet."[144] They elaborate that

[138] *Id.* at 17.
[139] *Id.* at 11, 18.
[140] *Id.* at 26–27 (identifying "initial design principles meant to guide our decisions about accounting standards").
[141] Azgad-Tromer, *supra* note 80, at 345–46.
[142] *See* SERAFEIM ET AL., *supra* note 131, at 17–25.
[143] Kering SA, *Group: Discover Kering*, https://www.kering.com/en/group/discover-kering/. *See also* KERING SA, ENVIRONMENTAL PROFIT & LOSS (EP&L): 2018 GROUP RESULTS 13 (June 2019) [hereinafter KERING SA, GROUP RESULTS].
[144] Kering SA, *Group: Discover Kering*, *supra* note 143.

"sustainability has always been at the heart of Kering's strategy," and that "more than an ethical necessity, it is a driver of innovation and value creation" that is "represented at every level of our governance," including a distinct board-level sustainability committee.[145]

Kering has developed an "Environmental Profit & Loss (EP&L) account," which they describe as "a key enabler of a sustainable business model," and which they make available with the hope that it will become a model for their industry.[146] This represents part of a broader sustainability effort through which Kering is "continuing to reduce our environmental impacts, advocating social welfare inside and outside the Group, and creating innovative game-changing platforms."[147] As to their environmental performance, Kering's goal is to achieve a 40 percent reduction in "EP&L intensity"—essentially a measure of environmental impact relative to revenues—by 2025.[148] Kering's EP&L "measures carbon emissions, water consumption, air and water pollution, land use, and waste production along the entire supply chain" in order to render "the various environmental impacts of the Group's activities visible, quantifiable, and comparable,"[149] in line with the broader aims of impact-weighted accounting initiatives. Indeed, identified impacts are "converted into monetary values to quantify the use of natural resources," which Kering can then use "to guide its sustainability strategy, improve its process and supply sources, and choose the best-adapted technologies."[150] This includes a modeling function to assess the potential impacts of projects under consideration.[151]

Kering's methodology involves dividing the supply chain into distinct tiers, "working backward from operations and sales to raw materials' production," and then mapping the supply chain "to determine where and how action can be taken to make the company more competitive" and to "clarify all the risks and related factors" involved.[152] They then identify relevant data and establish a system for collecting it, including both "environmental and non-environmental

[145] Kering SA, *Sustainability: Crafting Tomorrow's Luxury*, https://www.kering.com/en/sustainability/crafting-tomorrow-s-luxury/. *See also* Kering SA, *Sustainability: Governance*, https://www.kering.com/en/sustainability/crafting-tomorrow-s-luxury/governance/.

[146] Kering SA, *Our EP&L*, https://www.kering.com/en/sustainability/measuring-our-impact/our-ep-l/. *See also* KERING SA, GROUP RESULTS, *supra* note 143, at 4; Kering SA, *Methodology*, https://www.kering.com/en/sustainability/measuring-our-impact/our-ep-l/methodology/; SERAFEIM ET AL., *supra* note 131, at 20; Azgad-Tromer, *supra* note 80, at 346; Nicholls, *supra* note 57, at 19.

[147] KERING SA, GROUP RESULTS, *supra* note 143, at 2.

[148] *Id.* at 2, 5.

[149] Kering SA, *Our EP&L*, *supra* note 146. *See also* Kering SA, *What is an EP&L?*, https://www.kering.com/en/sustainability/measuring-our-impact/our-ep-l/what-is-an-ep-l/.

[150] Kering SA, *Our EP&L*, *supra* note 146. *See also* Kering SA, *What is an EP&L?*, *supra* note 149; Kering SA, *Why Develop an EP&L?*, https://www.kering.com/en/sustainability/measuring-our-impact/our-ep-l/why-develop-an-ep-l/.

[151] *See* Kering SA, *Our EP&L*, *supra* note 146.

[152] Kering SA, *Methodology*, *supra* note 146.

data from suppliers and the brands," as well as supplementary external data.[153] Finally, they seek to reveal "changes in the environment and the costs incurred by the public due to their impact"; to "convert the data into impacts on human well-being," including "where the impact occurs to account for differences between urban and rural populations, dry and wet countries, and so on"; to assess "the environmental impact and its consequences for human wellbeing"; and to analyze "costs and environmental benefits" through the EP&L's results.[154] Their "digital EP&L" contains their methodology and the underlying data, and results of this analysis indicate that Kering's greatest overall impacts relate to greenhouse gas emissions—particularly through raw materials production and processing, which also create outsized impacts in other areas, notably water consumption and pollution.[155] Accordingly, these areas have become their focus for improvement,[156] including through regenerative agriculture,[157] which involves "a system of farming focused on improving soil fertility—allowing the soil to then increase biodiversity and store carbon," curbing greenhouse gas emissions.[158]

Kering's efforts are certainly noteworthy relative to prevailing sustainability reporting practices. Although greenwashing and inconsistent disclosure practices remain problems across the fashion industry, Kering has been cited as a positive outlier—particularly given that "the majority of brands reveal next to nothing."[159] Transparency has been particularly lacking in the high-impact area of raw materials, exacerbated by distance of the brands themselves from realities on the ground,[160] which renders Kering's disclosures and resulting operational focus on this area all the more significant.

At the same time, however, substantial doubts have been voiced regarding the degree to which impact-weighted accounting efforts can actually be expected to achieve their ambitious goals. Beyond the practical challenges involved in gathering relevant data across complex and far-flung global value chains,[161] these efforts are rife with conceptual challenges as well. Voluntary initiatives that are not audited from the perspective of those on the ground render it "much

[153] *Id.*

[154] *Id.*

[155] Kering SA, *Results*, https://www.kering.com/en/sustainability/measuring-our-impact/our-ep-l/results/.

[156] *See* KERING SA, GROUP RESULTS, *supra* note 143, at 6–12.

[157] *See id.* at 3.

[158] Rachel Cernansky, *Where Fashion's Transparency Falls Short*, VOGUE BUS., Apr. 30, 2020, https://www.voguebusiness.com/sustainability/where-fashion-transparency-falls-short-raw-materials.

[159] Alden Wicker, *The Flawed Ways Brands Talk about Sustainability*, VOGUE BUS., Apr. 16, 2020, https://www.voguebusiness.com/sustainability/the-flawed-ways-brands-talk-about-sustainability-coronavirus (citing Adidas as another leader).

[160] *See* Cernansky, *supra* note 158.

[161] *See, e.g.*, Salminen, *supra* note 34; Villiers, *supra* note 34; Zhao, *supra* note 34. *See also* Cernansky, *supra* note 158 ("Because of the way supply chains today are structured, brands are far removed from how raw materials are produced.").

harder for resulting accounts to drive decisions and much easier for them to be criticised as subjective, incomplete and inaccurate." Embedding all of this within an accounting structure that remains focused on shareholder value means that, from an evaluative perspective, "information on social and environmental outcomes only matters if it affects decisions relating to the interests of investors."[162] Bringing non-financial considerations more fundamentally to bear upon assessments of corporate performance through accounting-based strategies would require auditors focused on impacts for other stakeholders affected by corporate decisions.[163] This would probably require some form of counterfactual analysis "to avoid overclaiming positive outcomes and under-reporting negative outcomes." A host of technical decisions, then, would be required to determine the corporate law ramifications of various balance sheet impacts—notably with respect to how they affect capacity to make distributions.[164]

The most significant challenge, however, is also the most obvious—whether we can, in fact, meaningfully value the full range of environmental and social impacts of corporate production in monetary terms. If values are assigned in a manner that disregards "the relative preferences of those affected," then they will not provide a useful guide for corporate decision-making.[165] At the same time, the problem of netting noted earlier—the possibility that negatives in one area and positives in another might cancel each other out from an accounting perspective—further complicates corporate decision-makers' use of such accounts.[166] More fundamentally, however, there is reason to doubt that higher magnitude harms can be valued in monetary terms at all—the problem of incommensurability. The precautionary principle embraced in environmental science is fundamentally motivated by this insight—the core idea being that we should err on the side of caution, leaning toward preventive action, precisely where threats of harm are uncertain, meaning that stable probabilities cannot be assigned to potential outcomes, and incommensurate, meaning that potential harms cannot be measured by reference to the same scale as potential outcomes associated with another course of action.[167] Climate change exemplifies these conditions because scientific understanding of the range of potential outcomes is constantly evolving, and because the potentially catastrophic losses from climate change differ in kind from any gains that declining to mitigate climate change

[162] Nicholls, *supra* note 57, at 10.

[163] *See id.* at 13–14. *See also* Mähönen, *supra* note 100, at 27–30 (describing a proposal for robust auditing of EU sustainability disclosures issued by the Sustainable Market Actors for Responsible Trade [SMART] project).

[164] *See* Nicholls, *supra* note 57, at 17–20.

[165] *See id.* at 12.

[166] *See id. See also* SERAFEIM ET AL., *supra* note 131, at 11; Mähönen, *supra* note 100, at 8 ("In strong sustainability offset between capitals is not acceptable as critical natural capital cannot be replaced by other forms of capital. . . .").

[167] *See generally* Aldred, *supra* note 19. *See also supra* Chapter 6.A.

might offer (say, marginally greater near-term economic benefits).[168] These realities present fundamental problems for impact-weighted accounting because the most consequential harms likely are not amenable to monetary valuation at all. At the same time, values placed upon other corporate impacts may differ considerably depending upon idiosyncratic preferences of various stakeholders and the differing contextual realities they face.[169]

There is certainly value in exploring potential ways to quantify the full range of corporate impacts, and reason to believe that this might improve corporate decision-making to some degree, at least for certain types of corporate impacts in certain contexts. There is likewise reason to doubt, however, that accounting structures alone could comprehensively resolve problems related to corporate sustainability. Ultimately, we need to alter the incentives of various corporate actors in more fundamental ways, and this can be tackled more directly through structural reforms keyed to the various governance dynamics discussed earlier.[170] The remainder of the book explores ways to re-calibrate corporate governance, and to reorient it toward sustainability, through industry-based strategies as well as approaches applied across entire corporate governance systems.[171]

168 *See* Aldred, *supra* note 19, at 132, 136–38.
169 *See* Nicholls, *supra* note 57, at 12–13.
170 *See supra* Chapter 5.
171 *See infra* Chapter 7, Chapter 8.

7

Re-Calibrating Governance: Industry-by-Industry Approaches

Although widely described by reference to a fixed and rigid set of characteristics that are strongly associated with a dominant finance-driven paradigm, we have seen that the corporate form has historically exhibited great flux and dynamism; that corporate governance models in fact vary considerably around the world in response to persistent contextual drivers of difference; and that fundamental issues of power, purpose, and risk-taking remain contested.[1] In response, I have argued that the corporation is more accurately conceptualized as a flexible form of governance technology, and that renewed attention to the wide range of governance structures that it can accommodate would offer great potential to address persistent pathologies of corporate production and to re-calibrate corporate governance toward more sustainable models.[2]

It is increasingly recognized that vexing governance-related problems will require creative governance-related solutions,[3] and that this will in turn require capacity to think beyond the hidebound conceptions of the corporate form and corporate law that dominate contemporary corporate governance debates.[4] The remaining chapters of the book apply the foregoing insights toward that end. This chapter explores concrete examples—either adopted or proposed—in various industries, highlighting both the costs of the status quo and the potential benefits of revisiting prevailing approaches to corporate governance. These include the historical approach to constraining risk-taking in financial firms by adjusting upward the governance levers for board liability exposure and shareholder

[1] *See supra* Chapters 3–4.

[2] *See supra* Chapters 5–6.

[3] *See, e.g.*, RANA FOROOHAR, MAKERS AND TAKERS: THE RISE OF FINANCE AND THE FALL OF AMERICAN BUSINESS 315 (2016); KATE RAWORTH, DOUGHNUT ECONOMICS: SEVEN WAYS TO THINK LIKE A 21ST CENTURY ECONOMIST 197–98 (2017); Christopher M. Bruner, *Conceptions of Corporate Purpose in Post-Crisis Financial Firms*, 36 SEATTLE U. L. REV. 527, 560–61 (2013); David Gindis, *Conceptualizing the Business Corporation: Insights from History*, 16 J. INSTITUTIONAL ECON. 569, 574 (2020); Ron Harris, *A New Understanding of the History of Limited Liability: An Invitation for Theoretical Reframing*, 16 J. INSTITUTIONAL ECON. 643, 660–61 (2020); Colin Mayer, *Shareholderism versus Stakeholderism—A Misconceived Contradiction* 9–10 (ECGI Law Working Paper No. 522/2020), https://ssrn.com/abstract=3617847.

[4] *See* Christopher M. Bruner, *Corporate Governance Reform and the Sustainability Imperative*, 131 YALE L.J. (forthcoming 2022).

The Corporation as Technology. Christopher M. Bruner, Oxford University Press. © Christopher M. Bruner 2022.
DOI: 10.1093/oso/9780197635179.003.0007

financial firms	banks and other types of entities involved in provision of financial services
essential non-financial firms	other industries that raise similar concerns in terms of systemic risk and moral hazard
hazardous industries	industries involving a substantial risk that externalized costs will exceed a given firm's value

Figure 11 Industry-by-Industry Approaches

liability exposure, while adjusting downward the shareholder orientation lever—adjustments that impact other governance levers as well. The relevant history has been discussed earlier, and this chapter engages with creative proposals to revive such strategies in response to the excessive risk-taking that has come to characterize contemporary financial markets. In so doing, the analysis focuses particularly on design features of such proposals with an eye toward discerning lessons of broader application. The analysis then turns to forms of non-financial firms thought to raise similar systemic concerns, and other companies engaged in inherently hazardous industries where there is substantial risk of generating significant negative externalities—in each case including consideration of the degree to which regulatory rationales and design features explored in the context of financial firms might offer benefits in these additional industry settings as well. For convenience, the categories discussed are summarized in Figure 11.

A. Financial Firms

The most prominent governance-related effort to constrain risk-taking in financial firms took the form of multiple liability rules in the nineteenth and early twentieth centuries—rules that increased shareholders' personal liability exposure following bank failures for the benefit of depositors.[5] As Jonathan Macey and Geoffrey Miller explain, while a wide range of approaches emerged in the early nineteenth century, multiple liability rules became widespread in the United States starting in the 1860s. In the National Banking Act of 1863 (NBA), Congress provided that each shareholder in a national bank "shall be liable to the amount of the par value of the shares held by him, in addition to the amount invested in such shares"—an approach referred to as double liability.[6] By 1931, most states had adopted double liability provisions that "were closely modeled

[5] *See supra* Chapter 4.A, Chapter 4.B.iii.

[6] Jonathan R. Macey & Geoffrey P. Miller, *Double Liability of Bank Shareholders: History and Implications*, 27 WAKE FOREST L. REV. 31, 36 (1992)(quoting the statute).

on the [NBA]."[7] Shareholder liability in failed national banks was assessed pro rata, "without regard to whether the insolvency or absence of other shareholders would reduce the amounts recoverable by the receiver below the full amount of the creditors' claims," and "liability followed ownership"—although in cases where "the true owner of the stock was shown to be someone other than the record holder, the general rule was that both could be assessed at the discretion of the receiver."[8] At the same time, courts generally looked through holding company structures and ignored sham transactions aimed at avoiding the double liability regime.[9]

Other countries, meanwhile, adopted multiple liability regimes as well, including Australia, Canada, and the United Kingdom.[10] Unlimited liability for U.K. bank shareholders lasted well into the nineteenth century, because "well-established banks considered that by staying with the unlimited liability system," even after banks and insurers gained statutory capacity to limit shareholder liability in 1862, "they would inspire greater trust in their customers." As Charles Goodhart and Rosa Lastra explain, bank shareholders and depositors alike "believed that unlimited liability made for a more stable banking system because the liability of shareholders was an effective constraint on risk shifting and excessive risk-taking."[11] Following the 1878 failure of the City of Glasgow Bank, however, which ruined most of the bank's shareholders, legislation was enacted to permit multiple liability as a more measured alternative to entirely unlimited liability.[12]

As Macey and Miller recount, the extremity of U.S. bank failures from 1929 to 1933 "placed heavy strains on the double liability system and ultimately precipitated its downfall." These events triggered heavy assessments of retail bank shareholders who were already struggling, while at the same time suggesting that the double liability regime had "failed to fulfill its intended purpose" of preventing bank failures. At the same time, the newly created system of federal deposit insurance struck many as "a far more effective remedy for the problems of the banking system" moving forward.[13] Between the early 1930s and the early

[7] *Id.* at 37. *See also* DAVID A. MOSS, WHEN ALL ELSE FAILS: GOVERNMENT AS THE ULTIMATE RISK MANAGER 97–100, 115 (2002); Bruner, *supra* note 3, at 540, 546–47.

[8] *See* Macey & Miller, *supra* note 6, at 39–45.

[9] *See id.* at 45–48.

[10] *See generally* Lewis T. Evans & Neil C. Quigley, *Shareholder Liability Regimes, Principal-Agent Relationships, and Banking Industry Performance*, 38 J. L. & ECON. 497 (1995); John D. Turner, *"The Last Acre and Sixpence": Views on Bank Liability Regimes in Nineteenth-Century Britain*, 16 FIN. HIST. REV. 111 (2009). *See also* Charles A.E. Goodhart & Rosa M. Lastra, *Equity Finance: Matching Liability to Power*, 6 J. FIN. REG. 1, 32–38 (2020).

[11] Goodhart & Lastra, *supra* note 10, at 32–33.

[12] *See id.* at 33–38.

[13] Macey & Miller, *supra* note 6, at 37–38. *See also* Bruner, *supra* note 3, at 553–54; Steven L. Schwarcz, *The Governance Structure of Shadow Banking: Rethinking Assumptions about Limited Liability*, 90 NOTRE DAME L. REV. 1, 9 (2014).

1950s, federal and state governments gradually dismantled U.S. double liability rules,[14] and such regimes attenuated in other countries around the same time.[15] As of 1992, Macey and Miller reported that "double liability for bank shareholders is a dead letter everywhere."[16]

Double liability rules were expressly aimed at reducing risk-taking in the banking system,[17] and although enforcement proved challenging, this approach appears to have been more effective than accounts of its demise suggest. Macey and Miller have found that, from 1865 to 1934, "the overall level of shareholder compliance with assessment orders was relatively high," netting on average approximately 51 percent of the assessed amount under the U.S. federal regime, representing approximately 28 percent of losses by creditors of national banks during that period.[18] Meanwhile, risk incentives were improved, in that shareholders facing such liability were prompted to liquidate struggling banks to avoid insolvency,[19] and banks subject to double liability were able to maintain a lower ratio of capital to assets—presumably because creditors anticipated less risk-taking and, in any event, could look to shareholder assessments as an additional form of "equity cushion."[20] In this light, Macey and Miller argue that "double liability was a success," and that it was a mistake to abandon it for deposit insurance, which improves depositor confidence at the cost of substantial moral hazard, promoting risk and diminishing creditor monitoring.[21]

[14] *See* Macey & Miller, *supra* note 6, at 38–39.

[15] *See, e.g.*, Goodhart & Lastra, *supra* note 10, at 37–38 (observing that double liability "remained a feature of British banking until the mid-1950s," and that double liability in Canada was similarly "phased out between 1934–1950").

[16] Macey & Miller, *supra* note 6, at 39. This is not strictly true today, as double liability remains prevalent "in many (if not all) of the states of the former Soviet Union," although its retention in that context has been criticized for contributing to abuses at the hands of centralized authorities with insufficient legal checks on their power. *See generally* Andrii Zharikov, *Litigation Under Double Liability of Banks Regime: Case Study of Ukraine*, 29 INT'L COMPANY & COM. L. REV. 729 (2018).

[17] *See* MOSS, *supra* note 7, at 93; Goodhart & Lastra, *supra* note 10, at 29–30; Schwarcz, *supra* note 13, at 6.

[18] *See* Macey & Miller, *supra* note 6, at 55–57. *See also* Howell E. Jackson, *Losses from National Bank Failures during the Great Depression: A Response to Professors Macey and Miller*, 28 WAKE FOREST L. REV. 919, 921 (1993) (arguing that "losses imposed on depositors in national banks that failed during the 1930–34 period were much higher than those reported by Macey and Miller"); Jonathan R. Macey & Geoffrey P. Miller, *Double Liability of Bank Shareholders: A Look at the New Data*, 28 WAKE FOREST L. REV. 933, 937 (1993) (responding to Jackson that "the conclusion that *depositors would have been worse off without double liability* seems impossible to refute").

[19] *See* Macey & Miller, *supra* note 6, at 53–55, 57–58.

[20] *See id.* at 59–61.

[21] *See id.* at 32–35. *See also* Jonathan R. Macey & Maureen O'Hara, *The Corporate Governance of Banks*, 9 ECON. POL'Y REV. 91, 97–99 (2003); Patricia A. McCoy, *A Political Economy of the Business Judgment Rule in Banking: Implications for Corporate Law*, 47 CASE W. RES. L. REV. 1, 14–15 (1996); Schwarcz, *supra* note 13, at 9–11 (rejecting critiques focusing on inability to prevent Depression-era bank failures, as the "magnitude of the Great Depression . . . does not make it an appropriate test; its impact overwhelmed even many prudent banks").

In the context of investment banking, techniques for limiting risk-taking persisted decades longer. In that setting, however, risk reduction through liability exposure took the more extreme form of unlimited liability resulting from the predominant general partnership form of business organization. "Until the 1980s," as Claire Hill and Richard Painter explain, "most investment banks were general partnerships run by partners who were personally liable for debts of their firms," such that "if the business failed, the partner paid."[22] While operating in this form, partners were strongly incentivized to exercise great care in the admission of new partners and to limit risk-taking in the investment bank's business.[23]

Although not remotely the norm today, remnants of these historical liability structures still exist. For example, the oldest bank in the United Kingdom, C. Hoare & Co., "has been owned and directed by members of the Hoare family since it was founded by Richard Hoare in 1672."[24] The family owners, now in the eleventh generation, refer to themselves as "partners" and have unlimited liability,[25] although the bank is in fact a U.K. unlimited company—a form of company in which shareholders remain personally liable for corporate debts.[26] Their "principal activity" is "provision of banking and ancillary services to a predominantly high net worth customer base,"[27] and they attribute the bank's survival for 350 years to "its focus on customer service; the strength of its conservative balance sheet; and its unique ownership structure."[28] They report that "the balance sheet continues to reflect a tradition of prudence, with £1.2bn on deposit at the Bank of England" as of March 31, 2020. "Capital reserves remain robust," they add, "with the common equity tier 1 capital ratio at 21.5%,"[29] far exceeding the minimum capital requirement of 8 percent of total risk-weighted assets.[30]

Recall that in the archetypal public company today, limited liability for shareholders and various liability protections for boards of directors go hand in hand, in so far as limited liability leaves shareholders preferring more risk

[22] Claire Hill & Richard Painter, *Berle's Vision Beyond Shareholder Interests: Why Investment Bankers Should Have (Some) Personal Liability*, 33 SEATTLE U. L. REV., 1173, 1177 (2010).

[23] *See id.* at 1179–81. *See also* Bruner, *supra* note 3, at 541; Peter Conti-Brown, *Elective Shareholder Liability*, 64 STAN. L. REV. 409, 459–60 (2012); Schwarcz, *supra* note 13, at 12–13.

[24] C. Hoare & Co., *Our History*, https://www.hoaresbank.co.uk/our-history. As a point of reference, the Bank of England was founded over twenty years later, in 1694. Bank of England, *Our History*, https://www.bankofengland.co.uk/about/history (updated Jan. 22, 2021).

[25] C. HOARE & CO., ANNUAL REPORT AND CONSOLIDATED FINANCIAL STATEMENTS: YEAR ENDED 31 MARCH 2020, at 10, 16–17 (May 21, 2020). *See also* Goodhart & Lastra, *supra* note 10, at 22 & n.56.

[26] *See* C. HOARE & CO., *supra* note 25, at 10; Companies Act 2006, c. 46, § 3(4) (U.K.) ("If there is no limit on the liability of its members, the company is an 'unlimited company.'"). For background on U.K. unlimited companies, see Johnathan Korchak, *What Is an Unlimited Company?*, INFORM DIRECT, Aug. 30, 2017, https://www.informdirect.co.uk/company-formation/unlimited-company-what-is-it/.

[27] C. HOARE & CO., *supra* note 25, at 10.

[28] *Id.* at 1.

[29] *Id.*

[30] *See id.* at 14–15.

while protections against duty of care suits free up management to take the risks that shareholders prefer.[31] In this light, it is hardly surprising that, in the commercial banking context, where we historically sought to constrain risk-taking, enhanced liability exposure for shareholders would ultimately go hand in hand with enhanced liability exposure for directors. As Patricia McCoy recounts, business judgment rule protections for U.S. bank directors have long been reduced in order to limit risk-taking,[32] and judges began to show greater regard for depositors in the late nineteenth century.[33] By the 1890s the National Banking Act was interpreted to have "furnished a common-law standard of care" rooted in tort, and this approach would soon be taken with state banks as well—in some cases, focusing directly on depositor interests.[34] In the early 1930s, then, the same developments that effectively undercut multiple liability rules prompted greater reliance on the duty of care, with correlatively diminished business judgment rule protection, as a means of constraining risk-taking in banks. As McCoy explains, it was "when bank losses came to be shifted onto a party with political muscle—the federal government—that the business judgment rule in banking began to unravel."[35] The significance of these dynamics was vividly illustrated in the wake of widespread bank failures in the late 1980s, when "courts second-guessed financial institution decisions with respect to a new range of loan activities that had previously gone unquestioned."[36]

Recent decades have witnessed a sea change in the governance structure of banking, however, with substantial deregulation, growth in the scale and scope of financial firms, and an increasing tendency to conceptualize their governance as if they were any other form of for-profit business. Since the 1970s, regulations that had previously limited the size, geographic scope, and operations of commercial banks have been dismantled, enabling these entities to grow larger and considerably more complex, in turn fueling fierce competition and intense focus on stock prices in public markets. Investment banks, meanwhile, gradually abandoned the partnership form and became publicly traded companies themselves, with limited liability for shareholders prompting correlatively greater appetite for risk-taking. These streams of financialization came together through the 1999 Gramm-Leach-Bliley Act, which endorsed the emergence of financial holding companies engaged in both commercial and investment banking under one roof.[37] While heightened directors' duties may continue to apply in banks

[31] *See supra* Chapter 5.A.ii, Chapter 5.A.vii.
[32] *See* McCoy, *supra* note 21, at 12, 21–22. *See also* Bruner, *supra* note 3, at 536–40, 545–46; Macey & O'Hara, *supra* note 21, at 99–100.
[33] *See* McCoy, *supra* note 21, at 29–33.
[34] *See id.* at 35–39.
[35] *Id.* at 40–43.
[36] *See id.* at 48–55. *See also* Macey & O'Hara, *supra* note 21, at 100–01.
[37] *See* Bruner, *supra* note 3, at 549; Macey & O'Hara, *supra* note 21, at 96–97.

themselves, this does not mean that they will apply at the financial holding company level, where risk-management challenges and associated systemic concerns have become increasingly salient—particularly given the extraordinary size and complexity of the largest holding companies, which now have multi-trillion-dollar balance sheets.[38] In terms of oversight duties under Delaware corporate law, directors of these holding companies need only show that some sort of monitoring system was in place to escape personal liability for compliance failures—a very low standard of conduct indeed for the governance of institutions that occupy such a central position in the financial system and the broader economy.[39]

While there was historically little concerted empirical research in the area,[40] the global financial crisis brought substantially greater attention to corporate governance in financial firms. This is not the place for a dissection of the crisis.[41] For present purposes it will suffice to say that mortgage securitization—aimed principally at boosting profits and stock prices of U.S. and U.K. financial institutions—resulted in an extraordinary build-up of complex and highly interconnected risks on the balance sheets of large financial institutions, leaving them vulnerable following the collapse of the housing markets on which these paper structures were built and ultimately bringing debt and stock markets to their knees, with far-reaching systemic effects throughout the global economy.[42] Empirical studies following the crisis have tended to associate higher degrees of shareholder-centrism with greater risk-taking preceding the crisis and worse performance in its wake. For example, Rüdiger Fahlenbrach and René Stulz found evidence suggesting that "banks led by CEOs whose interests were better aligned with those of their shareholders had worse stock returns and a worse return on equity" during the crisis, and they suggest that a "plausible explanation for these findings is that CEOs focused on the interests of their shareholders in

[38] *See* Bruner, *supra* note 3, at 550. *See also* Federal Financial Institutions Examination Council, *Large Holding Companies*, https://www.ffiec.gov/npw/Institution/TopHoldings (updated Mar. 31, 2021).

[39] *See In re* Caremark Int'l Inc. Derivative Litig., 698 A.2d 959, 971 (Del. Ch. 1996); Stone v. Ritter, 911 A.2d 362, 369 (Del. 2006). *See also generally In re* Citigroup Inc. Shareholder Derivative Litig., 964 A.2d 106 (Del. Ch. 2009). *See also* Bruner, *supra* note 3, at 550–51 (describing case law in this area); Alessandro Romano et al., *Extended Shareholder Liability for Systemically Important Financial Institutions*, 69 AM. U. L. REV. 967, 981–82, 989–90 (2020) (observing the lack of a tort remedy for failure of a large financial institution); Schwarcz, *supra* note 13, at 21–22 (observing the same with shadow banking firms).

[40] *See* Bruner, *supra* note 3, at 552; Klaus J. Hopt, *Corporate Governance of Banks and Financial Institutions: Economic Theory, Supervisory Practice, Evidence and Policy*, 22 EUR. BUS. ORG. L. REV. 13, 16–17 (2021); Macey & O'Hara, *supra* note 21, at 91; McCoy, *supra* note 21, at 2.

[41] For a detailed overview, see generally ROBERT POZEN, TOO BIG TO SAVE? HOW TO FIX THE U.S. FINANCIAL SYSTEM (2010).

[42] *See* Christopher M. Bruner, *Corporate Governance Reform in a Time of Crisis*, 36 J. CORP. L. 309, 311–16 (2011).

the build-up to the crisis and took actions that they believed the market would welcome."[43] Andrea Beltratti and Stulz similarly found that "[b]anks with a shareholder-friendly board performed worse during the crisis," and suggest that "the most likely explanation is that shareholder-friendly boards positioned banks in ways that they believed maximized shareholder wealth, perhaps by taking advantage of implicit or explicit governmental guarantees, but left them more exposed to risks that manifested themselves during the crisis and had an adverse impact on banks." Stated another way, "shareholder-friendly boards created more value for shareholders through their decisions before the crisis, but during the crisis these decision were associated with poor outcomes."[44] Similarly, Renée Adams found that banks that received funds under the U.S. Troubled Asset Relief Program (TARP) exhibited a higher degree of board independence—typically regarded as a shareholder-friendly attribute—which may have left the board with insufficient expertise to monitor executives effectively and to appreciate the build-up of risk that was taking place.[45]

In light of such findings, one might have expected a re-examination of the sorts of governance structures associated with such risk-taking, and pursuit of post-crisis reforms departing from these highly shareholder-centric paradigms—yet the policy results were precisely the opposite. This was exemplified by the Dodd-Frank Act in the United States—which includes say-on-pay and golden parachute votes, enhanced compensation disclosures keyed to "financial performance," and authority for the Securities and Exchange Commission to enact a proxy access regime[46]—and by the push for shareholder "stewardship" in the United Kingdom, which calls upon shareholders to exert greater oversight yet provides no explanation of why one might expect risk-reduction efforts to be championed by the corporate constituency most desiring risk.[47] I have argued

[43] Rüdiger Fahlenbrach & René M. Stulz, *Bank CEOs and the Credit Crisis*, 99 J. FIN. ECON. 11, 12 (2011). *See also* Luc Laeven & Ross Levine, *Bank Governance, Regulation and Risk-Taking*, 93 J. FIN. ECON. 259, 273 (2009) (finding that "banks with more powerful owners tend to take greater risks").

[44] Andrea Beltratti & René M. Stulz, *The Credit Crisis Around the Globe: Why Did Some Banks Perform Better?*, 105 J. FIN. ECON. 1, 2 (2012).

[45] *See* Renée Birgit Adams, *Governance and the Financial Crisis*, 12 INT'L REV. FIN. 7, 32–36 (2012). On the trade-off between independence and expertise, see Christopher M. Bruner, *Corporate Governance Reform in Post-Crisis Financial Firms: Two Fundamental Tensions*, 60 ARIZ. L. REV. 959, 974–85 (2018); Hopt, *supra* note 40, at 25–26.

[46] *See* Dodd-Frank Wall Street Reform and Consumer Protection Act, H.R. 4173, 111th Cong. §§ 165(h), 951, 953, 956, 971 (2010). *See also* Adams, *supra* note 45, at 35; Bruner, *supra* note 45, at 976. On the inability of reforms in the Dodd-Frank Act to end bailouts, see Conti-Brown, *supra* note 23, at 417–25; Romano et al., *supra* note 39, at 974–78.

[47] *See* DAVID WALKER, A REVIEW OF CORPORATE GOVERNANCE IN U.K. BANKS AND OTHER FINANCIAL INDUSTRY ENTITIES: FINAL RECOMMENDATIONS 13, 25–27 (2009). *See also* FINANCIAL REPORTING COUNCIL, THE UK STEWARDSHIP CODE 2020 at 15 (2020) (urging signatories to "systematically integrate stewardship and investment," without explanation). For background on the stewardship movement, see Dionysia Katelouzou, *Shareholder Stewardship: A Case of (Re)Embedding the Institutional Investors and the Corporation?*, *in* THE CAMBRIDGE HANDBOOK OF CORPORATE LAW, CORPORATE GOVERNANCE AND SUSTAINABILITY 581 (Beate Sjåfjell & Christopher M. Bruner eds.,

elsewhere that this reflects a flawed crisis narrative, pinning the risk-taking that precipitated the crisis entirely on financial firm managers without inquiring more deeply into the ultimate sources of those incentives, coupled with widespread incapacity to think creatively about how governance structures might be re-calibrated to tackle such incentive structures at their ultimate sources.[48]

Intriguing reform proposals have been advanced, however, that focus on the governance-related dimensions of excessive risk-taking in financial firms, taking direct aim at related incentive structures through creative re-calibration of related levers of corporate governance. Hill and Painter, for example, have proposed requiring a "Joint Venture/Partnership Agreement" for certain entities and employees to reduce risk-taking in financial institutions. This regime would apply to "categories of companies for which it would be desirable, from a societal perspective, for highly paid executives to be personally responsible for company liabilities," minimally to include "most firms that are federally insured banks or bank holding companies; firms that originate, buy, or sell mortgages; firms registered as broker-dealers or investment advisors . . .; and at least the larger hedge funds." Employees covered would include those paid $3 million or more annually, "broadly defined to include, among other things, stock options and phantom stock." Personal liability related to a defined category of "financial risk" would be triggered only where the company itself could not meet its obligations—including upon "bankruptcy, receivership, and similar events"—but they would exempt up to "$1 million in personal assets that would not be subject to attachment" in order to limit overall liability exposure.[49] They further suggest that, alternatively or perhaps together with the foregoing, compensation above $1 million paid to any employee in covered companies might be limited to assessable stock—that is, stock assessable for its fair market value as of the date of issuance following similar triggering events, again with up to $1 million in personal assets remaining exempt.[50]

Peter Conti-Brown, observing that extant regulatory structures "privatize the benefits of bank behavior while socializing the costs,"[51] argues that we need either less risk-taking or more bank capital. Accordingly, he proposes an "elective shareholder liability" regime under which shareholders in systemically important financial institutions (SIFIs)[52] would "elect between shareholder liability in

2019); Iain MacNeil & Irene-marié Esser, *From a Financial to an Entity Model of ESG*, EUR. BUS. ORG. L. REV., at 22–24 (forthcoming 2021), https://ssrn.com/abstract=3834529.

48 *See generally* Bruner, *supra* note 3; Bruner, *supra* note 42. *Cf.* Conti-Brown, *supra* note 23, at 454–58 (arguing that shareholders have been overlooked in reform discussions because limited liability is treated like a "sacred cow").

49 Hill & Painter, *supra* note 22, at 1189–92.

50 *Id.* at 1192–95.

51 Conti-Brown, *supra* note 23, at 427.

52 *See id.* at 412–13.

the case of a bailout, or a fifteen to twenty-five percent capital adequacy requirement." Should they elect shareholder liability, then in the event of a bailout the government would issue an assessment on a pro rata basis, and would "have authority to declare efforts to evade liability through corporate ownership—using limited liability entities to own shares in non-limited liability SIFIs—null and void." Shareholders would also be liable for treble damages and litigation costs if they were to challenge the assessment and lose.[53] As with the historical double liability regime already discussed, one could expect recovery rates to be "far from perfect,"[54] but Conti-Brown emphasizes that the true aim is ex ante risk reduction and cost internalization,[55] and he argues that this could be achieved largely through familiar market mechanisms—even without substantial shareholder activism to pressure management to do so. Notably, publicly traded shares in SIFIs subject to this regime would presumably trade at a discount due to the risk of bailouts, for which those shares would be subject to assessment. This inherently "forces firm management to monitor risk, since the failure to do so would result in prohibitive equity costs." At the same time, derivatives markets might develop instruments providing a form of quasi-insurance against such liabilities, which would represent an additional market mechanism for monitoring associated risks.[56]

In a similar spirit, Steven Schwarcz argues that concerns regarding risk-taking and cost externalization also arise in the context of "shadow banking." This "refers to the decentralized provision of financing outside of traditional banking channels"—a category including special purpose entities used in securitization, as well as "finance companies, hedge funds, money market mutual funds, nonbank government-sponsored enterprises, securities lenders, and investment banks."[57] Schwarcz argues that such entities give rise to heightened concerns in so far as they "are often managed directly by their primary investors," who accordingly "have strong incentives to take risks that could generate large profits," and because they engage in bank-like activities but are not subjected to solvency and prudential regulations applicable to banks.[58] Much like Hill and Painter's approach, Schwarcz would impose liability on "investor-managers" in shadow banks in order to link liability with control (and to spare passive investors), while capping their overall exposure (e.g. through double liability) to balance risk reduction with promotion of investment.[59] He adds that "capital flight" could be

[53] *Id.* at 428–29. For additional background, see *id.* at 429–35.
[54] *Id.*at 434.
[55] *See id.* at 436.
[56] *See id.* at 436–40.
[57] Schwarcz, *supra* note 13, at 2.
[58] *See id.* at 17–22.
[59] *See id.* at 23–24, 29–30.

managed domestically through federal law, and internationally through cooperative cross-border efforts.[60]

Goodhart and Lastra similarly seek to distinguish bank and SIFI shareholders who can influence decision-making from those who cannot,[61] drawing "a distinction between a class of 'insiders', who should be subject to multiple liability, and 'outsiders', who would retain limited liability." The former would include directors, executives, and other "key" employees, identified by rank or salary, as well as large shareholders—although they could elect to be treated as outsiders if they "undertake not to exercise voting rights" or otherwise influence decision-making.[62] The "base to which the liability should apply would be the remuneration of all those counted as 'insiders' (dividends in the case of large inside shareholders), cumulated from the date that they took on that role," and such liability would be triggered "when loss or misconduct occurred, and not just in the event of insolvency and closure."[63] Like Conti-Brown, Goodhart and Lastra would give firms subject to this regime a choice between "the alternatives of much higher capital requirements, or adopting a two-tier equity system along the lines outlined." They would seek to limit "avoidance measures" by forcing any "large-scale operation" to operate through "a separately capitalized subsidiary, where the managers of that subsidiary would, in turn, be subject to multiple liability."[64]

Focusing on SIFI bailouts, as Conti-Brown does, Alessandro Romano, Luca Enriques, and Jonathan Macey propose an "extended shareholder liability" regime.[65] The key difference from the proposals described earlier is that liability exposure under their approach would be scaled based on the "centrality" of a given financial institution within the financial system. The idea is that the greater an institution's centrality, the greater the systemic externalities that the institution's failure could create—in which case there is greater need for shareholder liability exposure to incentivize effective risk management.[66] Essentially they would start with the institution's average stock price during a defined window prior to its failure, and then apply "a multiplier that reflects the risk that the individual SIFI imposes on the system," scaling shareholders' exposure up to a maximum of two times the average stock price. For this purpose, the institution's centrality—and hence the multiplier—would be defined by reference to "a network-based (normalized) indicator of the firm's systemic relevance, such as the DebtRank

[60] *See id.* at 25.
[61] *See* Goodhart & Lastra, *supra* note 10, at 1, 18.
[62] *Id.* at 13–14.
[63] *Id.* at 14–15.
[64] *Id.* at 22–23.
[65] *See* Romano et al., *supra* note 39, at 969–72.
[66] *See id.* at 979–80.

Score."[67] The resulting extended liability would apply pro rata and, similar to Conti-Brown's proposal, exposure could be reduced to the extent that the institution exceeded the minimum capital requirement. Romano, Enriques, and Macey similarly foresee the emergence of derivatives providing quasi-insurance against such exposure,[68] and would provide for veil piercing sufficient to cover shareholders' liability obligations to prevent end runs through strategic use of limited liability entities.[69]

While, as the foregoing suggests, proposals along these lines have mainly focused on shareholder liability, it is important to note that proposals have also been advanced to bolster the effectiveness of director liability as a constraint on risk-taking. McCoy, for example, has proposed a federal statutory negligence action against bank directors. Critically, the "business judgment rule would be eliminated as a defense to proven violations," and the claim would accrue "to the FDIC directly, rather than to the agency standing in a failed institution's shoes."[70] The claim would be limited to "losses caused by negligent, reckless, or knowing violations of state and federal rules and statutes on bank safety and soundness," improving consistency and deterrence through "code-based standards." At the same time, "banks would have a political opportunity to shape conduct standards through the notice-and-comment process and through legislation."[71]

Macey and Maureen O'Hara, in a similar spirit, argue that "directors of federally insured depository institutions should have a legal obligation to consider the impact of their decisions on the safety and soundness of the bank." They further call for heightened duties in the oversight context, arguing that directors should have "a continuing obligation to develop and maintain a detailed and elaborate system for monitoring and oversight," with no capacity for exculpation of liability in duty of care cases. Furthermore, Macey and O'Hara argue that "bank creditors (including the FDIC) should be able to sue bank directors for violations of the fiduciary duty of care and loyalty if they suffer losses . . . that are attributable to the violation of one of these fiduciary duties."[72]

It is not my aim to evaluate such proposals against one another here, so much as to evaluate them collectively against typical discourse in corporate law and

[67] *See id.* at 994–97. DebtRank is a measure "inspired by feedback centrality, that takes recursively into account the impact of the distress of an initial node across the whole network." The result "is a number measuring the fraction of the total economic value in the network that is potentially affected by the distress or the default of [an institution]," which can in turn "be used to construct a ranking." Stefano Battiston et al., *DebtRank: Too Central to Fail? Financial Networks, the FED and Systemic Risk*, SCI. REP., no. 541, 2012, at 1, 3. For additional background, see Stefano Battiston et al., *DebtRank and the Network of Leverage*, 20 J. PRIV. EQUITY 58 (2016).

[68] *See* Romano et al., *supra* note 39, at 998–1005.

[69] *See id.* at 1011.

[70] McCoy, *supra* note 21, at 61.

[71] *Id.* at 65–67.

[72] Macey & O'Hara, *supra* note 21, at 102–03.

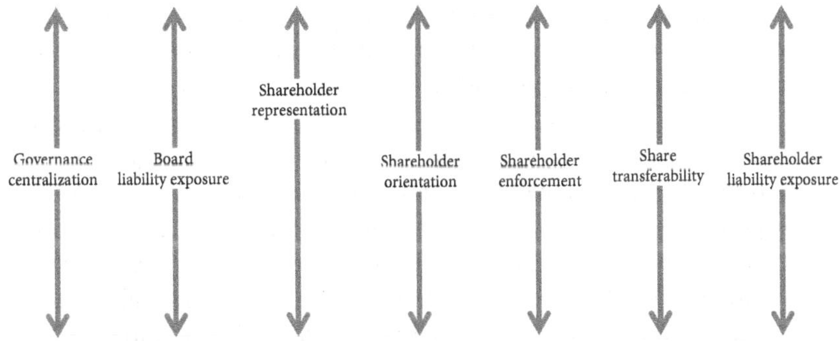

Figure 12 Financial Firm Reform Proposals

governance. What is most critical to observe of these proposals is the creative capacity that they exhibit regarding the role that corporate governance reform might play in responding to sustainability-related problems. Standing back from the foregoing, and considering what they represent in light of the mode of conceptualizing the corporation presented in prior chapters, we can see what a substantial impact these sorts of proposals would have on the overall calibration of the various governance levers that the corporate form embodies. Recall that the archetypal public company that now prevails in the United States—and, to varying degrees, in other financially driven markets—generally involves strong boards elected by shareholders; greater emphasis on generating financial returns for shareholders, who enjoy substantial capacity to further prioritize their own interests through shareholder lawsuits; a high degree of investment liquidity for shareholders; and limited liability exposure for boards and shareholders alike. In sharp contrast with this calibration, robust adoption of reforms along the foregoing lines would amount to significant re-calibration of various governance levers. As Figure 12 reflects, increasing board and shareholder liability exposure and extending duties to depositors would reduce governance centralization, due to enhanced shareholder monitoring; reduce shareholder orientation, due to enhanced prioritization of depositors, a category of creditors; reduce shareholder enforcement, because another stakeholder group (e.g. depositors or the government itself, as backstop of the banking system) could advance their own interests through assessment actions or related litigation; and reduce share transferability, because shareholders' exposure would prompt discounting—a systemic benefit, to the extent that it counteracts overinvestment and forces firms to internalize costs.[73] To be sure, different combinations of reforms selected from the menu of options that the foregoing proposals present would result in

[73] *See supra* Chapter 1, Chapter 5.B.

differing re-calibrations along these lines, but in any case the divergence from the status quo would be substantial, and would tend to have an overall moderating effect relative to the archetypal U.S. public company.

To be sure, any proposal that involves increasing liability exposure for shareholders and/or boards of directors, in particular, will encounter a host of generic responses. For example, those who object to increasing shareholders' liability exposure often argue that doing so would impose potentially bankrupting liability upon innocent shareholders who lack capacity to monitor effectively, result in equity investment drying up, and involve great practical difficulties in defining the reach of such a regime.[74] Likewise, those who object to increasing directors' liability exposure typically assume that debilitating risk aversion would result for a few reasons. First, directors holding a small percentage of the company's stock lack the shareholders' strong-form incentive to take big, and hopefully profitable, business risks in the first place; second, the scale of corporate operations and the correlative costs of a potential business decision gone awry could result in bankrupting liabilities; and third, hindsight bias might lead courts to see negligence, or worse, simply because a business decision that was in fact reasonable at the time it was taken happened not to pan out.[75]

There are important features to observe about such proposals that render them considerably more moderate, however, than such generic objections suggest. First, and most significantly, these are not all-or-nothing propositions. There is in fact substantial capacity for fine-grained calibration of degrees of liability exposure—for example, keying liability exposure to a multiple of stock investment, specifying another form of liability cap, and/or providing asset exemptions.[76] Second, while such regimes might apply to all shareholders in a given institution, they need not do so—for example, the regime might apply solely to those in a position to control the institution or influence its governance.[77] Third, they might apply to a broader or narrower range of entities—for example, banks, SIFIs, shadow banks, and/or other forms of market actors.[78] Fourth, the fundamental aim being to deter excessive risk-taking and promote ex ante cost internalization, it is certainly not fatal to such proposals that they are unlikely to achieve perfect

[74] *See, e.g.*, Romano et al., *supra* note 39, at 1008 (summarizing such objections).

[75] For discussion of such objections, see Christopher M. Bruner, *Good Faith, State of Mind, and the Outer Boundaries of Director Liability in Corporate Law*, 41 WAKE FOREST L. REV. 1131, 1137–47 (2006); Christopher M. Bruner, *Is the Corporate Director's Duty of Care a "Fiduciary" Duty? Does It Matter?*, 48 WAKE FOREST L. REV. 1027, 1039–45 (2013).

[76] *See, e.g.*, Hill & Painter, *supra* note 22, at 1191; Romano et al., *supra* note 39, at 984; Schwarcz, *supra* note 13, at 23, 29.

[77] *See, e.g.*, Goodhart & Lastra, *supra* note 10, at 13–14; Hill & Painter, *supra* note 22, at 1190; Schwarcz, *supra* note 13, at 24.

[78] *See, e.g.*, Conti-Brown, *supra* note 23, at 412–13; Goodhart & Lastra, *supra* note 10, at 1; Hill & Painter, *supra* note 22, at 1189–90; Romano et al., *supra* note 39, at 969, 974; Schwarcz, *supra* note 13, at 2.

compensation following an institution's failure.[79] Fifth, such proposals can work in tandem with other strategies and regulatory regimes—for example, they might be presented as alternatives, permitting institutions to avoid increased liability exposure by electing to comply with higher capital requirements instead.[80] Finally, sixth, such proposals might reinforce other regimes that similarly aim to correct flawed incentives—for example, approaches focusing on the design of executive pay packages in financial institutions.[81] Accordingly, it is not a significant objection that any single reform strategy could not resolve every problem on its own.

B. Essential Non-Financial Firms

There are compelling reasons to take seriously proposals like those discussed earlier, each of which fundamentally advocates a re-calibration of governance levers of the corporate form—but this prompts a further question. Is there really any intrinsic reason why such re-calibration of corporate governance levers would prove beneficial solely in financial firms?

It is a common refrain in the literature that banks are "special" due to their "liquidity production function," uniquely legitimating deviations from the archetypal model for public company governance. Notably, peculiarities of their business models and balance sheets are said to render banks particularly unstable, requiring a higher degree of prudence in their management.[82] The fundamental aims of proposals like those discussed earlier, however—which focus on reducing risk-taking and forcing internalization of costs—are not limited to the banking context. Indeed, as we have seen, these proposals themselves would reach well beyond banks to include a range of other types of entities involved in the broader financial system.[83] As McCoy argues, "it is wrong to treat the banking precedents as special," because the core problem "goes much deeper and is based on general principles of corporate capital structure."[84] Minimally, McCoy suggests that "other firms or industries with capital structures similar

[79] *See, e.g.*, Conti-Brown, *supra* note 23, at 434, 465; Goodhart & Lastra, *supra* note 10, at 24; Hill & Painter, *supra* note 22, at 1189; Romano et al., *supra* note 39, at 993.

[80] *See, e.g.*, Conti-Brown, *supra* note 23, at 429–31; Goodhart & Lastra, *supra* note 10, at 23.

[81] *See, e.g.*, Bruner, *supra* note 3, at 561 n.136; Goodhart & Lastra, *supra* note 10, at 11, 25–26; McCoy, *supra* note 21, at 76–77. On the significance of compensation structures, see generally Lucian A. Bebchuk & Holger Spamann, *Regulating Bankers' Pay*, 98 GEO. L.J. 247 (2010); Frederick Tung, *Pay for Banker Performance: Structuring Executive Compensation for Risk Regulation*, 105 NW. U. L. REV. 1205 (2011).

[82] *See* Macey & O'Hara, *supra* note 21, at 94–99. *See also* Hopt, *supra* note 40, at 15–16; McCoy, *supra* note 21, at 67.

[83] *See, e.g.*, Hill & Painter, *supra* note 22, at 1189–90; Schwarcz, *supra* note 13, at 2.

[84] McCoy, *supra* note 21, at 68.

to those in banking," such as insurance and investment management, might benefit from similar board liability structures.[85] Goodhart and Lastra, for their part, suggest that the expanded liability for SIFI "insiders" that they advocate—including both managers and certain shareholders—might ultimately "be extended, to other financial institutions, such as insurance undertakings, and also to FinTech companies." Indeed, they even suggest that it might "be applied to all public corporations."[86] The remainder of this chapter takes up these suggestions, considering additional industry and market settings where re-calibrating the levers of corporate governance, along the lines described earlier, might offer similar benefits.

It is well recognized that there are substantial interlinkages between banks and other types of entities that engage in, or support, financial services more generally. For example, the Financial Stability Oversight Council (FSOC)—created by the Dodd-Frank Act to provide more holistic oversight of the highly fragmented U.S. financial system, and particularly to limit systemic risks[87]—can subject a non-bank financial company to supervision by the Federal Reserve. This authority was exercised in the cases of American International Group, General Electric Capital Corporation, Prudential Financial, and MetLife. FSOC can also designate a financial market utility as "systemically important," similarly imposing heightened regulation—authority exercised in the cases of the Depository Trust Company, the Chicago Mercantile Exchange, the Clearing House Payments Company, and others.[88] Given existing statutory recognition of these sorts of interlinkages, and the risks that various forms of non-bank entities can impose on the financial system as a whole, extension of the sorts of proposals discussed earlier to these categories of entities would appear straightforward.

It is important to recognize at the same time, however, that the sorts of dynamics ascribed to banks and other types of entities directly involved in the financial system that purportedly render such entities "special" in fact arise in a broader range of industries. As McCoy presciently observed in 1996, "corporate America in general" was coming to resemble the banking industry in pertinent respects, including "increased leveraging of American companies"—which renders shareholders' preference for risk-taking "a heightened risk in the general corporate context." She added that, to the degree "these economic problems cut

[85] *See id.* at 76–77. *See also* Hopt, *supra* note 40, at 20–21 (observing that the "interplay between stock corporation law, bank supervisory law and insurance supervisory law in corporate governance is considered more rarely," and that "[c]orporate governance of banks may even pave the way to a self-contained law covering financial intermediaries and their corporate governance" in Europe).

[86] Goodhart & Lastra, *supra* note 10, at 23.

[87] *See* U.S. Department of the Treasury, *About FSOC*, https://home.treasury.gov/policy-issues/financial-markets-financial-institutions-and-fiscal-service/fsoc/about-fsoc.

[88] U.S. Department of the Treasury, *Designations*, https://home.treasury.gov/policy-issues/financial-markets-financial-institutions-and-fiscal-service/fsoc/designations.

across most industries, it is a serious mistake to dismiss the banking cases as aberrant."[89]

Today, we see these dynamics vividly displayed in the marketplace, and they have taken on heightened salience in the wake of the COVID-19 pandemic. Many companies found themselves struggling due to generalized deterioration of the economy following widespread shutdowns. As Kathryn Judge observes, however, the "decision by so many large corporations to take on so much debt in recent years did not cause COVID-19, but it did reduce the capacity of the corporate sector to weather this storm."[90] Specifically, large public companies have taken on extraordinary levels of debt in order to engage in stock buybacks for the benefit of shareholders, contributing to "record-breaking levels of nonfinancial corporate debt" that represents "a potential source of systemic risk." The prospect of bailouts "to protect productive enterprises and their employees" in turn creates moral hazard dynamics closely resembling those in banking. In this light, Judge suggests that U.S. government support be directed to small and medium-sized businesses, leaving large public companies to the Chapter 11 bankruptcy process.[91]

To a great extent, the challenge with circumstances like these is simply that there are so many companies struggling at once, but the matter becomes considerably more acute with companies that are essential to the provision of an important service or the performance of the economy more generally. Boeing, for example, may represent "the most prominent example of corporate financial engineering failure," having "spent $43.4B on share buybacks over the last six years," and having "aggressively hiked its dividend with a 5-year growth rate of 23%."[92] Following the onset of the pandemic, then, the airplane manufacturer found itself facing substantially lower demand for its planes and a consequent "liquidity crisis."[93] Some have suggested letting even such important companies fail in order to promote "more prudent capital allocation." As Stefan Redlich observes, such companies "deliberately opted not to save some cash for rainy days, or in this case a tsunami," and accordingly he argues that they should not be bailed out after the fact.[94]

This is easier said than done, however, with companies that provide essential services or are highly significant to the economy as a whole. For example,

[89] McCoy, *supra* note 21, at 69.

[90] Kathryn Judge, *The Truth about the COVID-19 Bailouts*, FORBES, Apr. 15, 2020, https://www.forbes.com/sites/kathrynjudge/2020/04/15/the-covid-19-bailouts/.

[91] *See id.*

[92] *Id.*

[93] Stefan Redlich, *This Time It Is "Too Many to Fail" Rather Than "Too Big to Fail,"* SEEKING ALPHA, Mar. 20, 2020, https://seekingalpha.com/article/4333214-this-time-is-too-many-to-fail-rather-too-big-to-fail.

[94] *Id.*

U.S. airlines have become very concentrated through mergers, and have been very profitable over the last decade, but they have "spent 96 percent of their cash profits on stock buybacks to enrich investors and their own executives," leaving them with insufficient cash on hand following the onset of the pandemic.[95] The moral hazard dilemma is obvious, because "America won't let the airlines fail, and the people who run the airlines know it." As Henry Grabar observes, the "mergers that helped the companies throw off such big profits have left us with corporations so fundamental to American life they are basically utilities." The simple reality is that "letting the planes go down would put nearly a million people out of work and deprive the country of nearly all its long-distance travel infrastructure."[96]

So, what are the alternatives in response to moral hazard dilemmas involving such companies, where the government cannot credibly commit to refraining from bailouts? Tellingly, Grabar advocates responses that resonate with proposals contemplated in the banking context—force the companies in question either to reform their governance to eliminate excessively risky, shareholder-driven practices of this sort, or force them to hold more cash on hand as a downside buffer. "The question for Congress," Grabar writes, "is not whether to save the airlines—but how to redraw corporate governance to fix its bad incentives," including conditioning bailout funds to maintain services and employment rather than enriching shareholders and executives. At the same time, the "central condition of any assistance has got to require airlines [to] keep their profits in the bank for the next time this happens (as was required for automakers after the 2008 crash—Ford has $37 billion in reserve)."[97]

It is well established in the economics literature that moral hazard can be expected to arise in any social or market context where people can expect the government to step in with a bailout after the fact,[98] and circumstances like the foregoing vividly illustrate that banks are not unique in this respect. In this light, Oscar Couwenberg and Stephen Lubben focus on "real economy" companies that are regarded as "too big to fail"—notably "national champions" that are "of substantial size relative to the local economy"—and argue that we need similar responses in those contexts because the problems of moral hazard and excessive risk are exactly the same.[99] While in "an ideal world, the kind of world

[95] Henry Grabar, *Why Do the Airlines Need a Bailout?*, SLATE, Mar. 17, 2020, https://slate.com/business/2020/03/airlines-bailout-coronavirus.html.

[96] *Id.*

[97] *Id. See also* Jesse Hamilton, *Fed Extends Dividend, Buyback Cap on Wall Street Banks*, BLOOMBERG L. NEWS, Oct. 1, 2020 (describing "constraints on dividend payments and share buybacks for the biggest U.S. banks").

[98] *See generally* Louis Kaplow, *Incentives and Government Relief for Risk*, 4 J. RISK & UNCERTAINTY 167 (1991).

[99] *See* Oscar Couwenberg & Stephen J. Lubben, *Not a Bank, Not a SIFI; Still Too Big to Fail*, 35 EMORY BANKR. DEV. J. 53, 53–58 (2019). For discussion of historical examples, see *id.* at 58–70.

most academic theories inhabit, all cases would be resolved under the traditional bankruptcy process" to preclude implicit subsidies of such firms, "the political costs" often prove too great.[100] To resolve such moral hazard problems, some means of ensuring that losses fall on shareholders rather than taxpayers must be found, and in light of the political realities surrounding failure of "national champion" non-financial firms that are too big to fail, they suggest as a "second best" the use of normal bankruptcy procedures, "with the government stepping in to provide for any gaps in the funding market"—notably if "the lending markets are severely disrupted," or "the broader economy is in distress, such that all potential asset buyers are apt to leave the market for the debtor's assets."[101]

Couwenberg and Lubben's analysis is highly suggestive in emphasizing that issues of moral hazard and excessive risk often associated with financial firms in fact arise with many non-financial firms as well. Indeed, bailouts for major automakers following the financial crisis provide a vivid example.[102] This leads Shlomit Azgad-Tromer to focus more intently on what she calls "socially important non-financial institutions," or SINFIs—"corporations positioned as monopolies providing essential social functions, typically situational monopolies of an essential industry, or major employers positioned as exclusive employers due to geographical or social circumstances." While banks "are essential because they perform necessary monetary services and provide credit," SINFIs may likewise be essential because they "fill key societal roles by supplying public utilities, providing public transportation, or running major hospitals."[103]

Such circumstances tend to arise, Azgad-Tromer observes, in markets where "we would expect consumers to purchase as a social moral baseline"; where there are "insufficient substitutes for their goods," creating a captive market; and where purchases are "constrained in time and are unlikely to be deferred." Although these categories may prove blurry at the margin, she adds that subsidies and price regulation serve as helpful proxies because they "signal the state's interest in making the subsidized service or product accessible to consumers, suggesting that policymakers consider the industry politically essential."[104] In such industries, we can reasonably expect substantial moral hazard to arise because, "like the too-big-to-fail SIFIs, the too-important-to-fail SINFIs impose social costs driven by the implied subsidy." Just like in the financial context, then, we can expect that in such industries the "probability of rescue . . . distorts the

[100] *Id.* at 74.

[101] *Id.* at 75–76.

[102] *See* CHRISTOPHER M. BRUNER, CORPORATE GOVERNANCE IN THE COMMON-LAW WORLD: THE POLITICAL FOUNDATIONS OF SHAREHOLDER POWER 283–85 (2013); Couwenberg & Lubben, *supra* note 99, at 67–68; Shlomit Azgad-Tromer, *Too Important to Fail: Bankruptcy versus Bailout of Socially Important Non-Financial Institutions*, 7 HARV. BUS. L. REV. 159, 168 (2017).

[103] Azgad-Tromer, *supra* note 102, at 161–62. *See also id.* at 164–69.

[104] *Id.* at 169–71.

organizational incentives of the SINFI's management well before failure occurs, increasing the taste for leverage and excessive risk taking."[105]

When failure of such an entity occurs, bailouts would appear unavoidable because private investors would not be able to capture the full value of positive externalities that effectively represent public goods—meaning that the traditional bankruptcy approach to their resolution would lead to insufficient investment and "a suboptimal equilibrium."[106] In response, Azgad-Tromer rightly focuses on the corporate governance-related sources of these problems among SINFIs, which are not materially different from those already considered in the context of financial institutions, and which produce similar problems—notably excessive leverage and risk-taking.[107] Consequently, such companies are prime candidates for precisely the sorts of corporate governance reforms already described, according to rationales and strategies that match very closely those explored in the context of financial institutions. This includes potential to work in tandem with other regulatory strategies that are typically directed at these industries due to their intrinsic public significance and the sorts of associated market constraints described earlier.[108]

C. Hazardous Industries

The foregoing discussion of essential non-financial firms, and the potential for beneficial re-calibrations of the levers of corporate governance in that context, has already suggested that banks are not in fact so special in this regard as they are often said to be. In a sense, a convergence of sorts is reflected in the increasing tendency over recent decades to approach the governance of financial firms as if they were any other form of public company.[109] As I have argued, however, we would likely have been better off if we had done exactly the opposite—taking historical governance structures in banking as a starting point to explore ways to curb pathologies associated with financialization, excessive risk, and cost externalization in a wider array of industry settings.

Apart from financial firms and other categories of essential firms where similar systemic risk concerns and moral hazard dilemmas arise, another category of companies where re-calibrating the levers of corporate governance could prove beneficial would be those engaged in industries that are inherently hazardous. In

[105] *Id.* at 163–64.
[106] *See id.* at 177–79.
[107] *See id.* at 181–82.
[108] *See supra* notes 80–81 and accompanying text (regarding such regulatory interactions in the financial context); notes 103–05 and accompanying text (regarding such regulatory interactions in the non-financial context).
[109] *See supra* Chapter 7.A.

a 1991 law review article widely regarded as the first in "the modern debate" to challenge limited liability generally,[110] Henry Hansmann and Reinier Kraakman called for greater shareholder liability exposure in the tort context. Observing that because limited liability "permits cost externalization, a corporation engaged in highly risky activities can have positive value for its shareholders, and thus can be an attractive investment, even when its net present value to society as a whole is negative." Accordingly, limited liability "encourages excessive entry and aggregate overinvestment in unusually hazardous industries,"[111] as well as "widespread reorganization of business firms to exploit limited liability to evade damage claims"—notably by "placing hazardous activities in separate subsidiaries."[112] Citing the U.K. and U.S. historical experiences with various shareholder liability regimes[113]—as well as the widely accepted normative position that limited liability is less compelling as applied to "involuntary creditors" in tort, who were afforded no ex ante opportunity to assess and negotiate their risk exposures[114]—Hansmann and Kraakman propose "a regime of unlimited pro rata shareholder liability for corporate torts"[115] that would apply to "any tort claim to which the state's tort law applies, regardless of the state of incorporation of the corporate defendant."[116]

The pro rata approach, Hansmann and Kraakman argue, would provide some insulation for passive shareholders in large public companies and preserve the viability of liquid trading markets.[117] Those concerned about such exposure could diversify[118] and take advantage of the insurance market for such risks that they predict would arise.[119] Meanwhile, society would benefit through greater board-level monitoring of risk with an eye toward bolstering stock price[120]—although Hansmann and Kraakman are not inclined to take the further step of augmenting directors' liability exposure as an additional means of reducing risk-taking.[121] As to administration, a modified "claims-made" rule, attaching liability to "persons who are shareholders when—or somewhat before—the tort claim is filed," would

[110] Romano et al., *supra* note 39, at 981.

[111] Henry Hansmann & Reinier Kraakman, *Toward Unlimited Shareholder Liability for Corporate Torts*, 100 YALE L.J. 1879, 1883 (1991).

[112] *Id.* at 1881. *See also id.* at 1925–26.

[113] *See id.* at 1924–25.

[114] *See id.* at 1919–21. The point is generally acknowledged by scholars in the law and economics tradition otherwise favorably disposed toward robust limited liability. *See, e.g.*, FRANK H. EASTERBROOK & DANIEL R. FISCHEL, THE ECONOMIC STRUCTURE OF CORPORATE LAW 58–59 (1991); Frank H. Easterbrook & Daniel R. Fischel, *Limited Liability and the Corporation*, 52 U. CHI. L. REV. 89, 112 (1985).

[115] Hansmann & Kraakman, *supra* note 111, at 1880.

[116] *Id.* at 1922.

[117] *See id.* at 1894–95.

[118] *See id.* at 1905.

[119] *See id.* at 1899–1901, 1926.

[120] *See id.* at 1907–09.

[121] *See id.* at 1928–29.

prevent evasion and would arguably be no more complicated to administer than typical bankruptcy collections.[122] While collections under such a regime might not be complete, they could plausibly be sufficient to "force public corporations to bear the bulk of their expected liability costs" and to "make share prices reflect tort costs."[123] If some companies were unable to finance their operations under such a regime, then so much the better, as there would be "no reason to suppose that unlimited liability would discourage shareholder investment except in firms that . . . impose net costs on society."[124]

As we saw in the context of financial firms, there is ample capacity to fine-tune such proposals in terms of the degree of liability exposure, categories of shareholders exposed, and categories of firms to which such a regime might apply.[125] In this spirit, Nina Mendelson similarly focuses on shareholder liability for corporate torts, but focuses intently on those circumstances in which a corporation is dominated by a controller. Mendelson similarly observes historical flexibility regarding shareholder liability regimes;[126] increasing use of subsidiaries and corporate group structures to cordon off risky activities and shield assets;[127] growing potential for excessive risk-taking and externalization of costs, particularly through "defective products, toxic substances, and environmental injuries";[128] and inability of extant structures "to blunt the effect of limited liability's moral hazard."[129] At the same time, however, she emphasizes the growing concentration of share ownership in the hands of institutions[130] and the differing postures that minority and controlling shareholders inhabit. While "efficiency-based justifications" for limited liability might have some force as applied to a "less wealthy individual shareholder holding a tiny fraction of corporate equity," they are considerably weaker "when the shareholder is a corporation or institution, is relatively wealthy, or is in a position to control the corporation"—because the latter categories of shareholders likely have better access to corporate information, can better monitor corporate decision-making, and

[122] *See id.* at 1896–1901. *See also id.* at 1926 (observing that collecting from shareholders would be easier than in earlier times due to "procedural reforms, improved communications, and improved record-keeping"). They would further seek to prevent evasion by "denying the right to conduct certain types of business within the United States to any firm incorporated in a nation that refuses to recognize unlimited liability for corporate torts, or requiring the posting of bond or proof of adequate insurance for potential tort damages by such a corporation before it can conduct business." *Id.* at 1922–23.

[123] *Id.* at 1901–03.

[124] *Id.* at 1933.

[125] *See supra* Chapter 7.A.

[126] *See* Nina A. Mendelson, *A Control-Based Approach to Shareholder Liability for Corporate Torts*, 102 COLUM. L. REV. 1203, 1209–11 (2002).

[127] *See id.* at 1204–05, 1246.

[128] *See id.* at 1235–47.

[129] *See id.* at 1259–71.

[130] *See id.* at 1215–17, 1227–32.

are better positioned to bear risk.[131] Indeed, the problem of excessive risk-taking may well loom larger where there is a controlling shareholder in a position to extract greater benefits from the controlled corporation and capable (by definition) of enforcing its preferences.[132] In contrast with Hansmann and Kraakman's preferred approach of holding all shareholders pro rata liable for corporate torts, then, Mendelson advocates holding only controllers liable (with an occurrence-based rule),[133] akin to some of the proposals in the financial firm context that focus on control and managerial relationships.[134] While ascertaining control could raise thorny factual issues,[135] Mendelson concludes that this approach would still likely prove more efficient overall, because it would reduce litigation costs and incentivize controllers to push for adequate insurance and/or capitalization, and more generally to monitor corporate risk-taking.[136]

Others have suggested approaches that would expand shareholder liability while effectively capping it—again resembling proposals discussed earlier in the financial firm context[137]—while introducing scaling features that might differentiate among categories of firms based on the degree of concern they raise regarding risk-taking and cost externalization. Robert Rhee acknowledges that limited liability is particularly problematic in the tort context, that it may lead to excessive risk-taking and cost externalization,[138] and that promoting internalization of the full costs of corporate activity is normatively desirable,[139] yet he observes that dynamics of charter competition may render it less likely that limited liability would be substantially curtailed in a generalized way.[140] Accordingly, Rhee holds the basic structure constant as a political matter and advocates what he terms "bonded limited liability," effectively creating "a risk retention arrangement akin to group self-insurance against excess liability" for the benefit of "third-party tort creditors."[141] For the sake of administrability and political feasibility, Rhee proposes that private companies pay a small bond on the order of $2,000, and that public companies pay something on the order of

[131] *See id.* at 1219–27.

[132] *See id.* at 1247–58. This dynamic is likewise generally acknowledged by scholars in the law and economics tradition. *See, e.g.*, EASTERBROOK & FISCHEL, *supra* note 114, at 56–57; Easterbrook & Fischel, *supra* note 114, at 110–11.

[133] *See* Mendelson, *supra* note 126, at 1271–79.

[134] *See, e.g.*, Goodhart & Lastra, *supra* note 10, at 13–14; Hill & Painter, *supra* note 22, at 1190; Schwarcz, *supra* note 13, at 24.

[135] *See* Mendelson, *supra* note 126, at 1272–78. Hansmann and Kraakman identify resulting evasion concerns as a point in favor of their more embracing proposal. *See* Hansmann & Kraakman, *supra* note 111, at 1931–32.

[136] *See* Mendelson, *supra* note 126, at 1285–96.

[137] *See, e.g.*, Hill & Painter, *supra* note 22, at 1191; Romano et al., *supra* note 39, at 984; Schwarcz, *supra* note 13, at 23, 29.

[138] *See* Robert J. Rhee, *Bonding Limited Liability*, 51 WM. & MARY L. REV. 1417, 1423–35 (2010).

[139] *See id.* at 1446–50.

[140] *See id.* at 1437–40.

[141] *See id.* at 1450–63.

"50 basis points of the average market capitalization of a defined period," which would amount to a modest amount for most public companies.[142] The resulting fund would be available solely to "tort plaintiffs who prevailed on the merits" in actions filed prior to insolvency, without punitive damages, and subject to limitations periods.[143] The regime would be managed at the state level for private companies and at the federal level for public companies,[144] and the bond would be forfeited upon insolvency but redeemable "upon dissolution without an unmet liability claim."[145] Rhee acknowledges that bonded limited liability would be "less onerous on companies than a rule of pro rata unlimited liability,"[146] and accordingly might prove insufficient to address mass torts,[147] pointing to the straightforward trade-off between the rigors of the system and the robustness of resulting incentive effects.

The foregoing would effectively require companies to purchase limited liability protection (by contributing to a compensation fund), and the prices for public companies would be scaled by size, reflected in market capitalization[148]—which essentially functions as a rough proxy for predilection toward risk-taking and cost externalization under Rhee's proposal. This prompts the question of whether prices could feasibly be calibrated more precisely and, from this perspective, Michael Simkovic conceptualizes limited liability as "mispriced insurance" for corporate risk-taking.[149] While private insurance typically is "not readily available for unknown or unknowable risks" of the sort that give rise to the greatest concerns in the corporate context,[150] a public regime could be structured to elicit internal corporate risk estimates through what Simkovic styles as a "limited liability tax." While it may be difficult to know the correct initial price to charge for limited liability, he observes that as long as the pricing process is "iterative" in nature, this difficulty could be overcome in time. "When limited liability comes at a cost," he explains, "those who believe that they are engaged in riskier activities will be more likely to opt into limited liability, while those who believe their actions are comparatively benign will be more likely to forego it," effectively revealing private risk estimates that regulators could use "to more closely study and eventually regulate or insure high-risk activities." Indeed, this might even lead to industry-based pricing, imposing a higher tax on particularly

[142] *Id.* at 1463–66.
[143] *See id.* at 1475–77.
[144] *See id.* at 1474.
[145] *Id.* at 1478.
[146] *Id.* at 1465.
[147] *See id.* at 1471.
[148] *See id.* at 1463–66.
[149] *See* Michael Simkovic, *Limited Liability and the Known Unknown*, 68 DUKE L.J. 275, 288–89 (2018).
[150] *See id.* at 309–11.

hazardous industries following an iterative "optimization process."[151] Initially, limited liability might be priced at around 4 to 5 percent of the greater of revenue or cost, reflecting the "size of economic activity," and then adjusted moving forward as "risk-uniform" groups emerged. This might culminate in industry-specific pricing of limited liability keyed to commonly used taxonomies, such as the North American Industry Classification System (NAICS).[152] While some businesses might decline to pay the tax or conduct business without limited liability, Simkovic is comfortable that this would "likely improve efficiency by shutting down socially harmful firms."[153]

One could certainly imagine such an approach eliciting useful information about risk perceptions within companies, but we need not start from scratch—because several peculiarly hazardous industries have already been identified through extant regulatory efforts that could plausibly serve as an alternative basis for re-calibrating the degree of limited liability protection that shareholders in such companies receive. For example, under a U.S. statute titled the Comprehensive Environmental Response, Compensation, and Liability Act (CERCLA), liability for environmental clean-up costs and damages can be imposed on "any person who at the time of disposal of any hazardous substance *owned or operated* any facility at which such hazardous substances were disposed of."[154] It is widely understood that casting the net to reach not only those who "owned" the facility, but also those who "operated" it, could effectively carve back at limited liability protections for shareholders that would otherwise apply under state corporate law—say, where a corporate subsidiary owns the facility but the parent determines its operation in pertinent respects.[155]

The practical potential for this statute to function as a means of calibrating risk incentives along the lines already described was effectively cabined, however, by the U.S. Supreme Court's 1998 *Bestfoods* decision,[156] which tethered the federal statutory analysis to state law principles of limited liability.[157] CERCLA does not provide substantive definitions for the key terms, rendering unclear the scope of parent liability for pollution at a subsidiary's facility.[158] In *Bestfoods*, the Court

[151] *Id.* at 312–14. Simkovic's regime would apply to all entity forms providing limited liability, and would be administered federally to avoid impediments arising from interstate competition. *See id.* at 325, 330.

[152] *See id.* at 314–20. Such industry classification systems have similarly been identified as a structural framework for implementing other types of proposed governance reforms. *See, e.g.*, Bruner, *supra* note 45, at 983–84 (proposing NAICS classifications as a basis for requiring that independent directors in public companies have industry-relevant expertise).

[153] Simkovic, *supra* note 149, at 316.

[154] 42 U.S.C. § 9607(a) (emphasis added).

[155] *See, e.g.*, Hansmann & Kraakman, *supra* note 111, at 1928; Mendelson, *supra* note 126, at 1265.

[156] United States v. Bestfoods, 524 U.S. 51 (1998).

[157] *See* Mendelson, *supra* note 126, at 1266–68.

[158] *See Bestfoods*, 524 U.S. at 55–56.

held that—in light of preexisting common-law principles not expressly displaced by the statute—a parent corporation could be held liable as an "owner" only if the test for veil piercing were met under applicable state corporate law, and could be held liable as an "operator" only if it were shown to have directed the polluting facility's operations through its own agents in a manner exceeding "accepted norms of parental oversight." These norms minimally permit monitoring performance, supervising finances and budgeting, and establishing general policies and procedures without exposing the parent to such liability.[159]

This interpretation of CERCLA's reach has led some to conclude generally that "statutory law imposing direct liability is unlikely to substantially broaden responsibility for corporate shareholders,"[160] but experience elsewhere suggests that this is not necessarily the case. Norway provides a vivid counterexample, demonstrating how such a regime could enhance shareholder liability exposure in the context of hazardous industries. Norway's Pollution Control Act permits the government to require "any person" engaging in pollution "to arrange or pay for any investigations or similar measures" required to assess the matter.[161] Much like under CERCLA, then, the Pollution Control Act permits the government to remediate polluted sites and subsequently pursue "the person responsible" for costs and damages.[162] The same issue of parent liability for polluting subsidiary facilities arose in Norway, and the Norwegian Supreme Court stated, in its 2010 *Hempel* decision, that an investigation order under the Pollution Control Act has "a public utility function that is to ensure that important societal interests are taken care of," justifying "a restrictive interpretation of the company law limitation of liability."[163] Consistent with this posture, the court held that the parent could be held liable for associated costs.[164]

As Beate Sjåfjell observes, while it is not entirely clear doctrinally whether the Norwegian court is applying environmental law or corporate law, it effectively does not matter. Either way, the case makes clear that shareholders' limited liability protections may be curtailed "when that will further environmental

[159] *Id.* at 61–73. The court further clarifies that the involvement of dual directors and officers will not, in and of itself, expose the parent to liability for decisions taken at the subsidiary level. *See id.* at 68–70.

[160] Mendelson, *supra* note 126, at 1268–69.

[161] Lov om vern mot forurensninger og om avfall [Act of 13 March 1981 No. 6 Concerning Protection Against Pollution and Concerning Waste], § 51 (Nor.), https://www.regjeringen.no/en/dokumenter/pollution-control-act/id171893/ (translation, as of June 20, 2003, by the Norwegian Ministry of Climate and Environment) [hereinafter Pollution Control Act].

[162] *Id.* §§ 74, 76.

[163] Beate Sjåfjell, *Environmental Piercing of the Corporate Veil: The Norwegian Supreme Court Decision in the* Hempel *Case*, 7 EUR. COMPANY L. 154, 156 (2010). Here the court quotes a decision of the Ministry of Environment regarding the complaint. *Id.* Sjåfjell notes that the case, titled *Hempel AS v. the Norwegian State*, was decided on March 10, 2010, and is available only in Norwegian. *See id.* at 154 n.1.

[164] *See id.* at 154.

protection or other . . . significant societal interest," prompting companies "to internalize the environmental costs stemming from earlier activity as well as related to new acquisitions."[165] The court's reasoning was subsequently applied to clean-up costs in further *Hempel* litigation, extending the reach of this approach and the correlative benefits.[166] The manner in which the Norwegian court conceptualized and addressed these issues amply demonstrates that there is no structural impediment to such a statutory approach, which might work in tandem with strategies pursued under corporate law itself to re-calibrate shareholders' liability exposure as a means of encouraging more effective risk monitoring and internalization of the costs of corporate production.

[165] *Id.* at 158–60.

[166] *See generally* Beate Sjåfjell, *The Courts as Environmental Champions: The Norwegian Hempel Cases*, 13 EUR. COMPANY L. 199 (2016).

8
Re-Imagining Corporate Accountability

Prior chapters examined various calibrations of the levers of corporate governance in a range of legal, cultural, market, and historical contexts, toward a variety of ends. This chapter addresses more directly an overarching issue that affects all of these topics—the nature and scope of corporate accountability. Here, I explore further strategies for advancing corporate sustainability through various additional mechanisms.

First, I assess the nature and scope of directors' accountability through the composition of the board, which naturally provides one reflection of how a given society believes corporate decision-making ought to be oriented—even if directors' duties are formulated by reference to the entity itself. Here we find movement in a corporate governance lever held constant through many of the foregoing analyses—the shareholder representation lever, which is calibrated quite differently in systems where non-shareholder constituencies have some measure of direct board representation. I also examine other ways of thinking about board composition and its potential to advance corporate sustainability. These include initiatives aimed at increasing the diversity of directors in publicly traded companies, and speculation that boards of directors might be augmented, or even replaced entirely, by emerging technologies such as artificial intelligence—which could have profound sustainability-related consequences.

Next, we turn to another significant aspect of the nature and scope of corporate accountability—the degree to which legal responsibility for the impacts of global value chains ought to flow up to entities, and perhaps even management, at the top of those chains, whether they are organized through parent-subsidiary relationships or through nominally arms'-length contractual relationships. This section assesses the apparent trend toward expanded responsibility along these lines, and the potential for such reforms to improve corporate sustainability in the context of multinational production.

Finally, this chapter assesses the nature and scope of corporate accountability through a striking national effort to re-imagine corporate governance along more sustainable lines, enlisting some (though by no means all) of the strategies discussed in this book—the corporate governance system of post-apartheid South Africa. This provides a vivid case study through which to assess pitfalls and opportunities that may arise in pursuing greater sustainability through corporate governance.

The Corporation as Technology. Christopher M. Bruner, Oxford University Press. © Christopher M. Bruner 2022.
DOI: 10.1093/oso/9780197635179.003.0008

A. Corporate Stakeholders and the Structure of the Board

From an economic perspective, nothing intrinsically links shareholder status with board representation—let alone exclusive board representation. Fundamentally, Henry Hansmann observes that "nearly all privately-owned firms" can be conceptualized as forms of "cooperatives," broadly construed to mean firms in which one or another group of "patrons" possess "the right to share in the organization's profits and the right to share in control of the organization."[1] From this broader economic perspective, the typical "business corporation, or joint stock company" might be conceptualized as a form of "capital" cooperative,[2] but of course the relevant "patron" group might just as straightforwardly consist of some other group of "customers or suppliers"—notably "employees" supplying labor.[3]

Hansmann argues that business corporations typically take the form of "capital cooperatives"—with shareholders alone represented on the board of directors—because, in large-scale production, a single patron group is more efficient; "it is easy," he suggests, "to structure the terms of investment so that all investor-owners have highly homogeneous interests . . . while it is much harder to induce such homogeneity among the interests of customers, employees, or suppliers of other inputs."[4] He adds that "governmental regulation often develops to mitigate the market imperfections that permit firms to exploit their [other] patrons,"[5] a position resembling that associated with the nexus of contracts view of the corporation. As already discussed, these assumptions of shareholder homogeneity and the sufficiency of external regulation to protect other stakeholders are likely flawed,[6] casting doubt on Hansmann's specific claims. His more general insights, however, remain sound and significant—notably, who we choose to favor with board representation might reasonably turn, to some degree, on who we regard as requiring substantial protection from "exploitation by the firm," and who can "govern the firm most effectively,"[7] bearing in mind "the surrounding legal and institutional environment."[8] Given the wide variety of ways in which stakeholder groups might be defined, in which boards of directors might be structured, and

[1] Henry Hansmann, *All Firms Are Cooperatives—and so Are Governments*, 2 J. ENTREPRENEURIAL & ORGANIZATIONAL DIVERSITY 1, 2 (2014). For comparison of corporations with prevailing forms of cooperatives, see generally Ville Pönkä, *The Cooperative as a Platform for Sustainable Business Operations*, *in* THE CAMBRIDGE HANDBOOK OF CORPORATE LAW, CORPORATE GOVERNANCE AND SUSTAINABILITY 682 (Beate Sjåfjell & Christopher M. Bruner eds., 2019); Ville Pönkä, *Are Cooperative Societies Transforming into Cooperative Companies? Reflections on the Finnish Cooperatives Act* (2017), https://ssrn.com/abstract=3072280.

[2] Hansmann, *supra* note 1, at 2.

[3] *Id.* at 3, 5.

[4] *Id.* at 5.

[5] *Id.* at 6–7.

[6] *See supra* Chapter 2.B.iii, Chapter 4.B.

[7] Hansmann, *supra* note 1, at 4.

[8] *Id.* at 8.

in which societies might formulate their goals, there is in fact no reason to expect that these factors will always break the same way,[9] although the argument in favor of employee governance power appears particularly strong given the firm-specific nature of their investments, the residual nature of their claims, and their centrality to economic conceptions of business firms.[10]

Germany's corporate governance system represents the paradigmatic example of deviation from the shareholder-centric board structure prevailing elsewhere. As already discussed, in large German companies, employees have substantial representation on the supervisory board, which in turn elects the management board. Notably, companies with over 2,000 employees are subject to quasi-parity co-determination, giving employees and shareholders equal representation while reserving a tie-breaking vote for the shareholder-elected chair. Coal, iron, and steel companies with over 1,000 employees, meanwhile, are subject to full-parity co-determination, with the tie-breaking vote going to a neutral member.[11] At the same time, employees may do even better through unique arrangements at particular companies. Notably, at Volkswagen there is a "de facto worker majority" on the supervisory board through seats reserved for officials of the government of Lower Saxony, who have "tended to side with the employees."[12] This approach to board structure clearly reflects a broader conception of whose interests require protection, and a differing perspective on the efficiency of shared governance.[13]

The structural emphasis that German corporate governance places on employee interests is further reflected in a formulation of directors' duties that similarly deviates from exclusive focus on shareholder interests. German directors "have to take into account equally the interests of shareholders, employees and the public," and "this pluralistic view of directors' duties is still considered to be the generally accepted, yet not undisputed, view."[14] This interpretation is

[9] *See generally* CHRISTOPHER M. BRUNER, CORPORATE GOVERNANCE IN THE COMMON-LAW WORLD: THE POLITICAL FOUNDATIONS OF SHAREHOLDER POWER (2013).

[10] *See* GRANT M. HAYDEN & MATTHEW T. BODIE, RECONSTRUCTING THE CORPORATION: FROM SHAREHOLDER PRIMACY TO SHARED GOVERNANCE 96–102, 145–60 (2020).

[11] *See supra* Chapter 2.B.ii. The European company form, Societas Europaea (SE), is "more flexible on employee co-determination." Christoph H. Seibt & Sabrina Kulenkamp, *Corporate Governance and Directors' Duties in Germany: Overview*, THOMSON REUTERS PRAC. L., June 1, 2020, at 3. However, the German Aktiengesellschaft (AG) "has so far defended its leading position among German companies." Andreas Rühmkorf et al., *Evolution of German Corporate Governance (1995–2014): An Empirical Analysis*, 19 CORP. GOVERNANCE 1042, 1044 (2019). Moreover, while SEs can choose either a one-tier or two-tier board structure, "most German SEs opt for the two-tier board system." Seibt & Kulenkamp, *supra*, at 6.

[12] Grant M. Hayden & Matthew T. Bodie, *Codetermination in Theory and Practice*, 73 FLA. L. REV. 321, 333 (2021).

[13] *See* HAYDEN & BODIE, *supra* note 10, at 172–83; Ewan McGaughey, *The Codetermination Bargains: The History of German Corporate and Labor Law*, 23 COLUM. J. EUR. L. 135, 140–46, 174–76 (2016).

[14] Rühmkorf et al., *supra* note 11, at 1045. *See also* JOHN W. CIOFFI, PUBLIC LAW AND PRIVATE POWER: CORPORATE GOVERNANCE REFORM IN THE AGE OF FINANCE CAPITALISM 82 (2010);

reinforced by the German Corporate Governance Code, which keys directors' duties to "the needs of the shareholders, the employees and other stakeholders, with the objective of sustainable value creation."[15] Although German corporate governance began to place greater emphasis on shareholders starting in the 1990s in an effort to attract foreign capital and spur the flagging economy,[16] reforms adopted during this period left the broader stakeholder orientation of the system intact.[17] Co-determination remains "an entrenched feature of Germany company law that has survived the pressures of globalisation and the legislative changes since the 1990s"[18]—in part because the better performance of German companies following the onset of the financial crisis led to "renewed appreciation of its consensus-based approach," which is thought to "prevent the pursuit of short-term gains to the detriment of long-term financial viability of companies."[19]

Overall, strong-form convergence toward a more shareholder-centric model remains unlikely,[20] and other features of the German corporate governance system strongly distinguish the typical large German company from the archetypal U.S. public company already described. While the shareholders do get to vote on some important matters,[21] shareholder voting has long been dominated by banks (holding proxy voting power over their brokerage clients' shares),[22] and "the combination of bank voting power, long-term relational lending, and direct shareholding" has traditionally netted out to an "institutional identity as lenders first and shareholders second."[23] Although greater foreign equity investment has increased the potential for shareholder activism in German companies,[24] it remains the case that greater reliance is placed on co-determined supervisory boards to control management.[25] Meanwhile, the German system has

Andreas Rühmkorf, *Stakeholder Value versus Corporate Sustainability: Company Law and Corporate Governance in Germany*, *in* THE CAMBRIDGE HANDBOOK OF CORPORATE LAW, CORPORATE GOVERNANCE AND SUSTAINABILITY, *supra* note 1, at 232, 233–35.

[15] Rühmkorf, *supra* note 14, at 235 (quoting the official translation of provision 4.1.1).

[16] *See* CIOFFI, *supra* note 14, at 141–42; Rühmkorf et al., *supra* note 11, at 1046, 1049–50.

[17] *See* CIOFFI, *supra* note 14, at 155–57.

[18] Rühmkorf et al., *supra* note 11, at 1045. *See also* McGaughey, *supra* note 13, at 137, 172–73.

[19] Rühmkorf et al., *supra* note 11, at 1050. *See also* CIOFFI, *supra* note 14, at 220–21; HAYDEN & BODIE, *supra* note 10, at 179–81. This is further reflected in executive compensation structures. *See* Rühmkorf, *supra* note 14, at 238–40. *See also* Seibt & Kulenkamp, *supra* note 11, at 11 (observing that compensation structures in listed German companies "must be focused on the sustainable growth of the company," and that performance-based pay "should have essentially forward-looking characteristics" and "should not encourage the recipients to take unreasonable risks").

[20] *See* Rühmkorf et al., *supra* note 11, at 1043.

[21] *See* Seibt & Kulenkamp, *supra* note 11, at 13.

[22] *See* CIOFFI, *supra* note 14, at 46, 71, 155.

[23] *Id.* at 71.

[24] *See* Seibt & Kulenkamp, *supra* note 11, at 4.

[25] *See* Rühmkorf et al., *supra* note 11, at 250–51. *See also* Rühmkorf, *supra* note 14, at 240–41.

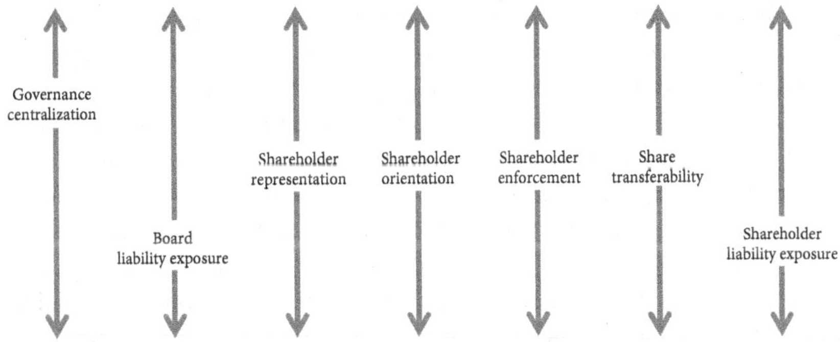

Figure 13 German Public Company (Aktiengesellschaft) Subject to Quasi-Parity Co-Determination

traditionally emphasized institutional bargaining over litigation, constraining shareholders' enforcement capacity.[26] Limited reforms have not fundamentally changed this orientation.[27]

The German system amounts to a very different calibration of the levers of corporate governance, contrasting starkly with the archetypal U.S. public company, as Figure 13 reflects.

Relative to the U.S. public company, this depiction of the German public company (AG) subject to quasi-parity co-determination reflects the substantial moderating effects of various features of the German corporate governance system. Governance centralization remains high (considering supervisory and management boards together in this respect), and board and shareholder liability alike remain low, as in the United States (due mainly to the far less active litigation environment).[28] However, all of the remaining levers of governance are calibrated

[26] *See* CIOFFI, *supra* note 14, at 68–69, 81–84.

[27] *See id.* at 174–78, 241–42. *See also* Seibt & Kulenkamp, *supra* note 11, at 22 (summarizing the limited minority shareholder actions available). Although employee-appointed directors on supervisory boards face the same exposure for breach of duty, concerns about excessive risk aversion arising from lesser capacity to bear losses may be mitigated due to diminished reliance on litigation. *See* Willi Joachim, *The Liability of Supervisory Board Directors in Germany*, 25 INT'L LAW. 41, 60–61, 67 (1991); Gerhard Wagner, *Officers' and Directors' Liability Under German Law—A Potemkin Village*, 16 THEORETICAL INQUIRIES IN L. 69, 77–80, 84–89 (2015). Additionally, directors and officers (D&O) liability insurance policies for supervisory board members are not required to include the substantial deductible required for management board D&O policies. *See* Aktiengesetz [AktG] [Stock Corporation Act], Sept. 6, 1965, *last amended* July 17, 2017, arts. 93, 116 (Ger.), https://www.gesetze-im-internet.de/englisch_aktg/englisch_aktg.html (translation by Samson Übersetzungen GmbH, Dr. Carmen von Schöning, published by the Federal Ministry of Justice and Consumer Protection). *See also* Wagner, *supra*, at 80–84, 89–91.

[28] Exculpation is not permitted, but members of both boards "can (and regularly do) obtain directors' and officers' liability (D&O) insurance" at the company's expense. While "a deductible of at least 10% of the loss of up to 1.5 times the fixed annual remuneration" is required for management board members, they "can get insurance coverage for that deductible on their own cost." Seibt & Kulenkamp, *supra* note 11, at 17–18.

lower in Germany than they are in the United States. Shareholder representation is lower in large German companies due to co-determination (although the degree differs based on the number of employees and the industry); shareholder orientation is lower due to both co-determination and a more stakeholder-oriented conception of corporate purpose; shareholder enforcement is lower due to the far less active litigation environment; and share transferability is lower due to the persistent concentration, and resulting stability, of share ownership. Overall, this calibration of the levers of governance more closely resembles the approach historically taken in U.S. financial firms[29] than it does the modern U.S. public company—producing moderating effects that help explain, for example, why German companies fared better in the wake of the financial crisis than their U.S. and U.K. counterparts did.[30]

This is not to suggest, however, that the German approach to corporate governance—and co-determination, in particular—necessarily renders Germany's large companies more sustainable in all respects. While co-determination would straightforwardly be expected to impact social and economic aspects of corporate sustainability,[31] the Volkswagen emissions scandal—occurring in a company with an exceptionally strong form of co-determination—vividly underscores that stakeholder-oriented corporate governance does not inherently promote environmental sustainability.[32] "No multinational companies have governance that is quite as worker-friendly as Volkswagen," Matthew Bodie observes. Yet, the emissions scandal "demonstrates that high levels of worker participation in corporate governance do not guarantee good behavior or sustainable practices."[33] This reflects the fact that reorienting the board of directors toward other stakeholders may yet fail to promote sustainability in all of its complex dimensions—and in this light, some have advocated broader board duties owed to the public writ large,[34] or keyed to a more embracing conception of sustainability in all of its dimensions.[35]

[29] *See supra* Chapter 7.A.

[30] *See supra* note 19 and accompanying text.

[31] *See, e.g.*, Rühmkorf, *supra* note 14, at 237–38.

[32] *See generally* Matthew T. Bodie, *Worker Participation, Sustainability and the Puzzle of the Volkswagen Emissions Scandal*, *in* THE CAMBRIDGE HANDBOOK OF CORPORATE LAW, CORPORATE GOVERNANCE AND SUSTAINABILITY, *supra* note 1, at 246. Volkswagen embedded a "defeat device" within their cars' software to "reduce emissions to legal levels during emissions testing, but then . . . release those constraints during normal driving." *Id.* at 246.

[33] *See id.* at 257–59.

[34] *See, e.g.*, BARNALI CHOUDHURY & MARTIN PETRIN, CORPORATE DUTIES TO THE PUBLIC 4–5, 83 (2019).

[35] *See, e.g.*, BEATE SJÅFJELL ET AL., SECURING THE FUTURE OF EUROPEAN BUSINESS: SMART REFORM PROPOSALS 34–38, 42–43 (2020), https://ssrn.com/abstract=3595048. *See also* Andrew Johnston et al., *Corporate Governance for Sustainability Statement* (2020), https://ssrn.com/abstract=3502101. While such proposals are consistent in spirit with the "trust firm" advocated by Colin Mayer, the latter differs fundamentally in that it focuses on corporate stakeholders and remains voluntary as to both the nature of the values pursued and the structure of the board. *See* COLIN MAYER, FIRM

Notwithstanding such limitations, the potential social and economic benefits of broadened board representation have led some to ask whether the United States should consider moving in this direction—particularly given growing disenchantment with strong-form shareholder orientation.[36] For example, Senator Elizabeth Warren's 2018 bill proposing a new "Accountable Capitalism Act" would effectively require U.S. businesses with over $1 billion in gross receipts to obtain a federal charter, identify a public benefit to be pursued in tandem with the pursuit of profit, and provide at least 40 percent board representation to employees.[37] Although the empirical literature on the impacts of co-determination remains mixed[38]—mainly due to methodological challenges including the difficulty of distinguishing between correlation and causation, and overreliance on event studies focused solely on financial impacts for shareholders[39]—Grant Hayden and Bodie observe a trend toward a more positive assessment of co-determination's effects, including its ability to buffer crisis impacts, benefits it offers for a range of stakeholders (not limited to employees), and its ability to "promote a well-functioning democracy and help prevent social division—in particular, the division between labor and capital."[40] Critics have argued that German companies have co-determination only because it is mandatory, and that the lack of voluntary adoption elsewhere reflects the market's judgment that shared governance is inefficient, but this ignores the fact that co-determination first arose through negotiated agreements in Germany—only later becoming formalized in law—and that German labor at the relevant times benefited from a stronger negotiating position than U.S. labor possesses today.[41] More subtly, some have suggested that while co-determination may be workable in Germany, it would not be workable in the United States, where greater emphasis has been placed on flexible corporate law through a market for charters, and where there is greater appetite for high levels of entrepreneurial risk[42]—an argument that

COMMITMENT: WHY THE CORPORATION IS FAILING US AND HOW TO RESTORE TRUST IN IT 199–206, 264–69 (2013).

[36] *See, e.g.*, Hayden & Bodie, *supra* note 12, at 357–58.

[37] *See* Accountable Capitalism Act, S. 3348, 115th Cong. §§ 4–6 (2018). For additional background, see Matthew T. Bodie, *Labor Interests and Corporate Power*, 99 B.U. L. REV. 1123, 1143–44 (2019); Jens Dammann & Horst Eidenmüller, *Codetermination: A Poor Fit for U.S. Corporations*, 3 COLUM. BUS. L. REV. 870, 886–89 (2020); Hayden & Bodie, *supra* note 12, at 330.

[38] *See, e.g.*, CIOFFI, *supra* note 14, at 74; Dammann & Eidenmüller, *supra* note 37, at 889–900; Hayden & Bodie, *supra* note 12, at 349–57; McGaughey, *supra* note 13, at 137.

[39] *See* Dammann & Eidenmüller, *supra* note 37, at 889–900. *See also* George S. Georgiev, *The Human Capital Management Movement in U.S. Corporate Law*, 95 TUL. L. REV. 639, 704–05 (2021) (observing similar methodological difficulties in the context of human capital management).

[40] *See* Hayden & Bodie, *supra* note 12, at 349–57. *See also* HAYDEN & BODIE, *supra* note 10, at 177–82.

[41] *See* Hayden & Bodie, *supra* note 12, at 338–44; McGaughey, *supra* note 13, at 154–70, 174–76. *See also* HAYDEN & BODIE, *supra* note 10, at 174–77.

[42] *See* Dammann & Eidenmüller, *supra* note 37, at 922–39.

assumes the optimality of shareholder-driven risk metrics.[43] This argument has an ironic ring to it, however, in the wake of a financial crisis driven by excessive risk-taking in U.S. and U.K. financial markets.[44]

Overall, there is good reason to take the German model as an opportunity to "reimagine the possibilities for a more efficient and more just framework for corporate law,"[45] particularly given recent work associating growing U.S. inequality with a decline in worker power and growing shareholder primacy.[46] Even some who doubt the political viability of full-blown co-determination in the U.S. context have developed moderate suggestions in this direction. Leo Strine, former Chief Justice of the Supreme Court of Delaware, concludes that the "American corporate governance system has failed to encourage long-term investment, sustainable business practices, and fair pay for workers"—shortcomings that he attributes to having "made public companies more responsive to the stock market's desires."[47] In response, Strine calls for a raft of reforms that include giving workers "more voice within the corporate boardroom."[48] While, in Strine's view, "it is not clear that codetermination fits with our economy," he suggests that shop floor-level works councils might be, and that single-tier boards in large U.S. companies might be required to have "a committee focused on workforce concerns," charged with addressing "fair gainsharing between workers and investors, training that assures continued employment, and maintaining a safe, inclusive, and tolerant workplace."[49] This would be a modest reform from which we could presumably expect only modest benefits,[50] but the emerging trend toward such committees in U.S. public companies is nevertheless a welcome development.[51]

[43] *See* Hayden & Bodie, *supra* note 12, at 348.

[44] *See generally* Christopher M. Bruner, *Corporate Governance Reform in a Time of Crisis*, 36 J. CORP. L. 309 (2011).

[45] Hayden & Bodie, *supra* note 12, at 358.

[46] *See generally* Zohar Goshen & Doron Levit, *Common Ownership and the Decline of the American Worker* (ECGI Law Working Paper No. 584/2021), https://ssrn.com/abstract=3832069; Anna Stansbury & Lawrence H. Summers, *The Declining Worker Power Hypothesis: An Explanation for the Recent Evolution of the American Economy* (NBER Working Paper No. 27193, 2020), https://www.nber.org/system/files/working_papers/w27193/w27193.pdf. *See also* HAYDEN & BODIE, *supra* note 10, at 184–85.

[47] Leo E. Strine, Jr., *Toward Fair and Sustainable Capitalism* 3 (Roosevelt Institute Working Paper, Aug. 2020), https://rooseveltinstitute.org/publications/toward-fair-and-sustainable-capitalism/.

[48] *Id.* at 5.

[49] *Id.* at 9–10. "For public companies," Strine notes, "integrating concerns of workers into their existing—and mandated—compensation committee would shift the board's focus away from just the senior management's compensation to broader discussions around the company's strategy regarding fair gainsharing amongst all its workers and stockholders." *Id.* at 10. As George Georgiev observes, there is already a trend in this direction, Georgiev, *supra* note 39, at 674–75, but he advocates assigning this responsibility to its own committee or to an "ESG or sustainability committee." *Id.* at 708–09. A committee with such responsibilities (among others) has been adopted in South Africa. *See infra* Chapter 8.C.

[50] *See* HAYDEN & BODIE, *supra* note 10, at 187.

[51] *See* Georgiev, *supra* note 39, at 673–76.

Debates regarding the merits of co-determination implicitly reflect an approach to board structure that focuses on groups defined by reference to economic inputs of one form or another—notably, shareholders providing equity capital, and workers providing labor.[52] At the same time, greater attention has been paid to board composition along different lines entirely, including the diversity of the directors themselves. Over recent decades, this has focused principally on achieving greater gender diversity on corporate boards, but more recently there have been growing calls for greater diversity in terms of race and sexual orientation as well.

Following Norway in 2003, several countries around the world have imposed mandatory quotas requiring specified categories of companies to achieve minimum levels of female board representation—sometimes framed as a floor for the representation of each gender.[53] For example, Norway and France both impose 40 percent floors.[54] Germany, meanwhile, has adopted a 30 percent floor for listed companies subject to co-determination, a quota that "applies to the entire board"—although, "if this principle is objected to by either the employee or the employer representatives on the supervisory board," it "applies to each side separately."[55] Sociological literature has identified a "critical mass" threshold of 35 percent for meaningful minority representation in group decision-making, below which "the majority can simply ignore a minority's presence,"[56] presumably prompting quotas in the neighborhood of this figure. California's gender diversity quota, however, varies depending on the size of the board; listed corporations headquartered in California are required to have one self-identified female director if the board has four or fewer directors, two if the board has five directors, and three if the board has six or more directors[57]—meaning that the percentage floor can vary considerably based on the size of the board. Many other jurisdictions, meanwhile, have adopted soft-law guidance aimed at promoting greater gender diversity on corporate boards along similar lines,[58] and several large investors have vocally pushed for improved gender diversity in the companies in which they invest—including the big index fund operator State

[52] *Cf.* Hansmann, *supra* note 1 (describing systems involving shareholder election of directors and employee election of directors, respectively, as differing forms of "producer cooperatives").

[53] *See* Institutional Shareholder Services, *Gender Parity on Boards Around the World*, HARVARD LAW SCHOOL FORUM ON CORPORATE GOVERNANCE, Jan. 5, 2017, https://corpgov.law.harvard.edu/2017/01/05/gender-parity-on-boards-around-the-world/. *See also* Darren Rosenblum & Daria Roithmayr, *More Than a Woman: Insights into Corporate Governance After the French Sex Quota*, 48 IND. L. REV. 889, 889–90 (2015).

[54] *See* Rosenblum & Roithmayr, *supra* note 53, at 889–90, 894, 897–98.

[55] Seibt & Kulenkamp, *supra* note 11, at 7.

[56] Rosenblum & Roithmayr, *supra* note 53, at 905–06.

[57] *See* CAL. CORP. CODE § 301.3(a)–(b). For corporations incorporated elsewhere, the California quota expressly applies "to the exclusion of the law of the jurisdiction in which the . . . corporation is incorporated." CAL. CORP. CODE § 2115.5.

[58] *See* Institutional Shareholder Services, *supra* note 53.

Street[59] and Norway's sovereign wealth fund (the world's largest).[60] These market pressures are now apparent at the initial public offering stage as well; Goldman Sachs has stated that "it wouldn't underwrite public offerings for any companies that lack a diverse board after July 1, 2020," and the "percentage of female directors rose to 24% among the companies with the 25 largest U.S. [IPOs]" that year, comparing with 21 percent in 2019 and 12 percent or less over the prior five years.[61]

There is certainly evidence suggesting that quotas have prompted greater gender diversity on corporate boards. Norway has the highest percentage of women on boards, with over 42 percent as of 2016.[62] France likewise saw a jump in female board representation following adoption of a quota,[63] as did California.[64] At the same time, however, it can be difficult to isolate the impact of quotas from other variables, including general social values. For example, Sweden also has a high percentage of women on boards, with over 36 percent as of 2016, exceeding all but a handful of countries in the world. Yet, Sweden does not have a quota, suggesting that culture may be a significant driver in Nordic countries, regardless of regulation.[65] Conversely, other countries with quotas may exhibit minimal compliance "in name only," suggesting that regulation alone may not achieve substantive diversity aims where not supported by prevailing cultural attitudes.[66] At the same time, however, it has been suggested that quotas may accelerate change in jurisdictions where cultural attitudes are shifting toward greater equality, as in the United States[67]—where, in 2019, women accounted for 45 percent of new board seats in Russell 3000 companies (up from just 12 percent in 2008), and 19 percent of all Russell 3000 board seats.[68]

[59] *See* Michal Barzuza et al., *Shareholder Value(s): Index Fund ESG Activism and the New Millennial Corporate Governance*, 93 S. CAL. L. REV. 1243, 1265–69 (2020).

[60] *See* Lars Erik Taraldsen & Ott Ummelas, *Norway Wealth Fund Asks Boards to Set Gender Diversity Goals*, BLOOMBERG L. NEWS, Feb. 16, 2021.

[61] Jeff Green, *Just One Major U.S. IPO Debuted with an All-Male Board in 2020*, BLOOMBERG L. NEWS, Feb. 22, 2021.

[62] *See* Institutional Shareholder Services, *supra* note 53.

[63] *See* Rosenblum & Roithmayr, *supra* note 53, at 899.

[64] *See* Anne Steele, *California Rolls Out Diversity Quotas for Corporate Boards*, WALL ST. J., Oct. 1, 2020, https://www.wsj.com/articles/california-rolls-out-diversity-quotas-for-corporate-boards-11601507471. For additional background, see ALEX PADILLA, CALIFORNIA SECRETARY OF STATE OFFICE, WOMEN ON BOARDS: MARCH 2020 REPORT (2020); Subodh Mishra, *U.S. Board Diversity Trends in 2019*, HARVARD LAW SCHOOL FORUM ON CORPORATE GOVERNANCE, June 18, 2019, https://corpgov.law.harvard.edu/2019/06/18/u-s-board-diversity-trends-in-2019/; Cydney Posner, *New Report on California Board Gender Diversity Mandate*, HARVARD LAW SCHOOL FORUM ON CORPORATE GOVERNANCE, Mar. 18, 2020, https://corpgov.law.harvard.edu/2020/03/18/new-report-on-california-board-gender-diversity-mandate/.

[65] *See* Institutional Shareholder Services, *supra* note 53.

[66] *See id.* (citing the example of India, where many companies have one female director, often related to a male board member, suggesting that they "are bringing on one female director to meet the minimum requirement").

[67] *See id.*

[68] *See* Mishra, *supra* note 64.

This is thought to have been driven by both growing investor demands and the California quota.[69] While lawsuits have been filed challenging the California law on constitutional grounds, California businesses generally "appear to have accepted the requirements of the legal mandate."[70]

As with studies examining the effects of co-determination, empirical literature on the effects of gender diversity on corporate boards remains mixed, and fraught with similar methodological challenges—notably, the difficulty of distinguishing between correlation and causation.[71] Much of this literature explores the "business case" for diversity through quotas, and studies focused on financial impacts (measured by reference to various metrics) point in different directions—meaning that "the existing empirical literature does not uniformly support a positive association between sex diversity and improved corporate performance,"[72] although "the relationship between diversity on executive teams and the likelihood of financial outperformance has strengthened over time."[73] Theoretical perspectives on why diversity might have a substantive impact on corporate decision-making often focus on the process—notably, reducing the likelihood of lapsing into groupthink-type consensus seeking—but also suggest further possibilities such as greater sensitivity to consumer and employee interests.[74] This suggests by contrast that traditional corporate governance theories may be "overvaluing consensus in the boardroom."[75]

Ultimately, it remains difficult to isolate the effects of gender as such. For example, based on interviews with directors and others following enactment of the French gender quota, Darren Rosenblum and Daria Roithmayr found a prevailing perception that, to the extent it affected board decision-making, it had less to do with gender and more to do with new female directors disproportionately being "outsiders"—specifically, they often "came from different countries, different schools, and with different areas of expertise."[76] This resonates with recommendations in the business literature to diversify boards through recruitment of "cognitively diverse 'outsiders'" who have "experience in areas that are required on the board," drawn from "new talent pools" beyond existing "board member networks and historical recruitment practices," providing "new views and perspectives and different approaches to problem solving."[77] It is also

69 *See id.*
70 *See* Posner, *supra* note 64.
71 *See* Rosenblum & Roithmayr, *supra* note 53, at 901.
72 *See id.* at 900–03. *See also* Taraldsen & Ummelas, *supra* note 60.
73 Sundiatu Dixon-Fyle et al., *Diversity Wins: How Inclusion Matters*, MCKINSEY & CO., May 19, 2020, https://www.mckinsey.com/featured-insights/diversity-and-inclusion/diversity-wins-how-inclusion-matters#.
74 *See* Rosenblum & Roithmayr, *supra* note 53, at 903–06.
75 HAYDEN & BODIE, *supra* note 10, at 134. *See also supra* Chapter 2.B.iii.
76 *See* Rosenblum & Roithmayr, *supra* note 53, at 906–27.
77 *See* Jared L. Landaw, *How Diverse Is Your Board, Really?*, HARV. BUS. REV., June 11, 2020, https://hbr.org/2020/06/how-diverse-is-your-board-really.

broadly consistent with recent empirical trends in the United States, which—in addition to greater gender and racial diversity—include "director appointments focus[ing] on non-financial skillsets, with an increased proportion of directors having international experience, ESG expertise, and background in human resources."[78]

Other forms of board diversity have not received the same level of attention, but this is starting to change. In 2019, 15 percent of new board seats in Russell 3000 companies were filled by non-white nominees, and non-white Russell 3000 directors overall "crossed the 10-percent threshold for the first time in 2019, compared to approximately 8 percent in 2008." Accordingly, "the rate of change is considerably slower than the trend in board gender diversity," and the foregoing figures fall "well below the proportion of the non-White population in the U.S. of approximately 40 percent."[79] Recently, however, board-level racial diversity has received greater attention as the "focus on social justice and racism . . . has prompted a wave of businesses to examine diversity within their ranks more closely."[80] In 2020, California enacted "the first quota in the world to address racial inequality, sexual orientation and gender identity."[81] The structure broadly resembles California's gender quota, applying to the same range of listed companies headquartered in California, and basing the requirement on the size of the board,[82] but it differs in two important respects. First, the size brackets differ, requiring fewer directors under the new quota in several situations.[83] Second, it lumps together two forms of diversity; the quota applies to "underrepresented communities," defined to include various racial minorities as well as LGBT people.[84] When the bill was passed, "dissenters said it would violate equal protection provisions of the law,"[85] suggesting that legal challenges resembling those brought against the gender quota will be pursued—although, once again,

[78] *See* Mishra, *supra* note 64.

[79] *Id. See also* Peter Eavis, *Diversity Push Barely Budges Corporate Boards to 12.5%, Survey Finds*, N.Y. TIMES, Sept. 15, 2020, https://www.nytimes.com/2020/09/15/business/economy/corporate-boards-black-hispanic-directors.html; Steele, *supra* note 64.

[80] Steele, *supra* note 64.

[81] Darren Rosenblum, *California Pioneers New Quotas for People of Color & LGBT People*, FORBES, Oct. 5, 2020, https://www.forbes.com/sites/darrenrosenblum/2020/10/05/california-pioneers-new-quotas-for-people-of-color--lgbt-people/.

[82] *See* CAL. CORP. CODE, §§ 301.4(a)–(b), 2115.6.

[83] *See id.* § 301.4(b) (requiring one director from an "underrepresented community" if there are four or fewer directors, two if there are five to eight directors, and three if there are nine or more directors).

[84] *See id.* § 301.4(e)(1). For additional background, see California Assembly Bill No. 979, § 1 (amending Corporations Code § 301.3, and adding §§ 301.4 and 2115.6) (2020) (summarizing legislative findings).

[85] Steele, *supra* note 64.

businesses themselves appear to be moving in the direction of pursuing greater racial diversity.[86]

Meanwhile, California's approach appears to have inspired similar approaches in other settings. In late 2020, Nasdaq proposed listing rules to "require most Nasdaq-listed companies to have, or explain why they do not have, at least two diverse directors, including one who self-identifies as female and one who self-identifies as either an underrepresented minority or LGBTQ+," and this proposal was approved by the U.S. Securities and Exchange Commission (which oversees U.S. listing rules).[87] This broadly tracks the California approach by creating a distinct gender quota while lumping together other forms of diversity in a combined quota,[88] yet it differs in its disclosure-based, comply-or-explain rule structure.[89] Nasdaq's extensive proposal cites wide-ranging calls for board diversity as an impetus,[90] noting that "the U.S. still lags behind other jurisdictions that have focused on board diversity."[91] The proposal cites "an extensive body of empirical research [that] demonstrates that diverse boards are positively associated with improved corporate governance and company performance," and further argues that investor calls for board diversity reflect that "investor confidence is undermined when a company's board room is homogenous [sic] and when transparency about such efforts is lacking."[92] While "Republicans on the Senate Banking Committee urged the Securities and Exchange Commission to reject" this initiative, their position was "at odds with that of some public companies,

[86] *See* Board Challenge, *Take the Pledge*, https://www.theboardchallenge.org ("Commit to add a Black director to your board of directors within the next year. . . . If your organization has at least one Black director, pledge to foster continued efforts for change."). *See also* Tiffany Stecker, *California Governor Oks Bill Mandating Corporate Board Diversity*, BLOOMBERG L. NEWS, Sept. 30, 2020; Eavis, *supra* note 79.

[87] Press Release, Nasdaq, Nasdaq to Advance Diversity through New Proposed Listing Requirements (Dec. 1, 2020), https://www.nasdaq.com/press-release/nasdaq-to-advance-diversity-through-new-proposed-listing-requirements-2020-12-01; Self-Regulatory Organizations, The Nasdaq Stock Market LLC, Order Approving Proposed Rule Changes, as Modified by Amendments No. 1, to Adopt Listing Rules Related to Board Diversity and to Offer Certain Listed Companies Access to a Complimentary Board Recruiting Service, Exchange Act Release No. 34-92590 (Aug. 6, 2021). *See also* Peyton Forte, *Republicans Urge SEC to Reject Nasdaq's Proposed Diversity Rule*, BLOOMBERG L. NEWS, Feb. 16, 2021; Erica T. Jones, *ESG on the Books: NASDAQ Proposed Rules Require Board Diversity*, NAT'L L. REV., Feb. 2, 2021, https://www.natlawreview.com/print/article/esg-books-nasdaq-proposed-rules-require-board-diversity.

[88] *See* Nasdaq Stock Market LLC, Form 19b-4 Amendment No. 1 (Feb. 26, 2021), at 9–10. *See also id.* at 61–62 (discussing the California model).

[89] *See id.* at 92–101. For the text of listing rule 5605(f), including various exceptions and effective dates, see *id.* at 343–48. Nasdaq has also adopted a new listing rule 5606, requiring board diversity disclosures. *See id.* at 348–49.

[90] *See id.* at 6–8.

[91] *Id.* at 12.

[92] *Id.* at 13–15.

including Facebook Inc. and Microsoft Corp.," which "urged the SEC to approve Nasdaq's proposal,"[93] broadly tracking the varied responses to California's efforts.

Observers have acknowledged that California "bravely serves as a laboratory for change" and expressed "hope [that] the experiment succeeds in diversifying corporate leadership," while at the same time expressing reservations about certain aspects of California's approach. For example, including two forms of diversity in the same quota means that compliance can be achieved solely by reference to one, without regard to the other.[94] Yet, this aspect of the California board quota structure appears to have been replicated in the comply-or-explain board diversity rule adopted by Nasdaq.

At the same time, questions have arisen regarding the degree to which board-level quotas can be expected to promote broader diversity-related impacts throughout corporate enterprises. Proponents had hoped that more diverse boards would in turn lead to more diverse senior management[95]—not an unreasonable expectation, given that appointing executive officers is among the most consequential tasks for any board of directors to undertake.[96] Yet, this has not occurred in Norway, the jurisdiction enacting one of the world's first and most aggressive board gender quota requirements.[97] Indeed, it is becoming clear that the C-suite presents an entirely distinct set of dynamics. For example, as of 2017, just 4 percent of S&P 500 CEOs were women,[98] and as of 2021, there were a total of just five Black CEOs in S&P 500 companies, of whom just one was a woman.[99] Accordingly, while board-level diversity may offer substantial benefits in its own right, achieving greater diversity among senior management is increasingly thought to require distinctive solutions—including through hiring for positions "with division responsibility for profit and loss," which represents "the traditional track to be a big-company CEO."[100]

There is every indication that the nature and scope of directors' accountability through the composition of the board will receive sustained attention in coming years, and that achieving greater board-level and executive-level diversity along the foregoing lines will increasingly be prioritized. At the same time, there is growing speculation that human boards of directors might be augmented, or even replaced entirely, by emerging technologies such as artificial intelligence (AI)—which could have profound sustainability-related consequences. Although not

[93] Forte, *supra* note 87.
[94] *See* Rosenblum, *supra* note 81.
[95] *See* Steele, *supra* note 64.
[96] *See, e.g.*, STEPHEN M. BAINBRIDGE, CORPORATE LAW 89 (2d ed. 2009).
[97] *See* Steele, *supra* note 64.
[98] *See* Institutional Shareholder Services, *supra* note 53.
[99] *See* Jeff Green, *Black CEO Ranks Dwindle with Ken Frasier's Exit from Merck*, BLOOMBERG L. NEWS, Feb. 4, 2021 (describing Roz Brewer's appointment as CEO of Walgreens Boots Alliance Inc., effective Mar. 15, 2021).
[100] *See id.* (describing Roz Brewer's prior experience in "key jobs at Walmart Inc. and Starbucks").

typically brought to bear on the question of a board's capacity to represent various stakeholders' interests—in part because the technology remains nascent—it is nevertheless important to recognize that AI may ultimately have a significant impact on how boards operate, and the degree to which they can bring the interests of various constituencies to bear upon corporate decision-making.

It is often assumed in the discourse on emerging technologies and corporate governance that such developments will further reinforce exclusive focus on the interests of shareholders. For example, distributed ledgers and blockchain technologies are widely expected to reduce the costs of voting and trade clearance, and accordingly to make it more realistic for shareholders to be directly involved with management. AI, meanwhile, is widely expected to shrink the domain in which we remain reliant on human boards. However, such consequences are far from obvious—not solely because these technologies remain rife with legal, ethical, and practical problems, and accordingly have a long way to go before such heavy reliance upon them to discharge managerial functions would be remotely plausible, but also because there are various ways in which we might choose to develop and regulate these technologies.[101] In other words, we have choices to make about what these technologies ultimately become, and how they are deployed.

When it comes to board composition and capacity to represent various constituencies, we could readily imagine AI itself offering potential to effectively diversify board decision-making, beyond what could presently be achieved through literal composition of a board consisting of human directors. In much the same way that greater human diversity is thought to counteract effects of groupthink, for example, AI might similarly be employed as a tool by the board of directors to promote consideration of a wider range of perspectives and to encourage dissenting views to be voiced.[102] More generally, given that "AI can process and consider a much higher volume of complex information than humans," we could readily imagine AI facilitating greater practical capacity for boards to balance the competing interests of various stakeholders. To the extent such technological tools become available to boards, they might tend to undercut arguments to the effect that corporate law must focus on a single maximand because human decision makers cannot effectively handle more than that.[103]

It bears emphasizing that we are a long way from plausibly relying on AI to take over managerial functions outright. As I have explored elsewhere, " 'black

[101] *See generally* Christopher M. Bruner, *Distributed Ledgers, Artificial Intelligence and the Purpose of the Corporation*, 79 CAMBRIDGE L.J. 431 (2020).

[102] *See* Akshaya Kamalnath, *The Perennial Quest for Board Independence: Artificial Intelligence to the Rescue?*, 83 ALB. L. REV. 43, 51–52 (2019/2020).

[103] *See* Martin Petrin, *Corporate Management in the Age of AI*, 2019 COLUM. BUS. L. REV. 965, 1018–22 (2019).

box' algorithmic outcomes not susceptible to straightforward explanation create numerous legal and regulatory complexities in wide-ranging contexts, and there remains significant legal uncertainty regarding who ought to be liable when algorithms run amok." At the same time, a host of legal, ethical, and practical problems associated with AI remain to be addressed, including "consumer data protection, inability to model truly novel events and circumstances, industry dominance (relative to governments and academia), and replication of discriminatory biases" embedded in the underlying data and/or the algorithm itself.[104] In this light, it is undoubtedly for the best that corporate statutes generally continue to require that a director be "a natural person."[105] It would seem most likely that any near-term reliance on AI by boards of directors would involve employing the technology as a tool to aid human decision-making, with potential applications and ramifications that are only now beginning to receive sustained attention.[106] Nevertheless, the potential for these technologies to impact both corporate purpose debates and the nature of board representation is quite real, and it is entirely within the realm of possibility that AI could effectively diversify board decision-making further, reinforcing the practical effects of initiatives focused on human composition of the board.

B. Consolidating Corporate Accountability in Global Value Chains

We have already seen that one of the consequences of financialization—the reorientation of corporate strategy toward appealing to financial markets[107]—has been a relentless drive toward "maintaining the lightest possible base of assets and employment through spin-offs and layoffs," resulting in widespread outsourcing, offshoring, and reliance on contractors for production and distribution, a strategy that Gerald Davis has termed "Nikefication" after "the firm that pioneered this approach." This strategy "has spread widely across the economy, not just in clothing and consumer packaged goods but in electronics and pharmaceuticals" as well. In these instances, the "top-selling brands" recognized in affluent jurisdictions are typically "managed by corporations that do little or no production themselves and employ relatively few people directly"—basically

[104] *See* Bruner, *supra* note 101, at 442–44.

[105] *See, e.g.*, DEL. CODE ANN. tit. 8, § 141(b).

[106] *See* Bruner, *supra* note 101, at 442–46, 449–58. For additional background, see generally NIKITA AGGARWAL ET AL., AUTONOMOUS SYSTEMS AND THE LAW (2019); Luca Enriques & Dirk A. Zetzsche, *Corporate Technologies and the Tech Nirvana Fallacy*, 72 HASTINGS L.J. 55 (2020); Kamalnath, *supra* note 102; Petrin, *supra* note 103; Sergio Alberto Gramitto Ricci, *Artificial Agents in Corporate Boardrooms*, 105 CORNELL L. REV. 869 (2020).

[107] *See supra* Chapter 6.B.

just housing intellectual property, marketing, and management functions. Meanwhile, compensation for executives has exploded while workers' wages and benefits have stagnated, further amplifying inequalities in these jurisdictions.[108]

At the same time, these dynamics have resulted in a proliferation of increasingly global "value chains," organized through parent-subsidiary relationships under corporate law, or through buyer-supplier relationships under contract law.[109] Such arrangements account for approximately 80 percent of global trade, and have become staggeringly complex, obscuring much of the workforce and rendering production processes inherently difficult to monitor. As Charlotte Villiers observes, the "fragmented nature of the production processes leads many chains to require multiple layers of suppliers." Indeed, in the electronics industry, a value chain may involve fifty tiers of suppliers and vendors. As of 2015, "Apple had 785 suppliers in 31 countries worldwide contributing to the production of the iPhone."[110] Given their complexity and opacity, it is unsurprising that global value chains have raised significant concerns about environmental and social harms arising in distant jurisdictions where production actually occurs, far removed from consumer-facing companies in more affluent jurisdictions where end products are ultimately sold.[111] This raises a host of questions about what level of responsibility should reside with the corporate entities and managers effectively structuring and coordinating these value chains.

In a sense, these developments reflect straightforward Coasian dynamics driving the boundaries of business firms. Ronald Coase, in his seminal 1937 paper titled "The Nature of the Firm," distinguished between market-level coordination of production through the "price mechanism" and firm-level

[108] Gerald F. Davis & Suntae Kim, *Financialization of the Economy*, 41 ANN. REV. SOCIOLOGY 203, 209–13 (2015). *See also* Gerald F. Davis, *After the Corporation*, 4 POLITICS & SOC'Y 283, 287–95 (2013). For additional background, see GERALD F. DAVIS, THE VANISHING AMERICAN CORPORATION: NAVIGATING THE HAZARDS OF A NEW ECONOMY 69–94, 115–37 (2016); RANA FOROOHAR, MAKERS AND TAKERS: THE RISE OF FINANCE AND THE FALL OF AMERICAN BUSINESS 13–21, 152–78 (2016); Goshen & Levit, *supra* note 46; Stansbury & Summers, *supra* note 46. *Cf.* BRUNER, *supra* note 9, at 166–76 (arguing that threats to the capacity of public company employers to provide social welfare benefits have prompted counter-reactions against shareholder-centric policies, notably in the context of hostile takeovers). On rising inequality more generally, see THOMAS PIKETTY, CAPITAL IN THE TWENTY-FIRST CENTURY 23–27 (Arthur Goldhammer trans., 2014) (arguing that high rates of inequality have resulted from the rate of return on capital exceeding the growth rate of the economy); KATE RAWORTH, DOUGHNUT ECONOMICS: SEVEN WAYS TO THINK LIKE A 21ST CENTURY ECONOMIST 139–73 (2017)("Rather than accept growing inequality as a law of economic development, an inevitability that must be endured, twenty-first-century economists will regard it as a failure of economic design and will seek to make economies far more distributive of the value that they generate.").

[109] *See* Jaakko Salminen, *Sustainability and the Move from Corporate Governance to Governance through Contract*, *in* THE CAMBRIDGE HANDBOOK OF CORPORATE LAW, CORPORATE GOVERNANCE AND SUSTAINABILITY, *supra* note 1, at 57, 57.

[110] Charlotte Villiers, *Global Supply Chains and Sustainability: The Role of Disclosure and Due Diligence Regulation*, *in* THE CAMBRIDGE HANDBOOK OF CORPORATE LAW, CORPORATE GOVERNANCE AND SUSTAINABILITY, *supra* note 1, at 551, 552–53.

[111] *See id.* at 554.

coordination of production through managerial fiat[112]—a distinction mapping onto the respective legal definitions of independent contractors and employees, the latter involving direct control over how the work is done.[113] Coase offered an elegant framework to illuminate how firms choose between these differing mechanisms for coordinating production, resulting in smaller or larger firms, respectively. He argued that reliance on the command mechanism within firms can reduce costs of price discovery and contracting, which could be particularly beneficial where stable long-term relations are desirable. This results in larger firms to the extent that transactions otherwise carried out at arms'-length on the open market are brought in-house.[114]

By the same token, Coase further observed that firms might "revert" to reliance on the market-based pricing mechanism where that mode of organizing production offers lower costs[115]—and this latter observation becomes critical to understanding what has driven "Nikefication" of production over recent decades. To the extent that firms can substantially reduce costs associated with employment and regulatory compliance in this manner (to a degree exceeding costs of price discovery and contracting), there is every reason to expect that firms will take advantage of outsourcing and offshoring. This can be accomplished under corporate law by hiving off production in distinct subsidiaries, or—in more distinctly Coasian terms—under contract law by dealing with nominally distinct suppliers.[116] This mode of organizing production becomes all the more attractive to the extent that the divergence between global markets and domestic legislation permits regulatory competition, further driving down regulatory standards and correlatively reducing production costs by allowing them to be externalized onto workers and natural environments far removed from consumers in more affluent countries.[117]

Naturally, Nikefied firms headquartered in affluent jurisdictions will disclaim responsibility for what occurs at distinct entities in their value chains[118]—after all, their capacity to do so is effectively the legal source of their ability to reduce costs by fragmenting production. As Vivian Grosswald Curran sums it up, the

[112] *See* R.H. Coase, *The Nature of the Firm*, 4 ECONOMICA 386, 388–89 (1937).

[113] *See id.* at 403–04.

[114] *See id.* at 390–92.

[115] *See id.* at 392.

[116] *See* Salminen, *supra* note 109, at 59–60. *See also* Blanaid Clarke & Linn Anker-Sørensen, *The EU as a Potential Norm Creator for Sustainable Corporate Groups*, *in* THE CAMBRIDGE HANDBOOK OF CORPORATE LAW, CORPORATE GOVERNANCE AND SUSTAINABILITY, *supra* note 1, at 190, 193–95.

[117] *See* Christopher M. Bruner & Beate Sjåfjell, *Corporate Law, Corporate Governance and the Pursuit of Sustainability*, *in* THE CAMBRIDGE HANDBOOK OF CORPORATE LAW, CORPORATE GOVERNANCE AND SUSTAINABILITY, *supra* note 1, at 713, 715. *See also supra* Chapter 6.B.

[118] *See, e.g.*, Vivian Grosswald Curran, *Harmonizing Multinational Parent Company Liability for Foreign Subsidiary Human Rights Violations*, 17 CHI. J. INT'L L. 403, 406–07 (2017) (regarding subsidiaries); Kishanthi Parella, *Protecting Third Parties in Contracts*, AM. BUS. L.J., at 6 (2021), https://ssrn.com/abstract=3697273 (regarding suppliers).

result has been capacity for multinational businesses "to become both legally ubiquitous and yet legally invisible," able to exploit opportunities everywhere while remaining accountable nowhere.[119] This extraordinary accountability gap has prompted efforts to explore a range of existing legal theories, and to develop a range of reform strategies, through which corporate accountability might be consolidated and brought to bear upon those coordinating these structures.

With multinational corporate structures organized through parent-subsidiary relationships, in which the former hold controlling equity stakes in the latter, the core questions are how strong the protections of limited liability for parent corporations ought to be, and whether managers of parent corporations ought to have more substantial and direct responsibility for sustainability-related problems that arise at subsidiaries. In this regard, it is critical to recall that liability protections widely available to corporate shareholders and managers alike are not intrinsically absolute; for example, as discussed earlier, structures imposing greater liability exposure on financial firm shareholders and directors have historically represented important strategies to prevent this category of corporations from generating excessive risk and associated externalities,[120] and reforms along such lines might prove beneficial in the context of essential non-financial firms, and in the context of intrinsically hazardous industries as well.[121] In a similar spirit, there is growing consideration of whether such strategies should be applied in a more general way to constrain risk-taking and cost externalization in the context of multinational production through complex corporate groups.

As a threshold matter, the argument for limited liability is inherently weaker in the context of multinational corporate groups. Corporate shareholders are not risk averse to the degree that individual shareholders are, and accordingly do not need the same liability shield to induce them to invest. Additionally, in the context of multinational groups, the principal concerns relate to torts committed by subsidiaries in foreign jurisdictions. Tort victims, unlike contractual creditors, typically had no ex ante opportunity to negotiate the terms of their interactions with the subsidiary corporation and their associated risk exposure.[122] These weaknesses in the case for limited liability are commonly acknowledged in the law and economics literature.[123] The potential for harms in the multinational production context are augmented, however, by regulatory competition dynamics, and governments are sometimes complicit in human rights violations

[119] Curran, *supra* note 118, at 406. *See also* David Hess, *The Transparency Trap: Non-Financial Disclosure and the Responsibility of Business to Respect Human Rights*, 56 AM. BUS. L.J. 5, 11–12 (2019).

[120] *See supra* Chapter 4.A, Chapter 4.B.iii, Chapter 7.A.

[121] *See supra* Chapter 7.B, Chapter 7.C.

[122] *See* Curran, *supra* note 118, at 408–10.

[123] *See, e.g.*, FRANK H. EASTERBROOK & DANIEL R. FISCHEL, THE ECONOMIC STRUCTURE OF CORPORATE LAW 56–59 (1991).

and other corporate harms to attract and maintain investment by multinational corporations.[124] International law provides little protection, meaning that effective responses would have to arise at the national level[125]—and "because alleged victims of human rights abuses at the hands of foreign subsidiaries of large multinationals are only very rarely able to have a realistic forum in the state in which the violation occurred,"[126] Curran argues that courts in jurisdictions where parent corporations are based should impose greater accountability. With respect to corporate law, she suggests that theories of "enterprise liability" might be "reinvigorated," such that "all entities that share the same commercial objective within a corporation of a complex structure" would be "liable as if they constitute a single corporation,"[127] effectively ignoring their distinct corporate existence in such circumstances.

Although not going so far as this, emerging case law in various jurisdictions indicates some potential for greater parent company liability exposure. For example, in *Chandler v. Cape plc*, the Court of Appeal (Civil Division) for England and Wales held a parent company liable to a former employee of a dissolved subsidiary for harms resulting from exposure to asbestos in the course of his employment.[128] In her opinion, Lady Justice Arden "emphatically reject[ed] any suggestion that this court is in any way concerned with what is usually referred to as piercing the corporate veil," stating that there can be "no imposition or assumption of responsibility by reason only that a company is the parent company of another company."[129] Rather, the court concluded that, given the parent's "superior knowledge about the nature and management of asbestos risks" and the fact that the parent gave the subsidiary "instructions as to how it was to operate with which . . . it duly complied," there was "a direct duty of care" owed by the parent to the subsidiary employees.[130] In 2019, then, in *Vedanta Resources plc v. Lungowe*, the U.K. Supreme Court applied this theory in the multinational context to claims brought against a U.K. parent company by local communities surrounding a copper mine, operated by a Zambian subsidiary, for alleged toxic discharges into their water sources.[131] Lord Briggs' opinion acknowledged that *Chandler* provides "[h]elpful guidance as to relevant considerations" in

[124] *See* Curran, *supra* note 118, at 411–13.
[125] *See id.* at 415, 423–24.
[126] *Id.* at 440.
[127] *Id.* at 425–26.
[128] Chandler v. Cape plc [2012] EWCA (Civ) 525, ¶¶ 1–5, 62–84 (Eng.).
[129] *Id.* ¶ 69.
[130] *Id.* ¶¶ 78–80. *See also* Jingchen Zhao, *Extraterritorial Attempts at Addressing Challenges to Corporate Sustainability*, *in* THE CAMBRIDGE HANDBOOK OF CORPORATE LAW, CORPORATE GOVERNANCE AND SUSTAINABILITY, *supra* note 1, at 29, 35–36. That parent companies have power to control their subsidiaries is a straightforward incident of their equity stake. *See, e.g.*, Jonathan R. Macey, *Corporate Law as Myth*, 93 S. CAL. L. REV. 923, 954–69 (2020).
[131] Vedanta Resources plc v. Lungowe [2019] UKSC 20, ¶¶ 1–5, 42–62 (U.K.).

determining whether a parent company assumes a direct duty to those harmed by activities of a subsidiary,[132] and (applying a summary judgment standard) concluded that it was "well arguable that a sufficient level of intervention by Vedanta in the conduct of the operations at the Mine may be demonstrable at trial."[133] Critically, for U.K. jurisdictional purposes, the court also found adequate support for the lower court's conclusion that "funding and local legal resources were insufficient to enable the claimants to obtain substantial justice in Zambia."[134] Case law similarly suggesting potential for expanded duties by parent companies owed directly to those harmed by their subsidiaries' operations—including in the context of multinational corporate groups—has emerged in other jurisdictions as well.[135]

Contractual supply chains, however, present greater impediments to such litigation strategies. Here, the focus falls upon the consumer-facing "lead firm," typically headquartered in an affluent jurisdiction, which coordinates outsourced production through contractual requirements governing the work of far-flung suppliers located in other jurisdictions around the world.[136] As Kishanthi Parella observes, litigation "concerning externalities produced by supply chain contracts" virtually always fails due to "a lack of judicial recognition of duties that contracting parties owe to various third parties"—specifically, the lack of a duty for lead firms to monitor their value chains or to exercise care toward those affected by their suppliers' conduct.[137] Often, buyers generate substantial leverage over suppliers through nonexclusive, short-term, high-volume contracts, which create foreseeable risks of "practices in the supply chain that result in harmful externalities to third parties," as suppliers cut corners and squeeze workers to reduce costs and speed up production. While buyer-generated "codes of conduct," annexed to supply contracts, might nominally target such abuses, the realities of geographic distance and commercial incentives have prompted growing skepticism regarding their effectiveness.[138] Such dynamics have in turn prompted calls

[132] *Id.* ¶¶ 49–50 (quoting Sales LJ in AAA v. Unilever plc [2018] EWCA (Civ) 1532, ¶ 36).

[133] *Id.* ¶ 61.

[134] *Id.* ¶¶ 88–101. For additional background, see Curran, *supra* note 118, at 436–38.

[135] *See* Curran, *supra* note 118, at 438–42 (discussing developments in the Netherlands and Canada). *Cf.* Diederik Baazil & Laura Millan Lombrana, *What a Dutch Court Ruling Means for Shell and Big Oil*, BLOOMBERG QUICKTAKE, June 4, 2021, https://www.bloomberg.com/news/articles/2021-06-04/what-a-dutch-court-ruling-means-for-shell-and-big-oil-quicktake (describing a Dutch court's reliance on a general "duty of care" under Dutch law as a basis for requiring Royal Dutch Shell to reduce emissions more aggressively). The United States, meanwhile, appears to be trending in the opposite direction. *See* Adam Liptak, *Supreme Court Limits Human Rights Suits Against Corporations*, N.Y. TIMES, June 17, 2021, https://www.nytimes.com/2021/06/17/us/supreme-court-human-rights-nestle.html; Greg Stohr & Kimberly Robinson, *Supreme Court Backs Nestle, Cargill on Child-Slavery Suit*, BLOOMBERG L. NEWS, June 17, 2021.

[136] *See* Salminen, *supra* note 109, at 61–62.

[137] *See* Parella, *supra* note 118, at 6, 13–19. *See also* Salminen, *supra* note 109, at 62–63.

[138] *See* Parella, *supra* note 118, at 10–13. This is not to suggest, however, that such instruments have no impact whatsoever. For a discussion of supply chain contracting and its impact on domestic

for more robust lead-firm duties to monitor for abuses in their supply chains and to take effective actions to combat them.[139]

Statutory responses aimed directly at supply chain governance have begun to emerge, but they vary considerably in their scope and rigor.[140] Some are relatively weak, relying fundamentally on disclosure-based strategies and reputational sanctions, as with the regimes adopted in the United Kingdom, Australia, and California.[141] The U.K.'s Modern Slavery Act 2015 requires companies doing business in the United Kingdom with total turnover of £36 million or more to "prepare a slavery and human trafficking statement for each financial year" and to make the statement publicly available.[142] The Act clearly invites a relatively comprehensive statement regarding how the company seeks to prevent slavery and human trafficking; it provides that the company "may" address its supply chain structure, relevant policies, its "due diligence process," its training activities, steps taken to assess the risk that such abuses are occurring in its supply chain, and the effectiveness of the company's responses.[143] Critically, however, this invitation is expressly illustrative and permissive. The Act makes clear that a company may either describe "the steps the organisation has taken" along the foregoing lines, or simply indicate that "the organisation has taken no such steps"—and the latter is fully sufficient to satisfy the statutory obligation.[144] Accordingly, it is unsurprising that the "results of the Modern Slavery Act have been modest so far," with few companies providing meaningful disclosures about their supply chain practices.[145] Australia's Modern Slavery Act 2018 similarly requires companies doing business in Australia with revenue of AU$100 million or more to make a public statement annually,[146] and appears somewhat more prescriptive

attitudes regarding "corporate social responsibility" in China, see generally Li-Wen Lin, *Mandatory Corporate Social Responsibility? Legislative Innovation and Judicial Application in China*, AM. J. COMP. L. (2021), https://ssrn.com/abstract=3361448.

[139] *See, e.g.*, SJÅFJELL ET AL., *supra* note 35, at 11, 73; Parella, *supra* note 118, at 19–22.

[140] *See* Salminen, *supra* note 109, at 68–70.

[141] *See* Parella, *supra* note 118, at 26–29. *See also* Hess, *supra* note 119, at 45–47; Villiers, *supra* note 110, at 555–59.

[142] Modern Slavery Act 2015, c. 30, § 54(1)–(3), (7)–(8), (12) (U.K.); Modern Slavery Act 2015 (Transparency in Supply Chains) Regulations 2015 (2015 No. 1833), reg. 2 (U.K.).

[143] Modern Slavery Act 2015, *supra* note 142, § 54(5).

[144] *Id.* § 54(4). *See also* Iris H.-Y. Chiu, *Disclosure Regulation and Sustainability: Legislation and Governance Implications*, *in* THE CAMBRIDGE HANDBOOK OF CORPORATE LAW, CORPORATE GOVERNANCE AND SUSTAINABILITY, *supra* note 1, at 521, 526–28; Zhao, *supra* note 130, at 32–34.

[145] Villiers, *supra* note 110, at 557. *See also* Press Release, U.K. Home Office, Home Office Tells Business: Open Up on Modern Slavery or Face Further Action (Oct. 18, 2018), https://www.gov.uk/government/news/home-office-tells-business-open-up-on-modern-slavery-or-face-further-action.

[146] Modern Slavery Act 2018 (No. 153, 2018) §§ 5(1), 13, 18 (Austl.). *See also* Australian Government, Department of Home Affairs, *Modern Slavery*, https://www.homeaffairs.gov.au/criminal-justice/Pages/modern-slavery.aspx# (updated June 9, 2021).

regarding its contents.[147] Sanctions, however, remain similarly weak, effectively amounting to public shaming through a register indicating noncompliance.[148] California's Transparency in Supply Chains Act, meanwhile, requires any retailer or manufacturer doing business in California with gross receipts exceeding $100 million to publicly disclose its "efforts to eradicate slavery and human trafficking from its direct supply chain for tangible goods offered for sale."[149] Although in California's case the regime is enforceable (exclusively) through "an action brought by the Attorney General for injunctive relief," the mandatory disclosures remain minimal, requiring only that the company disclose "to what extent, if any," it undertakes various efforts to combat slavery and human trafficking.[150] At the U.S. federal level, a bill has been introduced that would require any public company with gross receipts exceeding $500 million to conduct annual audits of its supply chains "to investigate the presence or use of forced labor by the covered business entity or its suppliers, including by direct suppliers, secondary suppliers, and on-site service providers," and to file a public report containing "the results of such audit and efforts," subject to injunctive relief as well as substantial civil and punitive damages for noncompliance.[151] The fate of this bill, however, remains uncertain.[152] Otherwise, U.S. federal-level action to date remains limited, typically involving targeted actions under trade laws.[153]

More demanding statutory structures, requiring real action to address sustainability-related concerns throughout corporate groups and threatening real liabilities for noncompliance, have been adopted elsewhere. Statutory structures aimed at increasing corporate accountability for environmental hazards are discussed earlier, and they do contemplate potential for parent liability where a subsidiary's facility causes environmental harms—although they depend to varying degrees on corporate veil piercing doctrines and/or direct operation of the facility, rendering parent liability both less predictable and less likely.[154] Some jurisdictions, however, are moving more aggressively in the global

[147] *See* Modern Slavery Act 2018, *supra* note 146, § 16 (describing the topics the statement "must" address).

[148] *See id.* § 16A. *See also id.* § 25 (clarifying that implementing regulations may not "create an offence or civil penalty" or "impose a tax").

[149] CAL. CIV. CODE § 1714.43(a)(b).

[150] *Id.* § 1714.43(c)–(d).

[151] Slave-Free Business Certification Act, S. 4241, 116th Cong. §§ 2–4 (2020).

[152] *See* David Sparkman, *Targeting Slavery in the Supply Chain*, MATERIAL HANDLING & LOGISTICS, Dec. 4, 2020, https://www.mhlnews.com/labor-management/article/21149570/targeting-slavery-in-the-supply-chain.

[153] *See id.*; Parella, *supra* note 118, at 4–5.

[154] *See supra* Chapter 7.C. On the U.S. regime, see 42 U.S.C. § 9607(a); United States v. Bestfoods, 524 U.S. 51 (1998). On the Norwegian regime, see Lov om vern mot forurensninger og om avfall [Act of 13 March 1981 No. 6 Concerning Protection Against Pollution and Concerning Waste], §§ 51, 74, 76 (Nor.), https://www.regjeringen.no/en/dokumenter/pollution-control-act/id171893/ (translation, as of June 20, 2003, by the Norwegian Ministry of Climate and Environment); Beate Sjåfjell, *The Courts as Environmental Champions: The Norwegian Hempel Cases*, 13 EUR. COMPANY L. 199 (2016).

value chain context, imposing more rigorous requirements on parent companies in corporate groups and lead firms in supplier relationships alike.

In response to the 2013 Rana Plaza disaster, in which "a factory in Bangladesh collapsed killing 1,000 people"—a tragedy that "highlighted the responsibility of companies like Mango and Benetton in their dealings with subcontractors"[155]—the French Parliament in 2017 adopted a new Corporate Duty of Vigilance Law.[156] This law employs a disclosure strategy, but it does so as a means of advancing more fundamental reforms, requiring large French companies to "establish and implement an effective vigilance plan" including "reasonable vigilance measures to allow for risk identification and for the prevention of severe violations of human rights and fundamental freedoms, serious bodily injury or environmental damage or health risks resulting directly or indirectly from the operations of the company and of the companies it controls . . . as well as from the operations of the subcontractors or suppliers with whom it maintains an established commercial relationship, when such operations derive from this relationship." Critically, the plan must include "[a]ppropriate action to mitigate risks or prevent serious violations," and "any person with a legitimate interest" can petition the government to pursue enforcement, or directly seek damages in court.[157] As the European Coalition for Corporate Justice explains, French law defines the concept of an "established business relationship" quite broadly, reaching "all types of relations between professionals, defined as stable, regular relationships, with or without contract, with a certain volume of business, creating a reasonable expectation that such relation will last." Based on stated employee thresholds, the law covers "an estimated 100–150 large companies."[158]

The French Corporate Duty of Vigilance Law is regarded as "the most effective response to date to the existing business and human rights governance gaps,"[159] although enforcement presents challenges. Notably, those seeking damages bear the

[155] Cécile Barbière, *France Leads EU on Duty of Care Requirements for Multinationals*, EURACTIV, Feb. 22, 2017, https://www.euractiv.com/section/global-europe/news/france-leads-eu-on-duty-of-care-requirements-for-multinationals/ (translated by Samuel White).

[156] *See* Respect, *French Corporate Duty of Vigilance Law (English Translation)*, https://respect.international/french-corporate-duty-of-vigilance-law-english-translation/.

[157] Loi 2017-399 du 27 mars 2017 relative au devoir de vigilance des sociétés mères et des entreprises donneuses d'ordre [Corporate Duty of Vigilance Law], arts. 1–2 (Fr.) (translation by the European Coalition for Corporate Justice), https://respect.international/french-corporate-duty-of-vigilance-law-english-translation/. *See also* Véronique Magnier, *Old-Fashioned Yet Innovative: Corporate Law, Corporate Governance and Sustainability in France*, *in* THE CAMBRIDGE HANDBOOK OF CORPORATE LAW, CORPORATE GOVERNANCE AND SUSTAINABILITY, *supra* note 1, at 276, 281–83; European Coalition for Corporate Justice, *French Corporate Duty of Vigilance Law: Frequently Asked Questions* (revised Mar. 24, 2017), FAQs 1–6.

[158] European Coalition for Corporate Justice, *supra* note 157, at FAQs 3–4. The law applies to any company that, "at the end of two consecutive financial years, employs at least five thousand employees within the company and its direct and indirect subsidiaries, whose head office is located on French territory, or that has at least ten thousand employees in its service and in its direct or indirect subsidiaries, whose head office is located on French territory or abroad." Corporate Duty of Vigilance Law, *supra* note 157, art. 1.

[159] European Coalition for Corporate Justice, *supra* note 157, at FAQ 8. *See also* Sandra Cossart & Lucie Chatelain, *What Lessons Does France's Duty of Vigilance Law Have for Other National*

burden of proof, "meaning victims will still need to prove fault by the company and a causal link between the fault and the damage they have suffered."[160] As initially proposed, the law would have placed the burden on companies, "which would have ensured a more effective corporate liability regime," but this was dropped in the final version.[161] Likewise, "the original bill was softened during the long debate, with criminal prosecutions for company bosses among the measures removed from the final version," in addition to reducing the range of companies covered by the law.[162] "In the absence of an official list of companies covered," meanwhile, "it is often difficult to assess whether a company meets the thresholds provided by the law."[163] At the same time, plaintiffs have faced jurisdictional challenges. In 2019, the first lawsuit under the Corporate Duty of Vigilance Law was brought by "six environmental groups in France and Uganda" against "the French multinational energy company Total," charging Total with "violating human rights and endangering the environment" in connection with a large oil project in Uganda.[164] The Tribunal de Grande Instance in Nanterre decided that the case belonged in the Commercial Court, however, and in late 2020 the Versailles Court of Appeal arrived at the same conclusion—a result that NGOs involved have criticized for treating such matters as commercial in nature rather than as human rights and environmental matters.[165] In light of such challenges, the long-term effectiveness of the French law remains to be seen.[166]

Meanwhile, similar laws are taking shape in other jurisdictions. In 2019, the Dutch Senate approved a new Child Labor Due Diligence Law,[167] which requires any company that "sells or supplies goods or services to Dutch end users" to undertake due diligence to determine "whether there is a reasonable suspicion that

Initiatives?, BUS. & HUM. RTS. RESOURCE CTR., June 27, 2019, https://www.business-humanrights.org/en/blog/what-lessons-does-frances-duty-of-vigilance-law-have-for-other-national-initiatives/ (characterizing the law as "a milestone" and "unprecedented"). *See also* Hess, *supra* note 119, at 47–48.

[160] European Coalition for Corporate Justice, *supra* note 157, at FAQ 7. *See also* Magnier, *supra* note 157, at 284–85.

[161] Cossart & Chatelain, *supra* note 159.

[162] Barbière, *supra* note 155.

[163] Cossart & Chatelain, *supra* note 159.

[164] *Total Sued Under France's New Duty of Vigilance Law*, ENV'T NEWS SERV., Oct. 23, 2019, https://ens-newswire.com/total-sued-under-frances-new-duty-of-vigilance-law/.

[165] *See* Ed Reed, *Court Backs Total in Uganda Vigilance Case*, ENERGY VOICE, Dec. 10, 2020, https://www.energyvoice.com/oilandgas/africa/ep-africa/285055/total-uganda-vigilance-appeal/.

[166] Another lawsuit was filed in October 2020 by representatives of the indigenous Zapotec community Unión Hidalgo and human rights organizations from Mexico and France against Electricité de France (EDF), alleging human rights violations and environmental harms in connection with construction of a wind farm by EDF's Mexican subsidiaries on Unión Hidalgo land. *See* European Center for Constitutional and Human Rights, *Case Report: Wind Farm in Mexico: French Energy Firm EDF Disregards Indigenous Rights* (last updated Nov. 2020).

[167] Michael R. Littenberg et al., *Dutch Child Labor Due Diligence Act Approved by Senate—Implications for Global Companies*, ROPES & GRAY, June 5, 2019, at 1, https://www.ropesgray.com/en/newsroom/alerts/2019/06/Dutch-Child-Labor-Due-Diligence-Act-Approved-by-Senate-Implications-for-Global-Companies.

the goods or services to be supplied have been produced using child labor." If such reasonable suspicion exists, then the company must implement a "plan of action" in response.[168] The Act permits "[a]ny natural person or legal entity whose interests are affected by the actions or omissions of a company relating to compliance" to submit a complaint to the government,[169] which may result in administrative or criminal actions—including against a director of the subject company.[170] This is the first law "to introduce criminal sanctions for a failure to exercise human rights due diligence,"[171] and it is expected to take effect in 2022.[172] Once again, there are open questions regarding how the regime will operate, including which regulator will be appointed to oversee it, what the required plan of action must include, and whether any categories of companies will be exempted,[173] all of which could impact the Act's effectiveness. Germany likewise contemplates a new Supply Chain Act, expected to require large companies based in Germany to "ensure that their suppliers also comply with human rights, in particular forced labor, child labor, discrimination, violation of freedom of association, violation of occupational health and safety, problematic employment and working conditions . . ., violation of land rights, damage to health and soil or air pollution." If approved, the law would require "remedial actions," which could include "the duty to conduct investigations or terminate business relationships," and violations could trigger fines "and possibly exclusion from public tenders." The law would take effect in 2023 for companies with over 3,000 employees, and in 2024 for companies with over 1,000 employees.[174] Human rights due diligence legislation is also anticipated for EU companies.[175]

[168] Wet zorgplicht kinderarbeid van 7 februari 2017 [Child Labor Due Diligence Act], arts. 4–5 (Neth.) (translation commissioned by Ropes & Gray LLP), https://www.ropesgray.com/en/newsroom/alerts/2019/06/Dutch-Child-Labor-Due-Diligence-Act-Approved-by-Senate-Implications-for-Global-Companies.

[169] *Id.* art. 3.

[170] *See id.* arts. 7–9. For additional background, see *Mandatory Human Rights Due Diligence Laws: The Netherlands Led the Way in Addressing Child Labour and Contemplates Broader Action*, ALLEN & OVERY, Sept. 2, 2020, https://www.allenovery.com/en-gb/global/news-and-insights/publications/mandatory-human-rights-due-diligence-laws-the-netherlands-led-the-way-in-addressing-child-labour-and-contemplates-broader-action; Anneloes Hoff, *Dutch Child Labour Due Diligence Law: A Step Towards Mandatory Human Rights Due Diligence*, OXFORD HUMAN RIGHTS HUB, June 10, 2019, https://ohrh.law.ox.ac.uk/dutch-child-labour-due-diligence-law-a-step-towards-mandatory-human-rights-due-diligence/; Littenberg et al., *supra* note 167, at 3–4.

[171] Hoff, *supra* note 170.

[172] *See Mandatory Human Rights Due Diligence Laws*, *supra* note 170.

[173] *See* Hoff, *supra* note 170; *Mandatory Human Rights Due Diligence Laws*, *supra* note 170.

[174] Désirée Maier et al., *Current Status Supply Chain Act (Germany)*, HOGAN LOVELLS, Feb. 19, 2021, https://www.hlregulation.com/2021/02/19/current-status-supply-chain-act-germany/. *See also German Government Reaches Agreement on Supply Chain Act—Sources*, REUTERS, Feb. 12, 2021, https://www.reuters.com/article/germany-companies-supply-chains/german-government-reaches-agreement-on-supply-chain-act-sources-idUSL8N2KI22O; Erika Solomon, *German Plan for Supply Chain Law Stirs Debate Over Human Rights*, FIN. TIMES, July 20, 2020, at 2.

[175] *See Mandatory Human Rights Due Diligence Laws*, *supra* note 170.

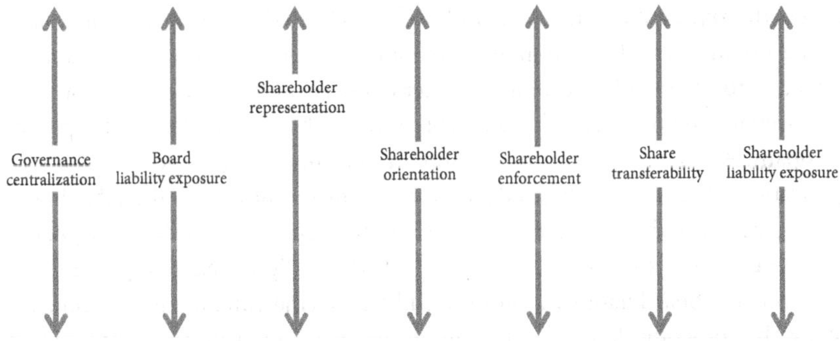

Figure 14 Due Diligence Laws and Multinational Subsidiaries

This new wave of due diligence laws moves well beyond the disclosure regimes discussed earlier, requiring multinational companies to exercise a higher level of care to detect and prevent abuses in their global value chains.[176] Only time will tell whether their aspirations are matched with robust enforcement[177]—particularly given the controversies and opposition from business groups that they have prompted.[178] Nevertheless, these developments demonstrate a trend toward imposing greater liability exposure upon multinational companies supplied by far-flung subsidiaries and contractors around the world—and even upon directors of those multinational companies—and the expectation is that this trend will continue.[179] In the context of parent-subsidiary relationships, enhanced liability exposure along these lines may effectively adjust the shareholder liability and board liability levers upward, as Figure 14 reflects.

Figure 14 reflects potential effects of due diligence laws like those described earlier from the perspective of a multinational subsidiary, based on some admittedly strong assumptions. Relative to the archetypal U.S. public company, the shareholder liability lever is adjusted upward, reflecting greater exposure for the subsidiary's parent company. As I have discussed in other contexts, this correlatively lowers the shareholder orientation lever, because it requires focusing on other constituencies and interests impacted by the subsidiary's operations, and

[176] *See, e.g.*, Littenberg et al., *supra* note 167, at 4; Parella, *supra* note 118, at 8–9, 27–29.

[177] *See, e.g.*, Magnier, *supra* note 157, at 285–86.

[178] For example, regarding business opposition in France, see Barbière, *supra* note 155; Curran, *supra* note 118, at 416–17. Regarding opposition in Germany, see *German Government Reaches Agreement on Supply Chain Act—Sources*, *supra* note 174; Solomon, *supra* note 174. Regarding opposition in the Netherlands, see Littenberg et al., *supra* note 167, at 1.

[179] *See, e.g.*, *Mandatory Human Rights Due Diligence Laws*, *supra* note 170 (observing "a wider legislative trend" to this effect); Sparkman, *supra* note 152 ("You can expect more U.S. legislation to be introduced in the future and if your company operates internationally, you already come under other countries' laws in this regard.").

lowers the shareholder enforcement lever as well, to the degree that these laws create broader standing for non-shareholders to pursue enforcement and/or remedies for their violation. Share transferability is lower because, by hypothesis, this scenario involves concentrated share ownership in the hands of a parent company. At the same time, this re-calibration would lower the governance centralization lever, due to enhanced parent company monitoring of the subsidiary's management, and might incentivize the parent company to demand greater exposure for the subsidiary's directors to further align their risk preferences, adjusting the board liability lever upward.[180] Differing combinations of reforms along the foregoing lines could naturally result in differing re-calibrations of the levers of governance, but this illustration suffices to convey the potential for substantial divergence from the status quo, and particularly for an overall moderating effect in terms of risk incentives and the overall orientation of decision-making in multinational subsidiaries.

At the same time, it is critical to recall that due diligence laws can have analogous effects for lead firms vis-à-vis their contractual suppliers. This is an important strength of this legal strategy for promoting corporate accountability in global value chains, given the turn to nominally arms'-length contractual structures that present substantial impediments to the pursuit of corporate sustainability through traditional legal avenues.[181]

C. Governing for Sustainability: Corporate Law and Governance in South Africa

Throughout the book we have examined a host of strategies for improving corporate accountability toward the goal of enhancing corporate sustainability. This chapter concludes with examination of a striking national effort to re-imagine corporate accountability along such lines, enlisting some (though by no means all) of the types of strategies examined in this book—the corporate governance system of post-apartheid South Africa. The South African experience provides a vivid case study through which to assess both pitfalls and opportunities that may arise in pursuing corporate sustainability through corporate governance.

The emergence of South Africa's contemporary corporate governance system is, to a great extent, a product of what comparative constitutional scholars describe as a "founding moment"—an historical circumstance where "landmark

[180] For discussion of analogous re-calibrations of various levers of governance that would result from greater shareholder liability in the financial firm context, see *supra* Chapter 7.A. Note that shareholder representation remains high in Figure 14 on the assumption that the subsidiary is not subject to co-determination.

[181] *See supra* notes 136–39, 155–58, and accompanying text.

events . . . break ties with the *ancien régime* and lay the foundation for the establishment of a new constitutional order."[182] Such events can involve varying degrees of revolution,[183] and potentially "follow from the emancipation of a sizeable section of citizens."[184] Such a founding moment effectively creates a new system of "sociological legitimacy,"[185] and "an enormous new wave of constitution-making" along such lines arose in the early 1990s "with many countries experiencing their move away from authoritarianism close together in time."[186] South Africa was one of them and, as we will see, the emergence of South Africa's contemporary corporate governance system clearly bears the imprint of their constitutional founding moment, definitively rejecting racial apartheid and embracing principles of human dignity, equality, and human rights.

It bears emphasizing, however, that despite the volatility of such transition periods, and despite the deliberate forging of a new order, legal institutions arising from constitutional founding moments often bear nontrivial resemblance to those of the prior order in various regulatory fields, including corporate governance—with implications that can be good or bad, depending on the circumstances. In this respect, the Russian Federation—which similarly experienced a constitutional founding moment in the early 1990s following dissolution of the Soviet Union—provides an illuminating comparison. For example, Eugene Mazo observes a high degree of path dependence in post-Soviet constitution-making, exemplified by the fact that post-Soviet republics, including Russia, largely adopted "semi-presidential executive organs and structures, ones that created a role for a president to function alongside a prime minister"—largely because Mikhail Gorbachev had imposed such a structure in the waning moments of the Soviet Union itself.[187] Similar path dependencies would inhibit the effort to forge a new market-based capitalist system after the collapse of the Soviet Union, and this was exemplified by the disastrous effort to implement Anglo-American-style corporate governance structures and capital markets in the Russian Federation, despite the lack of foundational legal and institutional structures supporting them elsewhere.

As part of the Western-led "shock therapy" approach, aimed at implementing capitalist structures before backsliding toward communism could occur, formerly state-owned enterprises were privatized through "mass voucher

[182] FOUNDING MOMENTS IN CONSTITUTIONALISM (Richard Albert et al. eds., 2019)(cover text).

[183] Richard Albert & Menaka Guruswamy, *Introduction: Mapping the Foundation*, *in* FOUNDING MOMENTS IN CONSTITUTIONALISM, *id.* at 1, 1.

[184] *Id.* at 4.

[185] *Id.* at 2.

[186] Eugene D. Mazo, *Path-Dependence in Soviet and Russian Constitution-Making*, *in* FOUNDING MOMENTS IN CONSTITUTIONALISM, *supra* note 182, at 133, 133.

[187] *See generally id.* This reflected Gorbachev's unsuccessful effort to displace the Communist Party apparatus in order to solidify his own authority to pursue economic reforms. *See id.* at 137–51.

privatization" aimed at promoting private ownership and creating political support for capitalism in Russia.[188] However, most of the stock was ultimately acquired at low prices by former managers and, following a series of further "rigged" privatizations, a de facto "kleptocracy" emerged that substantially undercut public trust in free markets.[189] As Bernard Black, Reinier Kraakman, and Anna Tarassova observe in a retrospective analysis (having had a hand in the reforms they describe),[190] the core problem was that Russia lacked effective institutions to control self-dealing, which became endemic following mass privatization of corporate stock in a context long characterized by widespread corruption.[191] Although Russian corporate governance has developed significantly since the chaotic early days of mass voucher privatization,[192] these factors continue to present challenges today; corruption remains a significant problem,[193] and constraints on controller self-dealing remain weak.[194]

As the Russian experience illustrates, "writing good laws can take years and building good institutions takes decades"—they cannot be created overnight, in the midst of a constitutional founding moment, regardless of anyone's best intentions.[195] This suggests that, even as a country definitively breaks from the past and sets a different course by reference to a new system of "sociological legitimacy,"[196] there is nevertheless a substantial advantage in having strong legal and institutional building blocks from the prior regime from which to begin constructing a new one. These dynamics have loomed large for South Africa, where they have definitively rejected apartheid and set out to build an inclusive and egalitarian society, yet did not have to start literally from scratch in constructing the post-apartheid economy and associated legal structures. As

[188] *See* Bernard Black et al., *Russian Privatization and Corporate Governance: What Went Wrong?*, 52 STAN. L. REV. 1731, 1739–40 (2000).
[189] *See id.* at 1740–49.
[190] *See id.* at 1734 n.3.
[191] *See id.* at 1750–90.
[192] For discussion of contemporary Russian corporate governance, see generally ANNA S. VLASOVA & NATALIA M. UDALOVA, DOING CORPORATE BUSINESS IN RUSSIA: FROM CIVIL THEORY TO PRACTICE (2018); Carsten Sprenger, *Limited Demand, Limited Supply: Corporate Governance and Sustainability in Russia*, *in* THE CAMBRIDGE HANDBOOK OF CORPORATE LAW, CORPORATE GOVERNANCE AND SUSTAINABILITY, *supra* note 1, at 317; Evgenia Teterevkova et al., *Corporate Governance and Directors' Duties in the Russian Federation: Overview*, THOMSON REUTERS PRAC. L., June 1, 2020.
[193] *See, e.g.*, Transparency International, *Our Work in Russia*, https://www.transparency.org/en/countries/russia (ranking Russia 129th of 180 jurisdictions included in the 2020 Corruption Perceptions Index).
[194] *See, e.g.*, Merritt B. Fox, *Ongoing Issues in Russian Corporate Governance*, 52 COLUM. J. TRANSNAT'L L. 435 (2014); Sprenger, *supra* note 192, at 318–24. *See also* World Bank Group, *Ease of Doing Business in Russian Federation*, https://www.doingbusiness.org/en/data/exploreeconomies/russia#DB_pi (ranking Russia 72nd of 190 jurisdictions included in the 2020 Doing Business project in terms of minority investor protections); World Bank Group, *About Us*, https://www.doingbusiness.org/en/about-us (describing the Doing Business project).
[195] Black et al., *supra* note 188, at 1753.
[196] *See* Albert & Guruswamy, *supra* note 183, at 2.

opposed to building entirely new institutions from the ground up of a sort that no one in the country had previously experienced, the project was rather to reform existing institutions in order to open them up and make associated benefits available to the previously oppressed majority population. While this remains a work in progress, as we will see, it is critical to recognize that post-apartheid reforms to South Africa's system of corporate law and governance fundamentally involve building upon preexisting structures that are well familiar to Anglo-American corporate lawyers, toward the goal of constructing a more sustainable corporate governance system. As such, the South African experience represents a highly instructive case study for other jurisdictions.

South Africa is an extraordinarily diverse society in multiple respects. An estimated 80 percent of South Africans are Black, 9.6 percent are white, approximately 9 percent are multiracial, and 2.6 percent are "of Asian descent (predominantly Indian and Chinese)." As South African historian Gail Nattrass explains, however, "these are not homogenous [sic] groups."[197] Indeed, South Africa has eleven official languages, the most commonly spoken at home being Zulu (23 percent), Xhosa (16 percent), Afrikaans (13.5 percent), and English (9.6 percent)—although English represents "the language of business and commerce" throughout the country.[198] At the same time, South Africa remains "one of the most unequal societies in the world," a "legacy of a succession of white-minority governments whose policies of segregation and apartheid left the majority of people disadvantaged."[199]

South Africa's sustainability challenges today reflect its complex and troubled history, in terms of both resource dependence and racial inequalities. Dutch colonists arrived at the Cape in the mid-seventeenth century and British colonists arrived in the early nineteenth century,[200] and these groups increasingly moved inland over the course of the nineteenth century—first with the so-called "Great Trek" of the Boers, white Afrikaans-speaking farmers, in the 1830s–1840s, and later following discovery of diamonds in Kimberley in 1867 and gold in the Witwatersrand region in 1886.[201] This "mineral revolution," in particular, "led to the development of South Africa's infrastructure, its railways and harbours, and a more capital-intensive agriculture to meet growing markets

[197] GAIL NATTRASS, A SHORT HISTORY OF SOUTH AFRICA 6 (2019). *See also* Robert G. Eccles et al., *Integrated Reporting in South Africa* 3 (Harvard Business School case no. 9-413-038, rev. Nov. 20, 2012).

[198] *See* NATTRASS, *supra* note 197, at 6–7. *See also* S. AFR. CONST., 1996, § 6 (recognizing 11 official languages and further calling for promotion of "all languages commonly used by communities in South Africa").

[199] NATTRASS, *supra* note 197, at 7.

[200] *See id.* at 36–40, 46–51.

[201] *See id.* at 72–103.

and the needs of a growing population," but also led to the conquest and subjugation of preexisting African kingdoms.[202]

Following defeat of the Boers in what came to be called the Anglo-Boer War, the British declared sovereignty over the region in 1902 and the Union of South Africa was formed in 1910.[203] Not long afterward, the 1913 Land Act "made it illegal for blacks to purchase or lease land except in demarcated reserves," which effectively "restricted black occupancy to less than 8 per cent of South Africa's land"—a move that "laid the foundation . . . for the segregated homelands policy that followed," under which the Black population was restricted to just 14 percent of South Africa's land.[204] In 1948, the Afrikaner-led "Purified National Party" (PNP) rose to power and immediately proceeded to implement apartheid policies under which non-white people, "all generally referred to as 'blacks' by the authorities," were "excluded from any active or meaningful participation in government and were disadvantaged in terms of opportunity and education."[205] From 1948 until 1993, apartheid remained the official policy of the South African government, strictly segregating the country by race in essentially all domains of life.[206]

The precursor of the African National Congress (ANC) was established in 1912, and by the time the PNP took power in the late 1940s, the ANC (which adopted this name in 1923) had already "become a mass organisation."[207] Around that same time, the ANC's Youth League began to pursue "more decisive action," and facilitated the work of a number of young activists who would provide critical leadership in the anti-apartheid movement over coming decades, including Nelson Mandela, Walter Sisulu, and Oliver Tambo.[208] Their campaign of civil disobedience was modeled on that of Mohandas Gandhi, whose own social consciousness had been formed in part through his experience of discrimination in South Africa during his time there as a young lawyer for Indian traders.[209] Following the Sharpville Massacre in 1960—in which police killed 69 people and wounded about 180 who were protesting the requirement that Black people

[202] *See id.* at 84, 104–18.
[203] *See id.* at 120–38.
[204] *Id.* at 142–44, 169–71.
[205] *See id.* at 155–57, 167–68.
[206] *See* Frank Sampong et al., *"Apartheid-Induced" Corporate Social Responsibility in the Context of South Africa: A Review*, 8 DEVELOPING COUNTRY STUD. 62, 63–64 (2018); Collins G. Ntim & Teerooven Soobaroyen, *Black Economic Empowerment Disclosures by South African Listed Corporations: The Influence of Ownership and Board Characteristics*, 116 J. BUS. ETHICS 121, 122–23 (2013). For a vivid personal account of life among and between racial categories during the late apartheid era, see TREVOR NOAH, BORN A CRIME AND OTHER STORIES 25–38 (2017) ("During apartheid, one of the worst crimes you could commit was to have sexual relations with a person of another race. Needless to say, my parents committed that crime.").
[207] *See* NATTRASS, *supra* note 197, at 141–44.
[208] *See id.* at 176–77.
[209] *See id.* at 94, 177–79.

"carry documents allowing them to 'pass' into urban areas"—the ANC and other parties were banned.[210] In 1961, South Africa left the British Commonwealth following a referendum limited to white voters, and the newly independent Republic of South Africa imposed a series of increasingly draconian security laws.[211] At this point, the ANC "went underground and military wings were established" following "many decades of nonviolent resistance, which was met by increasingly brutal repression by the apartheid regime." Several leaders, including Mandela and Sisulu, were found guilty of treason, and became globally recognized figures who would spend decades in prison for their role in resisting apartheid.[212]

By the 1970s, economic strains were increasingly felt due to strikes, sanctions, boycotts, and economic inefficiencies, and the government increasingly responded to the anti-apartheid movement with systematic torture and assassinations.[213] At the same time, the Black Consciousness movement and the 1976 Soweto uprising—protesting a decree "that Afrikaans was to be the medium of instruction in African secondary schools"—captured increasing attention worldwide.[214] By the mid-1980s, under "both international and internal pressure," the government began to make limited concessions, including recognizing Black trade unions, and the Congress of South African Trade Unions (COSATU) was established. In 1987 there were over 1,100 strikes, "the most serious being a strike of the National Mine Workers (NUM) led by Cyril Ramaphosa."[215]

Around this same time, "a series of secret meetings began to take place" outside the country "between members of the ANC and church people, white business leaders and other influential whites," and these eventually included the government itself.[216] In 1990, then, due to "forces from within South Africa and pressure from the outside world," State President F.W. de Klerk announced that "open negotiations for a democratic constitution, equality before the law and the protection of minority and individual rights" would be held. Additionally, the ban on the ANC and other parties would be removed, and those imprisoned due to association with those parties, including Mandela, would be released. This led to negotiations between the government and the ANC, repeal of several discriminatory laws, and ultimately an election open to all races—which the ANC handily won, resulting in Nelson Mandela becoming "South Africa's

[210] *Id.* at 187–88.

[211] *Id.* at 188–89, 196.

[212] *See id.* at 191–94. Tambo went into exile and supported the movement from abroad. *See id.* at 188, 194.

[213] *See id.* at 199, 205–07, 216–17.

[214] *See id.* at 210–13. *See also* Sampong et al., *supra* note 206, at 64.

[215] NATTRASS, *supra* note 197, at 215. On the "important sociopolitical role" that unions played in the struggle against apartheid, see WORLD BANK, OVERCOMING POVERTY AND INEQUALITY IN SOUTH AFRICA: AN ASSESSMENT OF DRIVERS, CONSTRAINTS AND OPPORTUNITIES 91 (Mar. 2018).

[216] NATTRASS, *supra* note 197, at 217–18.

first democratically elected president." A new constitution was adopted in 1996, for which Cyril Ramaphosa acted as the chief ANC negotiator, and South Africa rejoined the British Commonwealth. President Mandela pursued what Nattrass describes as a "reconciliatory presidency" from 1994 to 1999, including a "Truth and Reconciliation Commission" designed to "deal with human rights abuses and heal some of the pain of the past."[217]

The foregoing history, although cursory, points toward several themes that are directly pertinent to achieving sustainability in post-apartheid South Africa, including in the corporate context. These include the extraordinary diversity of South Africa and its people; the persistent problem of inequalities stemming from the apartheid era; and a high level of dependence on resource extraction, which remains central to South Africa's economy today. All of these have significantly impacted how South Africa has come to approach corporate sustainability since the advent of democracy in 1994.

Recognition of these dynamics and challenges is amply reflected in the South African constitution adopted in 1996. The constitution expressly aims to "Heal the divisions of the past and establish a society based on democratic values, social justice and fundamental human rights,"[218] and expressly affirms "Human dignity, the achievement of equality and the advancement of human rights and freedoms" as core values.[219] The "Bill of Rights" included in the constitution emphasizes achievement of equality, including through affirmative action policies,[220] and provides more generally that courts interpreting South African legislation and developing its common law "must promote the spirit, purport and objects of the Bill of Rights."[221] The Bill of Rights expressly addresses various subjects that relate directly to corporate sustainability, including rights to freely choose one's occupation, to enjoy "fair labour practices," and to participate in a trade union,[222] as well as the right to environmental protection "for the benefit of present and future generations." This includes "measures that . . . secure ecologically sustainable development and use of natural resources while promoting justifiable economic and social development,"[223] gesturing toward tensions and trade-offs across these dimensions of sustainability in a highly resource-dependent economy like South Africa's.

Strikingly, there is express provision for anyone "alleging that a right in the Bill of Rights has been infringed or threatened" to seek "appropriate relief"

[217] *See id.* at 219–32.
[218] S. AFR. CONST., 1996, Preamble.
[219] *Id.* §§ 1, 7.
[220] *See id.* §§ 9 (Equality), 25 (Property), 29 (Education). *See also id.* § 217 (permitting affirmative action in public procurement).
[221] *See id.* § 39.
[222] *See id.* §§ 22–23.
[223] *Id.* § 24.

in court,[224] and this could have particular significance in the context of corporate sustainability, because the Bill of Rights expressly binds both "natural" and "juristic" persons.[225] Although it may remain debatable "whether private parties—particularly multinational corporations—ought to have human rights obligations" in the "international law context,"[226] this constitutional structure "expressly imposes human rights obligations on private persons" as a matter of domestic South African law, toward the goal of "dismantling the legacy of colonialism and apartheid."[227]

This constitutional context has had a profound impact on South Africa's post-apartheid company law, but comprehending its structure and sustainability-related features requires additional context on the evolution of South African corporate governance norms. The challenges that faced South Africa in the wake of the apartheid era were extreme, but unlike in the case of Russia, in South Africa these challenges were "tempered by the country's solid institutions, democratic traditions, and well-respected constitution."[228] In the context of corporate governance, these institutional dynamics have been reflected in the evolution of the King Code—the product of a committee chaired by Mervyn King—the first iteration of which (King I) was issued in 1994.[229] Subsequent iterations of the King Code would be released in 2002 (King II), 2009 (King III), and 2016 (King IV). Although South Africa's company law had long tracked highly shareholder-centric English models, the King Code "advocated an integrated approach to good governance in the interests of a wide range of stakeholders," advancing concepts now widely associated with integrated reporting and corporate sustainability more generally.[230] The King Code also identifies as one of its "fundamental concepts" the "African concept of *Ubuntu* or *Botho*, captured by the expressions *uMuntu ngumuntu ngabantu* and *Motho ke motho ka batho*—I am because

[224] *Id.* § 38.

[225] *See id.* § 8. For background on application of the Bill of Rights to "juristic" persons, see STUART WOOLMAN & MICHAEL BISHOP, CONSTITUTIONAL LAW OF SOUTH AFRICA 31-39–31-42, 31-62–31-63, 31-74–31-75 (2d ed. 2014); M. Gwanyanya, *The South African* Companies Act *and the Realisation of Corporate Human Rights Responsibilities*, 18 POTCHEFSTROOM ELECTRONIC L.J. 3102, 3114 (2015). *See also* Fred Khumalo and Others v. Bantubonke Harrington Holomisa (53/01) [2002] (S. Afr.) (O'Regan J., Constitutional Court of South Africa).

[226] Mbuyiseli Madlanga, Justice, Constitutional Court of South Africa, The Human Rights Duties of Companies and Other Private Actors in South Africa, Stellenbosch Human Rights Lecture (Aug. 30, 2018), at 3–4, https://www.sun.ac.za/english/Documents/PDF_Stellenbosch%20University_Annual%20Human%20Rights%20Lecture%20_2018%20-%20for%20delivery.pdf.

[227] *Id.* at 6–12.

[228] *See* Eccles et al., *supra* note 197, at 4.

[229] *See* Michael Barrier, *Principles, Not Rules: Thanks to Codes Drafted Under Mervyn King, South Africa Has Taken the Lead in Defining Corporate Governance in Broadly Inclusive Terms*, 60 INTERNAL AUDITOR (2003) (interview with Mervyn King).

[230] *See* Tshepo H. Mongalo, *The Social and Ethics Committee: Innovating Corporate Governance in South Africa*, *in* THE CAMBRIDGE HANDBOOK OF CORPORATE LAW, CORPORATE GOVERNANCE AND SUSTAINABILITY, *supra* note 1, at 360, 360–61. *See also* Stephen D. Girvan, *The Antecedents of South African Company Law*, 13 J. LEGAL HIST. 63, 67–72 (1992).

you are; you are because we are." As King IV explains, these "imply that there should be a common purpose to all human endeavours (including corporate endeavours) which is based on service to humanity."[231] In the business context, as Zenzo Dube observes, this "implies that the organisation foremost and above all sees its commitment in a holistic way, a commitment which encompasses the interests of both shareholders and non-shareholding stakeholders."[232] In the King Code, this orientation takes the form of express regard for "sustainable development" and "stakeholder inclusivity," with longer-term orientation in board decision-making,[233] creating an obvious tension with South Africa's historical embrace of English-style, shareholder-centric company law models.[234]

Broadly speaking, the King Code can be viewed as balancing "pressures from international governance standards and institutional investors" with "pressures emanating from the transformation of South African society,"[235] and is now widely considered "ground-breaking" in its "aspiration to set international standards of best practice as South Africa sought to become internationally competitive and simultaneously foster an inclusive approach to the role of business."[236] As King himself would observe in a later interview, "[r]ather than focusing just on the financial aspects of governance, like the United Kingdom's 1992 Cadbury Code, we went for an integrated approach that looked at stakeholders as a whole who were linked through the company, and at how the board should deal with those stakeholders. It was the first time anyone had taken an integrated approach in articulating governance guidelines," and this included addressing "what became known as affirmative action," prior to the adoption of formal legislation in the area.[237] In this respect, King explains that the committee's "remit was wider than that of the Cadbury Committee and embraced issues other than the financial aspects of governance"—but he emphasizes the significance of context in this regard, adding that in "the new South Africa, it would have been an act of commercial folly for directors to have directed their companies on an exclusive basis, thereby ignoring all stakeholders other than the providers of capital."[238]

[231] INSTITUTE OF DIRECTORS SOUTHERN AFRICA, KING IV: REPORT ON CORPORATE GOVERNANCE FOR SOUTH AFRICA 24 (2016) [hereinafter KING IV]. *See also* Zenzo L. Dube, *The King Reports on Corporate Governance in South Africa: An* Ubuntu *African Philosophy Analysis*, *in* CORPORATE GOVERNANCE IN AFRICA 199, 203–05 (K.E. Howell & M.K. Sorour eds., 2016); Sampong et al., *supra* note 206, at 65.

[232] Dube, *supra* note 231, at 201.

[233] *See* KING IV, *supra* note 231, at 22–26.

[234] *See* Dube, *supra* note 231, at 207–08, 214–15. *See also* Stefan Andreasson, *Understanding Corporate Governance Reform in South Africa: Anglo-American Divergence, the King Reports, and Hybridization*, 50 BUS. & SOC'Y 647, 655–56, 660 (2011); Richard Croucher & Lilian Miles, *Corporate Governance and Employees in South Africa*, 10 J. CORP. L. STUD. 367, 370–77 (2010).

[235] Andreasson, *supra* note 234, at 656.

[236] Eccles et al., *supra* note 197, at 5.

[237] Barrier, *supra* note 229 (interview with King).

[238] MERVYN E. KING, THE CORPORATE CITIZEN: GOVERNANCE FOR ALL ENTITIES 8–9 (2006). *See also* Henk Kloppers, *CSR, Corporate Governance, and the King Reports*, *in* SUSTAINABILITY AND

King IV represents "a set of voluntary principles and leading practices," and "aspires to apply to all organisations, regardless of their form of incorporation," although it "includes supplements for specific sectors."[239] Significantly, King IV also calls upon institutional investors to "promote the good governance and the creation of value" at investee companies,[240] reflecting the fact that—in sharp contrast with other jurisdictions[241]—South African pension fund regulations affirmatively require them to "consider any factor which may materially affect the sustainable long term performance of the asset including, but not limited to, those of an environmental, social and governance character."[242] King IV's principles adopt an "apply and explain" standard, reflecting "the less prescriptive approach adopted," while at the same time placing "greater emphasis on transparency with regards to how judgment was exercised when considering the practice recommendations" presented.[243] Substantively, King IV's approach is expressly associated with "integrated reporting" and "integrated thinking," emphasizing environmental, social, and economic sustainability through focus on six distinct capitals involved in the production of value—"financial, manufactured, intellectual, human, social and relationships, and natural capitals."[244]

King himself has long remained opposed to fixing corporate governance principles in legislation, favoring flexible soft-law approaches tailored to a given business,[245] but the King Code nevertheless has various forms of direct and indirect impact upon hard law. King IV itself acknowledges that such recommended practices may impact how courts develop standards of director conduct under company law,[246] and the King Code has itself been referenced in South African case law as a benchmark for "sound corporate governance."[247] In a more directly

SOCIAL RESPONSIBILITY: REGULATION AND REPORTING 55, 55 (G. Gal et al. eds. 2018) (observing that apartheid had "caused many international brands to withdraw from the country in protest to the situation").

[239] KING IV, *supra* note 231, at 35. *See also id.* at 40–73 (setting seventeen principles and recommended practices associated with them).

[240] *Id.* at 73.

[241] *See supra* Chapter 6.B.

[242] Pension Funds Act, 1956: Amendment of Regulation 28 of the Regulations Made Under Section 36, No. R. 183, reg. 28(2)(c)(ix) (S. Afr.). *See also* KING IV, *supra* note 231, at 32–33, 73.

[243] KING IV, *supra* note 231, at 27.

[244] *Id.* at 23–26. *See also* Eccles et al., *supra* note 197, at 9–12; Michael Judin et al., *Corporate Governance . . . Innovative Thinking in South Africa's Latest Code*, 2017 BUS. L. TODAY 1 (2017); Kloppers, *supra* note 238, at 75–76. For an example of such a report by a prominent South African company, see generally ANGLO AMERICAN PLATINUM LIMITED, INTEGRATED REPORT: UNLOCKING OUR FULL POTENTIAL (2018). *See also* Croucher & Miles, *supra* note 234, at 381 ("Anglo American is an exceptional company in that, unlike its competitors, it played a role in opposition to apartheid.").

[245] *See* Barrier, *supra* note 229 (interview with King). *See also* Andreasson, *supra* note 234, at 663; Kloppers, *supra* note 238, at 58.

[246] *See* KING IV, *supra* note 231, at 35.

[247] Minister of Water Affairs and Forestry v. Stilfontein Gold Mining Company Limited and Others (7655/05) [2006] ZAGPHC 47 ¶¶ 16.7–16.9 (S. Afr.) (Hussain J., High Court of South Africa, Witwatersrand Local Division). *See also* Croucher & Miles, *supra* note 234, at 373; Irene-marié

regulatory spirit, meanwhile, the Johannesburg Stock Exchange (JSE) has made compliance with certain elements of the King Code compulsory for listed companies.[248] Indeed, "South Africa was the first country to mandate integrated reporting for all companies listed on [the JSE]," and the King Code "was further institutionally validated in 2005 when the JSE launched its Social Responsibility Index . . . making South Africa the first emerging market and exchange in the world to bring sustainability issues to the fore."[249] At the same time, the King Code has impacted statutory reforms to company law as well.[250]

Before turning to that, however, another essential element of the context for understanding South African company law is affirmative action legislation, along the lines contemplated by the constitution.[251] As in other areas of law, South African labor law was largely racialized during the apartheid era, effectively amounting to "a dual system of labour relations based on race," with distinct union structures.[252] Although Black trade unions were largely restricted in the 1960s, "unregistered black trade unions took hold" in the 1970s. By the late 1980s, COSATU had formed and become a major force—not solely in collective bargaining, but in the struggle to end apartheid more generally.[253] As discussed, the Bill of Rights includes labor provisions,[254] and affirmative action policies have been pursued in the corporate context as a means of realizing the constitutional

Esser & Piet Delport, *The Protection of Stakeholders: The South African Social and Ethics Committee and the United Kingdom's Enlightened Shareholder Value Approach: Part 1*, 2017 DE JURE 97, 106–07 (2017); Nereus L. Joubert, *Reigniting the Corporate Conscience: Reflections on Some Aspects of Social and Ethics Committees of Companies Listed on the Johannesburg Stock Exchange*, *in* ESSAYS IN HONOUR OF FRANS MALAN 183, 187 n.19 (Coenraad Visser et al. eds., 2014); Judin et al., *supra* note 244; Judith Katzew, *Crossing the Divide Between the Business of the Corporation and the Imperatives of Human Rights—The Impact of Section 7 of the Companies Act 71 of 2008*, 128 SOUTH AFRICAN L.J. 686, 707 (2011). More generally, South African case law has articulated a broad conception of what "corporate governance" involves. *See* Mthimunye-Bakoro v. Petroleum Oil and Gas Corporation of South Africa (SOC) Limited and Another (12476/2015) [2015] ZAWCHC 113 (S. Afr.) (Davis J., High Court of South Africa, Western Cape Division, Cape Town) (describing "the animating idea" of corporate governance as being "to ensure net gains in wealth for shareholders, protect the legitimate concerns of other stakeholders and improve efficiency, organisational performance and resource allocation").

[248] *See* Johannesburg Stock Exchange Limited, Listings Requirements ¶ 3.84. *See also* Andreasson, *supra* note 234, at 663; Croucher & Miles, *supra* note 234, at 376–77; Judin et al., *supra* note 244. Although South Africa has three capitals—Cape Town being the legislative capital, Bloemfontein the judicial capital, and Pretoria the administrative capital—Johannesburg remains the largest city in South Africa and "its economic center." Eccles et al., *supra* note 197, at 2.

[249] Eccles et al., *supra* note 197, at 1–8. *See also* Sampong et al., *supra* note 206, at 65.

[250] *See* Esser & Delport, *supra* note 247, at 105.

[251] *See* Kloppers, *supra* note 238, at 62–63.

[252] *See* DEBBIE COLLIER ET AL., LABOUR LAW IN SOUTH AFRICA: CONTEXT AND PRINCIPLES 19–26 (2018).

[253] *See id.* at 26–29.

[254] *See id.* at 28.

principle of equality—notably through the Employment Equity Act (EEA) and the Broad-Based Black Economic Empowerment Act (B-BBEEA).[255]

Apartheid's "defining feature" having been "the use of race to restrict and severely control access to the economy by black persons,"[256] the EEA and the B-BBEEA both expressly aim to enhance economic opportunities. Under the EEA, enacted in 1998, "[e]very employer must take steps to promote equal opportunity in the workplace by eliminating unfair discrimination in any employment policy or practice," and "affirmative action measures" are expressly permitted.[257] Certain larger employers, however, are required to implement affirmative action measures, and must also consult with employees and prepare employment equity plans, among other statutory requirements.[258]

The B-BBEEA, enacted in 2003, focuses on equity ownership and managerial power. For purposes of this statute, the term "black people" is defined broadly to include non-white people, and "broad-based black economic empowerment" is defined to mean "the viable economic empowerment of all black people . . . through diverse but integrated socio-economic strategies," including "increasing the number of black people that manage, own and control enterprises and productive assets."[259] This regime involves scoring companies based on ownership, management, skills development, enterprise and supplier development, and socioeconomic development,[260] and listed companies, among others, are required to publicly file reports "on their compliance with broad-based black economic empowerment."[261]

Both the EEA and the B-BBEEA contemplate public enforcement and seek to incentize compliance through preferential public procurement programs,[262] although realizing the aims of these statutes has remained a challenge. For example, in the Black economic empowerment context, concerns have been raised

[255] *See id.* at 479–91. Industry-specific regimes have also been implemented. *See, e.g.*, Mineral and Petroleum Resources Development Act 28 of 2002 § 2 (S. Afr.); Mineral and Petroleum Resources Development Regulations, No. R. 527 of 2004, regs. 40–46 (S. Afr.); Mongalo, *supra* note 230, at 369–70.

[256] Irene-marié Esser & Adriette Dekker, *The Dynamics of Corporate Governance in South Africa: Broad Based Black Economic Empowerment and the Enhancement of Good Corporate Governance Principles*, 3 J. INT'L COM. L. & TECH. 157 (2008). *See also* Okechukwu C. Iheduru, *Black Economic Power and Nation-Building in Post-Apartheid South Africa*, 42 J. MOD. AFRICAN STUD. 1, 4 (2004).

[257] Employment Equity Act 55 of 1998 §§ 5–6 (S. Afr.).

[258] *See id.* §§ 12–27.

[259] Broad-Based Black Economic Empowerment Act 53 of 2003 § 1 (S. Afr.). *See also* COLLIER ET AL., *supra* note 252, at 289–90.

[260] *See* Norton Rose Fulbright, *Broad-Based Black Economic Empowerment—Basic Principles* (July 2018), https://www.nortonrosefulbright.com/en/knowledge/publications/fe87cd48/broad-based-black-economic-empowerment---basic-principles.

[261] Broad-Based Black Economic Empowerment Act 53 of 2003 § 13G (S. Afr.).

[262] *See* COLLIER ET AL., *supra* note 252, at 487–90; Natania Locke, *Enhanced Accountability, in* CORPORATE GOVERNANCE REVIEW 2012 65, 116–17 (Michele Havenga & Irene-marié Esser eds., 2012); Norton Rose Fulbright, *supra* note 260; Sampong et al., *supra* note 206, at 67.

about empowering a politically connected "small black elite" to the exclusion of the majority of the population.[263] Further concerns have been raised about "fronting," which refers to various practices that may create the appearance of compliance without in fact providing substantive managerial or economic rights and benefits.[264]

Constitutional principles, evolving corporate governance norms reflected in the King Code, and affirmative action legislation together represent the backdrop against which the Companies Act 2008 was adopted.[265] Given the historical reliance on English company law models,[266] it might have been tempting to track the U.K. Companies Act 2006, regardless of contextual fit—say, in an effort to attract foreign investment.[267] South Africa long tracked English statutory models with only limited departures and "continually referred to English cases for guidance when interpreting provisions of companies legislation,"[268] resulting in strong-form shareholder-centrism,[269] but it was abundantly clear by the early 1990s that the "political future of the country will undoubtedly play a major role in shaping the development of its company law," and that it would come to reflect "the socio-political process at present under way."[270]

In 2004, when the Department of Trade and Industry (DTI) published its "guidelines" for reform of South Africa's company law, the undertaking was expressly framed by reference to the "fundamental legal developments" that had unfolded since the Companies Act 1973 was enacted, of which the "most important change was the adoption of the Constitution of 1996." The DTI further cited the ongoing effort "to dismantle apartheid social relations and create a democratic society based on equity, equality, non-racialism and non-sexism."[271]

[263] *See* Ntim & Soobaroyen, *supra* note 206, at 123. *See also* Croucher & Miles, *supra* note 234, at 385; Esser & Dekker, *supra* note 256; Iheduru, *supra* note 256, at 2–3, 15–25; Sampong et al., *supra* note 206, at 66.

[264] *See* Broad-Based Black Economic Empowerment Act 53 of 2003 §§ 1, 13J (S. Afr.); Aubrey Sibanda, *Weighing the Cost of "BEE Fronting" on Best Practices of Corporate Governance in South Africa*, 29 SPECULUM JURIS 23 (2015). *See also* COLLIER ET AL., *supra* note 252, at 490–91; Iheduru, *supra* note 256, at 23; Locke, *supra* note 262, at 117.

[265] *See* DENNIS DAVIS ET AL., COMPANIES AND OTHER BUSINESS STRUCTURES 4 (4th ed. 2019); DEON ROSSOUW, THE SOCIAL AND ETHICS COMMITTEE HANDBOOK: A GUIDEBOOK FOR SOUTH AFRICAN COMPANIES 9–10 (2d ed. 2018); Gwanyanya, *supra* note 225, at 3107–09; Ruth Jebe et al., *Fostering Corporate Sustainability through Directors' Duties: South Africa's Attempt to Align Corporate Governance with Its Constitution*, 25 ILSA J. INT'L & COMP. L. 117, 134–38 (2018).

[266] *See* Mongalo, *supra* note 230, at 360.

[267] *See, e.g.*, James Thuo Gathii, *Lessons from the Transplantation of Kenya's 2015 Companies Act From the U.K.'s Companies Act of 2006*, AFRONOMICSLAW, Apr. 11, 2020, https://www.afronomicslaw.org/2020/04/11/lessons-from-the-transplantation-of-kenyas-2015-companies-act-from-the-u-k-s-companies-act-of-2006/# (describing such a move per such a rationale in Kenya).

[268] *See* Girvin, *supra* note 230, at 67–73.

[269] DAVIS ET AL., *supra* note 265, at 10.

[270] Girvin, *supra* note 230, at 74 (writing in 1992).

[271] REPUBLIC OF SOUTH AFRICA DEPARTMENT OF TRADE AND INDUSTRY, NOTICE 1183 OF 2004, SOUTH AFRICAN COMPANY LAW FOR THE 21ST CENTURY: GUIDELINES FOR CORPORATE LAW REFORM 16 (May 2004).

DTI argued that "South African law needs to take into account the unique South African context, including the best interests of South Africa and its citizens and the mandates of the Constitution," and accordingly proposed that "the company law needs to take account of stakeholders such as the community in which the company operates, its customers, its employees, its suppliers and the environment in certain situations," rejecting shareholder primacy in a manner consistent with the constitution and the King Code.[272] "While the harmonisation of new South African Company law with that of international jurisdictions may be desirable," the DTI added, "it may not always be appropriate for South African conditions."[273]

To be sure, significant aspects of the Companies Act 2008 build directly upon historical English models. For example, shareholders in a South African company retain strong statutory powers to amend the memorandum of incorporation unilaterally,[274] to call special meetings,[275] to elect directors and remove them by ordinary resolution,[276] and to approve use of takeover defenses[277]—forms of governance authority that clearly resemble those available to U.K. shareholders.[278] The directors' duty of loyalty, meanwhile, remains rooted in "the best interest of the company,"[279] a concept traditionally understood in English law to mean the best interests of shareholders—although the term is not expressly defined in the Companies Act 2008, and there is some debate regarding whether this interpretation remains valid in light of broader structural changes to South African company law adopted in the statute.[280]

Notwithstanding adherence to historical English models on these points, the Companies Act 2008 introduces several significant developments that depart markedly from the prior shareholder-centric paradigm. As a threshold matter, the statute reflects the constitutional reality that a company is regarded as a "juristic person,"[281] and expressly conditions interpretation and application

[272] *Id.* at 27. *See also id.* at 21–29.

[273] *Id.* at 30–31. *See also* Jebe et al., *supra* note 265, at 127–30.

[274] *See* Companies Act 71 of 2008 §§ 15–16, 65 (S. Afr.).

[275] *See id.* § 61.

[276] *See id.* §§ 68, 71.

[277] *See id.* § 126. This is likely of greater theoretical than practical significance, however, because a "large proportion of Johannesburg Stock Exchange (JSE) listings are effectively controlled by groups with a pyramidal ownership structure." Samuel Fosu, *Capital Structure, Product Market Competition and Firm Performance: Evidence from South Africa*, 53 Q. REV. ECON. & FIN. 140, 141 (2013).

[278] *See* BRUNER, *supra* note 9, at 29–36.

[279] *See* Companies Act 71 of 2008 § 76(3) (S. Afr.).

[280] *See, e.g.*, KING IV, *supra* note 231, at 26; MALEKA FEMIDA CASSIM, THE NEW DERIVATIVE ACTION UNDER THE COMPANIES ACT: GUIDELINES FOR JUDICIAL DISCRETION 74–77 (2016); FAROUK H.I. CASSIM ET AL., CONTEMPORARY COMPANY LAW 514–17 (2d ed. 2015); HENOCHSBERG ON THE COMPANIES ACT 71 OF 2008 at 298(9)–298(19) (P.A. Delport ed., updated May 2019) [hereinafter HENOCHSBERG]; Esser & Delport, *supra* note 247, at 107–08; Jebe et al., *supra* note 265, at 140–43.

[281] *See* Companies Act 71 of 2008 §§ 1, 19 (S. Afr.). *See also* HENOCHSBERG, *supra* note 280, at 81–83.

by reference to purposes that include "promot[ing] compliance with the Bill of Rights" and "reaffirm[ing] the concept of the company as a means of achieving economic and social benefits."[282] Significantly, it has been argued that directors' duties should accordingly be interpreted to require "balancing" the pursuit of profit with "policies to ensure that the social, transformative purpose of the company as set out in s 7 of the Companies Act and the Constitution, are achieved."[283] At the same time, whereas board powers under the Companies Act 1973 were limited to those delegated by shareholders, South African boards under the Companies Act 2008 possess direct statutory authority "to exercise all of the powers and perform any of the functions of the company"[284]—a change that represents a transition from a more shareholder-centric, English-style conception of corporate governance authority toward a more board-centric, American-style conception.[285] Additionally, the Companies Act 2008 requires various categories of large companies to have "social and ethics committees,"[286] discussed later in the chapter.

Strikingly, the statute empowers various non-shareholder constituencies to pursue powerful remedies of a sort that are typically reserved for shareholders. Derivative standing has been extended well beyond shareholders; a derivative action can now be pursued by a director, a prescribed officer, "a registered trade union that represents employees of the company, or another representative of employees of the company," or anyone else who "has been granted leave of the court . . . if the court is satisfied that it is necessary or expedient to do so to protect a legal right of that other person."[287] Express derivative standing for employee representatives "appears to be unique to South African law,"[288] and it has been argued that the catch-all category may bring actual or potential human rights violations within the ambit of derivative litigation.[289] Meanwhile, other causes of action under the Companies Act 2008 appear even more open-ended. "One or more shareholders, directors or prescribed officers of a company, or a trade union representing employees of the company, may take proceedings to restrain the

[282] *See* Companies Act 71 of 2008 §§ 5, 7 (S. Afr.); John Frederick Booysen v. Jonkheer Boerewynmakery (Pty) Ltd and Daniel Terblanche (10999/16) [2016] ¶¶ 41–46 (S. Afr.) (Sher A.J., High Court of South Africa, Western Cape Division, Cape Town). *See also* DAVIS ET AL., *supra* note 265, at 6; 2 WALTER D. GEACH, GUIDE TO THE COMPANIES ACT AND REGULATIONS 1–35 (updated 2019); HENOCHSBERG, *supra* note 280, at 49–52; 1 J.L. YEATS ET AL., COMMENTARY ON THE COMPANIES ACT OF 2008 1-41–1-46 (2018).

[283] Katzew, *supra* note 247, at 704–05. *See also* HENOCHSBERG, *supra* note 280, at 54(1); Gwanyanya, *supra* note 225, at 3109.

[284] *See* Companies Act 71 of 2008 § 66(1) (S. Afr.).

[285] *See* Mongalo, *supra* note 230, at 367–68.

[286] *See* Companies Act 71 of 2008 § 72(4)–(10) (S. Afr.); Companies Regulations, 2011, Reg. 43.

[287] *See* Companies Act 71 of 2008 § 165(2) (S. Afr.). *See also* HENOCHSBERG, *supra* note 280, at 594–95; 2 J.L. YEATS ET AL., COMMENTARY ON THE COMPANIES ACT OF 2008 at 7-30–7-31 (2018).

[288] CASSIM, *supra* note 280, at 14–15.

[289] *See* Gwanyanya, *supra* note 225, at 3111–12.

company from doing anything inconsistent with this Act."[290] Conversely, then, and more generally yet, "[a]ny person who contravenes any provision of this Act is liable to any other person for any loss or damage suffered by that person as a result of that contravention."[291] Together with the board-related reforms described, these structures all reinforce the conclusion that the Companies Act 2008 marks "a dramatic shift" away from the stark shareholder primacy of historical English models toward a more stakeholder-oriented approach.[292]

The social and ethics committee is a particularly remarkable and unique governance structure that underscores the shift toward a broader conception of corporate purpose.[293] The Companies Act 2008 authorizes regulations requiring specified categories of companies to establish such committees, and regulations have been enacted that generally require this in state-owned companies, listed companies, and various others with a sufficiently high "public interest score" based on factors including the number of employees and beneficial investors, and the extent of third-party liabilities and turnover.[294] The statute specifies that a social and ethics committee "is entitled to . . . require from any director or prescribed officer . . . any information or explanation necessary for the performance of the committee's functions"; to "request" such information from employees; to "attend any general shareholders meeting"; and to "be heard at any general shareholders meeting . . . on any part of the business of the meeting that concerns the committee's functions."[295] Regulations, then, establish a very broad substantive mandate for social and ethics committees to "monitor" corporate activities in a host of operational and regulatory domains—"social and economic development," including "the company's standing" under the UN Global Compact and OECD recommendations on corruption, as well as the EEA and the B-BBEEA; "good corporate citizenship," including "promotion of equality, prevention of unfair discrimination, and reduction of corruption," as well as "contribution to development of the communities in which its activities are predominantly conducted" and the company's "record of sponsorship, donations and charitable

[290] Companies Act 71 of 2008 § 20(4) (S. Afr.). *See also* YEATS ET AL., *supra* note 282, at 2-105–2-106.

[291] Companies Act 71 of 2008 § 218(2) (S. Afr.). *See also* GEACH, *supra* note 282, at 1-211–1-213; HENOCHSBERG, *supra* note 280, at 298(20), 641–43; YEATS ET AL., *supra* note 282, at 2-1278–2-1280; YEATS ET AL., *supra* note 287, at 9-5.

[292] *See* GEACH, *supra* note 282, at 1-1–1-3. *See also* CASSIM ET AL., *supra* note 280, at 517–21; Jebe et al., *supra* note 265, at 130–34. Moreover, the Companies Act 2008 applies to companies formed under prior legislation. *See* DAVIS ET AL., *supra* note 265, at 22.

[293] *See* Michele Havenga, *The Social and Ethics Committee in South African Company Law*, 78 J. CONTEMP. ROMAN-DUTCH L. 285, 285 (2015); Mongalo, *supra* note 230, at 372.

[294] *See* Companies Act 71 of 2008 § 72(4) (S. Afr.); Companies Regulations, 2011, Regs. 26(2), 43(1). On the calculation of public interest scores, see also ROSSOUW, *supra* note 265, at 19–20; Irene-marié Esser & Piet Delport, *The Protection of Stakeholders: The South African Social and Ethics Committee and the United Kingdom's Enlightened Shareholder Value Approach: Part 2*, 2017 DE JURE 221, 222–23 (2017).

[295] Companies Act 71 of 2008 § 72(8) (S. Afr.).

giving"; "the environment, health and public safety," including impacts of both corporate activities and products or services sold; "consumer relationships"; and "labour and employment," including "the company's standing" under International Labour Organization standards, as well as "the company's employment relationships, and its contribution toward the educational development of its employees." Additionally, the regulations empower the committee "to draw matters within its mandate to the attention of the Board as occasion requires," and "to report . . . to the shareholders at the company's annual general meeting on the matters within its mandate."[296]

As encompassing as the social and ethics committee's mandate may be, the degree to which this structure ultimately promotes corporate sustainability will turn on how these committees actually operate and what the nature and extent of their governance authority is determined to be—matters that remain unclear. The advent of this structure was "not uniformly welcomed by companies listed on the JSE,"[297] and initially there were many applications for exemptions, although the structure has since "become widely accepted" and the number of such applications has "drastically reduced."[298] Although requiring a social and ethics committee could create complications due to potential "overlap" with other committees (notably the audit committee), as well as broader "ambiguities and uncertainties" regarding its "institutional nature,"[299] it has been argued that this structure could "benefit a company's reputation, enhance its sustainability and improve its management of risk and legal compliance"—particularly given its resonance with constitutional parameters for company law—and thereby "increase shareholder, stakeholder and investor confidence."[300]

There is an ongoing debate regarding the scope and nature of the social and ethics committee's authority, and particularly whether it ought to be regarded as subsidiary to the board or a distinct power structure in its own right.[301] One

[296] Companies Regulations, 2011, Reg. 43(5). On the breadth of the committee's mandate, see also CASSIM ET AL., *supra* note 280, at 461–62, 522–23; DELOITTE & TOUCHE, THE COMPANIES ACT: THE SOCIAL AND ETHICS COMMITTEE AND THE MANAGEMENT OF THE ETHICS PERFORMANCE OF THE COMPANY (2014); HENOCHSBERG, *supra* note 280, at 284–86; Locke, *supra* note 262, at 109–18; Bonray Marsellus Botha, *Evaluating the Social and Ethics Committee: Is Labour the Missing Link? (1)*, 79 J. CONTEMP. ROMAN-DUTCH L. 580, 589–90 (2016); Havenga, *supra* note 293, at 288–91; Joubert, *supra* note 247, at 187–88; H.J. Kloppers, *Driving Corporate Social Responsibility (CSR) through the* Companies Act: *An Overview of the Role of the Social and Ethics Committee*, 16 POTCHEFSTROOM ELECTRONIC L.J. 166, 171–85 (2013).

[297] Joubert, *supra* note 247, at 194.

[298] Mongalo, *supra* note 230, at 363. The statute expressly permits such applications, notably where other legislation already requires a corporate structure that performs similar functions, or where it is otherwise deemed "not reasonably necessary in the public interest" to require it "having regard to the nature and extent of the activities of the company." Companies Act 71 of 2008 § 72(5) (S. Afr.).

[299] Joubert, *supra* note 247, at 194–95. *See also* HENOCHSBERG, *supra* note 280, at 285.

[300] Havenga, *supra* note 293, at 290–91.

[301] *See* Esser & Delport, *supra* note 294, at 223–24; Joubert, *supra* note 247, at 190–91; Mongalo, *supra* note 230, at 363–64.

prominent treatise, for example, observes that the "question remains whether the social and ethics committee is a board committee or a company committee," and argues in favor of the latter characterization based on the regulation's reference to appointment by the "company" itself—interpreted to mean the shareholders—and the committee's apparently greater reporting responsibilities vis à vis the shareholders.[302] Others, however, have argued that this committee is in fact a board committee based on the fact that this structure arises under a section of the Companies Act 2008 focused on "board committees,"[303] and that this characterization is bolstered by the expectation that a committee with such significant responsibilities would ordinarily be subject to fiduciary duties (which would not apply if this were a company committee).[304] Given this uncertainty, it remains unclear "whether the board may refuse to comply with an instruction from this committee."[305] Tshepo Mongalo argues that, to realize the specific aims within the committee's mandate and the broader aims of South African company law, it ought to be regarded as a board committee that effectively functions as "the company's second board," and as "the final arbiter regarding matters within its competence," although "this interpretation has yet to be tested in court."[306] Given this uncertainty, the long-term impacts of the social and ethics committee remain unclear.[307] As a matter of corporate governance practice, however, it is noteworthy that King IV endorses a relatively robust conception of this structure to "progress beyond mere compliance to contribute to the creation of value,"[308] and that the JSE in turn draws attention to the King Code in appointing these committees.[309] These factors may lead companies to imbue this structure with "a more proactive and forward-looking role."[310]

Expressed by reference to the levers of corporate governance, where do the foregoing structures leave South African corporate governance today, and how does this state of affairs differ from what we have encountered elsewhere? Figure 15 summarizes corporate governance in South African listed companies, based on certain assumptions subsequently detailed.

[302] *See* HENOCHSBERG, *supra* note 280, at 282–83. *See also* Esser & Delport, *supra* note 294, at 228–29.

[303] *See* Joubert, *supra* note 247, at 190 n.33.

[304] *See* Mongalo, *supra* note 230, at 364–67.

[305] Botha, *supra* note 296, at 590. *See also* Esser & Delport, *supra* note 294, at 230.

[306] Mongalo, *supra* note 230, at 370–71. Others suggest that, if the social and ethics committee lacks such authority, its impact would essentially derive from capacity to persuade shareholders to pressure the board to act in accordance with the committee's recommendations. *See* HENOCHSBERG, *supra* note 280, at 285–86.

[307] *See, e.g.*, CASSIM ET AL., *supra* note 280, at 522–23; Gwanyanya, *supra* note 225, at 3113–14; Joubert, *supra* note 247, at 194.

[308] KING IV, *supra* note 231, at 29. *See also id.* at 57.

[309] *See* Johannesburg Stock Exchange Limited, Listings Requirements ¶ 3.84(c).

[310] ROSSOUW, *supra* note 265, at 31.

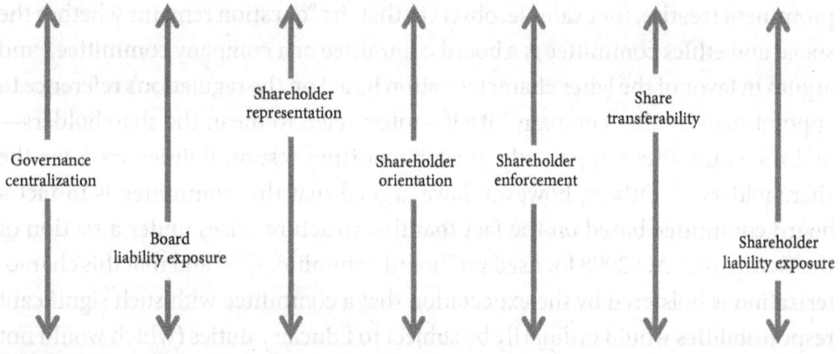

Figure 15 South African Listed Company

Overall, Figure 15 reflects the relatively mixed picture resulting from the combination of shareholder-centric structures, carried over from historical English models, with sustainability-related innovations introduced through the Companies Act 2008, the King Code, and JSE listing requirements. Board and shareholder liability exposure generally remain low, as boards benefit from a codified form of business judgment rule[311] and shareholders benefit from limited liability,[312] although it remains possible that open-ended causes of action described earlier for contravention of the statute could alter the liability landscape moving forward. Meanwhile, shareholder representation remains high because the Companies Act 2008 retains the exclusive shareholder franchise of prior statutes, and share transferability remains high because the JSE provides a relatively liquid market for shares and shareholders retain exclusive authority to determine the outcome of hostile takeover bids. The configuration of these levers remains broadly consistent with that reflected by the archetypal U.S. public company described earlier in this book, and what one would likewise expect such a depiction of a U.K. public company to look like. The remaining governance levers, however, deviate markedly.

To the extent corporate litigation occurs moving forward, it is conceivable that the shareholder enforcement lever will be calibrated lower in South Africa, as the Companies Act 2008 makes various forms of robust causes of action available to employee representatives, and in some cases other non-shareholder constituencies. Although such actions may impose "significant procedural hurdles," they minimally "provide employees and their representatives"—and potentially

[311] Companies Act 71 of 2008 § 76(4) (S. Afr.).
[312] *Id.* § 19(2).

other stakeholders—"with leverage possibilities."[313] Accordingly, the depiction in Figure 15 assumes some degree of take-up of these causes of action, and/or that non-shareholder constituencies are able to advance their interests more effectively in negotiations with corporate management before the backdrop of the remedies these structures offer. Such dynamics can prove difficult to identify and measure empirically because they will often not be publicly observable, but are thought to have been operative in other jurisdictions where a particular constituency possesses strong corporate governance powers or ability to sue.[314] To the extent this occurs with other stakeholders in South Africa, it would effectively dilute the ability of shareholders to advance their exclusive interests through this mechanism.

The governance centralization and shareholder orientation levers, meanwhile, are perhaps the most intriguing in the South African context, and their calibration will depend to a substantial degree on the impact of social and ethics committees. Overall, given the combination of shareholder-centric and stakeholder-centric structures, it remains unclear whether the Companies Act 2008 is better described as aiming for a form of "enlightened shareholder value" or a limited form of "pluralism,"[315] but King IV plainly rejects the historical approach of equating the company's interests with those of shareholders. Rather, King IV advocates a "stakeholder-centric approach" under which "the board considers other stakeholders not merely as instruments to serve the interests of shareholders, but as having intrinsic value for decision-making in the best interests of the company over time."[316] Figure 15 presents both the governance centralization and shareholder orientation levers being calibrated lower on this basis, and on the further assumption that a more robust interpretation of the social and ethics committee's role and authority will take shape, consistent with the more proactive and strategically oriented role that the King Code endorses.

[313] Croucher & Miles, *supra* note 234, at 373, 387. With respect to derivative actions, for example, the *Henochsberg* treatise cites no cases involving non-shareholder constituencies. *See* HENOCHSBERG, *supra* note 280, at 594(1)–95. The High Court of South Africa has, however, recognized the significance of expanded derivative standing, observing that "provisions which give standing to directors and employee representatives are no doubt reflective of the modern recognition that persons other than shareholders have a legitimate and cognisable interest in the assertion or defence of a company's legal interests." Lewis Group Limited v. David Farring Woollam and Others (9900/16) [2016] ¶ 33 (S. Afr.) (Binns-Ward J., High Court of South Africa, Wester Cape Division, Cape Town).

[314] *See, e.g.*, BRUNER, *supra* note 9, at 29–35 (discussing such dynamics associated with strong governance powers for U.K. shareholders), 101–02 (discussing such dynamics associated with strong capacity for U.S. shareholders to sue directors).

[315] *See, e.g.*, Esser & Delport, *supra* note 247, at 100–03, 108–09. *See also* CASSIM ET AL., *supra* note 280, at 518–21; HENOCHSBERG, *supra* note 280, at 54; Botha, *supra* note 296, at 582–83; Joubert, *supra* note 247, at 192 n.47.

[316] KING IV, *supra* note 231, at 26.

Specifically, this assumes a robust legal interpretation of the social and ethics committee's formal powers, concerted use of those powers, and real engagement with the full board and shareholders alike. Should the social and ethics committee evolve along these lines, one could readily imagine this structure effectively reducing both governance centralization and shareholder orientation, even if shareholders were regarded as the sole beneficiaries of fiduciary duty—because this committee would be fulfilling functions otherwise defaulting to the full board (or a board committee with a differing mandate); because a core governance structure would be focused on priorities expressly distinct from maximizing profits; and because such matters would be brought to bear on overall corporate decision-making, including the formulation of strategy. It of course remains possible, however, that things could unfold otherwise, in which case these governance levers would be calibrated differently. If, for example, the social and ethics committee were to become the narrowly conceived, compliance-oriented, box-ticking exercise that King IV opposes, then it would not be difficult to imagine such a structure making little practical difference.

Viewed from a global perspective, there are plainly weaknesses and strengths of the South African approach—as with any other extant regime. Correlatively, there are pitfalls and opportunities that emerge from the foregoing analysis that merit consideration by other jurisdictions that contemplate sustainability-oriented corporate governance reforms and expanded corporate accountability. Notably, maintaining various shareholder-centric structures from preexisting models and then grafting onto them various stakeholder-centric structures has raised thorny questions about the nature of directors' duties—in particular, whether "the best interests of the company" continue to reflect solely the interests of shareholders, or now embrace a broader range of stakeholders and concerns.[317] Meanwhile, the lack of clarity regarding the specific responsibilities and powers of the social and ethics committee raises correlative, and equally thorny, questions about how this committee is intended to function vis-à-vis the board of directors, particularly where priorities and perspectives differ.[318] These lacuna in the Companies Act 2008 suggest that the broader shift toward stakeholder interests, and sustainability more generally, remains less than fully theorized, inviting further questions and critique—including, for example, whether the apparent aim of advancing employee interests reflected in the structures described in this chapter might have been better realized by ensuring employee

[317] *See, e.g.*, Esser & Delport, *supra* note 247, at 104–10; Gwanyanya, *supra* note 225, at 3121; Jebe et al., *supra* note 265, at 143.

[318] *See, e.g.*, Esser & Delport, *supra* note 294, at 228–31, 241; Kloppers, *supra* note 296, at 187.

representation on the social and ethics committee,[319] or even on the board of directors itself.[320]

Notwithstanding these shortcomings, however, South Africa is rightly viewed today as a global leader in sustainable corporate governance.[321] South Africa's corporate governance regime plainly demonstrates the viability of placing environmental, social, and economic sustainability considerations front and center—not solely in the corporate governance context, but also in the legal system more generally, and even in the constitutional order. Overall, these structures reflect keen recognition of "a strong and growing societal view that financial performance and efficiency should not necessarily always trump other aspects that society values, such as the environment and human dignity"—dynamics "punctuated" in the South African context "by the complex challenges of historical social and economic inequalities, the resource intensity of many South African industries, water scarcity, and the unique richness of the country's natural resources and biodiversity."[322] South Africa's corporate governance innovations

[319] *See generally* Bonray Marsellus Botha, *Evaluating the Social and Ethics Committee: Is Labour the Missing Link? (2)*, 80 J. CONTEMP. ROMAN-DUTCH L. 1 (2017). COSATU actually called for such representation in a public hearing on the Companies Bill. *See* Parliamentary Monitoring Group, *Companies Bill: Submission by COSATU; Department's Preliminary Response to Public Hearings*, Aug. 20, 2008, https://pmg.org.za/committee-meeting/9521/ (summarizing submission by Prakashnee Govender, Parliamentary Liaison Officer, Congress of South African Trade Unions) (calling for "every Board to have a social and ethics committee drawn from trade unions and relevant communities").

[320] Prominent trade unions reportedly sought co-determination on the German model. *See* Parliamentary Monitoring Group, *supra* note 319; Sabinet, *Cosatu Presents Labour Movements' Views on Corporate Regulatory Regime*, Aug. 24, 2017, https://legal.sabinet.co.za/articles/cosatu-presents-labour-movements-views-on-corporate-regulatory-regime/. Such an approach "was mooted . . . but not adopted." COLLIER ET AL., *supra* note 252, at 362. *See also* REPUBLIC OF SOUTH AFRICA DEPARTMENT OF TRADE AND INDUSTRY, *supra* note 271, at 39 (proposing a unitary board with "stakeholder representation"); DELOITTE & TOUCHE, *supra* note 296 (describing the social and ethics committee as "a compromise" in lieu of co-determination). South African law does make a form of co-determination available through workplace forums, but these have been regarded as ineffective in the absence of board-level representation. *See* COLLIER ET AL., *supra* note 252, at 355–62; Edward Webster & David Francis, *The Paradox of Inequality in South Africa: A Challenge from the Workplace*, 101 TRANSFORMATION 11, 19–21 (2019). Meanwhile, collective bargaining remains an entrenched feature of South African industrial relations. *See* WORLD BANK, *supra* note 215, at 91–92.

[321] *See, e.g.*, Andreasson, *supra* note 234, at 654; Eccles et al., *supra* note 197, at 1, 5, 12; Judin et al., *supra* note 244. For additional background, see Mohamed Adib & Zhang Xianzhi, *Board Characteristics and Corporate Social Performance Nexus—A Multi-Theoretical Analysis—Evidence from South Africa*, 21 IOSR J. BUS. MGMT. 24 (2019); Eccles et al., *supra* note 197, at 12–15; Claudia Kitsikopoulos et al., *Limited Progress in Sustainable Development: Factors Influencing the Environmental Management and Reporting of South African JSE-Listed Companies*, 27 BUS. STRATEGY & ENV'T 1295 (2018); Collins G. Ntim & Teerooven Soobaroyen, *Corporate Governance and Performance in Socially Responsible Corporations: New Empirical Insights from a Neo-Institutional Framework*, 21 CORP. GOV. INT'L REV. 468 (2013).

[322] Joubert, *supra* note 247, at 184–85. On persistent challenges relating to inequality and resource dependency, see COLLIER ET AL., *supra* note 252, at 480–92; NATTRASS, *supra* note 197, at 6–7, 81–84; NATIONAL PLANNING COMMISSION, REPUBLIC OF SOUTH AFRICA, NATIONAL DEVELOPMENT PLAN 2030: OUR FUTURE—MAKE IT WORK, EXECUTIVE SUMMARY (2012); WORLD BANK, *supra* note 215; Aroop Chatterjee, *Measuring Wealth Inequality in South Africa: An Agenda*, 36 DEV. SOUTHERN AFRICA 839 (2019); David Francis & Edward Webster, *Poverty and Inequality in South Africa: Critical Reflections*, 36 DEV. SOUTHERN AFRICA 788 (2019); Webster & Francis, *supra* note 320.

and broader conception of corporate accountability demonstrate both a high degree of commitment to sustainability-related considerations and a high degree of creativity in exploring differing calibrations of the levers of corporate governance, offering real potential to elevate such concerns in corporate decision-making and to promote more sustainable corporate operations.

9
Conclusions

The corporate form is widely described by reference to a fixed and rigid set of characteristics strongly associated with a dominant finance-driven paradigm. As we have seen throughout this book, however, the corporation and corporate law have historically exhibited great flux and dynamism; corporate governance models continue to vary considerably around the world in response to persistent contextual drivers of difference; and fundamental issues of power, purpose, and risk-taking remain contested.[1] In response to these realities, I have argued that the corporation is better conceptualized as a flexible form of governance technology, and that engaging directly with the extraordinary diversity of governance structures that the corporate form can accommodate could help us to address persistent pathologies of corporate production and to re-calibrate corporate governance for a more sustainable future.[2]

It is increasingly clear that governance-related problems will require governance-related solutions, and the latter chapters of the book have applied the foregoing insights toward that end. Creative industry-by-industry approaches—some applied historically, and others proposed in response to recent crises—could re-calibrate the levers of corporate governance to constrain risk-taking and cost externalization in financial firms, essential non-financial firms, and companies that are engaged in inherently hazardous industries.[3] More generally, then, we have considered various ways to re-imagine corporate accountability as a means of improving corporate sustainability, surveying the landscape through various lenses—notably board composition, legal responsibility in global value chains, and holistic national efforts to re-imagine corporate governance along more sustainable lines.[4] As these analyses demonstrate, the corporate form and corporate law offer real potential to promote governance structures that are more environmentally, socially, and economically sustainable, offering real cause for hope that the multitude of interconnected crises we now face can ultimately be overcome.

1 *See supra* Chapters 2–4.
2 *See supra* Chapters 5–6.
3 *See supra* Chapter 7.
4 *See supra* Chapter 8.

The Corporation as Technology. Christopher M. Bruner, Oxford University Press. © Christopher M. Bruner 2022.
DOI: 10.1093/oso/9780197635179.003.0009

What stands in our way? Simply put, the principal impediments we face are flawed metaphors that short-circuit nuanced and creative thought about the corporate form, corporate law, and potential governance structures. For example: The corporation is the shareholders' property, so corporate law should focus on maximizing their wealth. Or: The corporation is a nexus of contracts, so corporate law should focus on what direct participants would likely bargain for, left to themselves. Or: The corporation is a legal person, so corporate law should focus on the entity's rights rather than social obligations. And so on.[5]

To move beyond such cramped metaphors, it is essential to recognize and respond to their underlying rhetorical function in debates about corporate governance. In the context of argumentation, metaphors can be employed to convey "self-validating claims that increase the chances of their being accepted"—that is, to "self-legitimate their conceptual mapping" of a given field.[6] They can only accomplish this, however, through an implicit form of circular reasoning—effectively begging the question by assuming the conclusion in the framing of the metaphor itself. This might occur because a model offering limited utility in a particular doctrinal domain has been pushed too far and applied too broadly. As Margaret Blair observes, this reflects the risk that "a scholar or policy advocate may become seduced by the elegance or charm of a particular model so that he or she begins to believe in it too much, treating it as a literal, fully accurate, and complete description."[7] Alternatively, however, such metaphors might be used strategically, despite their descriptive weaknesses, to advance preferred normative visions for the field without defending their underpinnings—in which case they essentially substitute for reasoned argument about the true underlying issues, which may be perfunctorily dismissed or ignored altogether.[8]

The metaphors that have largely driven corporate law discourse in recent decades bear different implications, but they have in common that each tends to be deployed rhetorically to place large public companies "on the private side of the fundamental divide between public and private." Accordingly, discussion

[5] *See supra* Chapters 2–3. For discussion of such corporate metaphors and their consequences, see generally Margaret M. Blair, *On Models, Metaphors, Rhetoric, and the Law*, 41 TULSA L. REV. 513 (2006); Kent Greenfield, *From Metaphor to Reality in Corporate Law* (Boston College Law School Public Law and Legal Theory Research Paper No. 2001–10, 2001), https://ssrn.com/abstract=254117; Daniel J.H. Greenwood, *Introduction to the Metaphors of Corporate Law*, 4 SEATTLE J. SOC. JUST. 273 (2005); David Millon, *The Ambiguous Significance of Corporate Personhood*, 2 STAN. AGORA 39 (2001).

[6] Steve Oswald & Alan Rihs, *Metaphor as Argument: Rhetorical and Epistemic Advantages of Extended Metaphors*, 28 ARGUMENTATION 133, 133–35 (2014).

[7] Blair, *supra* note 5, at 513.

[8] *See id.* at 516; Greenfield, *supra* note 5, at 4–5, 10–12.

framed by reference to such metaphors often "treats corporations as values in themselves . . . and not mere tools for a greater end,"[9] without fully defending this normative preference. Indeed, in some cases their proponents may be so ready to leap to preferred normative conclusions that they fail to recognize, let alone grapple with, the ambiguities of their own metaphors. For example, even if one accepts that a corporation may be coherently conceptualized as a legal "person" in limited respects, this does not, in and of itself, logically determine the optimal or desirable balance between rights that such a person ought to enjoy, on the one hand, and obligations that such a person ought to bear, on the other.[10] As David Millon observes, resolving such an underlying debate "is not a matter of observation and description." Rather, it requires some account of what "the ties of obligation that bind people together" amount to in a given society. In this light, rhetorical resort to corporate metaphors too often amounts to "normative arguments masquerading as positive assertions."[11]

Achieving a fuller and more accurate understanding of what the corporate form in fact is—and a more comprehensive appreciation of what it could be, and how it might better advance broader public goals—requires casting such metaphors aside.[12] In this book, I have argued that conceptualizing the corporation as a flexible form of governance technology offers a superior means of advancing both descriptive understanding and normative deliberation, substituting for inapt metaphors a more literal descriptor that can accommodate flux and dynamism in response to a host of contextual drivers of difference.[13] As to how normative deliberation ought to proceed moving forward, I have advanced corporate sustainability, including environmental, social, and economic dimensions, as a superior framework for evaluating our options in the field of corporate governance—one that focuses more intently on what is truly at stake, acknowledging both the good that the corporate form can facilitate and the pathologies that, if unchecked, could impose extraordinary harms on society and the planet.[14]

Although perhaps an effective deflection device in the short-term, no amount of privatizing rhetoric can obscure the broader public implications of corporate governance for long. Grappling with the environmental, social, and economic

[9] Greenwood, *supra* note 5, at 275–76.

[10] *See* Millon, *supra* note 5, at 47–49.

[11] *Id.* at 56. *See also* Blair, *supra* note 5, at 522 (observing that models can "lead to confusion and misunderstanding if the scholar is not careful to articulate what assumptions were made and the underlying reasons"); Greenfield, *supra* note 5, at 5 (observing that "these metaphors are so powerful that they are taken not as placeholders but as arguments themselves, thus not only describing the law but shaping it as well"); *supra* Chapter 2.

[12] *See, e.g.*, Blair, *supra* note 5, at 522; Greenfield, *supra* note 5, at 12–13; Greenwood, *supra* note 5, at 283–84, 293–94; Millon, *supra* note 5, at 56–58; *supra* Chapter 2.

[13] *See supra* Chapters 1, 5.

[14] *See supra* Chapters 1, 6.

impacts—both positive and negative—requires a nuanced understanding of the various ways in which the levers of corporate governance can be calibrated and re-calibrated to respond to a dynamic landscape. The sustainability of corporate operations will turn, in large part, on our capacity to engage in this form of collective introspection and to reckon honestly with the results.

Index

For the benefit of digital users, indexed terms that span two pages (e.g., 52–53) may, on occasion, appear on only one of those pages.

Note: Page numbers followed by *f* indicate a figure on the corresponding page.